The New England Pantry

BEACH PLUMS

Beach plums grow on shrub bushes in sand dunes all along the New England coast. The bushes only produce fruit every few years, and the plums are preceded by stunning white blossoms. Because the fruit is quite bitter, the plums are not eaten out of hand, but the flavor works well when combined with other fruits in jelly, especially when served with meat or game.

BLUEBERRIES

Wild blueberries are small, tart berries quite distinct from their cultivated cousins. Almost all wild blueberries are grown in two counties in eastern Maine (Washington and Hancock), where low bushes on barren or burned land yield fruit during a short season late in the summer. Wild blueberries can be enjoyed in traditional New England desserts like blueberry grunt, slump, or pandowdy, all of which combine the sweetened fruit with a baked biscuit dough. Cultivated blueberries come from the same general regions and are plumper and juicier than their wild cousins.

CLAMS

Several varieties of clam can be dug, or "raked," along the shores of New England. Quahogs are hard-shell clams best eaten young. Tiny littlenecks and slightly larger cherrystones are often served on the half shell. Razor clams are not as well known in the U.S., and most are exported to Japan for sashimi. For the traditional New England clambake (see page 24), use the soft-shell clams known as long-necks or steamers. Clams are also often fried or cooked in creamy New England clam chowder (see page 19).

COD

This is the abundant Atlantic fish that created the New England "Codfish Aristocracy." Cod was often dried and salted for preservation or trade, which brought tea, spices, brandy, and molasses to New England. "Scrod" isn't a distinct fish, but was a term invented in the 1800s at the Parker House restaurant in Boston to refer to young cod, which are split, deboned, dredged in bread crumbs, and broiled.

CRANBERRIES

This versatile, sour berry appears throughout New England's culinary history. Native Americans used it for pemmican, a jerky made of cranberries, venison, and fat. The cranberry's high vitamin C content made it popular with medicine men and with colonial sailors eager to prevent scurvy. Wild cranberries grow on dense springy mats in sand dunes. The members of the Ocean Spray growers collective also cultivate them in salt marsh bogs. Cape Cod produces much of the world's cranberries, providing us with our Thanksgiving sauce and year-round juices.

FIDDLEHEADS

These young vegetables, the first of the spring, are the curled fronds of wild ostrich ferns. They grow along shady streams in Maine, New Hampshire, and Vermont. It is important to remove the brown, leafy covering from fiddleheads before using. After blanching, add them to soups, sautés, and salads. Fiddlehead fans describe the taste as a cross between asparagus, artichoke, and broccoli.

FISH

The Atlantic waters boast several other fish that appear prominently in traditional New England cooking. Shad, a bony fish native to the East Coast, is known for its roe. Alewife, a herring, gets its fame as the fertilizer that the Native Americans encouraged the pilgrims to use in their cornfields. Alewife roe is just as delicious as shad roe. Haddock, pollack, mackerel, and bluefish are also popular fish for boiling, broiling, and frying.

LOBSTER

These delicious crustaceans are trapped year-round off the New England coast, but are especially plentiful during the summer. Lobsters are classified by size as chickens, quarters, selects, and jumbos. Maine is famous for the big-clawed *Homarus americanus*. The cornerstone of a New England clambake (see page 24), lobsters can be enjoyed simply boiled or steamed, or elegantly prepared in salads, mousse, bisque, or other delicacies.

MAPLE

Put real maple syrup on your breakfast pancakes, and you'll never want to go back to pallid imitations. Native Americans and settlers alike tapped these lovely trees for the thin sap, thirty gallons of which will boil down to one gallon of thick, sweet syrup. Maple gives flavor to many New England recipes, from glazed hams or carrots to maple sugar candy, maple sugar pie, and the great childhood favorite: maple syrup poured on fresh snow.

MUSHROOMS

Many wild mushrooms grow in the damp New England woods. Springtime morels, midsummer chanterelles, trumpets, puff balls, and meadow mushrooms can all be used in sauces, stuffings, salads, or alone.

MUSSELS

This "poor-man's" bivalve was avoided by New England colonists and, therefore, is not seen in many traditional recipes. Today their low price and wide availability make them a popular alternative to clams.

OYSTERS

Native East Coast oysters are named according to location, as in the Blue Points, Cotuits, and Chincoteagues. The Bélon oyster, also called the European flat, was brought to America from France and does very well in New England waters. Oysters are enjoyed on the half shell, smoked, in turkey stuffing for Thanksgiving, and in Christmas Eve stew.

POULTRY AND GAME BIRDS

Chicken varieties developed in New England over the last two centuries include Rhode Island Reds, Plymouth Rocks, and New Hampshires. When a Plymouth Rock was crossed with a Cornish game hen, the Rock Cornish game hen resulted, providing single-serving birds for roasting. Ducks were brought to Connecticut from Peking. Today Long Island is the largest duck-producing region in the United States. As hunting becomes less common and hunting land more scarce, game birds like turkey, geese, squab, pheasant, and quail are raised domestically.

PUMPKIN

This king of the squash family has played an important role in early and current New England cooking. Pumpkin pie (see page 35), a traditional American dessert favorite, was served at the second Thanksgiving in 1623. The colonists made frequent use of this large vine-ripened vegetable. They made soup as well as beer from it, and they also roasted and ate the seeds.

SCALLOPS

Three kinds of scallops are harvested in New England. The large sea scallops (also called smooth or giant) are available year-round and are an excellent all-purpose scallop. Bay scallops are cork-shaped, smaller, and sweeter. They are less plentiful and are in season only from October to May. The cape scallops found around Nantucket Island during the winter months are best enjoyed raw.

The Recipes

VERMONT CHEDDAR SOUP

ADAPTED FROM A RECIPE BY JASPER WHITE, JASPER'S
RESTAURANT, BOSTON, MASSACHUSETTS

Serves 8

Cheddar cheese was named for a village in Somerset, England. The Vermont version is a sharp cheese made from cow's milk. It is yellowish, dense, and ages well. This traditional soup is easy to make, loaded with flavor, and perfect for a chilly New England day.

- 8 tablespoons (1 stick) butter
- 3 small leeks, halved lengthwise, cleaned, and sliced
- 2 medium celery stalks, diced
- 1 medium carrot, diced
- ¼ cup all-purpose flour
- 4 cups chicken stock
- 1 cup half-and-half (light cream)
- ½ pound Vermont sharp cheddar, shredded
- 1 teaspoon dry mustard
- 1 teaspoon Worcestershire sauce
- Cayenne pepper to taste
- Salt and freshly ground black pepper
- 1 Pippin apple, peeled, cored, and finely diced

Melt 6 tablespoons of the butter in a medium saucepan over medium heat. Add the leeks, celery, and carrot and sauté until tender, about 3 minutes. Sprinkle the flour over the vegetables and stir for 3 minutes. Add the chicken stock, 1 cup at a time. Stir after each addition. Bring to a boil over medium-high heat, then reduce the heat and simmer uncovered for 40 minutes.

Purée the soup in a blender or food processor. Strain into a clean saucepan. Bring to a simmer. Add the half-and-half, cheese, mustard, and Worcestershire sauce. Stir until the cheese is melted. Season to taste with salt, pepper, and cayenne pepper.

Melt the remaining 2 tablespoons of butter in a small skillet. Sauté the apple until it starts to turn brown, about 3 minutes. Serve the soup and garnish each serving with a sprinkling of the apple.

NEW ENGLAND CLAM CHOWDER

Serves 8 (6 as a main course)

The term chowder, which refers to a hearty soup, comes from the French term for a large pot or caldron, chaudière. *A good clam chowder should be like a stew with extra liquid.*

- ¼ cup finely diced slab bacon
- 3 leeks, white parts only, halved lengthwise, cleaned, and sliced ¼-inch thick
- 3 cups finely diced russet potatoes (about 1½ pounds)
- 3 stalks celery, finely diced
- 2 medium carrots, finely diced
- 2 teaspoons finely chopped fresh thyme *or* 1 teaspoon dried thyme
- 2 quarts chopped fresh clams and their liquor reserved
- 1 bay leaf
- 3 cups heavy cream
- Bottled clam juice, as needed
- Salt and freshly ground black pepper
- Chopped fresh parsley and paprika for garnish

In a heavy, wide saucepan, render the bacon until it begins to crisp. Add the leeks, potatoes, celery, and carrots. Sauté for 3 minutes or until the vegetables have softened. Add the thyme.

Pour the reserved clam liquor into a 4-cup measure. Add enough bottled clam juice to make 3½ cups total. Add to the vegetables. Add the bay leaf and simmer for 25 minutes.

Add the heavy cream. Bring to a boil over medium-high heat. Reduce heat and simmer for 20 more minutes.

Remove and discard the bay leaf. Ladle about 2 cups of the soup (at least half of this should be vegetables) into a blender. Purée and blend it back into the soup. Add the clams and heat through. Season to taste with salt and pepper (be careful with salt because the clams may provide enough saltiness).

Serve hot, garnished with parsley and paprika.

Chef Jasper White

Jasper White, with his wife, Nancy, opened Jasper's in 1983 in what was an old molasses warehouse on Boston's waterfront. The restaurant has been lauded for its renditions of New England cookery, and thanks to careful research on the region's foods, Chef White has become a spokesman for New England cooking.

His sensibilities were shaped by having spent his youth on a farm. Hunting and fishing, along with farming, gave him a solid respect for food in its purest state. After honing his skills in San Francisco, Seattle, and Montana, Chef White came to Boston, where he introduced contemporary cuisine to some of the city's finest hotels.

Chef White won the James Beard Award for "Best Chef in the Northeast" in 1991. His first cookbook, Jasper White's Cooking from New England, *was published in 1989.*

STUFFED CHERYSTONE CLAMS
ADAPTED FROM A RECIPE BY JASPER WHITE, JASPER'S RESTAURANT, BOSTON, MASSACHUSETTS

Serves 6 as an appetizer

Hiding a few inches under the sand at the bottom of New England's shallow bays, hard-shell cherrystone clams quietly live out their lives until they are dug up by clammers of both the professional and amateur variety. Although delicious raw, cherrystones are so difficult to open that they are more easily handled when cooked.

- ¼ pound slab pancetta or bacon, finely diced
- 18 cherrystone clams, scrubbed
- ½ cup bottled clam juice
- 6 tablespoons unsalted butter
- ¼ cup olive oil
- 1 medium onion, finely chopped
- 6 cloves garlic, minced
- ½ teaspoon red pepper flakes
- 2½ cups fresh bread crumbs
- ⅔ cup (2 ounces) grated Parmesan cheese
- 2 tablespoons chopped fresh basil
- 2 tablespoons chopped fresh Italian parsley
- 1 tablespoon chopped fresh oregano
- 1 tablespoon snipped fresh chives
- Lemon wedges

Preheat the oven to 400°F. In a small skillet over medium heat, sauté the pancetta until crisp. Drain on a paper towel–lined plate and set aside.

Place the clams and clam juice in a large saucepan; cover and place over medium-high heat and steam until they open, about 6 minutes. With a slotted spoon, remove the clams to a large bowl. Remove the cooked clams from their shells; chop the clams into ½-inch pieces and set aside. Separate each clam shell into 2 halves to make 36 halves; reserve. Strain the clam juice through a fine strainer and set aside.

Melt 2 tablespoons of the butter with the olive oil in a small skillet over medium heat; add the onion, garlic, and red pepper flakes. Cook, stirring constantly, until the onion is translucent, about 5 minutes. Spoon the mixture into a medium bowl. Add 1 cup of the bread crumbs, the Parmesan cheese, basil, parsley, oregano, chives, and the reserved pancetta, clams, and clam juice; stir to combine. Spoon the mixture into the clam shells and place on a 10 x 15 inch jelly roll pan; set aside.

Melt the remaining ¼ cup of butter in a medium skillet over medium heat; stir in the remaining 1½ cups of bread crumbs and toss until coated with the butter and lightly toasted. Sprinkle evenly over the clams and bake 10 minutes.

Preheat the broiler. Broil the clams until the bread crumbs are golden brown, about 1 minute. Serve with lemon wedges.

CHEDDAR CROQUETTE AND SPINACH SALAD

Serves 6

New England food has a reputation for being heavy and old-fashioned. Here is a salad that should please even the trendiest eaters. It is a combination of typical northeast ingredients that produce a very contemporary salad.

- 3 tablespoons cranberry *or* red wine vinegar
- 1 shallot, minced
- ½ cup olive oil
- Salt and pepper
- 1½ cups (6 ounces) shredded sharp cheddar cheese
- ¾ cup ricotta cheese
- 2 tablespoons chopped fresh thyme
- 1½ cups fresh bread crumbs
- ½ cup all-purpose flour
- ½ cup milk
- 1 egg
- Vegetable oil, for frying
- 2 (10-ounce) packages fresh, cleaned spinach leaves
- 2 Granny Smith apples, peeled, cored, and sliced
- 1 cup toasted walnuts, coarsely chopped

To make the vinaigrette: Place the vinegar and shallot in a small bowl. Slowly whisk in the olive oil. The vinaigrette will thicken slightly. Season with salt and pepper. Set aside.

Place the cheeses and thyme in a food processor fitted with a metal blade; process until smooth. Season with salt and pepper. Place the bread crumbs and flour in 2 separate bowls. Mix egg and milk in another bowl. Form the cheese mixture into 24 quarter-size balls. Coat the balls with flour. Dip into the egg mixture and then into the bread crumbs, coating completely. Place on a baking sheet lined with aluminum foil.

Pour vegetable oil into a large, heavy skillet to a depth of 1 inch. Heat the oil until it reaches 350°F. Fry the croquettes in batches until golden brown, about 1 minute, turning occasionally. Using a slotted spoon, transfer to a paper towel–lined baking sheet and keep warm.

In a large bowl, toss the spinach, apples, and walnuts with the vinaigrette. Divide among 6 salad plates. Top each with 4 warm croquettes.

NANTUCKET BAY SCALLOPS
WITH BROWN BUTTER–LEMON CHIVE SAUCE
ADAPTED FROM A RECIPE BY JASPER WHITE, JASPER'S RESTAURANT, BOSTON, MASSACHUSETTS

Serves 4

There is nothing sweeter and more delicate in flavor than bay scallops.
This recipe provides a simple glorification of this exquisite mollusk.

- ⅓ cup all-purpose flour
- ¼ teaspoon salt
- ⅛ teaspoon white pepper
- 1 pound Nantucket bay scallops
- 6 tablespoons unsalted butter

- 3 tablespoons lemon juice
- 2 cloves garlic, minced
- 3 tablespoons snipped chives
- 2 teaspoons grated lemon zest

Combine flour, salt, and white pepper in a pie plate; add the scallops and toss to coat completely.

Melt 2 tablespoons of the butter in a medium skillet over medium-high heat. Remove the scallops from the flour mixture, shaking off excess. Add scallops to the skillet and sauté until opaque throughout and brown on all sides, about 3 to 4 minutes. Remove the scallops from the skillet. Set them aside and keep warm.

Reduce the heat to medium-low and add the remaining 4 tablespoons of butter. Cook the butter slowly, swirling or stirring it so that it cooks evenly. When the butter begins to foam, pay very close attention, as it will also begin to brown. When the butter has a rich brown color and a nutty aroma, remove it immediately from the heat. Add the lemon juice to stop the cooking and to flavor the butter. Add the garlic, and let the mixture cook off the heat for 1 minute. Stir in the chives, lemon zest, and reserved scallops. Gently warm through over low heat. Serve immediately.

CODFISH CAKES

Serves 4 (8-9 cakes)

The North Atlantic off the coast of New England offers one of the richest fishing grounds in the world. Fish are plentiful, and the variety of species is amazing. Cod is a very common food fish, and these easy cakes are an excellent way of making something delicious out of leftovers (you can also make these without leftovers, but you will have to poach or bake the fish first). Although cod is generally the fish of choice, you can substitute any other firm white-fleshed fish.

- 1½ pounds cooked cod, flaked
- 1 cup riced, boiled potatoes (about ¾ pound)
- 1 teaspoon Dijon-style mustard
- 2 tablespoons finely chopped green onions (scallions)
- ½ teaspoon Worcestershire sauce
- Salt and freshly ground black pepper
- 2 tablespoons peanut oil
- Chopped fresh parsley for garnish

In a large bowl, mix the cod, potatoes, mustard, scallions, Worcestershire sauce, salt and pepper. Form the mixture into flattened cakes, 2½ inches in diameter. Heat the oil over medium heat in a medium skillet. Sauté the cakes until golden brown, about 2 minutes on each side. Sprinkle with parsley and serve with the tartar sauce (see below).

TARTAR SAUCE

Makes 1½ cups

- 1 cup mayonnaise
- 2½ tablespoons chives, finely chopped
- 1 tablespoon capers, finely chopped
- 1 tablespoon parsley, finely chopped
- 2 tablespoons cornichons or sweet pickles, finely chopped
- 1 tablespoon freshly squeezed lemon juice

Mix all the ingredients thoroughly in a small bowl. Serve immediately or cover and refrigerate until ready to serve.

The American Lobster

The American lobster—often called the "Maine" lobster—is found in beds all along the New England coastline. This speckled, black, clawed shellfish is unlike its European or tropical counterparts, the "spiny" lobster found in Florida, California, and Hawaiian waters. Its most distinguishing feature, besides its tender claw meat, is the fact that it turns red when cooked. The spiny variety is a lighter-colored, clawless creature that provides meat only from the tail.

There is debate about the best way to prepare lobster. Some people like to broil it, some grill it, some boil it, and some steam it; others use a combination of techniques. The problem with dry-heat methods such as broiling and grilling is that, if not used with caution and skill, they can dry out the meat and make it stringy and tough. Boiling is better, but if overdone can wash away flavor. Steaming seems ideal to keep the lobster moist and tender.

Lobsters generally weigh between 1 and 5 pounds. The smaller ones are called "chicken" lobsters because they are so tender. The best size for an individual serving is between 1½ and 2½ pounds. Female lobsters—identified by the fact that the claws under the tail and close to the body are feathery and small—are preferable because they often contain the coral, or bright red roe. Lobsters of both genders contain the tomalley (pancreas and liver), a creamy, rich, light green substance.

When buying lobster be sure that they are alive, and the livelier the better. Put about an inch of water in the bottom of a large roasting pan or stock pot. (Some people like to add beer, white wine, or fish fumet to the liquid.) Place a low rack or a vegetable steamer in the pot to keep the lobster above the boiling liquid. Bring the liquid to a boil and then, holding it by the body, insert the lobster head first. Cover and cook for five minutes per half pound of weight. If you are cooking more than one lobster in the same pot, DO NOT increase the cooking time; two 2-pounders should cook for the same amount of time—20 minutes—as one. Meanwhile, melt some butter.

When done, remove the lobsters from the pot and rinse them briefly with cold water. Let them rest in the sink for five minutes. Turn them over and cut down the tail with a large sharp knife. Split the lobster from end to end. Remove the sac right behind the lobster's eyes and discard it. Serve the lobster with lemons, melted butter, crusty bread, crisp white wine, and nutcrackers (for the claws).

OYSTER PAN ROAST
ADAPTED FROM A RECIPE OF THE OYSTER BAR,
GRAND CENTRAL TERMINAL, NEW YORK

Serves 2

This rich and luscious dish is a wonderful way to appreciate the briny, delicate flavor of oysters.

- 1 jar (10 ounces) shucked small oysters *or* 20 in-shell oysters, shucked, and oyster liquor reserved
- Clam juice, as needed
- 1 cup half-and-half
- ¼ cup chili sauce
- 2 tablespoons unsalted butter
- 1 tablespoon Worcestershire sauce
- 1½ teaspoons paprika
- Celery salt
- Snipped chives

Drain the oysters, reserving the oyster liquor. Place the oysters in the top of a double boiler. Measure the oyster liquor and add enough clam juice to yield ½ cup liquid. Add this to the saucepan along with the half-and-half, chili sauce, butter, Worcestershire sauce, and paprika. Place the saucepan over simmering (not boiling) water being careful not to let the pan touch the water. Cook, stirring constantly, until the oysters are slightly firm to the touch, their edges have curled, and the liquid is hot. This will only take 2 to 3 minutes. DO NOT LET BOIL. Season with the celery salt and spoon into soup plates. Sprinkle with chives.

The New England Clambake

Another useful technique the early settlers learned from their Native American neighbors was the clambake. This efficient way of cooking clams and other mollusks also became the focus of colonial social gatherings, a tradition that continues today.

The method is simple: dig a pit on the beach (back far enough so that it won't be doused when the tide comes in) and fill it with dry driftwood, hardwood, and kindling. Top with smooth, flat igneous rocks. Alternately add more wood and then more rocks until the pile is three or four feet high. Ignite the pile (you can use charcoal starter) and let it burn for two or three hours, or until the stones are very hot. The idea is to let the stones fall into the pit as the wood burns away, and you may need a rake to round up errant rocks. You should be left with a pit full of hot rocks and charcoal embers.

When the fire pit is intensely hot, top the stones with a layer of damp seaweed (experts suggest it be from 5 to 10 inches in thickness). Place the clams and mussels on top of the first layer of seaweed and cover with a second, thin layer of seaweed. Place lobsters and crabs at the next level. Cover with another thin layer of seaweed and top with vegetables—ears of corn, potatoes, and onions. (Racks can be used to separate the layers, but are not essential.) Finally, top with one more thin layer of seaweed and cover with a layer or two of thick, wet canvas. Build up sand around the canvas so that no steam can escape. Plug any holes in the pile with wet seaweed. Bake undisturbed for about 1½ hours.

Uncover and transfer the vegetables to warm platters. Dig down, being careful not to burn your hands (work gloves are helpful, or use the rake), and remove the other cooked ingredients to other platters. Serve with crackers, plenty of melted butter, and paper towels. The clambake can be approximated using a kettle-style barbecue grill, although the procedure loses some of its inherent romance.

NEW ENGLAND BOILED DINNER

Serves 8 (with leftovers)

Although it is traditional to cook this hearty New England classic in one pot, the different ingredients can be boiled separately so that each is cooked for an optimum time.

- 1 corned beef brisket, about 6 pounds
- 1 leek, halved lengthwise, cleaned, and sliced
- 2 carrots, diced
- 1 celery stalk, diced
- 10 beets, 1½ inches in diameter
- 16 small boiling onions
- 12 small boiling potatoes
- 3 parsnips, cut into wedges about the size of the potatoes
- 16 baby carrots
- 1 cabbage (preferably Savoy) cut into 6 wedges without removing the core
- 2 tablespoons butter
- 1 cup chicken stock

Fill a large pot with enough water to cover corned beef by at least 2 inches. Bring to a boil and simmer for 20 minutes, skimming the foam off when necessary. Add the leek, carrots, and celery stalk. Simmer for 3½ hours. Test meat's tenderness with a fork. Simmer if necessary.

Meanwhile, preheat the oven to 350°F. Scrub the beets and trim their tops to ¾ of an inch. Put them in an oven-proof pot, add an inch of water, cover and cook in the oven for 45 minutes. Drain, cool, and peel.

Cut an X at the base of each onion with a small paring knife. In a medium-sized pot filled with water, boil the onions for 20 minutes or until tender. Remove with a slotted spoon, cool, and peel. In the same water, simmer the potatoes and parsnips for about 25 minutes or until tender. Remove with a slotted spoon. Next, add the baby carrots and simmer 5 minutes or until tender. Remove with a slotted spoon. Finally, add the cabbage wedges and simmer approximately 5 minutes or until tender. Drain.

When the corned beef is tender, reheat all the vegetables in a large skillet in which you have melted the butter. Add half of the chicken stock, and when reduced to several tablespoons, add the rest of the stock and reduce again to a glaze. Arrange the meat on a platter surrounded by the vegetables, sprinkle with chopped parsley, and serve with Horseradish Cream and several varieties of mustard.

CORNED BEEF HASH

Serves 8

This may be the perfect vehicle for leftovers. It is so good that the original dish may be just a momentary diversion on the road to perfect hash.

- 2 tablespoons butter
- 2 tablespoons olive oil
- 2 onions, diced
- ½ red bell pepper, diced
- ½ yellow bell pepper, diced
- 3 cups boiled potatoes, diced
- 4 cups leftover corned beef, diced
- 1 tablespoon chopped fresh thyme
- 1 tablespoon snipped fresh chives
- Salt and freshly ground black pepper
- ¼ cup chopped fresh parsley

Heat the butter and oil in a medium skillet over medium heat. Sauté the onions until they begin to brown, about 3 minutes. Add the peppers and sauté, stirring, another 2 minutes. Add the potatoes, corned beef, thyme, and chives. Press the mixture flat with a spatula.

Cook 25 to 30 minutes, turning with a spatula after the first 10 minutes and as often as needed, until a brown crust has formed. Season with salt and pepper.

Serve, garnished with the parsley. Another common garnish is to top each serving with a poached egg.

NOTE: As a follow-up to a New England Boiled Dinner, this hash can easily accommodate a cup or two of leftover vegetables.

HORSERADISH CREAM

Makes 2 cups

- ½ cup heavy cream
- 1 cup sour cream
- 1 small white onion, grated
- 3 tablespoons prepared horseradish
- Salt
- Snipped chives

In a medium bowl, whip the cream to soft peaks. Gently fold in the sour cream, onion, and horseradish. Season with salt. Spoon into a serving bowl and sprinkle with the chives.

TURKEY WITH MOLASSES GLAZE

Serves 12 (with leftovers)

This is a basic, foolproof method for preparing turkey. The glaze gives the bird a deep mahogany color and adds flavor to the skin.

- 1 16-pound turkey, fresh *or* fully defrosted
- Salt and freshly ground pepper
- 1 recipe Cornbread Stuffing (see right)
- 2 tablespoons molasses
- 2 tablespoons soy sauce

Preheat the oven to 325°F. Rinse the turkey inside and out with cold water. Dry thoroughly with paper towels. Sprinkle the cavity with salt and pepper. Stuff loosely and close the opening with metal skewers. Also stuff the neck cavity and skewer it closed. (Place the leftover stuffing in a buttered soufflé dish and bake it alongside the turkey for the last hour of its cooking time, basting the stuffing occasionally with pan juices.)

Tie the turkey's legs together and place it on a rack set in a large roasting pan.

Mix the molasses and soy sauce in a small dish. With a pastry brush, paint the turkey with the mixture, lifting it up to reach the underside.

Place the turkey in the center of the preheated oven and roast, basting occasionally with accumulated pan juices, until a thermometer inserted into the thickest part of the thigh registers 170°F and juices run clear. This should take between 4½ and 5 hours. The turkey skin should be quite dark. Check at the 4-hour point and, if skin is not dark enough, brush again with the molasses mixture.

Transfer the turkey to a platter or carving board and let it rest for 20 minutes before carving.

CORNBREAD STUFFING

Makes 8 cups

Some Americans like stuffing even better than the turkey for which it is usually made. This basic version combines flavors and textures in a nicely balanced way. The addition of water chestnuts prevents a mushy texture—there is nothing worse than mushy stuffing.

- ¼ cup chicken *or* turkey fat, *or* butter
- 3 medium onions, chopped
- 2 cloves garlic, minced
- 1 cup chicken *or* turkey broth
- 2 eggs, well-beaten
- ½ cup fresh parsley, finely chopped
- 4 cups crumbled cornbread (see recipe on page 61, or use 1 (28-ounce) bag of packaged cornbread stuffing. Adjust the seasoning accordingly.)
- ½ cup walnuts, chopped
- ½ cup water chestnuts, chopped
- Salt and freshly ground pepper

Melt the fat or butter in a medium skillet over medium heat. Sauté the onions and garlic until the vegetables are translucent but not brown. Remove from the heat. Add the broth, eggs, and parsley. Stir to combine.

In a large bowl place the cornbread and add the broth mixture from the skillet. Add the walnuts and water chestnuts. Season with salt and pepper. Toss to combine, being careful not to compress the stuffing any more than necessary. Keep it fluffy. Cover the bowl and refrigerate until ready to use.

Turkey: The All-American Bird

The turkey was strutting about North America more than eight million years before human beings made their first appearance. Domesticated turkeys were part of the diet of the peoples of the Southwest at the same time that Julius Caesar ruled Rome.

Great flocks of turkeys were found in most of the original Atlantic seaboard colonies. In fact, in the 1820s wild turkeys were so common that they were actually disdained by gourmets. But European connoisseurs, who had been given less opportunity to become blasé about these tasty birds, raved about turkey when they visited the United States.

The modern turkey industry has made it easy to shop for turkey. The uniformity and high quality of the birds in the butcher shops and supermarkets mean there is really very little need to be concerned about such things as freshness, tenderness, and flavor. Just buy from a reliable merchant and you should have no problems. Your most important consideration may be size. How big a turkey should you buy?

Obviously, the size of your turkey is directly related to the number of people you will be feeding, but there are other factors that should influence your choice. Do you want leftovers? Are your guests going to be mostly hungry adults, or will there be a substantial number of children?

The best way to estimate the size of the turkey needed is to allow 1 to 1½ pounds of uncooked weight for every person (allow 2 pounds per person if the turkey weighs less than 10 pounds). This rule of thumb should leave a goodly amount left over and also provide enough white and dark meat to satisfy any preferences. Of course, you don't have to buy just one turkey. If you are having thirty people and find that a husky 30-pound tom will not fit in the oven, buy two 15-pound birds instead.

All turkeys today are classified as "young turkey." A useful sub-category, "fryer-roaster," is usually reserved for a very young bird weighing 6 to 9 pounds and under sixteen weeks old. This size is excellent for a small group and for barbecuing.

If you are selecting a frozen turkey, make sure it is wrapped in tight packaging that is completely free of holes and tears. Also be aware of expiration or "sell by" dates.

Take your fresh or frozen turkey home immediately after purchase and keep it frozen or refrigerated. If you are using a fresh turkey that is not enclosed in a tight plastic wrap, take it out of its wrappings and, after removing the bag containing the giblets, rinse it under cold running water. Then pat it dry with paper towels, rewrap it in fresh, new waxed paper and place it in a large, tightly sealed plastic bag in the refrigerator. Make the turkey the last thing you buy before heading home so that it will not be left unrefrigerated for too long.

Poultry must be handled in a clean environment. Make sure that utensils, platters, cutting boards, counter tops, and hands are soap-and-hot-water clean. After handling fresh poultry, wash your hands again so as not to transfer bacteria to other foods.

A fresh turkey—and any other uncooked meat, for that matter—should never be left unrefrigerated for more than two hours. The key temperatures to remember are 40°F and 140°F. If you are keeping the turkey cold it must be at 40°F or lower. If you are heating food, it must be 140°F or higher. The temperatures in between are ideal for the growth of bacteria and the production of toxins in food.

If you are using frozen turkey, the best way to defrost it is in the refrigerator. This method is slow, but the bird loses very little of its moisture and will, therefore, cook up as tender and juicy as possible.

Put the frozen turkey—still in its original wrap—on a platter or tray in the refrigerator. Allow five hours per pound of turkey for defrosting. This means that if you are preparing a 15-pound turkey, it will take seventy-five hours to defrost. If you need to defrost your turkey a little faster, place the still-wrapped bird in the sink the day before it is to be cooked and cover with cold water. Change the water frequently during the day and allow about ½ hour per pound. Refrigerate immediately. The next morning the turkey will be ready to prepare for cooking.

Although it may seem a tempting way to avoid the time and work of these two methods, never defrost a turkey at room temperature. The bird will become a breeding place for bacteria.

Small turkeys can also be defrosted in the microwave oven. The bird must be unwrapped and placed in the same roasting pan you will eventually cook it in. Shield thin or bony areas with small pieces of aluminum foil and rotate the bird several times during defrosting. Consult the oven manufacturer's instructions for thawing times.

Frankly, a fresh turkey is preferable. As much as modern technology has perfected the flash-freezing method, a fresh-killed bird is superior to its frosty cousin. Do not take delivery of a fresh turkey more than twenty-four hours before you plan to cook it. Home refrigerators—no matter how efficient they may be—do not offer the right degree of cold or humidity for any lengthy storage. When you bring your turkey home, immediately change the bird's wrappings.

Before cooking, rinse the turkey thoroughly under cool running water and pat dry with paper towels. If you want to bring the turkey to room temperature before cooking, drape it with waxed paper and let it sit on a well-ventilated kitchen counter for no more than one hour.

After rinsing and drying, the easiest method for preparing a turkey is to secure the flap over the neck opening with a poultry pin or round wooden toothpick. Place the drumsticks in the pre-cut band of skin, or tie them together loosely. Tuck the wing tips back under the shoulders of the bird to allow the turkey to rest more solidly on the roasting rack (this also prevents over-browning of the wing tips during roasting).

Place the turkey breast side up on a V-shaped roasting rack set in an open, shallow roasting pan. The rack should hold the bird at least ½-inch above the bottom of the pan to allow the oven heat to circulate evenly.

Place the turkey in the center of a pre-heated 325°F oven. The relatively low roasting temperature is the secret to a golden, juicy result. Drippings will not burn, and the meat will shrink less. Higher temperatures may cause the outside of the bird to cook faster than the inside, resulting in tough, dried-out meat that is difficult to carve.

Set the turkey in the middle of the oven, running lengthwise from side to side, not back to front. Halfway through the roasting process, turn the turkey around completely to insure even cooking.

If the turkey reaches the desired color before the roasting time is over, cover the bird with lightweight foil, shiny side down, to shield the skin against over-browning.

There is no exact formula for the amount of time a turkey should cook, but there are general guidelines. These times are inexact because there are a number of variables that affect the roasting process. Ovens vary in size; heat distribution can be different for each oven; turkeys have individual physical characteristics; and oven temperature is directly affected by the number of times the oven door is opened. If you are cooking a bird that has been defrosted, the exact degree of thawing will also have an impact.

Here are the approximate roasting times for a turkey in a 325°F oven:

Weight	Unstuffed	Stuffed	Weight	Unstuffed	Stuffed
6 pounds	2½ hours	2½ hours	16 pounds	4½ hours	4½ hours
8 pounds	3 hours	3½ hours	18 pounds	4½ hours	5 hours
10 pounds	3½ hours	4 hours	20 pounds	4½ hours	5½ hours
12 pounds	3½ hours	4½ hours	22 pounds	5 hours	5½ hours
14 pounds	4 hours	4½ hours	24 pounds	5½ hours	6 hours

The way to tell if your turkey is done is to take its temperature by inserting a thermometer—the instant-reading kind—in the upper thigh area. When the internal temperature of the meat is 170°F to 175°F, the turkey is done. Another way to tell is to look at the juices that flow from the spot where the thermometer punctures the skin. If they run clear, the turkey is done.

There are important rules that must be observed when dealing with stuffing: make sure the stuffing has been refrigerated or is, at least, cool before putting it into the turkey. Do not stuff a turkey until just before you are ready to cook it.

Spoon the stuffing in loosely. Don't overstuff. Stuffing expands during cooking and if it is too firmly packed, it may split the turkey. And don't forget to remove the giblet bag and neck from inside the turkey before stuffing.

If you are cooking all the stuffing or some of the stuffing outside of the turkey, put it into a buttered casserole or soufflé dish, being sure to keep it loosely packed. The stuffing should not be cooked as long as you cook the turkey. An hour or less at 325 °F should be enough to warm the stuffing through. To keep the stuffing moist, baste the casserole occasionally when basting the turkey.

NOTE: After dinner, if you have cooked the stuffing inside the turkey, remove all of it from the bird and store the leftovers in a separate container. Leaving stuffing in the turkey carcass is an invitation to spoilage.

Keeping the turkey moist while cooking is an important consideration. One way to insure this is to baste the bird. This procedure—occasionally spooning liquid over the turkey—keeps the turkey skin moist and tender and can also help the browning process.

Any number of liquids can be used for basting, but the most common is chicken or turkey stock. As the liquid runs off into the roasting pan it blends with the rich pan drippings from the turkey. If you use a bulb baster, you can suck up this enriched stock and baste the turkey with it in the latter stages of cooking.

The basting liquid in the bottom of the roasting pan helps to keep the oven environment humid (thus keeping the turkey from drying out), and it prevents drippings from burning in the pan and causing unwanted smoke and a burnt taste.

Basting is helpful, but don't overdo it. Basting the bird every twenty minutes or so is plenty. Remember, each time you open the oven door the temperature inside the oven is lowered and cooking time is lengthened.

If you purchase a bird that is labeled "self-basting," this doesn't mean that basting can be given up completely. The "self-basting" turkeys are injected with liquid that keeps the meat moist internally during cooking. But the skin still requires attention, and an occasional basting with stock and pan juices will keep it from drying out.

DOUBLE CRANBERRY-CHERRY RELISH

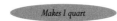
Makes 1 quart

This recipe is adapted from The Household Magazine, *a publication for "homemakers who are especially interested in food preparation," that was sold throughout the country from 1925 to 1942. This all-purpose relish is wonderful with turkey, chicken, pork, and other meats.*

- 1 (12-ounce) package fresh *or* frozen whole berry cranberries
- 2 cups golden brown sugar, packed
- ½ cup dried cranberries
- ½ cup dried tart cherries
- ½ cup cranberry *or* white wine vinegar
- 1 orange, cut into 8 wedges and thinly sliced
- 1 lemon, cut into 8 wedges and thinly sliced
- ½ teaspoon ground cinnamon
- ½ teaspoon ground cloves
- ½ teaspoon ground nutmeg
- 1 cinnamon stick

Place all ingredients in a large saucepan over medium-high heat. Bring to a boil, reduce the heat, and simmer for 15 minutes. Remove and discard the cinnamon stick. Cool the relish completely. Cover and refrigerate. This relish will keep in the refrigerator for up to 2 weeks.

MINTED ROASTED BEETS

Serves 6

Beets, a Mediterranean root vegetable, are often pickled. This time they are flavored with fresh mint.

- 2 pounds beets, trimmed of beet green tops (You should have about 1½ pounds of beets after trimming. Save the beet greens for the recipe on page 58.)
- 3 tablespoons unsalted butter
- 2 shallots, minced
- ⅓ cup apple jelly
- 2 tablespoons chopped fresh mint
- 2 teaspoons lemon juice
- Salt and freshly ground pepper

Preheat the oven to 350°F. Place the trimmed and scrubbed beets in a roasting pan and add enough water to reach ¼ inch high. Cover tightly with aluminum foil and roast about 45 minutes or until tender. Let the beets cool in the pan until cool enough to handle. Slide the skins off the beets and cut them into ½-inch wedges; set aside.

Melt the butter in a large skillet over medium heat; add the shallots and sauté, stirring, for 3 minutes.

Add the beets, apple jelly, mint, and lemon juice; heat through and cook until the beets are nicely glazed, about 10 minutes. Season with salt and pepper.

CHICKEN POT PIE

Serves 8

*Popular since Revolutionary times, this dish got its name from the deep pans or pots
in which it was baked by New England colonists.*

For the pastry:
- 2 cups all-purpose flour
- ¾ cup (6 ounces) very cold butter, in ½-inch slices
- 1 cup (4 ounces) shredded sharp cheddar cheese
- ½ cup ice water
- 1 egg, lightly beaten

For the filling:
- 2½ cups chicken stock
- 3 medium (about 12 to 14 ounces each) whole bone-in chicken breasts
- 1 (10-ounce) package fresh baby onions with skins
- 2½ cups 1-inch baby carrot pieces

- 3 cups (¾ pound) new potatoes cut into ½-inch cubes
- 2 stalks celery, cut into ½-inch slices
- 3 tablespoons butter
- 1 cup frozen baby peas, thawed

For the sauce:
- 6 tablespoons butter
- 7 tablespoons all-purpose flour
- ¾ cup half-and-half *or* heavy cream
- 3 tablespoons finely chopped fresh parsley
- 3 tablespoons minced fresh thyme
- 3 tablespoons snipped fresh chives
- Salt and freshly ground black pepper

To make the pastry: In a large mixing bowl cut the cold butter into the flour with two knives until the mixture resembles coarse meal. Sprinkle the cheese on top and cut it into the mixture until just blended. Sprinkle the ice water over the mixture and bring the pastry together into a ball, kneading lightly until just combined. Wrap the pastry in plastic wrap and refrigerate until needed.

To prepare the filling: In a large saucepan bring the chicken stock to a simmer and add the chicken breasts. Simmer, covered, 20 minutes or until cooked through and firm to the touch. Let cool; remove chicken and set stock aside for the sauce. Remove the chicken meat from the bones. Cut the meat into ¾-inch chunks. Set aside.

Bring two medium saucepans, ¾ full of lightly salted water, to the boil. To one of the saucepans add the onions and boil for 5 minutes. Then add the carrots and boil another 3 minutes. Drain, peel the onions, and set aside. To the second saucepan add the potatoes and boil for 8 minutes. Add the celery and boil 2 minutes longer. Drain and set aside.

Melt the butter in a medium skillet over medium heat. Sauté the onions and carrots, stirring occasionally, for 15 minutes. Set aside.

For the sauce: Melt the butter in a medium saucepan over medium heat. Sprinkle in the flour and whisk until the mixture is smooth and bubbling slightly, but not browned, about 3 minutes. Slowly add 2 cups of the reserved chicken stock, whisking until smooth, and bring to a simmer. Continue to simmer, stirring, for 4 to 5 minutes, or until the sauce thickens slightly, then add the half-and-half and cook for 5 more minutes, stirring occasionally. The sauce should coat the back of a spoon. Remove from the heat and stir in the herbs. Season with salt and pepper.

Preheat the oven to 400°F. Combine the sauce with the chicken, onions, carrots, potatoes, celery, and peas. Spoon the mixture into a 9 x 13 inch baking dish. Brush the edge of the dish with a little of the egg. Roll out the pastry to ¼ inch thick and fit it over the dish, pressing along the edge firmly. Trim edges and use leftover pastry to cut several small leaf shapes for decoration.

Brush the top of the pastry with the egg. Cut vents in the pie. Bake the pie in the preheated oven for 25 to 30 minutes, or until the pastry is crisp and golden brown. Let stand for 5 minutes before serving.

Boston Baked Beans

Serves 8

*Native Americans cooked their beans in holes dug
in the earth and taught this to the colonists.
The dish was originally made with maple sugar.*

- 1 pound dry, small white beans (white pea, Jacob's Cattle, navy, or Great Northern)
- ½ pound salt pork, cut into 2 equal pieces
- 2 medium onions, cut into ¼-inch dices
- 1 quart water
- ⅓ cup brown sugar, packed
- ⅓ cup dark molasses
- ¼ cup dry mustard
- 3 tablespoons apple cider vinegar
- 1½ teaspoons salt
- 1 teaspoon freshly ground black pepper
- ¾ teaspoon hot pepper sauce
- ¾ teaspoon ground ginger
- 1 bay leaf

In a large bowl, place the beans and add cold water until covered by at least 2 inches. Soak overnight, or at least 8 hours. Drain.

Score the pieces of salt pork every ½ inch, being careful not to cut all the way through. Put 1 piece of salt pork in a medium ovenproof pot over medium heat. Render the fat for 3 or 4 minutes. Add the onions and sauté until translucent and beginning to brown, about 10 minutes. Add the beans.

In a medium saucepan, combine the quart of water and all the rest of the ingredients. Bring to a boil over medium heat and pour over the beans. Stir to combine. Place the second piece of salt pork on top of the beans.

Preheat the oven to 250°F. Cover the pot and place it in the preheated oven. Bake for 5 hours, checking every hour or so to make sure the beans are not drying out. (If they are, add water ½ cup at a time.) Uncover and cook another ½ hour. Cut the pork into ½-inch cubes. Serve beans in individual bowls, topped with the pork.

Boston Brown Bread

Makes 1 loaf

This recipe is attributed to two Bostonians, Mr. Lately Gee and Mrs. Bennett. They adapted it from a steamed bread that the Native Americans made. It was quite useful when yeast was difficult to get. This brown bread is cooked in a cylindrical mold. A 12-ounce coffee can is a perfect substitute. This dense bread is the traditional accompaniment to Boston Baked Beans (see left).

- ½ cup yellow cornmeal
- ½ cup whole-wheat flour
- ½ cup rye flour
- 1½ teaspoons baking soda
- ½ teaspoon salt
- ⅓ cup dark molasses
- 1 cup buttermilk

Butter the inside of a 12-ounce coffee can or a cylindrical pudding mold. Combine the dry ingredients in a mixing bowl. Add the molasses and the buttermilk and mix well. Pour into the coffee can or mold.

If you still have the metal top of the can or if your mold has a top, butter its inside. Otherwise butter a sheet of aluminum foil and cover the top and part way down the sides, securing with string.

Place the can or mold in a deep pot. Pour boiling water down the sides of the pot until the water comes halfway up the sides of the can or mold.

Place the pot over low heat and simmer for 1½ hours. Keep checking the water level and add more boiling water if necessary.

Remove the can or mold from the pot and take off its lid. A cake tester or toothpick inserted in the center of the bread should come out clean. If it doesn't, re-cover and continue steaming for 5 more minutes.

Cool on a rack until the bread pulls away from the side of the can or mold. Tap the bread out. Cool further on the rack. Serve sliced into rounds.

GRAHAM'S BLUEBERRY GLAZE PIE
ADAPTED FROM A RECIPE OF GRAHAM'S RESTAURANT, MACHIAS, MAINE

Makes one 9-inch pie

Machias is located on the edge of the Bay of Fundy, not far from the New Brunswick border. The surrounding county, Washington, produces more blueberries than any other in the state. It is only fitting that this most delectable expression of fresh blueberries comes from a restaurant in this coastal town.

- 2 tablespoons cornstarch
- ¾ cup water
- 1 teaspoon lemon juice
- 4 cups fresh blueberries (this pie will *not* work with frozen berries)
- 1 tablespoon butter
- ¾ cup sugar
- Pinch of salt
- 1 recipe Super Flaky Pie Crust (page 34), baked blind

Mix the cornstarch, 2 tablespoons of the water, and the lemon juice in a small bowl. Stir until completely dissolved. Meanwhile, place 1 cup of blueberries and all the remaining water into a medium-sized saucepan over medium-high heat and bring to a boil. Cook until the berries begin to pop, about 3 minutes. Add the butter, sugar, salt, and the cornstarch mixture. Lower the heat and cook, stirring constantly, until the mixture is thick and clear, about 3 minutes. Remove from heat.

Fold the remaining fresh berries into the cooked berry mixture and pour into the baked crust. Refrigerate until ready to serve, then bring to room temperature. To bake a blind pie shell, see next page.

33

SUPER FLAKY PIE CRUST

Makes one 9-inch pie shell

This recipe can be doubled. If you are not going to use the second crust right away, the dough can be refrigerated for up to four days, or you can freeze it for up to three months.

- 1 cup unbleached all-purpose flour
- ¼ teaspoon salt
- Pinch of sugar
- 6 tablespoons chilled butter, cut into ½-inch slices
- 1½ tablespoons solid vegetable shortening
- 2 to 3 tablespoons ice water

Combine the flour, salt, and sugar in the bowl of a food processor fitted with a metal blade. Add the butter and the shortening. Pulse the processor on and off until the dough resembles coarse meal.

Transfer the mixture into a bowl and sprinkle a little at a time with 2 tablespoons of water. Toss with a fork until the mixture comes together in lumps and holds together when pressed. If necessary, add a bit more water, but avoid kneading.

NOTE: The entire procedure up to this point can be done by hand, just be careful not to overmix the ingredients.

Form the dough into a ball, wrap in plastic wrap and chill for at least 4 hours.

When ready, roll the dough into a ⅛-inch thick sheet (about 13 inches in diameter) on a cool surface dusted with flour. To lift, roll the dough onto the rolling pin and unroll it over a 9-inch Pyrex pie plate. Using your fingers, press the dough into the plate. Roll the edges over to make an even hem that extends about ½ inch beyond the rim of the plate. Crimp with the tines of a fork or with your fingers to form a decorative edge. Prick the bottom of the dough with a fork several times.

Put the finished, uncooked pie shell into the freezer for at least 20 minutes. (It will keep, tightly wrapped, in the freezer three months.) Preheat the oven to 450°F. Put the oven rack about one-third up from the bottom of the oven.

To bake a "blind" (unfilled) pie shell, place aluminum foil into the frozen shell. Press it into place. Fill the foil three-quarters full with rice, dried beans, or aluminum pellets that are specifically made for this purpose. (Most cooking stores carry them.)

Bake the shell for 10 minutes or until set and looking dry. Remove it from the oven and lift out the foil with its filling. Reduce the oven temperature to 400°F. Put the shell back in the oven for 10 more minutes, or until golden brown in color.

Remove from the oven and place on a rack. Cool to room temperature.

PEPPER PUMPKIN CUSTARD PIE

Makes one 9-inch pie

No New England Thanksgiving would be complete without pump-kin pie, but all pumpkin pies are not created equal. There are, of course, various things that can be done with seasonings, crusts, and other ingredients to make a particular pie unique and memorable. This pie may seem a bit unorthodox, but it is really delicious.

- 2 cups (1 large can) canned pumpkin
- 1½ cups heavy cream
- 3 eggs
- ¾ cup maple syrup
- 1 teaspoon freshly ground white pepper
- 1 teaspoon vanilla extract
- 1 recipe Super Flaky Pie Crust (page 34)

Preheat oven to 350°F. In a bowl mix the pumpkin, cream, eggs, and maple syrup until smooth. Stir in pepper and vanilla.

Pour the filling into the prepared pie shell and bake for 1 hour. The pie is done when a toothpick or cake tester inserted into the pie center comes away clean. (To avoid the unsightly mark of this test you can also shake the pie slightly. If the center is firm, the pie is done.) Cool on a wire rack.

VARIATION: This pie can be completely changed by varying the seasonings. A more traditional pie would result from eliminating the pepper and adding all of the following:

- 1 tablespoon brandy
- ½ teaspoon ground allspice
- ½ teaspoon freshly grated nutmeg
- ½ teaspoon ground ginger

LEMON MERINGUE PIE

Makes one 9-inch pie

Invented in England as lemon curd; perfected in New England.

- 3 eggs
- 5 egg yolks (save 4 egg whites, at room temperature, for meringue)
- ½ cup plus 1 tablespoon sugar
- Juice of 3 large lemons (½ cup)
- 9 tablespoons butter, cut into ½-inch pieces
- ½ teaspoon cream of tartar
- ½ cup superfine sugar
- ½ teaspoon vanilla extract
- 1 recipe Super Flaky Pie Crust (page 34), baked blind

In a heavy, nonreactive saucepan whisk the eggs, yolks, and granulated sugar until well combined. Whisk in the lemon juice and then stir in the butter. Cook, stirring constantly, over low heat until the mixture comes together and thickens enough to coat the back of a spoon. Remove from the heat. Allow to stand for 5 minutes, then whisk briefly to smooth. Set aside.

Preheat the oven to 350°F. Spread the lemon filling in the pie shell and bake 12 minutes or until the filling is just set. Raise oven temperature to 375°F.

To make the meringue, beat the egg whites until frothy. Add the cream of tartar and continue beating until stiff peaks form. Beat in the superfine sugar and the vanilla.

Spread the meringue over the lemon filling, making sure it meets the edge of the crust to make a seal. Swirl in a design or lift into random peaks with a knife or the back of a spoon. Bake about 10 minutes or until the meringue is lightly browned.

Allow to cool completely, 1 to 2 hours.

STRAWBERRY SHORTCAKES

Serves 8

This classic dessert uses a typical English shortbread biscuit, fresh strawberries, and whipped cream. It is so easy to make and so satisfying that its great popularity is not difficult to understand.

- 2 cups all-purpose flour
- 2 tablespoons granulated sugar
- 1 tablespoon baking powder
- ½ teaspoon salt
- 6 tablespoons chilled unsalted butter, cut into ½-inch pieces
- 2 cups heavy cream
- 2 pints strawberries, hulled and thickly sliced
- ½ cup plus 2 tablespoons powdered sugar
- 1 teaspoon vanilla extract
- Additional powdered sugar, for dusting
- Mint sprigs for garnish

Preheat the oven to 425°F. In a food processor fitted with a metal blade, combine the flour, granulated sugar, baking powder, and salt. Add the butter and pulse on and off until the mixture resembles coarse meal. With the motor running, slowly pour 1 cup of the cream through the feed tube. Process until the mixture becomes a soft dough.

Place the dough on a floured surface. Knead it with the heel of your hand, then roll it into a ½-inch thickness. Cut the dough into 3-inch rounds (or squares, if you like). Place them on an ungreased baking sheet, spacing them 2 inches apart. Bake in the preheated oven until their tops are light golden brown, 10 to 12 minutes. Cool on racks.

Toss the strawberries and ½ cup of the powdered sugar in a bowl. Set aside for 1 hour.

In a small bowl, whip the remaining 1 cup of cream to soft peaks. Gently fold in the remaining 2 tablespoons of powdered sugar and the vanilla. Cover and refrigerate until ready to serve.

To serve, split each shortcake in half horizontally, using a serrated knife. Place the bottom half on an individual dessert plate, spoon ½ cup of the strawberries and their juice onto it. Top with ¼ cup of whipped cream. Add the shortcake top, cut side down. Dust with additional powdered sugar (put the sugar into a fine, small strainer and tap gently to produce an even dusting). Garnish with mint sprigs.

TRIPLE GINGER GINGERBREAD CAKE WITH CARAMEL SAUCE

Makes one 10-inch cake (8-10 servings)

Ginger was brought to the colonies by English settlers. This uses powdered ginger, candied ginger, and fresh ginger—thus its name.

- 1¾ cups granulated sugar
- ½ cup unsalted butter, softened
- ½ cup vegetable shortening
- ¼ cup golden brown sugar
- 2 eggs
- 2 cups all-purpose flour
- 1 tablespoon instant espresso coffee powder
- 1 teaspoon powdered ginger
- 1 teaspoon cinnamon
- 1 teaspoon powdered sugar
- 1 teaspoon baking powder
- 1 teaspoon baking soda
- 1 cup dark molasses
- 1 cup boiling water
- ½ cup finely chopped candied ginger
- 2 teaspoons grated fresh ginger
- ¼ cup cold water
- ½ teaspoon lemon juice
- 2 cups heavy cream
- ½ teaspoon salt

Preheat the oven to 350°F. Lightly grease and flour a 10-inch bundt pan; set aside. In a large mixing bowl, cream together ¾ cup of the granulated sugar, the butter, shortening, and brown sugar. Beat in the eggs to combine completely. Add the flour, coffee powder, powdered ginger, cinnamon, powdered sugar, baking powder, and baking soda; mix just until combined.

Add the molasses, boiling water, candied ginger, and fresh ginger; mix just until combined. Pour the batter into the prepared pan; spread evenly. Bake about 40 minutes or until a cake tester or toothpick inserted into the cake comes out clean. Remove to a rack to cool 30 minutes. Turn the cake out of the pan onto a serving plate.

To make caramel sauce: In a medium saucepan, combine the remaining 1 cup of the granulated sugar, the cold water, and lemon juice. Place over medium heat to dissolve sugar. Increase heat. Cook until the sauce turns a deep golden color, swirling the pan to insure even cooking and coloration. Remove from heat. Stir in the cream and salt; return the pan to medium heat and cook, stirring constantly, until sauce is thickened and a deep golden brown color. Remove from heat; cool slightly.

To serve, slice the cake and serve with the warm sauce.

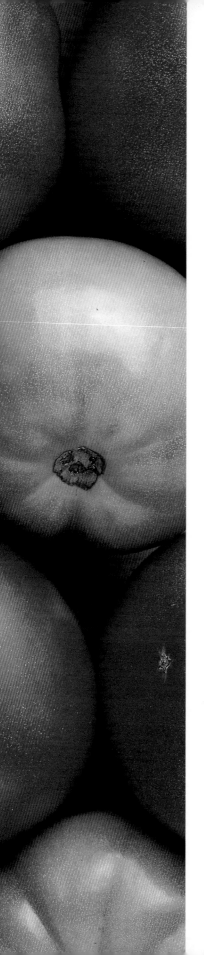

The South

More than any other American cuisine, the cooking of the South is the cumulative product of the tumultous history of the area. Southern cuisine is a living monument to the hard life, the pain, and the conflicts that have defined this region for nearly four hundred years.

The South, like New England, was founded by English emigrants who fled their native land for religious reasons. Like their New England counterparts, the colonists who settled the South were greatly aided by Native Americans, who quickly taught them how and what to farm. Much of the early cooking of the South was undertaken in large cast-iron fireplace kettles. Captain John Smith and his Jamestown settlers learned almost immediately about maize, or corn, from the local Powhatan Algonquian tribes. The English had been prescient enough to bring along some pigs, which thrived in their new environment. Within a few months the basis of Southern cooking had been established. For the nearly four centuries since 1607, corn and pork have been the foundation of the Southern kitchen.

The integration of the European and Native American culinary disciplines became a classic case of the whole being greater than the sum of the parts. The settlers brought sheep, cattle, goats, and chickens, as well as pigs. The Powhatans contributed turkeys, deer, rabbits, ducks, pigeons, possums, squirrels, geese, crabs, shrimp, clams, turtles, oysters, shad, mullet, herring, trout, and catfish. The settlers imported rye, barley, oats, wheat, turnips, cabbage, and apples. The Native Americans provided pumpkins, squash, greens, onions, berries, plums, cherries, peas, and beans.

African Inspiration

By the mid-1700s the ignoble slave trade had transported more than half a million Africans to America, mostly to the South, and a hundred years later there were four million. The influence of these African people on the food and style of cooking in the South was profound.

Many Africans brought with them foodstuffs for the lengthy Atlantic crossing, and a number of these were planted in Southern soil upon arrival. As a result, okra, black-eyed peas, yams, collard greens, watermelons, benne seeds (sesame), and peanuts became part of the southern pantry. In addition to being a source of new ingredients, Africans staffed the kitchens where the new cuisine emerged and provided hands-on culinary inspiration.

Southern food quickly took on a distinctive character all its own. Plain, bland English cooking was changed forever by Native American and African tastes, techniques, and seasonings. In addition, other influences—French, Spanish, German, and Dutch—brought in by subsequent immigrants, added texture and complexity to the new cuisine.

Southern Hospitality

The cash crops of the South were not food products. Landowners made their fortunes on cotton and tobacco, but these crops did little to feed the working class and the slaves, both of whom lived in comparative poverty until long after the Civil War.

Most of the British immigrants who came to the South weren't aristocrats; they were merchants and artisans. This fact did not prevent them from constructing a society modeled after the English class system; it only served to stimulate that great American tradition, upward mobility. Landowners and successful merchants became the new southern aristocracy.

One of the trappings of wealth and social ascendancy was the ability to serve elegant, elaborate, labor-intensive meals to guests. Most of the wealthiest families were fairly self-sufficient in the area of basic foodstuffs thanks to the ready supply of cheap labor. They also had the financial resources to import costly spices, wines, and preserved European foods.

Although the majority of white southerners did not own slaves or enjoy the opulent plantation life, this lifestyle set the tone and made "Southern Hospitality" a hallmark of life in the region that would eventually become the Confederacy. Even families who lived in poverty or modest circumstances prided themselves on being gracious and welcoming to guests. The door was open, and the focus of the welcome was the dinner table.

Offering the most basic food to family, friends, and strangers was the most meaningful and appreciated form of hospitality.

The French Influence

Southerners appreciated the support that the French gave to the revolutionaries in the War of Independence and, when it was over, embraced French culture, especially cooking techniques. America's greatest Francophile, Thomas Jefferson, served as an envoy to Paris during and after the war and brought many French food traditions back to Virginia.

At Monticello, Jefferson studied the ways he could produce and prepare the French foods he loved. He planned the gardens, kitchen, and dining room to duplicate his Gallic experiences and became an avid importer of French wines.

The Civil War and After

Fought mostly on Southern soil, the Civil War had a devastating effect on the region. Although many African-Americans moved north to the large industrial cities, a substantial number stayed put, doing what they had been doing before the war. The South was poor and rural. Food was the focus of everyday life because so much time had to be devoted to growing, gathering, and preparing it.

Ironically, the southern diet improved because of widespread poverty, at least by today's standards. People ate more vegetables and less meat. Vegetables could be grown at home in abundance; meat was harder to get and expensive to buy. While the northern industrialists were living on a fatty diet of meat and potatoes, the southern table was piled high with a colorful variety of vegetables and baked goods. "Putting up"—canning and preserving—became a vital part of the late summer and early fall.

Down Home

This preoccupation with food translated into communal feasts. Southern social life still values hospitality: big family Sunday dinners, church potlucks, pie suppers, fish fries, and political barbecues were regular occurrences. More than any other region, the food of the South is home food. The restaurants that have succeeded are generally places that recapture some of the "down home" flavor missing in modern lifestyles.

Southern cooking was born from a blend of English, Native American, and African influences. It was raised and matured with added complexity from other imported disciplines, but what truly forged it was hardship and deprivation. Genuine Southern food is the most unique and heroic of cuisines. Whites may call it "down home," and blacks may dub it "soul food," either way it is a way of life, a symbol of triumph over adversity.

The Southern Pantry

BEANS AND PEAS

Both have been daily staples for hundreds of years, and both are often cooked simply like greens (with a ham hock or piece of salt pork) and served with cornbread. But peas—more specifically, cowpeas—are the real southern specialty. The most familiar variety is the earthy black-eyed pea, introduced from Africa. Traditionally thought to bring good luck, black-eyed peas show up on every good southern New Year's Day menu. They are often combined with rice to make the popular Hoppin' John (see page 60).

BIBB LETTUCE

Good Kentucky soil has produced more than just superior bourbon. In 1865 Judge John Bibb capitalized on the soil's alkaline quality to propagate Bibb lettuce, a small, tender variety similar to Boston lettuce. Its flavor is subtle and delicious when dressed with a simple vinaigrette.

BLACK WALNUTS

Although black walnuts grow throughout the region, they are literally a "tough nut to crack," and are not widely available elsewhere. Many southerners, however, collect a gunnysack full every fall, "pound the heck out of 'em" with a hammer, and spend some winter evenings around the table picking out the tiny, pungent pieces to go into cake batter. If there are any left by summer, black walnuts add a rich flavor to homemade banana ice cream.

BUTTERMILK

Southerners drink more buttermilk than the rest of the country. This by-product of churning milk and cream into butter is thick, rich, "creamy," and fat-free. Many southerners still crumble their cornbread into buttermilk, and cooking with buttermilk adds a pleasing pungency to cornbread, biscuits, and certain cakes and pies.

CATFISH

According to the *Encyclopedia of Southern Culture*, "every Southern state proclaims at least one 'catfish capital of the world.'" It is a fish that is becoming more and more popular throughout the rest of the country as well. And while rising water pollution levels are causing concern about seafood in general, the catfish sold today is actually cleaner and—to most people—better tasting than it used to be, because it is farm-raised in clean water as opposed to growing up scavenging the murky bottoms of Southern rivers. Catfish stars at fish fries, with Hush Puppies (see page 60) and coleslaw, but you can now find this once-lowly scaleless fish, without its tough skin and whiskers, "pan-roasted" and served with elegant sauces and accompaniments in the finest restaurants in the land.

CHICKEN

Of course, people throughout the United States have always eaten chicken, but southerners love chicken more than most. Indeed, they produce almost 80 percent of the chickens the rest of the country consumes. Good Fried Chicken (see page 52), long a mainstay of the traditional Sunday dinner, embodies the flavor of the South. Other poultry classics include "smothered" chicken (browned, covered with gravy, then baked), Brunswick Stew (see page 54), and chicken and dumplings.

CORN

In the South corn has remained a staple since the Algonquian Indians showed the Jamestown settlers how to plant, harvest, and prepare it in the early 1600s. When in season, sweet corn is prized all over the region, but it is field corn that appears on tables in various forms year-round. Ground into cornmeal, it is the base for a number of batter breads popular in the South, such as Cornbread (see page 61), Spoonbread (see page 60), Hush Puppies (see page 60), and muffins. White cornmeal is used more than yellow in the South, but the two can usually be interchanged in recipes. Stone-ground cornmeal has more flavor and is actually a little more nutritious than the more common commercial meal that has been passed through rollers. Many cooks in the South use self-rising cornmeal—not to be confused with a cornmeal mix, which has flour, baking powder, and salt added.

Hominy is produced by soaking field corn in a lye (or limestone) solution, which loosens the outer husks from the kernels. The most visible form of hominy in the South today is the finely ground version known as grits (see pages 57 and 62)—the cornerstone of a good southern breakfast.

COUNTRY HAM

A cured ham epitomizes the original influences on the Southern diet: pork (contributed by English settlers) fattened originally on peanuts (contributed by Africans) and preserved with Native American methods. But many people in the United States—even those who consume ham regularly —have never set eyes on a southern country-cured ham. When confronted with the genuine article, in fact, some people turn squeamish at what looks like (and indeed is) mold covering the surface, and modern palates might actually reject the deep, smoky, salty flavor. That's because today's brine-injected supermarket hams have diluted our taste for this richest of all southern traditions: the dry-cured, smoked, and aged country ham. Smithfield, Virginia, was the birthplace of southern-style country hams and is still the leader in curing hams by the traditional method: with dry salt, then smoked over a hardwood fire and aged. These hams are salty, but that is why they taste so good with a spicy-sweet glaze, sliced thinly and piled in the middle of a warm biscuit or, best of all, fried in a cast-iron skillet and served with coffee-based red-eye gravy, biscuits, eggs, grits, and fried apples for breakfast.

GAME

Though not the necessity it was in past centuries, wild game continues to be popular, and hunters fill southern woods and fields during cold weather. Ducks, quail, doves, wild turkeys, and geese are the most sought-after birds. Bear and deer are the big game of choice. But a "critter supper" in the South features small quarry: rabbit, squirrel, raccoon, and, of course, opossum (just "possum" in the South). Game is usually roasted, fried, stewed, or "smothered."

GREENS

A "mess of greens" in their "pot likker" will take any displaced Southerner home. Greens in the regional vernacular are not the ones you put in a salad; they are turnip greens, beet greens, mustard greens, collards, kale, spinach, chard, dandelion greens, watercress, or the more exotic wild poke sallet, rapeweed, purslane, and others. These are simmered for a long time—traditionally with some form of pork (salt pork, ham hocks, fatback, slab bacon, or hog jowls) and sometimes other flavorings, such as onions and hot peppers—to release their bitterness and tenderize the leaves (see page 58). Of course, modern cooks sometimes compromise with a lean piece of meat and realize that cooking greens for hours destroys vitamins and other nutrients, but, on the other hand, some of those remain in the rich "pot likker," which is always sopped up with cornbread or biscuits.

OKRA

Avoided by many who consider it "slimy," okra is actually becoming more popular these days because of its use in such cuisines as Cajun. Okra has been a workhorse vegetable since the late 1700s, after being introduced by African slaves. Cooks actually take advantage of its mucilaginous characteristic—that slime—to thicken other dishes. They also control its gumminess by rolling it in cornmeal and frying it, boiling it whole, or pickling it, instead of slicing and boiling it.

ONIONS

There is a special onion that grows in Georgia: the Vidalia. It is yellow and sweet, allegedly because of the sandy loam around Vidalia, Georgia. Occasionally an impostor onion from somewhere else will try to trade on the Vidalia name, but it is never as mild and sweet and good for baking, topped with bread crumbs, cheese, and butter—a favorite regional dish.

A small wild cousin of the onion is a much-celebrated flavor in the mountains of Tennessee and North Carolina —the ramp. These are sometimes called "Tennessee truffles," even though they actually grow up and down the East Coast and all the way west to Minnesota. Southern cooks have always taken the most advantage of this scallion-like plant, often cooking it like other greens, either boiled with salt pork, or fried.

PEACHES

The climate in the South is perfect for peaches, and although California has the edge in growing this fruit, South Carolina and Georgia aren't far behind. Spanish explorers first planted peach trees in the region, and they were adopted and cultivated by the Native Americans. By the time English settlers came on the scene, they found peaches growing wild. Something about the soft summer evenings in the South reminds one of peaches and cream, which has long been a popular dessert combination. Other favorites are fresh peach pie (see page 67) and fresh peach ice cream.

PECANS

First grown on the east coast by Thomas Jefferson and George Washington, pecans are now found in most southern states, and almost every family has "the best" recipe for pecan pie (see page 65).

RICE

In some areas of the South rice is served more often than potatoes. And rice has been one of the South's most important crops. Though the first Virginia rice crop failed, Charleston's Henry Woodward tried again with grain from Madagascar. The result soon became known as "Carolina Gold." During the Revolutionary War, the British shipped one entire harvest to England, leaving no seeds to replant. But the inimitable Thomas Jefferson smuggled some rice out of Europe when he was ambassador to France, and brought it back to South Carolina, where it was grown successfully for the next one hundred years. But several events, including the Civil War and a series of weather-related disasters, caused rice production to move west to Louisiana and Arkansas.

SESAME SEEDS

Sesame seeds were brought from Africa in the 1600s by slaves, who called them by their original name, benne seeds. In South Carolina, cooks still occasionally use this term as they turn them into breads, cookies, and candies, the most traditional of which are small, crunchy, benne seed wafers.

SHELLFISH

From the largest estuary in North America, the Chesapeake Bay, south through the Low Country, around the Keys and along the Gulf Coast, southern waters produce prodigious amounts of shellfish. Crab and shrimp "boils" are one of the many food-oriented public gatherings famous in the region. For more elegant occasions cooks might offer baked, scalloped, or deviled shellfish.

When shrimp are the shellfish of choice for the "boil"—as they often are in the Carolina Low Country or in Georgia—the water is usually highly seasoned, most likely an influence of African or West Indian cooks. The shrimp are served with highly-seasoned red cocktail sauce and the same "down-home" accompaniments that appear in so many southern places: coleslaw, corn on the cob, and biscuits. Shrimp also often show up in casseroles and pilaus, which are the southern version of rice pilaf, also known in some areas as "perloo" (see page 49).

Chesapeake Bay's famous soft-shell crabs are really just hard crabs which have molted—that is, shed their shell to grow. This happens in the spring, and they have to be caught quickly, before they begin to develop a new shell. Like a lot of other seafood in the South, soft-shell crabs are often breaded and fried (see page 50), and then served with tartar sauce.

Oysters kept the Jamestown colonists alive during their early winters, and oysters have been associated with holiday celebrations ever since—in Thanksgiving stuffing or preceding a Christmas ham. The most common species goes by many names: Chincoteague, Apalachicola, Kent Island, and Blue Point (which is actually a generic term for all Atlantic oysters), but there are many different varieties from specific coastal areas. The old rule of thumb, "Only eat domestic oysters during the months which contain an 'r' in their names," is still a good general guideline. It is not that oysters are inedible or poisonous from May through August, but their texture is a little soft and mushy. In the fall they taste much better.

SWEET POTATOES

Sweet potatoes aren't yams, although the early slaves called them that. (The African word *unyamo* means "to eat.") They were a natural part of the combined Native American–English settler diet in the 1600s. Sweet potatoes are delicious baked, of course, and are also frequently made into pies or puddings, candied, or whipped into soufflés (see page 58). In any form they offer a sweet contrast to salty ham. Most of the sweet potatoes sold in markets all over the country come from North Carolina.

TOMATOES

Originally from South America, tomatoes had to overcome the worldwide myth that they were poisonous before they began to be grown in favorable climates during the 1700s. The reasonable explanation for this unreasonable belief is that tomatoes are a member of the nightshade family, all of which contain toxins in some part of the plant. This wariness led people to cook tomatoes for a very long time, once they began eating them at all. Many traditional southern preparations—stewed, baked, or scalloped—call for sugar to balance out the tomato's natural acidity. Ironically, green tomatoes (simply unripe tomatoes) do contain a harmless amount of poisonous solanine, but it is green tomatoes—dredged in flour, fried, and served with the gravy that also smothers the biscuits, ham, and grits at breakfast—that became a signature dish of the South (see page 48).

The Recipes

SHE-CRAB SOUP

Serves 8

This typical coastal bisque-like soup calls for immature female blue crabs, which are less meaty than their male counterparts, but may contain roe. This is a rich, smooth, and very elegant soup.

- 2 cups steamed meat from female blue crabs with roe (If necessary, you can use other types of crabmeat, such as Dungeness, rock, or golden.)
- 1 cup (2 sticks) butter
- ¼ cup all-purpose flour
- 3 cups heavy cream
- 2 cups milk
- 2 tablespoons Worcestershire sauce
- 2 teaspoons finely grated lemon zest
- ¼ teaspoon finely grated onion
- 1 teaspoon freshly ground white pepper
- Salt
- Madeira
- Paprika

Carefully pick over the crabmeat for shell. Set the roe aside.

Melt the butter in a large saucepan over low heat. Add the flour, stirring until it is completely dissolved. Cook for 2 minutes, stirring constantly with a whisk. Remove the pan from the heat and pour in the cream and milk, whisking to combine. Return the pan to the heat, whisking until the liquid is completely smooth.

Increase the heat to medium. Stir in the crabmeat, Worcestershire sauce, lemon zest, and onion. Reduce the heat and simmer for 20 minutes, stirring occasionally. Stir in pepper; season with salt.

To serve: Divide the roe (if you have it) among 8 soup plates, put 1 teaspoon of good Madeira into each bowl and ladle in the soup, making sure the crabmeat is evenly distributed. Garnish with a pinch of paprika on top of each serving.

FRIED GREEN TOMATOES

Serves 6

This traditional dish was popularized by the motion picture named after it. The choice of tomato used in making it is critical. There are a number of tomatoes that are green when fully ripe; they are wrong for this recipe. The green tomatoes required here are unripe red tomatoes. The tomato slices need to be crisp and firm in texture in order to hold their shape.

- 1 cup buttermilk
- 1 egg
- 1½ cups yellow cornmeal
- 1 teaspoon cayenne pepper
- ½ teaspoon salt
- ¼ teaspoon freshly ground pepper
- Bacon fat or vegetable oil, for frying
- 2 pounds green tomatoes, sliced ⅜ inch thick
- Hot pepper sauce

In a pie plate, whisk the buttermilk with the egg; set aside.

In another pie plate, combine the cornmeal, cayenne pepper, salt, and black pepper; set aside.

In a large heavy skillet, heat ¾ inch of bacon fat until hot but not smoking. Working in batches, dip the tomato slices in the buttermilk mixture and then dredge them in the flour mixture. Fry in the hot fat for about 5 minutes, turning once, until golden brown and crusty on both sides. Drain on a paper bag–lined baking sheet. Repeat with the remaining tomatoes. Serve hot, sprinkled with hot pepper sauce.

BIBB LETTUCE SALAD WITH COUNTRY HAM, STILTON CHEESE, AND CANDIED PECANS

ADAPTED FROM A RECIPE BY KATHY CARY, LILLY'S, LOUISVILLE, KENTUCKY

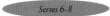

Serves 6–8

Bibb lettuce is named after amateur horticulturalist John B. Bibb from Frankfort, Kentucky. This modern salad combines this delicious and elegant lettuce with southern country ham and candied pecans framed by the tanginess of an English blue cheese.

- 3 tablespoons lemon juice
- 2 tablespoons red wine vinegar
- 2 tablespoons granulated sugar
- 2 teaspoons Dijon-style mustard
- ½ cup plus 1 tablespoon olive oil
- Salt and freshly ground black pepper
- 1½ tablespoons dark brown sugar, packed
- ⅔ cup coarsely chopped pecans
- ½ teaspoon cayenne pepper
- 2 to 3 heads Bibb lettuce (about ½ pound), washed, dried, and torn
- ⅓ pound smoked country ham, diced
- ⅓ pound Stilton cheese, crumbled
- 3 oranges, peeled and cut into sections
- 1 small red onion, thinly sliced

To make the vinaigrette: In a small bowl, whisk together the lemon juice, vinegar, granulated sugar, and mustard. Slowly whisk in ½ cup of the olive oil. Season with salt and black pepper. Set aside.

To prepare the pecans: In a small skillet, heat the remaining 1 tablespoon of olive oil and the brown sugar over medium heat. Stir in the pecans and cayenne pepper; sauté, stirring occasionally, until lightly toasted, about 3 to 4 minutes. Season with salt. Set aside to cool.

In a large salad bowl, combine the lettuce, ham, cheese, oranges, onion, and pecans. Pour the vinaigrette over and toss well. Serve immediately.

SHRIMP PERLOO

Serves 6

"Perloo" is a southern version of pilau, *a middle-eastern word that refers to a variety of rice dishes. Because the South was the source of most American rice in the nineteenth century, perloo became a standard dish, especially in the Carolinas. This version combines a number of indigenous southern ingredients.*

- 6 slices thick bacon, cut into ½-inch pieces
- 1 large onion, chopped
- 4 large tomatoes, seeded and chopped
- 1 teaspoon red pepper flakes
- 1½ cups rice
- 3 jars (8 ounces each) clam juice
- 1½ pounds medium shrimp, peeled and deveined
- ¼ cup chopped fresh parsley
- 2 tablespoons lemon juice
- Salt and freshly ground black pepper

In a Dutch oven, sauté the bacon over medium heat until crisp, stirring occasionally. Remove to a paper towel–lined plate and set aside. Drain all but 3 tablespoons of fat from the pan.

Add the onion and sauté, stirring occasionally, for 10 minutes. Stir in the tomatoes and red pepper flakes; sauté 5 minutes.

Stir in the rice and clam juice. Bring to a boil, reduce the heat, cover, and simmer 20 minutes. Fluff the rice while tossing in the shrimp. Remove from the heat, cover, and let sit 10 minutes (the heat of the rice will cook the shrimp).

Stir in the parsley, lemon juice, and the reserved bacon; season with salt and black pepper. Serve immediately.

SAUTÉED SOFT-SHELL CRABS WITH LEMON BUTTER SAUCE

Serves 4

Soft-shell crabs are common to the Chesapeake Bay, where they are harvested throughout the year. (Soft-shell crabs are also plentiful in Lake Ponchartrain, near New Orleans.) It is traditional to coat them in batter and deep-fry them, a technique that tends to overwhelm the delicate flavor of the crabs. In today's home kitchen, where deep-frying is messy and somewhat out of favor, it is preferable to sauté them quickly and serve them with a tangy lemon sauce.

- 8 soft-shell crabs
- 2 cups cold milk
- 1 cup all-purpose flour
- ¼ teaspoon salt
- 6 grindings of fresh black pepper
- ¼ teaspoon cayenne pepper
- 6 tablespoons butter

Clean the crabs (see note below) and rinse them in cold running water. Pat them dry with paper towels. Place them in one layer in a rectangular Pyrex dish that holds them snugly. Pour the milk over them and let them soak for 30 minutes.

Meanwhile, put the flour into a shallow bowl. Add the salt, pepper, and cayenne. Mix thoroughly.

Preheat the oven to 250°F. Line a platter with paper towels.

Remove each crab from the milk, draining it thoroughly. Dust with the flour mixture, shaking off any excess.

Melt the butter in a large nonstick skillet. When the foam begins to subside, add the first four crabs, belly down. Sauté for 2 minutes over medium heat. Turn and sauté for 2 more minutes; then turn them once more and finish for 1 minute. Remove the 4 crabs to the paper-lined platter and place them in the preheated oven. Repeat the procedure with the remaining 4 crabs.

Prepare the sauce (see right). Place 2 crabs on each plate, top with a tablespoon of sauce, and serve immediately.

NOTE: Most soft-shell crabs are sold already cleaned. If you find yourself with crabs that are fresh and/or uncleaned, simply remove the triangular apron flap on the belly side. With a small knife, scrape out the stomach and intestines underneath the apron. Lift the pointed ends of the shell carapace and remove the spongy, finger-shaped lungs. With scissors, cut just behind the eyes and remove the head of the crab. Squeeze the body gently until the gray sand sac pops out of the head opening. Discard it.

LEMON BUTTER SAUCE

Makes ½ cup

- Juice of 1 lemon
- 6 tablespoons chilled butter
- 2 tablespoons fresh chopped parsley

Over medium heat, in a non-aluminum saucepan, reduce the lemon juice to 1 tablespoon.

Remove the pan from the heat. Add two tablespoons of butter. Whisk until absorbed.

Place the pan over low heat. Whisk in the remaining butter, 1 tablespoon at a time, until absorbed. Stir in the parsley.

PAN-FRIED CATFISH WITH SPICY RED PEPPER SAUCE

Serves 6

*Catfish has been a traditional food in the South, where this freshwater bottom
feeder was plentiful in ponds and rivers. Because of its eating habits, wild catfish can
have a muddy flavor that makes it unpopular, but lately things have changed dramatically.
Almost all catfish is now grown in farms, mostly in Mississippi, where its sweet,
mild taste is unblemished by muddiness. Recently catfish has become a delicacy,
appreciated by gourmets all over the country.*

- 2 cups buttermilk
- 3¼ teaspoons salt
- 1 teaspoon freshly ground black pepper
- Hot pepper sauce
- 6 (6-ounce) catfish fillets
- 2 jars (7 ounces each) roasted red bell peppers, drained
- ¼ cup tomato paste
- 2½ tablespoons red wine vinegar
- 5 teaspoons sugar
- Cayenne pepper
- 1 cup vegetable oil
- 2 cups corn flour (*or* grind cornmeal in a food processor to a fine meal)
- Lemon wedges

In a large shallow dish, whisk together the buttermilk, 2 teaspoons of the salt, ½ teaspoon of the black pepper, and a dash of hot pepper sauce. Add the catfish and coat completely with the buttermilk mixture. Cover and refrigerate overnight.

To make the red pepper sauce: In a food processor fitted with a metal blade, purée the bell peppers and transfer to a medium saucepan. Set over low heat and add the tomato paste, vinegar, sugar, ¼ teaspoon of the salt, a generous dash of the hot pepper sauce, and a pinch of cayenne pepper. Cook, stirring occasionally, until heated through, about 8 minutes. Set aside until ready to serve.

Heat the oil in a 12-inch skillet over medium heat.

In a pie plate, mix the flour, the remaining 1 teaspoon salt, ½ teaspoon black pepper, and a generous pinch of cayenne pepper. Remove the catfish fillets from the buttermilk, draining well. Dredge the fillets in the flour mixture, shaking off any excess.

When the oil is hot, pan-fry the fillets until crisp and golden brown, about 4 minutes a side. Drain on a paper bag–lined baking sheet. Serve hot with the warm sauce and the lemon wedges.

Duncan Hines

Duncan Hines was the first "foodie." Born in Kentucky in 1880, he grew up on southern country cooking. Eventually his career took him to Chicago, but he spent much of his time on the road, driving from city to city as did many salesmen of that era. During his travels Hines developed into an avid gastronome. He kept notes on the places where he ate and eventually, in 1935, he published a booklet of his findings, which he circulated among his friends and colleagues.

The book was so well received he expanded it into a guidebook of restaurants throughout the regions he visited. This little red volume was called Adventures in Good Eating. *Based on its success, Hines expanded his operations to include hotel guides, cookbooks, a cooking school, a food institute, and food products, becoming the first food celebrity. In 1957, two years before he died, Duncan Hines sold his empire to Proctor & Gamble, the large Cincinnati soap company, which has immortalized his name on millions of boxes of cake mix.*

SMOTHERED PORK

Serves 6

"Smothering," in Dixie dialect, refers to the common practice of baking or braising meat or fish in a covered skillet with gravy and vegetables. This method of cooking assures that the main component of the dish will be moist and extremely tender.

- 6 center-cut pork loin chops, about 1 inch thick
- All-purpose flour, for dredging
- 6 tablespoons bacon fat *or* vegetable oil
- 6 leeks, white and light green parts only, halved lengthwise, cleaned, and thinly sliced
- 8 cloves garlic, slivered
- 1¼ cups chicken stock
- 1 cup dry white wine
- Salt and freshly ground pepper

Dredge the pork chops in the flour, shaking off any excess. Heat the bacon fat over medium heat in a 12-inch skillet. Add the pork chops and sauté until golden brown on both sides, about 5 minutes on each side. Remove the chops from the skillet and set aside.

Add the leeks and garlic to the skillet; sauté for 10 minutes, stirring occasionally. Return the chops to the skillet and add the stock and wine; stir and smother the chops with the leek mixture. Reduce the heat, cover and simmer 1 hour or until the chops are very tender. Season with salt and pepper.

SOUTHERN FRIED CHICKEN

Serves 4

There probably isn't a more all-American dish than this one. You may wince at the idea of lard, but you can't make real southern fried chicken without it.

- 2 cups buttermilk
- 1 teaspoon freshly ground pepper
- ⅛ teaspoon salt
- 3½- to 4-pound chicken, cut into 8 pieces
- 1¼ cups all-purpose flour
- 1½ teaspoons seasoned salt, such as Lawry's
- 1 pound lard
- ¼ pound (1 stick) butter

Place the buttermilk, ¼ teaspoon of the pepper, and the salt in a large bowl; stir to combine. Add the chicken pieces and coat with the buttermilk mixture. Refrigerate for 1 to 2 hours.

Combine the flour, seasoned salt, and the remaining ¾ teaspoon of pepper in a shallow baking dish; blend well. Remove the chicken pieces from the buttermilk, 2 or 3 at a time, and dip them into the flour mixture until well coated on all sides.

Over medium-high heat melt the lard and butter in a skillet, preferably a black iron skillet large enough to hold the chicken pieces in one layer without touching. Add the chicken, skin-side down, and cook until golden brown on one side, about 15 minutes. Watch closely so as not to burn. If the chicken is browning too quickly, reduce heat slightly. Turn the chicken over and continue cooking until pieces are golden brown and chicken juices run clear, about 15 minutes longer. Drain the chicken on a paper bag–lined baking sheet. Serve immediately.

BRUNSWICK STEW

Serves 10

Invented in Brunswick County, North Carolina, in the early nineteenth century, this hearty dish was originally made with squirrel. At the beginning of the twentieth century, the squirrel was replaced by chicken.

- 1 (5-pound) stewing chicken, quartered and giblets reserved
- 3 large onions, finely chopped
- 3 stalks celery, finely chopped
- 3 carrots, finely chopped
- 5 sprigs fresh parsley
- 2 sprigs fresh thyme
- 10 whole black peppercorns
- 2 (2-inch) pieces lemon peel
- 2 cloves garlic, lightly mashed with the broad side of a knife
- 2 small dried red peppers
- Water

- ½ pound thick-sliced bacon, cut into ½-inch pieces
- 2 large tomatoes, peeled, seeded, and chopped
- 2 tablespoons tomato paste
- 2 (10-ounce) packages frozen corn kernels, thawed
- 2 (10-ounce) packages frozen lima beans, thawed
- ¾ cup cooked rice
- Salt, freshly ground black pepper, and hot pepper sauce

Place the chicken in a large stockpot. Add one each of the onions, celery stalks, and carrots. In a piece of cheesecloth, tie the parsley, thyme, peppercorns, lemon peel, garlic, and dried red peppers; add to the pot along with enough water to barely cover the contents. Cover and bring slowly to a boil. Reduce the heat and simmer, partially covered, for 1½ hours. Remove from the heat and let the chicken cool in the broth until possible to handle. Remove the meat from the bones and discard the bones. Cut the meat into ½-inch pieces. Strain the broth and reserve it in the stockpot; discard the solids.

In a large skillet, cook the bacon over medium heat, stirring occasionally, until crisp. Remove to a paper towel–lined plate and set aside. Drain all but 3 tablespoons of fat from the skillet; add the remaining two each of the onions, celery stalks, and carrots. Sauté, stirring, about 10 minutes, until the vegetables are tender. Chop the reserved giblets and add them to the skillet along with the tomatoes and tomato paste. Sauté 5 minutes.

To the stock, add the corn, lima beans, chicken meat, sautéed vegetables, giblets, and bacon. Heat through.

Meanwhile, purée the rice with 1½ cups water; stir this into the stockpot to thicken the stew. Heat through; season with the salt, pepper, and hot pepper sauce.

GLAZED COUNTRY HAM

Serves 16 or more

This, including the cola, is the traditional way of preparing a true southern-style country ham. The most important consideration is the choice of the ham itself. The results will be disappointing if you use a canned ham or one that has been injected with lots of water.

- 1 (7- to 8-pound) ham
- Whole cloves
- ½ cup packed light brown sugar
- ¼ cup cola
- 1 tablespoon dry mustard
- 1 cup apple cider

Preheat the oven to 300°F. Using a sharp knife, cut off the skin and most of the fat from the ham, leaving a thin layer of fat on the ham's top side. Score the remaining layer of fat diagonally about ⅛ inch deep to make a diamond pattern. Place the ham in a shallow roasting pan. Cover securely with foil. Bake about 18 to 20 minutes per pound until internal temperature registers 160°F.

When the ham is done, remove it from the oven and increase the oven temperature to 350°F. Stud the corners of the diamond pattern with the cloves. In a small bowl, mix the brown sugar, cola, and dry mustard. Spoon the mixture over the ham. Return to the oven and bake about 30 more minutes until a glaze forms, basting occasionally. Add the cider to the pan and scrape up the brown bits that have formed on the bottom of the pan. Return to the oven for 10 more minutes. Remove from the oven; carve into thin slices and serve with the juices from the pan.

The Real Hams

To experience a true Virginia ham you have to go to the source. Here are the best mail-order purveyors of these delectable smoked legs:

Gwaltney of Smithfield, Ltd., C/O Basse's Choice Plantation, P.O. Box 1, Smithfield, VA 23431, (800) 292-2773 or (804) 357-9222.

H. P. Beale & Sons, Inc., P.O. Box 97, 16276 Ivor Road Courtland, VA 23837, (804) 653-9145, FAX: (804) 653-0348.

Pruden Packing Co. Inc., P.O. Box 1416, 1201 North Main Street , Suffolk, VA 23439, (804) 539-6261, FAX: (804) 925-4971.

Smithfield Ham & Products Co., Inc., P.O. Box 487, Smithfield, VA 23431, (800) 628-2242 or (804) 357-2121, FAX: (804) 357-5407.

S. Wallace Edwards & Sons, Inc., P.O. Box 25, Surry, VA 23883, (800) 222-4267 or (804) 294-3121, FAX: (804) 294-5378.

The E. M. Todd Company, 1128 Hermitage Road, Richmond, VA 23220, (800) 368-5026 or (804) 359-5051, FAX: (804) 359-5052.

NORTH CAROLINA BARBECUED RIBS

Serves 6-8

The beauty of this traditional preparation is its simplicity. Why hide the crispy deliciousness of these ribs with a heavy, sweet sauce? These are finger lickin' good just as they are.

- 2 tablespoons red pepper flakes
- 1 tablespoon salt
- 1 tablespoon cracked black pepper

- 6 pounds pork spareribs
- 1 cup apple cider vinegar
- ½ cup unsalted butter
- ¼ cup packed dark brown sugar

In a small bowl, combine 1 tablespoon of the red pepper flakes, the salt, and black pepper. Rub the mixture over the ribs and let marinate in the refrigerator for 2 hours.

Meanwhile, in a 1-quart saucepan combine the vinegar,

butter, sugar, and the remaining 1 tablespoon red pepper flakes over medium-high heat. Bring to a boil, reduce the heat, and simmer for 5 minutes. Use the sauce for basting the ribs while grilling and, afterward, as a dipping sauce. Grill the ribs over hot coals, basting occasionally with the warm sauce, for about 30 minutes or until cooked throughout and nicely charred.

To serve, slice the ribs between the bones and serve with the hot dipping sauce that remains.

MAVERICK GRITS

ADAPTED FROM A RECIPE BY FRANK LEE, SLIGHTLY NORTH OF BROAD, CHARLESTON, SOUTH CAROLINA

Serves 6

Grits can be an all-purpose backdrop for a variety of different ingredients from cheese to fruit. This combination, invented by Chef Lee, may well be the best use of grits ever invented.

- 1 quart water
- 1 cup stone-ground grits
- 1 cup (2 sticks) unsalted butter
- ½ cup heavy cream
- ⅓ cup (1 ounce) grated Parmesan cheese
- Salt and freshly ground black pepper
- ½ pound thinly sliced country ham, chopped
- ½ pound smoked pork sausage, sliced
- 1 pound medium shrimp, peeled and deveined
- ⅔ pound sea scallops, halved
- 2 tomatoes, seeded and chopped
- 4 cloves garlic, minced
- 1⅓ cups chicken stock
- 6 green onions (scallions), finely chopped

Bring the water to a boil in a large saucepan. Add the grits and ½ cup of the butter. Reduce the heat to medium-low and stir constantly until thickened. When thickened, remove from the heat and stir in the cream and cheese. Season with salt and pepper. Set aside; keep warm.

Melt 2 tablespoons of the remaining butter in a large skillet over medium-high heat. Add the ham and sausage; sauté, stirring constantly, until the sausage is well-browned, about 4 minutes. Add the shrimp, scallops, tomatoes, and garlic; sauté, stirring constantly, for 1 minute. Stir in the stock and continue to cook until the shrimp and scallops are opaque throughout and the stock has reduced slightly, about 2 minutes. Stir in the remaining 6 tablespoons of butter and cook until just melted. Stir in the green onions and season with salt and pepper.

To serve: Spoon equal amounts of the grits onto six plates. Top with the skillet ingredients and serve immediately.

CORN PUDDING

Serves 8

This recipe gets high marks from all the children around the table. Yes, it calls for canned creamed corn and evaporated milk, but the result is superb. Generally, things are better when made from scratch, but in this foolproof preparation, there is no perceptible improvement when it is made from fresh corn and whole milk.

- ½ cup (1 stick) unsalted butter
- 4 eggs, beaten
- 2 (17-ounce) cans creamed corn
- 2 (5-ounce) cans evaporated milk
- 2 tablespoons sugar
- 6 tablespoons cracker meal *or* matzo meal
- 1 tablespoon salt

Preheat the oven to 350°F. Grease a 3-quart casserole.

Melt the butter in a saucepan and let cool. In a large bowl, combine the remaining ingredients and stir in the cooled melted butter. Pour into the casserole.

Place the casserole in a large pan and fill with enough hot water to come up 1½ inches on the casserole's sides. Bake for 1½ hours, or until just set. Serve immediately.

Chef Frank Lee

Frank Lee is chef of the Slightly North of Broad restaurant in downtown Charleston, South Carolina. This comfortably elegant dining room is a popular choice for locals, who flock here for the unique, garden-fresh southern cooking. A South Carolina native, Chef Lee explores the local traditions while adhering to the highest standards of quality and culinary technique.

He began his gastronomic education at several small restaurants in Columbia, South Carolina. His training continued at Le Perroquet in Chicago under Chef Jovan Trboyevic and later with Chef Yannick Cam at Le Pavillon in Washington, D.C. Since he joined Slightly North of Broad, the restaurant has earned praise from the James Beard Foundation and has been featured in local newspapers, magazines, and cable television programs. Maverick Grits (see left) has been singled out by GQ as one of America's best dishes.

MESS O' GREENS, SOUTHERN STYLE

Serves 6

This cooks down into a kind of murky dark mush, but it tastes a lot better than it looks. The liquid in this dish is called "pot likker" and is rich in vitamins and nutrients.

- 3 pounds mixed greens (select from turnip greens, collard greens, mustard greens, beet greens, kale, and sorrel)
- ½ pound slab bacon, cut into ¼-inch cubes
- 2 stalks celery, finely chopped
- 1 onion, finely chopped
- 1 green bell pepper, finely chopped
- 1 ham hock (about ¾ pound)
- 2 tablespoons red wine vinegar
- ½ teaspoon red pepper flakes
- 1¼ cups water
- Salt and freshly ground pepper

Pick over the greens to remove any tough stems, veins, and yellow leaves. Wash and drain thoroughly. Cut the greens into 2-inch pieces and set aside.

Place the bacon in a stockpot over medium-high heat and cook, stirring, until it is browned (not crisp) and the fat has been rendered. Stir in the celery, onion, and bell pepper. Cook, stirring, 5 minutes.

Reduce the heat to medium and add the greens. Cover and cook, stirring occasionally, until the greens are wilted, about 10 minutes. Add the ham hock, vinegar, and pepper flakes. Cover and cook 15 minutes.

Add the water, cover, and simmer for 1½ hours, stirring occasionally. Season with salt and pepper.

ORANGE-SCENTED SWEET POTATOES

Serves 6-8

Sweet potatoes are native to the Americas and were actually much more common in colonial times than white potatoes. Later on, while the white potato flourished elsewhere, the sweet potato held sway in the South. Here is a recipe that combines two subtropical ingredients, sweet potatoes and oranges.

- 4 sweet potatoes, about 8 ounces each
- ½ cup packed dark brown sugar
- 6 tablespoons unsalted butter, melted
- 2 eggs, lightly beaten
- 2 tablespoons orange juice concentrate, thawed
- 2 teaspoons grated orange zest
- 2 teaspoons salt
- ½ teaspoon white pepper
- ½ cup pecan halves

Preheat the oven to 400°F. Pierce the potatoes with the tines of a fork. Bake about 35 minutes or until tender. Cool potatoes slightly, halve lengthwise, and scoop out the pulp into a medium bowl.

Reduce the oven to 350°F. Add ¼ cup of the sugar, 4 tablespoons of butter, the eggs, juice concentrate, orange zest, salt, and pepper to the potato pulp. Beat with an electric hand mixer until smooth. Spoon into a greased 2-quart casserole dish; arrange the pecans on top in a decorative fashion. Sprinkle with the remaining ¼ cup sugar and drizzle with the remaining 2 tablespoons butter. Bake about 20 minutes or until hot. Turn on the broiler and broil about 30 seconds just to brown the top slightly.

CARAMELIZED VIDALIA ONION PUDDING
ADAPTED FROM A RECIPE BY KATHY CARY, LILLY'S,
LOUISVILLE, KENTUCKY

Serves 8-10

Vidalia onions are treated like fine wine grapes. The name is protected by Georgia law, and the onions can only be grown in a limited area within the state. What makes them so special is how sweet and mild they are. Here is a lovely dish that makes good use of these special onions.

- ½ cup (1 stick) unsalted butter
- 6 medium Vidalia onions (or other sweet, mild onion variety such as Walla Walla or Maui), thinly sliced
- 6 eggs
- 2 cups heavy cream
- ¼ cup sugar
- 3 tablespoons all-purpose flour
- 1 tablespoon salt
- 2 teaspoons baking powder
- ½ teaspoon cayenne pepper

Preheat the oven to 350°F. Grease a 9 x 13 inch baking dish.

Melt the butter in a large skillet over medium heat. Add the onions; cook, stirring occasionally, until they are deep golden brown and caramelized, about 30 minutes. (If the onions are browning too quickly, reduce the heat to medium-low.)

In a medium bowl, beat the eggs, cream, sugar, flour, salt, baking powder, and cayenne pepper with an electric mixer. Stir in the caramelized onions. Pour into the prepared baking dish; bake for 35 minutes or until just set. Cut into squares and serve.

THE ULTIMATE POTATO SALAD
ADAPTED FROM A RECIPE FROM MRS. WILKES'S BOARDING
HOUSE, SAVANNAH, GEORGIA

Serves 12 (with leftovers)

Potato salad became very popular in the South in the second half of the nineteenth century. This particular version may very well be the most delicious potato salad ever; it is creamy, tangy, and loaded with rich flavors.

- 4 pounds red new potatoes
- 1½ cups chopped bread-and-butter pickles
- 6 hard-cooked eggs, chopped
- 1 medium red onion, chopped
- 3 stalks celery, diced
- 1 red bell pepper, diced
- 2 cups mayonnaise
- 5 tablespoons distilled white vinegar
- 3 tablespoons dry mustard
- 1 tablespoon celery seeds
- Salt and freshly ground black pepper
- Finely chopped fresh parsley

Place the potatoes in a stockpot or large saucepan. Cover them with water. Place over high heat and bring to a boil. Reduce the heat, cover, and simmer about 20 minutes until a sharp knife easily pierces the potatoes. Drain the potatoes. Cool completely. Cut the potatoes into ½-inch cubes.

In a large bowl, combine the potatoes, pickles, eggs, onion, celery, and bell pepper. Set aside.

In a medium bowl, whisk the mayonnaise, vinegar, mustard, and celery seeds. Pour onto potato mixture; combine gently. Season with salt and pepper and toss again. Sprinkle with parsley. Serve immediately or cover and refrigerate until ready to serve.

Chef Kathy Cary

Chef Kathy Cary draws on her Kentucky roots to create distinctive and progressive Southern regional cooking at Louisville's sleek Lilly's restaurant and at La Pêche, a gourmet carryout and catering business. Her menus typically include traditional Kentucky ingredients with innovative, contemporary twists.

Chef Cary learned to love food at an early age in her mother's kitchen, and when she was old enough, she moved on to apprentice under a Cordon Bleu–trained chef in Washington, D.C. She later started a small catering firm, and then became chef at a stylish Georgetown restaurant.

She returned to Louisville and opened La Pêche gourmet-to-go in 1979. Nine years later, she opened Lilly's next door. The restaurant has been receiving high praise in the local and national press ever since.

HOPPIN' JOHN

Serves 6

This delicious combination of rice and black-eyed peas (which are of African origin and sometimes known as "cowpeas") is easy to make. It is traditionally served on New Year's Day for good luck in the coming year. Hoppin' John was a staple for the Carolina Low Country slave.

- 8 slices bacon, coarsely chopped
- 1 stalk celery, finely chopped
- 1 carrot, finely chopped
- 1 yellow onion, finely chopped
- 1 (10-ounce) package frozen black-eyed peas (If you can find fresh peas, then certainly use them.)
- 2¾ cups chicken stock
- 1 clove garlic, minced
- 6 sprigs fresh thyme
- 1 bay leaf
- ¼ teaspoon red pepper flakes
- 1 cup rice, uncooked
- 2 tablespoons unsalted butter
- Salt and freshly ground black pepper
- 2 green onions (scallions), finely chopped

Place the bacon in a large saucepan over medium-high heat and cook, stirring often, until crisp, about 6 minutes. Add the celery, carrot, and yellow onion and cook, stirring, 1 minute.

Add the peas, 1¼ cups of the stock, the garlic, thyme, bay leaf, and red pepper flakes. Bring to a boil, reduce heat, and simmer 30 minutes, partially covered.

Stir in the rice and the remaining 1½ cups stock. Bring to a boil, reduce the heat, cover, and simmer about 20 minutes until the rice is tender and the stock has been absorbed. Remove and discard the thyme sprigs and bay leaf. Stir in the butter and season with salt and pepper. Serve hot, sprinkled with the green onions.

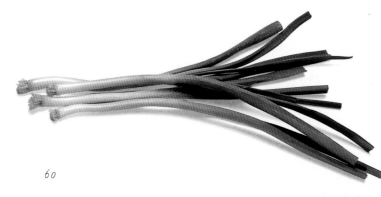

SPOONBREAD

Serves 6

This corn-based bread is almost pudding-like in texture.

- 2 cups milk
- ⅔ cup yellow cornmeal
- 1 teaspoon baking powder
- 1 teaspoon sugar
- 1 teaspoon salt
- 2 tablespoons unsalted butter
- 3 eggs, separated

Preheat the oven to 350°F. Scald the milk in a medium saucepan. In a small bowl, combine the cornmeal, baking powder, sugar, and salt; stir into the hot milk and bring just to a boil, stirring constantly. Remove from the heat and stir in the butter. In another small bowl, beat the egg yolks; stir in ¼ of the cornmeal mixture and then stir this back into the remaining hot mixture. Beat the egg whites to form stiff peaks; gently fold into the cornmeal mixture. Spoon into a well-greased 1½- to 2-quart soufflé dish. Bake about 30 minutes until puffed and golden brown. Serve immediately with fried chicken or ham.

HUSH PUPPIES

Serves 6

Southern tradition has it that family dogs would whimper and beg to be fed. To placate them—and hush them up—a little batter would be dropped into oil, fried, and fed to them. Thus the name.

- 2 cups white cornmeal, preferably stone-ground
- 1 tablespoon all-purpose flour
- 1 teaspoon baking powder
- 1 teaspoon salt
- ½ teaspoon baking soda
- 1 cup plus 3 tablespoons buttermilk
- 2 eggs, beaten
- 3 green onions, finely chopped
- Hot pepper sauce
- Vegetable oil, for frying

Into a large bowl, sift the dry ingredients. Stir in the buttermilk, eggs, and green onions. Season with the hot pepper sauce as your taste dictates. Place about a 2-inch depth of oil in a large skillet and heat to 375°F. Using a serving spoon, gently drop the batter by spoonfuls (about 2 or 3 teaspoons each) into the hot oil. Fry until golden brown. Drain on a brown paper bag and serve hot.

CORNBREAD

Makes one 12 inch round cornbread

The first settlers in the South were introduced to corn by the Native Americans living in the region. One of the recipes they were taught was for a basic bread called "pone," which was made of cornmeal, salt, and water. This basic bread became an integral part of southern cuisine. It became known more commonly as "cornbread."

- 2 cups yellow or white cornmeal
- 1 cup all-purpose flour
- ¼ cup sugar
- 2½ teaspoons baking powder
- 1 teaspoon salt
- 1¼ cups buttermilk
- 1¼ cups heavy cream
- ½ cup (1 stick) unsalted butter, melted and cooled slightly
- 2 eggs, separated
- 2 tablespoons bacon fat *or* vegetable shortening

Preheat the oven to 400°F. In a large bowl, combine the cornmeal, flour, sugar, baking powder, and salt. In another bowl, whisk together the buttermilk, cream, butter, and egg yolks; add to the dry ingredients and gently stir together with a wooden spoon. In a small bowl, beat the egg whites to form soft peaks; gently fold into the batter.

Grease a 12-inch black iron skillet with the bacon fat; pour in the batter. Bake about 20 minutes or until golden brown around the edges and a cake tester or toothpick inserted into the center comes out clean. Serve fresh from the oven, cut into wedges, with lots of sweet butter.

NOTE: If desired, try adding 1 cup shucked fresh corn kernels; ½ cup sliced green onions; diced, roasted Anaheim chiles; or crumbled, cooked bacon to the batter.

CHEDDAR GRITS

Serves 6

Grits are dried and hulled corn that has been finely ground. Often they are prepared as a breakfast food in the South, but they are equally effective as a southern version of Italian polenta.

- 3 cups water
- ¾ cup grits, preferably stone-ground
- 1½ cups (6 ounces) shredded extra-sharp cheddar cheese
- ¼ cup (½ stick) unsalted butter
- Salt and white pepper

Bring the water to a boil in a heavy saucepan. Reduce the heat to medium; add the grits and cook about 10 minutes or until the water has been absorbed. Stir in the cheese and butter until they melt. Season with the salt and pepper. Serve hot.

BEST-EVER BUTTERMILK BISCUITS

Makes 12 2-inch biscuits

Buttermilk, the creamy liquid left after butter has been made by churning milk, is used frequently in southern recipes. These biscuits are extremely simple to make and incredibly good.

- 2 cups all-purpose flour
- 4 teaspoons baking powder
- ½ teaspoon baking soda
- ½ teaspoon salt
- ¼ cup vegetable shortening
- 1 cup buttermilk

Preheat the oven to 475°F. Sift the flour, baking powder, baking soda, and salt into a large bowl. Cut in the shortening with a pastry blender or two knives until the mixture resembles coarse meal. Add the buttermilk and stir with a fork until just combined.

Turn the dough out onto a lightly floured surface. Roll to a thickness of ½ inch. Do not overhandle the dough as this will result in tough biscuits. Cut out the biscuits with a 2-inch round, floured cutter.

Place the biscuits, spaced so they don't touch, on an ungreased baking sheet. Bake about 12 minutes or until their tops are light golden brown. Serve piping hot with lots of sweet butter.

FROZEN MINT JULEP

Serves 1

There are as many mint julep recipes in Kentucky as there are people who make them. Some like to crush the mint leaves. Others use ice made from special spring water or lemons from a special tree. In any case, this traditional drink is a superb summer refresher and is a required accessory for watching the Kentucky Derby.

- 6 small mint leaves
- ¼ cup bourbon
- 2 tablespoons lemon juice
- 2 tablespoons sugar syrup
- 1 scoop crushed ice
- Mint sprigs

Muddle mint leaves with bourbon, lemon juice, and syrup in a bar glass. Remove mint leaves and pour mixture into a blender with finely crushed ice. Mix at high speed for about 15 seconds, or until the ice becomes mushy. Pour the blend into a chilled double old fashioned glass and garnish with the mint sprigs.

The Tradition of Breakfast

The great tradition of southern hospitality includes breakfast, which is often the biggest, most ambitious meal of the day, especially on Sundays or, in Kentucky, on Derby Day. Nineteenth-century landed gentry began each day with a julep—to ward off malaria—and sat down to a mid-morning breakfast of grits, sausages, ham, bacon, turkey, eggs, fried hominy, toast, preserves, and coffee.

The majesty of the southern breakfast was affirmed in 1936 when Governor "Happy" Chandler of Kentucky had the first official Derby Day breakfast. In Louisville it is now traditional on that first Saturday in May to eat burgoo, a close relation of Brunswick Stew (see page 54). Burgoo consists of lamb, chicken, vegetables, and seasonings and takes up to twelve hours to cook. Modern times have altered the southern breakfast but not obliterated it. There isn't time most weekdays to indulge in a long, leisurely feast, but on weekends there is. The Sunday breakfast is still very much a focus of southern social and culinary life.

Bourbon

It is a unique southern irony that as alcohol consumption—a well-established taste in this country from the beginning—waxed and waned, the South led the rest of the nation both in temperance fervor and in alcohol production. Even old recipes for punch intended to be served at church picnics included a bit of the strong stuff. The proudest of the southern distillates is bourbon, a beverage that much of the country associates with the Kentucky Derby. While a great deal is consumed at that event, bourbon has many uses in addition to the mint julep, both for drinking and cooking.

The South is not of one accord as to where bourbon was "invented." No one agrees on what state can claim credit. A Baptist preacher named Elijah Craig first produced this corn whisky—with a little rye and barley thrown in—in 1789 in what is now Bourbon County, Kentucky. But until 1792, Kentucky was part of Virginia, so naturally Virginia claims to be the birthplace. Today bourbon is made in Virginia, too, but many connoisseurs hold that the spring water bubbling through Kentucky limestone produces a superior beverage.

Americans have developed a love for assertively flavored country whiskey made from corn, rye, and barley. Hearty bourbon is whiskey made from at least 51 percent corn, and rye is whiskey made from at least 51 percent rye. Whether for sipping or flavoring a variety of recipes, it has always been an important ingredient in the southern kitchen.

RAISIN-BREAD PUDDING WITH WHISKEY SAUCE
ADAPTED FROM A RECIPE BY HOPPIN' JOHN TAYLOR
CHARLESTON, SOUTH CAROLINA

Serves 12

Bread pudding is an example of the southern penchant for being economical and using everything in the larder, even stale bread. Here, mundane ingredients are converted into a sumptuous dessert, something much more difficult to do than using the most expensive raw materials.

- ½ cup natural raisins
- ½ cup golden raisins
- ½ cup bourbon
- 8 cups torn and dried out bite-size pieces of French bread (about 1 pound)
- 5 cups milk
- 1 teaspoon vanilla
- 1 cinnamon stick
- 7 eggs
- 1½ cups sugar
- ½ cup (1 stick) unsalted butter, melted

To make the bread pudding: In a small bowl soak the raisins in the bourbon for at least 30 minutes or overnight, if possible.

Preheat the oven to 350°F. Grease a 9 x 13 inch baking dish. Put the bread in a large bowl. Drain the raisins, reserving the bourbon for making the sauce. Add the raisins to the bread.

In a medium saucepan, combine the milk, vanilla, and cinnamon stick; cook over medium heat until bubbles just begin to break the surface.

Beat 6 of the eggs with 1 cup of the sugar until well blended, then gradually whisk in the scalded milk. Pour the mixture over the bread and raisins, discarding the cinnamon stick. Let the bread soak for 10 minutes.

Spoon the mixture into the prepared baking dish, patting it evenly. Set the dish inside a larger roasting pan and pour enough hot water into the pan to reach 1 inch up the sides of the baking dish. Bake the pudding for 45 minutes or until a cake tester or toothpick inserted into the center comes out clean.

To make the sauce: Whisk the remaining 1 egg and ½ cup sugar in the top of a double boiler set over simmering water. Whisk until very light and nearly doubled in volume, about 3 minutes. Whisk in the melted butter, a little at a time; then whisk in the reserved bourbon. Remove the pan from the heat, but keep the sauce warm over the water.

Serve the bread pudding warm, drizzled with the warm sauce.

PERFECT PECAN PIE

Serves 8-12

Pecans are a staple in the south and the natural progression would be to make them into pie. Too many pecan pies are gummed up with gloppy cornstarch filling. Here is a version that celebrates the pecan with a minimum of filler.

- 1 recipe Super Flaky Pie Crust (page 34)
- ¼ cup (½ stick) unsalted butter, softened
- ¾ cup dark brown sugar, packed
- 3 eggs, at room temperature
- 1 teaspoon maple syrup
- 1 teaspoon vanilla extract
- 1½ tablespoons orange juice
- ¾ cup dark corn syrup
- 2½ cups coarsely chopped pecans
- 1½ cups unbroken pecan halves

Preheat the oven to 425°F. Roll the pastry into a round on a lightly floured surface. Line a 9-inch pie pan with the pastry, leaving a ½-inch overlap around the top. Fold the upper edge of the crust back, doubling the amount of crust at the rim of the plate. You can decorate the rim by fluting the edge: with your right index finger and thumb gently press forward, while at the same time pressing between them with the left index finger in the opposite direction. You can also use the tines of a serving fork to make a pattern.

Cover the pan with a sheet of parchment paper or foil and press to fit sides. Pour baking beads, beans, or rice into center of paper and distribute evenly.

Bake the crust for 10 minutes. Remove from the oven and lift out the paper and beans. Prick the pastry and let it cool 15 minutes.

In a mixer bowl, cream the butter and sugar until quite light in color, about 7 minutes. Add the eggs, one at a time, beating 2 minutes after each addition.

In a small bowl, combine maple syrup, vanilla, and orange juice.

With the mixer at medium speed, alternate adding the corn syrup and the juice mixture. Fold in the chopped nuts. Pour into the prebaked pie shell.

Place the whole pecans in neat concentric circles on top of the filling.

Reduce the oven temperature to 350°F and bake the pie in the center of the oven until the filling is set, about 50 minutes. If a cake tester or toothpick inserted into the center of the pie comes out clean, the pie is done. If the pecans on top brown too quickly, cover them with foil until the last 5 minutes of baking time. The pie will keep in the refrigerator for 2 days.

Southern Wines

America's first wines were made in the South. This may surprise those who think of the South as "bourbon and branch water" country. But in the mid-sixteenth century French Huguenot settlers in Florida made wines from Scuppernong grapes. Settlers at Jamestown produced their first vintage in 1609, only two years after their arrival in the New World.

Then, in the early 1700s, plantings of European varieties were made in various locations in the region. Despite the enthusiastic involvement of Lord Baltimore, Lord Delaware, William Penn, and Thomas Jefferson himself, vinifera grapes (European varieties such as cabernet sauvignon and chardonnay) proved too difficult to grow in the warm, humid southern climate. Eventually, vintners planted muscadine and native American varieties. There were also some successful native hybrids. In the early nineteenth century, Major John Adlum developed the Catawba grape in Maryland. His wine was sampled by Jefferson who pronounced it, "truly fine, of high flavor."

By the mid-1800s a commercial wine industry was thriving in the South. In fact, wine production was substantial until the temperance movement slowly took hold, culminating in national Prohibition in 1919. And Prohibition did not die easily south of the Mason-Dixon Line, making the reemergence of a Southern wine industry slow and late.

Important viticultural areas within the region include Virginia's Shenandoah Valley, Monticello, and the North Fork of the Roanoke River; the Catoctin Valley in Maryland; and parts of North Carolina, South Carolina, Georgia, Tennessee, Mississippi, and Florida. In fact, the only southern state without a serious wine industry is Louisiana. As demand and viticultural know-how increase, the region's wines are becoming more plentiful and of higher and higher quality. There are now more than 10,000 acres of wine grapes planted in the southeastern United States, and that figure is growing all the time.

CAROLINA RICE PUDDING

Serves 6

From the 1700s until the 1940s, most American rice was grown in the Carolinas, and rice pudding appears in an 1847 cookbook from the region. The pudding is often made with leftover rice, but here is a modern version cooked "from scratch."

- 1 cup golden raisins
- 5 cups half-and-half (light cream)
- 1 cup rice, uncooked
- ¾ cup sugar
- 1 teaspoon vanilla
- 2 egg yolks
- 2 tablespoons softened unsalted butter

Put raisins in a small saucepan and cover with water. Bring quickly to a boil, remove pan from heat, and allow raisins to soak for 30 minutes.

Put the cream and rice in a large saucepan and bring to a simmer over medium heat. Stirring often, simmer 18 minutes or until the rice is soft, but all the liquid is not absorbed. Continuing to stir, add the sugar a little at a time.

In a separate bowl, beat the vanilla into the egg yolks. Whisk a tablespoon of the hot rice mixture in the yolk mixture; then add the yolk mixture back to the rest of the rice mixture. Stir in the butter. Drain the raisins and stir them into the rice pudding. Serve warm.

DIXIE PEACH PIE

Makes one 9-inch pie

Georgia peaches are legendary for good reason. For several months each summer these luscious stone fruits are plentiful and superbly delicious. Here is a lovely way to showcase them without hiding their wonderful, fresh fruitiness.

- Double recipe of Super Flaky Pie Crust (page 34), adding 1 teaspoon cinnamon to the flour mixture
- 6 cups peeled, pitted, and sliced ripe peaches (about 6 *or* 7 large peaches)
- ¾ cup sugar
- 6 tablespoons all-purpose flour
- 2 tablespoons lemon juice
- ½ teaspoon cinnamon
- Pinch of ground nutmeg
- Pinch of salt
- 1 egg
- 1 tablespoon milk
- 2 tablespoons unsalted butter, softened

Prepare the double recipe of the Super Flaky Pie Crust, adding 1 teaspoon of cinnamon to the dough. Chill dough as directed.

Preheat the oven to 425°F. Remove the dough from the refrigerator and cut in half. On a lightly floured surface, roll one half of the dough to about 1½ inches larger than a 9-inch pie plate. Place the dough into the pie plate and press down lightly into the pan with your fingertips. Cut the edge of the pastry with kitchen shears so it hangs evenly about 1 inch past the outer edge of the pan. Fold the dough edge under itself so it is even with the edge of the pie plate. Crimp edge and freeze 15 minutes.

Meanwhile, on a lightly floured surface, roll out the remaining dough to about ⅛ of an inch thickness. With a 2- to 3-inch star cutter, cut out enough stars (about 20) to cover most of the pie when overlapping the stars slightly. Place on a baking sheet and chill in the refrigerator until ready to assemble the pie.

In a large bowl, gently toss together the peaches, sugar, flour, juice, the ½ teaspoon cinnamon, nutmeg, and salt. In a small bowl, whisk together the egg and milk.

To assemble the pie, remove the pie shell and stars from the freezer and refrigerator. With a slotted spoon, spoon the peach mixture into the shell, leaving any accumulated juices behind. Dot with the butter. Brush the stars with the egg mixture and arrange them, overlapping slightly, to cover most of the pie. (Make sure that you leave a few spaces here and there for air vents.) Brush the edge of the pie with the egg mixture. Bake in the middle of the oven for 20 minutes. Reduce the heat to 350°F and continue to bake another 20 to 25 minutes until the crust is crisp and golden brown and the peach juices are bubbling. (If the pie is browning too quickly, cover loosely with foil.) Remove to a rack. Serve warm or at room temperature with generous scoops of your favorite vanilla ice cream.

KILLER COCONUT CAKE

Serves 8-12

Simply beautiful and one of the best cakes ever invented.

Cake Layers:
- 3 cups sifted cake flour
- 4½ teaspoons baking powder
- ½ teaspoon salt
- ¾ cup (1½ sticks) unsalted butter, softened
- 1¾ cups superfine sugar
- 3 eggs, separated and at room temperature
- 1 tablespoon vanilla extract
- 1 tablespoon lemon juice
- 1½ cups milk
- 2 egg whites, at room temperature

Coconut Buttercream:
- 3 egg whites, at room temperature
- ⅔ cup granulated sugar
- 1¼ cups (2½ sticks) unsalted butter, softened
- ½ cup cream of coconut

Boiled Icing:
- 4 egg whites, at room temperature
- 1½ cups granulated sugar
- ⅔ cup light corn syrup
- 6 tablespoons water
- 2 teaspoons vanilla extract
- Shredded, sweetened coconut, as needed

To make the cake layers: In a bowl, mix the sifted flour, baking powder and salt. Sift again and set aside.

Preheat the oven to 375°F. Place the butter in the bowl of an electric mixer and beat until smooth. Gradually add the sugar and beat until the mixture has become light and most of the granulated quality of the sugar has disappeared. Beat in the 3 egg yolks, vanilla, and juice. On low speed, add some of the flour mixture and then some of the milk. Continue to alternate the flour mixture and milk until all these ingredients have been incorporated. Set aside.

In a medium bowl, beat the 5 egg whites with an electric hand mixer to form soft peaks; gently fold into the batter. Dividing equally, spoon the batter into 3 (9-inch) cake pans that have been greased and dusted with flour. Set the pans on the middle rack(s) in the center of the oven and bake about 30 minutes until the cakes have shrunk away from the sides of the pans and a toothpick inserted into the centers comes out clean. Remove to racks to cool 5 minutes. Turn the cakes out of the pans and cool another 5 minutes. Cover the cakes with light, clean dish towels until they are ready to be frosted. It is important to cover the cakes in time, before they become hard and crusty on the surface.

To make the buttercream: Combine the egg whites and sugar in the bowl of an electric mixer and whisk over a saucepan of simmering water until the whites are hot and the sugar is dissolved. Whip this mixture into meringue, with stiff peaks and a glossy texture. (The meringue should be cool at this time.) Incorporate the butter, 2 tablespoons at a time, to achieve a thick buttercream. On low speed, beat in the coconut cream. Cover and set aside in a cool place.

To make the icing: In a mixer bowl, beat the egg whites to form stiff peaks; reserve. Place the sugar, corn syrup, and water in a small saucepan and cover. Bring to a boil and remove the cover. Cook until the syrup spins a 6- to 8-inch thread when spun on the tines of a fork, about 4 to 5 minutes. The syrup has gone too far if it turns at all golden in color.

Pour the hot syrup over the egg whites, beating constantly until the icing holds stiff peaks. It is important to use the icing as quickly as possible or it will set up and harden.

To assemble the cake: Place 1 cake layer on a serving plate. Spread the top of the layer evenly with half of the buttercream. Top with a second cake layer and the remaining buttercream. Cover with the third cake layer. Frost the cake evenly with the icing, covering the top and sides completely. Gently press enough coconut onto the top and sides of the cake to cover completely. This cake will keep, covered, up to 1 week.

Florida

Florida cooking is the youngest of the nine regional cuisines of America. It has only recently developed as a distinct cuisine and is still very much evolving.

The cooking of the Sunshine State exploded with a new energy in the mid-1980s that seemed to coincide with Miami's emergence as a flashy, pasteled playground for the young and hip. Fashion models and movie stars gave this sun-soaked southland a much needed infusion of youthful style and attitude. And they demanded better food—refreshing, healthful, with plenty of flavor.

But few could imagine the extraordinary regional cuisine that would develop as a result. Almost overnight, a talented core of local chefs charted a bold new culinary course, inspired by the exotic ingredients and the cooking traditions of a huge immigrant population that has made south Florida a crossroads of the Caribbean and Latin America.

The Raw Ingredients

The Sunshine State certainly had all the prerequisites for exciting regional cooking: a rich ethnic tradition, year-round fruits and vegetables, abundant local seafood, and a dining public that was eager to move beyond the heavy continental fare that dominated much of the restaurant scene. In this fertile environment, chefs like Allen Susser, Doug Rodriguez, Robin Haas, Mark Militello, and Norman Van Aken developed a thrilling new tropical cuisine.

The first step was to take stock of what foodstuffs were currently available. In the ethnic markets of south Florida, they discovered an exotic array of fruits, vegetables, and seasonings. There were black sapotes, jack fruits, boniatos, chayote, and hearts of palm. The fish markets offered cobia, pompano, conch, and wahoo. And the chefs couldn't ignore Florida classics like stone crab, key limes, alligator meat, and Everglades frog legs. With this treasure chest of ingredients, they began creating dishes that reflected their tropical origins: fun, refreshing, and a far cry from the dull fare of the past.

Try Robin Haas's Grilled Pompano with Gingered Sticky Rice, Red Curry-Coconut Sauce, and Rum Glaze (see page 92) or Mark Militello's Yellowtail Snapper with Rum, Brown Butter, Mango, Ginger, and Mint (see page 89), and you will see why this cuisine has thrilled visitors from across the nation. There is nothing conservative or subtle about the flavors: they explode in your mouth. Yet there is an inherent balance here. Fiery Caribbean spices are tempered by sweet tropical fruit. This is healthy, clean cooking, reliant on marinating, grilling, and accompanied by light salsas and salads. A Florida meal leaves you refreshed and energized.

Cultural Input

Traditional hispanic recipes are a vital part of the New Florida Cuisine. Nicaraugan *tres leches* ("three milk") cake, Cuban breads, and Yucca Con Mojo (a popular tropical tuber stewed with orange juice, garlic, parsley, and oregano; see page 92) are fast becoming favorites outside the native communities. The ethnic dishes are getting a creative twist at restaurants like Yuca in Miami, where diners are captivated by refined "New Cuban" cooking. And Pascal Oudin, at the Grand Bay Hotel in Coconut Grove, has experimented with combining Florida ingredients and classic French techniques.

As Mark Militello explains, "We'll make a classic reduction, but instead of wine, we use rum and lime juice." It seems the only limit a chef in south Florida has is individual creativity.

Old Florida Cooking

While the current movement is not yet a decade old, its origins stretch back to the European discovery of the New World. In fact, Florida was a birthplace of American cooking, the setting where Old World foods first met the traditions of the Native Americans.

Ponce de Leon, in his search for the mythical Fountain of Youth and other material riches for Spain, opened the door for settlements along the Florida peninsula. Colonists brought not only foodstuffs, but also farm animals that would become the source of the state's current cattle industry. In turn the Spanish settlers learned from the Native Americans to eat local vegetables, including hearts of palm, and to catch and prepare a wide variety of seafood. This friendly interaction was confined to the northern parts of Florida, since the tribes to the south were more interested in shooting arrows than sharing culinary ideas.

The flavors of colonial Florida were not purely Spanish. Africans and West

Indians, first free and later as slaves, added sesame seeds, yams, eggplants, and okra to the local diet. Anglo settlers brought with them the quick breads so central to Southern-style cooking as well as a taste for sweets that would lead to the creation of such Florida delicacies as Key Lime Pie (see page 95).

It was not until the late nineteenth century that Florida began to develop as a tourist destination. Lavish winter resorts from Palm Beach to Miami Beach lined what would be aptly named the Gold Coast, and railroads were constructed to bring in the frostbitten vacationers. Actually, the year-round railroad workers and their families had the greatest impact on Florida cooking. They fixed New England chowder with stone crab, or substituted mangoes for apples in their pies. The recipes were disseminated through community cookbooks and home demonstrations. In combining native ingredients with traditional recipes, home cooks can rightly be considered the parents of the New Florida Cuisine.

Twentieth-Century Immigrants

A large Jewish population began to settle in south Florida in the 1920s, and delis and kosher markets in Miami Beach and other communities sustained the locals as well as the seasonal residents. Along the Caribbean "Sun Coast," in Tarpon Springs and Tampa, several Greek fishing and sponge-diving communities existed. These were largely unaffected by the culinary changes around them, and they became a source of Greek influence.

The immigrants who would have the greatest impact on Florida cooking were the Cubans, who began to flee the Communist Revolution in 1959. The *loncheria,* or Cuban snack bar, became a fixture on Miami street corners, joining a myriad of Cuban restaurants in the city. Perfect for a quick bite, the loncheria served Cuban coffee and tasty croquetas and buñuelos—fritters made of yucca and malanga dough.

A great number of Caribbean and Latin American immigrants have followed the Cubans, making south Florida a paradise of Hispanic dining. Miami restaurant books read like travel guides. On any given day, you can choose a Peruvian breakfast, Colombian lunch, Jamaican dinner, and Haitian midnight snack. Argentinian, Nicaraguan, Honduran, and Puerto Rican eateries also vie for your attention. With the intersection of all these lively cuisines, it was only a matter of time before young chefs started to fuse them into a uniquely Florida cuisine.

Ingredients and Geography

To most vacationers, the miles of Florida coastline represent nearly unlimited beachgoing possibilities. But to the Florida chef, all that littoral land means one thing: seafood. People of this peninsula have always relied upon the generosity of Floridian waters, and there is variety along the coast as well as among inland locales. In the northeast corner of the state, around the cities of Jacksonville and St. Augustine, oysters dug off Amelia Island may be roasted and enjoyed on the half shell or baked in a casserole or pie. Rock shrimp with their thick, rigid shell and firm meat are a local favorite. (Though not a "new" species, as is often proclaimed, rock shrimp have recently captured a national audience.)

Move inland toward the state capital in Tallahassee, and the food takes on an increasingly southern character with local menus featuring grits, hushpuppies, and pecan pie. Continue west to the Florida panhandle, and you enter a region that is literally and figuratively as far away from Miami's flashy New Florida Cuisine as you can get in the state. The food is definitely Old South, and served with a casual, friendly attitude. Peanut farms and tobacco fields suggest more than a passing affinity with neighbors Alabama and Georgia, and the copious Spanish moss draping area oaks completes the picture. The warm Gulf waters offer a ready supply of shrimp, crab, mullet, and mackerel. Wild game and venison add further variety to the panhandle pantry.

Farther south along the Gulf Coast, stone crabs, blue crabs, snapper, mullet, and game fish flourish offshore. Fresh hearts of palm, culled from private trees, are a special treat, as are the scallops gathered on the grassy flats along Cedar Key.

A few restaurants have followed the lead of their Gold Coast neighbors. Michael's on East in Sarasota is an outpost for the New Florida Cuisine with its modern and sophisticated approach to food and wine.

The oceans provide the bulk of Florida's seafood, but inland waterways contribute to the bounty as well. Dominating the southern third of the state is America's second-largest freshwater lake, Lake Okeechobee. Catfish is the prized catch here, and numerous local eateries offer delicious, freshly fried plates of the delicacy. Largemouth bass and bream are also likely to wind up on the end of a line cast into Okeechobee.

The land around the lake supports a tremendous variety of crops. If you serve fresh vegetables with your winter meals this year, odds are that they come from this part of Florida. Fields stretch in every direction, with rows of eggplant, lettuce, celery, green beans, peppers, and radishes bathing in the year-round sunshine.

Nearby to the south is Everglades National Park. Native tribes once relied on the rich hunting grounds of this amazing wetland, abundant in game, fish, and alligator. Early colonists also hunted gators, which they prized more for their skins than meat. Today, alligator is eaten as a novelty item in Florida, and the animals are mostly farm-raised. The Everglades are also a source of "swamp cabbage" (hearts of palm) and frog legs.

Moving north of Lake Okeechobee, through the center of the state, you enter the vast subtropical zone where many of the definitive Florida ingredients are grown. Chief among these, of course, is citrus. Oranges have become synonymous with the state, thanks in part to an aggressive publicity campaign by the Growers Association. The fruit was introduced to Florida sometime in the sixteenth century, and the seeds were rapidly spread by Native Americans who carried this beloved, sweet fruit with them wherever they went.

Wild orange trees were discovered by the early settlers, and it was not long before they began planting them. The Great Freeze of 1894–95 ruined many of the groves, and growers moved to locations farther south in the state. Today, Florida is second only to Brazil in worldwide production of oranges, and it is number one in grapefruit production. Lemons, limes, tangerines, and kumquats also flourish here. Central Florida is also home to a massive strawberry harvest and a modest cattle industry.

Nonetheless, the real action in Florida is still along the southeastern Gold Coast. Pulsating Miami, chic Coconut Grove, and opulent West Palm Beach drive the demand for first-rate, fashionable dining. Most of the useful ingredients are available within a few hundred miles. Joe's Stone Crab Restaurant in Miami Beach (see page 81) has made the local crustacean a national celebrity. Farther offshore, fisherman find yellowtail snapper, dolphin (mahimahi), and snook. South and slightly inland from Miami lies the town of Homestead. Originally founded by railroad workers, the area now produces a wealth of exotic tropical fruits. Mangos, star fruit, lychees, sapotes, mameys, and passion fruit are grown here, essential components of the succulent, refreshing New Florida Cuisine.

Island hop along the Keys until you reach Key West, birthplace of key lime pie and home to Florida lobster and conch—the giant, edible sea snail. The conch was so popular in Key West that it was hunted to near extinction and now enjoys protected status. Good news for the Key West conch; bad news for those in Costa Rica and the Bahamas, where the crop now originates.

A Flash in the Pan?

Even as some of the "newness" wears off and fickle trendsetters plot their next move, the fortunes of Florida cooking continue to rise. This youngest American cuisine is legitimate, and once the initial excitement cools, it will mature much the same way as Southwestern and Hawaiian regional cuisines have done. Perhaps in the future a definitive name for the movement will be agreed upon. Until then, look for references to Floribbean, New Florida, Caribbean Fusion, New World, and Haute Cuban. Whatever it is called, this colorful cooking bursts with unique taste sensations.

The Florida Pantry

ALLIGATOR

It tastes like a cross between pork and a freshwater fish such as perch. Traditionally deep-fried, alligator can also be roasted, stewed, or sautéed. Since gator can be a little tough and chewy, it is best when tenderized with a meat mallet and marinated in an acidic agent such as lemon juice. Alligator is exceptionally low in fat and cholesterol and has considerably fewer calories than beef or chicken. The meat can be found at select game shops throughout the country or ordered frozen by mail.

BLACK SAPOTE

A round, green fruit, two to six inches in diameter. When fully ripe, the green skin becomes black and shriveled. The pulp of a ripe fruit looks like chocolate pudding and tastes similar to dates or persimmons.

BONIATO

The "Caribbean sweet potato" is an elongated tuber with a taste similar to the dry sweetness of chestnuts. It has patchy, purplish skin and cream-colored flesh, but it is harder and drier than a typical American sweet potato. Look for hard, firm tubers free of mold, tiny worm holes, or soft spots.

CHAYOTE

Chayote ("shy-ó-tay") looks like a pale-skinned, slightly flattened avocado, though it is not edible raw. Also known as vegetable pear, chayote is squash-like when cooked. It is popular throughout the Caribbean and Latin America and can be found at West Indian and Hispanic groceries throughout Florida.

CITRUS FRUITS

Florida is the nation's largest producer of oranges, grapefruits, and tangerines. These plentiful and juicy fruits offer two types of flavors: the aromatic oils in the rind and the sweet-tart juice in the pulp. Oils are concentrated in the zest, the shiny outer peel of the fruit. The pleasantly bitter zest is used in drinks like martinis; simmered with milk, cream, or poached fruit; or finely chopped in a spice mill for other uses.

Orange, tangerine, and grapefruit juices are distinctive in salad dressings, but when used in cooking they are best boiled down in a nonreactive saucepan until reduced to about one-fourth of their original volume. This makes an intensely flavored concentrate or syrup. Florida citrus is available year-round, though oranges and grapefruits, which are the state's two largest citrus crops, are in their prime in the winter. The best way to store citrus fruit is loosely wrapped in a plastic bag in the refrigerator.

Some of the unusual varieties of citrus fruits being used in the New Florida Cuisine include:

Blood Orange: Smaller than more typical oranges, with a red pulp and a delicate, sweet flavor that has a hint of raspberry or strawberry. Used in salads, desserts, and as a garnish, it also makes delicious juice.

Calamondin: A native fruit of the Philippines now grown commercially in Florida. Calamondin looks like a miniature tangerine and is more or less inedible when uncooked, but delicious when prepared in jellies and jams.

Key Lime: A small, tart, and aromatic relative of the green lime. The juice of this yellowish variety is the essential ingredient in Key Lime Pie (see page 95), the signature dessert of the Florida Keys, which was developed by the British Tory settlers of the area.

Kumquat: Tiny, oblong citrus fruits that grow on hardy plants that thrive in the region. Quite bitter when eaten raw, kumquats are best when prepared

by poaching in sugar syrup for sauces, dressings, jellies, and jams.

Pomelo: An ancestor of the modern grapefruit. Large and thick-skinned, sweeter and drier than a grapefruit, it is eaten like a naval orange. The individual juice sacs can be separated and sprinkled on salads. They crunch when bitten into, like pomegranate seeds.

Sour Orange: Bumpy, green-orange fruit that looks like an irregular unripened orange. Used as a primary ingredient in Cuban and other Latino cuisines and in Mojo Sauce (see page 92).

Tangelo: A grapefruit-tangerine hybrid that looks like a dark-skinned orange with a nipple-like protrusion on one end. The most popular variety is the Minneola, named after a town that is a center of the citrus industry in central Florida. The tangelo is a large, quite juicy fruit with an aroma reminiscent of pineapple.

Ugli Fruit: Another cross between a tangerine and a grapefruit, this time from Jamaica. It is a pear-shaped, thick-skinned, green-yellow fruit with the honeyed fragrance of a tangerine and the juicy tartness of grapefruit.

CONCH

Pronounced "conk," this giant sea snail has meat similar to abalone, clams, and scallops in appearance and texture. It is a cornerstone of the Caribbean diet. Popular Florida dishes include Conch Fritters (see page 85), chowders (both tomato- and cream-

based), salad, and ceviche. As a consequence of the depletion of the conch population in the waters off of Florida, most of the conch served in Florida now comes from Costa Rica and the Turks and Caicos islands.

FISH

Florida has a longer coastline than California, and the warm waters that surround the state teem with many species of fish. Floridians thrive on seafood and eat meat only occasionally. Here are some of the types of fish commonly available:

Amberjack: A large, firm-fleshed, silvery-green fish with a distinctive brown stripe running from head to tail. Amberjack has a mild flavor similar to grouper and is prepared and served in much the same manner.

Catfish: A southern staple and a specialty of the Lake Okeechobee area. A freshwater fish, catfish are generally prepared by frying in a batter of cornmeal. Commercially available catfish from Florida are increasingly being grown on large fish-farms.

Cobia: A large, warm-water fish that resembles shark. Once considered a "trash fish," cobia is now widely appreciated for its firm, white, mild-flavored flesh. It is particularly good for chowders and ceviche.

Mahimahi: A member of the dolphin family and a distant cousin of "Flipper," this long, slender fish has a mild but rich flavor and is best prepared

broiled as a steak in the same manner as swordfish. Since the name "dolphin" might confuse consumers into thinking they are eating an endangered mammal, Floridians have adopted the Hawaiian name.

Grouper: A large, puffy-looking fish with firm, white, mild flesh. Often used in chowders and in fish sandwiches in Florida. Popular varieties of grouper include the red, gag, warsaw, corcy, and black.

Kingfish: A long, round-bodied, dark-fleshed fish, especially popular among Cubans and Central Americans. An oily fish that acquires a strong fishy flavor after a couple of days, kingfish is the traditional ingredient for making escabeche, a Cuban form of pickled fish.

Pompano: A flat, silvery fish yielding solid, mild-flavored fillets. Its texture is dry, almost sandy, without being firm or tough. Pompano is one of the mainstays of Florida cuisine (see pages 88 and 92).

Snapper: Harvested commercially in the shallow waters off the Keys, snapper is Florida's most popular fish. It is sweet, mild, and tender. Varieties include hog, mutton, and mangrove snapper.

Tuna: Several varieties of tuna are found in Florida waters. They range from the huge yellowfin tuna, which weigh between 500 and 600 pounds and have pinkish-red flesh, to the much smaller blackfin tuna, which weigh only 20 to 40 pounds and have dark, blood- red meat.

Wahoo: This long, round-bodied game fish resembles the kingfish and has grayish flesh much like the northeastern bluefish. The meat has a firm consistency with a flavor similar to kingfish or mackerel, though milder tasting and less oily.

FROG LEGS

The legs of frogs harvested in Florida's Everglades are heralded by the state's top chefs as the best and most flavorful. They are tender, succulent, mildflavored, and very sweet.

HEARTS OF PALM

The tender center of the white core, or heart, of the sabal or cabbage palm native to Florida. Because the entire tree must be sacrificed for the relatively tiny heart of the palm, commercial harvesting in Florida is now strictly regulated. Fresh hearts of palm are available in small numbers in farmers' markets throughout Florida, but most canned hearts are from South America. Popular uses are raw in salads, or as a side dish, boiled with a bit of smoked pork and a little sugar.

JACK FRUIT

A huge, armadillo-shaped fruit with a tough, scaly skin. The jack fruit tastes like a mixture of melon, apricot, and honey.

LOBSTER

The Florida lobster is of the spiny variety with giant antennae and no claws. It has crisp white meat in its tail. Also known as rock lobster, spiny lobsters can weigh up to 15 pounds, though the average is 1 to 2 pounds. They are sold whole or by the tail, fresh and frozen.

LYCHEE

The lychee nut, originally native to China, has been grown in Florida since the 1890s, but intensive commercial harvesting dates to about 1980. The mature lychee fruit measures 1¼ inches and has a rough, red, knobby skin that covers the white flesh underneath. There is a single shiny brown seed in the center. The flavor of the flesh of the lychee hints at honey and muscat grapes. It is used in sauces and eaten on its own.

MANGO

Floridians are fond of saying that mangos are to their state what peaches are to Georgia. There are literally hundreds of varieties of mango in Florida, each with its own distinct flavor. Used in sauces, soups, and salsas, mangos are rich in Vitamins A and C and the mineral potassium.

PASSION FRUIT

A lemon-sized fruit with a leathery yellow, brown, purple, or green casing. The orange flesh is tart and is filled with crunchy, black, edible seeds. The pulp is usually strained and enjoyed in juice form.

ROCK SHRIMP

This native of Florida waters has a hard, thick shell and a taste somewhere between shrimp and lobster. Only since 1988 has there been a device to shell rock shrimp commercially. They are more perishable than ordinary shrimp, so rock shrimp are best prepared or frozen soon after purchase.

SOFT-SHELL CRABS

These are not a species of crab; they are young crabs that have molted—shed their shells in order to grow larger. Soft-shell crabs are available all year long in Florida and they range in size from "mediums" (3 inches across the back), to "whales" (5 inches and over).

STONE CRABS

Though eaten in Cuba for generations, stone crabs didn't really catch on in the States until Joe Weiss, who founded Joe's Stone Crab Restaurant in Miami in 1913, began serving them chilled, thereby eliminating the stone crab's chief drawbacks: the mild iodine aftertaste and the slightly watery consistency of its meat even when boiled. Only the rock-hard claws are eaten. The rest of the crab is thrown back in the water and and will regenerate the missing claws in twelve to eighteen months. The claws are always sold cooked and are categorized in three grades: medium (eight to a pound), large (four to a pound), and jumbo (one to three to a pound). They are in season from mid-October to mid-April. If you want to sample this extraordinary delicacy, you can order them for overnight shipment from Joe's by calling 1-800-780-CRAB. Joe's will also send along a container of their exquisite mustard sauce.

Tropical Drinks

Refreshment is a top priority in the often steamy Sunshine State, and Floridians have a variety of colorful cocktails that are perfect as a midday thirst quencher or sunset toast. Cuba, where bartending is an art form, is responsible for many of the favorite drinks.

Mojita—The most popular mixed drink in Cuba and a top choice in Florida. Recipe: juice of ½ lime; 1 teaspoon superfine sugar; mint leaves, to taste; 1 scoop crushed ice; 2 ounces light rum; soda water; sprig of mint for garnish. Place lime juice and sugar in a highball glass and stir until sugar is dissolved. Add a few mint leaves, bruising them against the inside of the glass with a back of a spoon. Fill the glass with crushed ice and pour in the rum. Top off with soda water, stirring gently, and garnish with a sprig of mint.

Daiquiri—Invented in the late-nineteenth century by two copper mine engineers in the Cuban province of Oriente. The nearest town? Daiquiri, of course! Originally just rum, lime juice, sugar, and ice, the daiquiri has since been made with every fruit imaginable. The frozen (blended) daiquiri was invented at Havana's legendary La Floridita bar in the 1930s and was Ernest Hemingway's favorite drink. Original Version: 1 scoop crushed ice; juice of ½ lime; 2 teaspoons sugar; 1 ounce white rum. Mix vigorously in a shaker and strain into an iced cocktail glass. For a frozen daiquiri, mix all ingredients in a blender. Variations: Add one of the following: ½ banana, 3 or 4 strawberries, 3 or 4 mint leaves, ½ peeled peach, 1 slice pineapple, 2 splashes grenadine.

Mary Pickford—Many Cuban bartenders named their signature drinks after American movie stars, perhaps as a nod to their stateside patrons, or maybe to increase their own celebrity status. Recipe: 1½ ounces light rum; 1½ ounces pineapple juice; splash of grenadine; 1 scoop crushed ice; 1 maraschino cherry. Combine all the ingredients, except the cherry, in a shaker. Mix well and strain into a chilled cocktail glass. Garnish with the cherry.

El Presidente—1½ ounces light rum; ¼ ounce dry vermouth; 1 ounce sweet vermouth; splash of grenadine; maraschino cherry for garnish. In a stirring glass with ice, mix together the ingredients. Strain into an iced cocktail glass and add the cherry.

Cuba Libre—To toast the liberation of Havana after the Spanish-American War, this drink features the most American of ingredients: Coca-Cola. To 1 ounce of light rum, add Coca-Cola in a highball glass with a few ice cubes. Add a lime wedge, after giving it a light squeeze over the drink, and stir well.

Mulatta—1 scoop crushed ice; juice of ½ lime; ¼ ounce brown creme de cacao; 1 ounce white rum. Mix in a blender. Serve in an iced cocktail glass.

The Recipes

SCALLOP CEVICHE WITH CRISPY SPICED TORTILLA STRIPS
ADAPTED FROM A RECIPE FROM MICHAEL'S ON EAST, SARASOTA

Makes 6 appetizer servings

Ceviche—raw fish or shellfish marinated in fresh lime juice—is actually of Peruvian origin. The delicate seafood "cooks" in the acidic juice. This lovely Florida version adds regional spices and fruits to create a refreshing and visually interesting dish.

- 1 pound sea scallops, cut in quarters, or smaller if scallops are particularly large
- 2 tomatoes, seeded and chopped
- 1 small red onion, finely chopped
- 1 jalapeño pepper, seeded and minced
- 2 cups fresh lime juice (bottled juice will not work!)
- Olive oil, for frying
- 4 corn tortillas, cut into 3-inch x ⅛-inch strips
- Salt and cayenne pepper
- 2 oranges, peeled and cut into segments
- 1 pink grapefruit, peeled and cut into segments
- 1 avocado, peeled, seeded, and diced
- 1 mango, peeled, seeded, and diced
- 2 limes, peeled and cut into segments
- ½ cup chopped fresh cilantro
- 1 tablespoon sugar
- Freshly ground white pepper

In a medium stainless steel bowl, combine the scallops, tomatoes, onion, jalapeño, and lime juice. Cover and marinate in the refrigerator until the scallops are "cooked," about 3 hours.

Meanwhile, heat 1 inch of oil in a large skillet over medium-high heat. Add the tortilla strips and fry until crisp, stirring to make sure they don't stick together. Remove with a slotted spoon and drain on a paper towel–lined baking sheet. While still hot, season the tortillas with salt and cayenne pepper. Set aside.

Just before serving the scallops, drain off as much lime juice as possible. Add the oranges, grapefruit, avocado, mango, limes, cilantro, and sugar. Toss gently. Season with salt and white pepper.

Serve in balloon wine goblets and sprinkle with the tortilla strips.

STUFFED PLANTAINS
ADAPTED FROM A RECIPE BY EFRAIN VEIGA AND GUILLERMO VELOSO, YUCA RESTAURANT, MIAMI

Serves 6-8

This is a crispy, flavorful appetizer that offers Cuban spice in a neat package.

- 2 pounds ham hocks
- 4 semiripe plantains, peeled and sliced into large chunks
- 2 tablespoons olive oil
- 1 small onion, finely diced
- 1 red bell pepper, finely diced
- 1 green bell pepper, finely diced
- 2 cloves garlic, minced
- 2 tablespoons tomato paste
- 1 teaspoon chili powder
- Salt and freshly ground black pepper
- All-purpose flour, for dredging
- 3 eggs, beaten
- Seasoned bread crumbs, for dredging
- Vegetable oil, for frying

Place the ham hocks in a large pot and cover them with water. Bring to a boil and cook for 30 minutes or until the meat is falling off the bones. Drain the ham hocks and let cool slightly. Discard the fat and bones. Shred the meat and reserve.

Place the plantains in another large pot and cover them with water. Bring to a boil and cook for 15 minutes. Drain the plantains and purée them in a food processor fitted with a metal blade. Set aside.

Heat the olive oil in a large skillet over medium heat. Add the onion and bell peppers. Sauté, stirring, for 6 minutes. Add the garlic and sauté, stirring for 2 to 4 minutes. Stir in the shredded ham, tomato paste, and chili powder. Remove from the heat. Season with salt and pepper.

Put the flour, eggs, and bread crumbs in 3 different pie plates. Heat the vegetable oil in a Dutch oven to a depth of 3 inches and a temperature of 375°F. For each stuffed plantain, place a scant ⅓ cup plantain mixture in the palm of your hand and flatten to form a round disk. Spoon a scant ⅓ cup of the ham mixture onto the disk and roll up to form a torpedo and enclose the ham mixture. Dip into the flour, then into the eggs, and then into the bread crumbs. Deep fry until golden brown, about 2 minutes. Drain well on paper towel–lined plates. Serve immediately.

BLACK BEAN SOUP
ADAPTED FROM A RECIPE BY STEVEN RAICHLEN, MIAMI

Serves 8

Steven Raichlen

Steven Raichlen is an award-winning cookbook author, cooking instructor, and syndicated food columnist. His popular book Miami Spice *celebrates the vibrant cuisine of his home state. It won the 1994 Julia Child IACP Award for Best Regional American Cookbook. As a columnist for the* Los Angeles Times Syndicate, *he is read monthly in ninety-five newspapers by 14.5 million people.*

Raichlen also runs "Cooking in Paradise," a popular Caribbean cooking school on the French island of St. Barthélemy. Specializing in healthy West Indian cuisine, the school has been profiled by CNN, Bon Appétit, *and the* Hideaway Report.

Trained at the Cordon Bleu and La Varenne cooking schools in Paris, Raichlen's teaching and writing have done much to popularize the cooking of South Florida and the Caribbean.

The Cuban influence in Florida cooking is exemplified by this dark, dense soup that author Steven Raichlen calls the state's official soup.

- 1 pound dried black beans
- 2 yellow onions, finely chopped
- 2 red bell peppers, finely chopped
- 6 cloves garlic, minced
- 3 bay leaves
- 1 whole clove
- 6 slices bacon, cut into ¼-inch slivers
- 3 tablespoons extra virgin olive oil
- 2 stalks celery, finely chopped
- 1 carrot, finely chopped
- ½ cup dry white wine
- 1 tablespoon white wine vinegar
- 1 teaspoon ground cumin, or to taste
- 1 teaspoon dried oregano leaves, or to taste
- Salt and freshly ground black pepper
- ½ cup sour cream
- 2 green onions (scallions), finely chopped

The day before, rinse the beans in a colander under cold running water. Pick through them, looking for any pebbles. Place the beans in a large, heavy pot and add 8 cups of water. Let soak overnight.

Add 1 onion, 1 bell pepper, 3 cloves of garlic, 1 bay leaf, and the clove to the pot containing the beans. Bring to a boil, reduce the heat, loosely cover, and simmer, stirring occasionally, until tender, about 1 hour.

Meanwhile, in a large skillet, over medium heat, cook the bacon until crisp. Drain the bacon on a paper towel–lined plate. Discard the fat in the skillet.

In the same skillet, heat the oil over medium heat. Stir in the remaining onion, bell pepper, garlic and the celery and carrot. Sauté, stirring, until the vegetables are soft, about 10 minutes.

Stir the vegetables into the bean pot along with the bacon, wine, vinegar, cumin, oregano, and the remaining 2 bay leaves. Bring to a boil, reduce the heat, cover, and simmer 15 minutes.

Remove the 3 bay leaves and discard. Scoop 2 cups of the bean mixture into a bowl; mash with a potato masher and return to the pot. Season soup with salt and pepper.

To serve, spoon into soup bowls. Top with a dollop of sour cream and sprinkle with the green onions.

CONCH FRITTERS
ADAPTED FROM A RECIPE BY STEVEN RAICHLEN, MIAMI

Makes about 24 fritters

This popular Florida mollusk is rarely available in the rest of the country and can become very tough and rubbery if not handled exactly right. When properly prepared, however, conch is sweet and delicious. Nevertheless, substituting sea scallops is an excellent alternative. Serve these as a appetizer with tartar sauce (see page 23) or just a squeeze of lime.

- ½ pound conch
- 1 cup all-purpose flour
- 1 teaspoon sugar
- 1 teaspoon baking powder
- 1 egg, beaten
- 6 to 8 tablespoons buttermilk
- ¼ cup finely chopped onion
- ¼ cup finely chopped red bell pepper
- ¼ cup minced celery
- 1 pickled jalapeño pepper, seeded and minced
- 1 clove garlic, minced
- ¾ teaspoon salt
- ¼ teaspoon freshly ground pepper
- Vegetable oil for frying
- Lime wedges

Grind the conch finely in a food processor fitted with a metal blade. Set aside.

Combine flour, sugar, and baking powder in a large bowl. Add the egg and then stir in the buttermilk as necessary to obtain a thick batter. Stir in the conch and all the remaining ingredients except the oil and lime wedges.

Pour the oil to a depth of at least 1 inch in a small frying pan and heat to 350°F. Using spoons, drop 1-inch balls of batter into the oil. Fry, turning with a slotted spoon, until golden brown, about 2 minutes. Cook the fritters in several batches so as not to overcrowd the pan. Drain the fritters on a paper towel–lined plate. Then arrange the fritters on a platter and serve with lime wedges.

MANGOSPACHO
ADAPTED FROM A RECIPE BY STEVEN RAICHLEN, MIAMI

Serves 4

This easy summer soup demonstrates the playfulness that is typical of Florida cuisine. It combines Caribbean tropical fruit and a traditional European blended vegetable soup. .

- 3 large or 6 small ripe mangos, peeled and very finely diced (about 6 cups)
- 1 cup water
- ¼ cup rice wine vinegar
- ¼ cup light olive oil
- 1 cucumber, peeled, seeded, and very finely chopped
- ¼ cup very finely diced red onion
- ¼ cup finely chopped fresh cilantro
- 2 tablespoons snipped fresh chives
- 1 to 2 tablespoons sugar (optional)
- Salt and freshly ground black pepper

Combine half of the mango pulp (3 cups), the water, vinegar, and oil in a blender and purée. If the purée is too thick, add a little more water.

Transfer the mixture to a bowl. Stir in the cucumber, onion, cilantro, chives, and the remaining diced mango. Season with salt and pepper. If the soup is too tart, you may want to add a little sugar. The soup can be served right away, but it will be better if you refrigerate it for 1 hour to allow the flavors to blend. Adjust seasonings just before serving, if necessary.

The Cuban Sandwich

Even if you're not going to south Florida any time soon, you can still prepare Miami's favorite snack, the Cuban sandwich. These tasty, toasted sandwiches are served in Miami's streetcorner snack bars, called loncherias.

When preparing the sandwich at home, it's important to stick to the rules. Start with authentic Cuban bread. Pan cubano resembles a French baguette, but it is softer and chewier with a slightly flattened top. If there aren't any Cuban bakeries in your neighborhood, you can substitute a long, soft Italian loaf that's not too crusty. Split the bread lengthwise, spread it inside with mustard, and layer it with thinly-sliced roast pork, ham, Genovese salami, dill pickle, and Swiss cheese. This is not the place for leftover roast beef or chicken, Florida locals will tell you.

Next, brush the sandwich with butter or margarine on the outside and heat in a fold-down grill, called a plancha. This toasts the bread and flattens the sandwich for easy eating. You can toast the sandwich in a frying pan and flatten it with a skillet or other weight while it cooks. The Cuban sandwich makes a great, simple snack that kids love.

CARIBBEAN ANTIPASTO SALAD
ADAPTED FROM RECIPES BY ALLEN SUSSER, CHEF ALLEN'S, NORTH MIAMI

Serves 6 (8 appetizers)

The Caribbean islands have had a strong impact on Florida cooking. In fact, the term "Floribbean" is often used to indicate the fusion nature of this new style. Allen Susser is one of the best interpreters of the tropical aspects of this burgeoning cuisine. Here is a medley of his appetizers. They can be prepared separately, but they look wonderful on a big platter, arranged in a colorful design.

- **Jerked Calamari** (recipe follows)
- **Grilled Shrimp with Tangerine Barbecue Sauce** (recipe follows)
- **Green Papaya Slaw** (recipe follows)
- **Hearts of Palm Ceviche** (recipe follows)
- **1 large avocado,** peeled, seeded, and sliced
- **1 large mango,** peeled, seeded, and sliced

Prepare the Jerked Calamari, Grilled Shrimp with Tangerine Barbecue Sauce, Green Papaya Slaw, and Hearts of Palm Ceviche. Arrange on a large platter, placing one or two elements in the middle and arranging the others around them. Decorate with avocado and mango slices.

NOTE: "Jerked" is a term that refers to a Jamaican dish in which two different meats are combined and marinated in fiery hot chile spices and then grilled. It has been expanded to include just about any dish with a hot, spicy sauce.

NOTE: Green, unripe papaya is eaten frequently throughout Latin America and the Caribbean. It is crisper and less sweet than the ripe version and similar to the green tomatoes used in the South (see page 47). The Florida influence is represented by the use of tangerine in the shrimp sauce, as well as hearts of palm, which is a typical local ingredient.

JERKED CALAMARI

- 1 cup dry red wine
- ¼ cup olive oil
- 4 green onions (scallions), finely chopped
- 6 cloves garlic, minced
- 2 tablespoons chopped fresh cilantro
- 1 teaspoon minced Scotch bonnet chile
- 1 teaspoon ground cinnamon
- 1 teaspoon salt
- ½ teaspoon ground nutmeg
- ¼ teaspoon ground allspice
- 1 pound calamari, cleaned, with tentacles and mantles separated

In a medium bowl, whisk together all the ingredients except the calamari. Add the calamari. Cover and marinate in the refrigerator for 1 to 2 hours. Drain and discard the marinade.

Prepare the grill. Grill the calamari over high heat until just firm to the touch, about 1 minute. Serve hot or at room temperature.

NOTE: To clean a fresh squid, gently pull the tentacles, arms, and head away from the body. Remove the rigid "quill" from inside the body and clean out the cream-colored viscera. Rinse and then pull off the outer membrane. Locate the ink sac near the head. Reserve it if needed, otherwise discard it. Cut off the arms and tentacles and pinch out the hard beak.

GREEN PAPAYA SLAW

- 1 green (unripened) papaya, peeled, seeded, and grated
- 1 red bell pepper, julienned
- 1 carrot, julienned
- 1 small white onion, chopped
- 2 tablespoons olive oil
- 1 tablespoon minced fresh ginger
- 1 tablespoon lime juice
- 1 teaspoon celery seeds
- Salt and freshly ground white pepper

Combine all the ingredients in a medium bowl except the salt and pepper. Toss well. Season with salt and pepper. Let stand at room temperature before serving.

GRILLED SHRIMP WITH TANGERINE BARBECUE SAUCE

- 1 cup tangerine or orange juice
- ¼ cup prepared chili sauce
- 3 tablespoons molasses
- 2 tablespoons Dijon-style mustard
- 1 tablespoon red wine vinegar
- 1 green onion (scallion), minced
- 1 clove garlic, minced
- 1 teaspoon minced chipotle in adobo (page 197)
- ⅛ teaspoon ground cinnamon
- ⅛ teaspoon ground cloves
- 1 pound large shrimp, peeled and deveined

In a medium saucepan over medium heat, combine all the ingredients except the shrimp. Cook until the sauce is thick enough to coat the back of a spoon, about 15 to 20 minutes.

Prepare the grill. Place the shrimp on the grill and brush with some of the sauce. Grill until opaque throughout, about 3 minutes, turning once. Serve hot or at room temperature, with the remaining sauce.

HEARTS OF PALM CEVICHE

- 1 (14-ounce) can hearts of palm, drained
- 2 tomatoes, seeded and chopped
- 1 red onion, finely chopped
- ¼ cup lime juice
- 3 tablespoons chopped fresh cilantro
- 1 jalapeño pepper, seeded and minced
- 2 tablespoons olive oil
- ½ teaspoon ground cumin
- Salt and freshly ground black pepper

Thinly slice the hearts of palm on the bias. Place them in a medium bowl. Add all the remaining ingredients except the salt and pepper and toss well. Season with salt and pepper. Let stand at room temperature for 1 hour before serving.

GRILLED MARINATED LOIN OF PORK WITH JAMAICAN SPICES
ADAPTED FROM A RECIPE BY MARK MILITELLO,
MARK'S PLACE, NORTH MIAMI

Serves 4

Here is another use of the Jamaican "jerk" spices. In this recipe, Chef Militello uses a pork loin. The result is superbly delicious and remarkably subtle. Be very careful with the Scotch bonnet pepper, one of the hottest in the world. Wear rubber gloves when handling it.

• 1½ teaspoons ground cinnamon	• 2 teaspoons minced fresh ginger
• 1½ teaspoons ground nutmeg	• 1 Scotch bonnet chile, seeded and minced
• ½ teaspoon ground allspice	• ½ cup orange juice
• 4 green onions (scallions), chopped	• ½ cup olive oil
• 1 small yellow onion, chopped	• ¼ cup soy sauce
• 2 tablespoons fresh thyme leaves	• Salt and pepper
	• 8 (3-ounce) pork loin medallions

Place the cinnamon, nutmeg, and allspice in a small skillet over low heat. Cook until toasted and fragrant.

Place the spices, green onions, yellow onion, thyme, ginger, and chile in a food processor fitted with a metal blade. Process until finely chopped. Add the orange juice, oil, and soy sauce. Process until smooth. Season with salt and pepper. Place the marinade in a shallow dish. Add the pork and marinate in the refrigerator for 6 hours, turning occasionally.

Prepare the grill. Remove the pork from the marinade and discard the marinade. Grill the pork to desired doneness, turning once. Slice and serve.

COCONUT POMPANO WITH CITRUS BEURRE BLANC

Serves 4

Pompano is a highly prized fish. It weighs 1 to 2 pounds and does not need to be scaled. The fish is usually split in half and then filleted. The meat is firm and sweet. Here it is combined with coconut and the ever-present citrus.

• ¼ cup orange juice	• 1 pink grapefruit, peeled and cut into segments
• 1½ teaspoons sugar	• 2 tablespoons snipped fresh chives
• 1 tablespoon lemon juice	• Salt and freshly ground pepper
• 1 tablespoon lime juice	• 4 (6-ounce) pompano fillets
• ½ teaspoon grated orange zest	• ½ cup milk
• ¼ teaspoon grated lemon zest	• ½ cup all-purpose flour
• ½ cup (1 stick) plus 2 tablespoons unsalted butter, room temperature and cut into ½-inch pieces	• 3 eggs, beaten
	• 1 cup shredded, unsweetened coconut
• 1 orange, peeled and cut into segments	• 1 tablespoon olive oil

To make the sauce: Combine the orange juice, sugar, lemon and lime juices, and orange and lemon zests in a small saucepan. Bring to a boil, reduce the heat to medium and simmer the mixture, uncovered, until the liquid is reduced to about 1 tablespoon. Reduce the heat to low. Add 1 piece of the ½ cup of butter, whisking constantly. When the butter is nearly blended in, add another piece, still whisking. Continue adding 1 piece at a time, whisking constantly. After the ½ cup of butter is added and the sauce is thick, stir in the citrus segments and chives. Season with salt and pepper. Set aside and keep warm.

Put the milk, flour, and eggs in 3 different pie plates. Dip each pompano fillet in the milk, dredge in the flour, dip in the egg, and then cover with the coconut to coat completely. Season each with salt and pepper. Melt the remaining 2 tablespoons of butter with the oil in a large skillet over medium-high heat. Add the fillets and sauté until the fish is opaque throughout and the coconut is golden brown, about 8 minutes, turning once. Serve with the sauce.

YELLOWTAIL SNAPPER WITH RUM, BROWN BUTTER, MANGO, GINGER, AND MINT
ADAPTED FROM A RECIPE BY MARK MILITELLO, MARK'S PLACE, NORTH MIAMI

Serves 4

Here is an excellent example of the new Floribbean cooking. A fresh fish is augmented, but not overshadowed, by tropical spices and flavors.

- 4 (6- to 8-ounce) yellowtail, red, *or* mutton snapper fillets
- Salt and pepper
- 1 cup all-purpose flour
- ⅓ cup (⅔ stick) clarified unsalted butter (see note)
- ¼ cup (½ stick) unsalted butter
- 1 mango, peeled, pitted, and diced
- ⅔ cup loosely packed fresh mint leaves
- ½ cup chopped macadamia nuts
- 2 tablespoons julienned fresh ginger
- ¼ cup dark rum
- 3 tablespoons lemon juice

Run your fingers over the fish fillets, feeling for pin bones, and remove any you may find with pliers. Take care not to tear the flesh. Score the fillets on the diagonal through the skin-side 3 times with a sharp knife. Season the fish with salt and pepper. Lightly dust the fillets with the flour, shaking off the excess.

Heat the clarified butter in a large nonstick skillet over medium heat. Sauté the fish, starting skin-side down, about 8 minutes, until opaque throughout, turning once. Transfer the fish to a warm platter.

Add the remaining ¼ cup butter to the skillet and cook until lightly browned. Stir in the mango, mint, nuts, and ginger. Sauté for 1 minute. Stir in the rum and lemon juice and bring to a boil. Season with salt and pepper. Spoon the sauce over the fish and serve at once.

Note: Clarified butter is melted butter from which casein and other nonfat ingredients have been removed. Melt the butter and simmer slowly over a low flame. Skim the white scum that rises to the surface. Some of the white will also drop to the bottom of the pan. After a few minutes, you can pour off the pure, clear liquid.

PICKAPEPPA CHICKEN WITH RUM-GLAZED PLANTAINS
ADAPTED FROM A RECIPE BY NORMA SHIRLEY, NORMA'S, KINGSTON, JAMAICA

Serves 4

From the widespread use of tropical fruits and vegetables to the spices, condiments, and techniques of local island cooks, the Caribbean has had a profound influence on Florida's cuisine. This recipe comes from Norma Shirley, one of Jamaica's best cooks.

- ½ cup (1 stick) unsalted butter
- ¼ cup olive oil
- 2 onions, cut into thin wedges
- 1 jalapeño pepper, seeded and minced
- 2 cloves garlic, minced
- 4 chicken legs with thighs, skinned and split (about 2 pounds)
- 1 cup chicken stock
- 1 (5-ounce) bottle Pickapeppa sauce
- Salt and freshly ground pepper
- ¼ cup dark rum
- ¼ cup molasses
- 2 tablespoons lime juice
- 2 plantains, cut into ¼-inch thick slices
- 1 tablespoons chopped fresh parsley

In a large skillet, melt ¼ cup of the butter with the oil over medium-low heat. Add the onions and cook, stirring occasionally, until caramelized, about 30 minutes.

Stir in the jalapeño and garlic. Cook, stirring, 3 minutes. Push the onion mixture to the side of the skillet. Raise the heat to medium. Add the chicken pieces and cook until golden brown on both sides, about 8 minutes. Stir in the stock and Pickapeppa sauce. Bring to a boil, reduce the heat, cover, and simmer until the chicken is tender and its juices run clear, about 30 minutes. Transfer the chicken to a warm platter, cover with aluminum foil, and keep warm in a low oven.

Over high heat, reduce the sauce until it thickens slightly. Season with salt and pepper. Set the sauce aside and keep it warm.

In a medium skillet, melt the remaining ¼ cup butter with the rum, molasses, and lime juice over medium-high heat. Cook about 2 minutes until slightly thickened. Add the plantains and cook over medium heat until softened slightly and nicely glazed.

To serve, pour the sauce over the chicken and accompany with the plantains. Sprinkle with the parsley. If desired, serve over parsleyed rice.

Dining with Disney

Formidable American regional and international cuisine has been introduced to Orlando, where the most common question in restaurants used to be, "Do you want fries with that?"

Here are some of Walt Disney World's gastronomic highlights: Victoria & Albert's—Located in the Grand Floridian Hotel, this intimate spot offers the complete European dining experience. The sophisticated international menu changes daily and often shows an American regional touch. Narcoossee's —The open kitchen at this airy Grand Floridian eatery gives you a close-up view of the chefs in action. While there are steaks on the menu, the main attraction here is Florida regional cooking. Flagler's—This large, lively restaurant offers upscale Italian dining. Artist Point—Disney's Wilderness Lodge is home to this artsy dining room that features regional cooking from the Pacific Northwest. Chefs de France—When word leaked out that Paul Bocuse, Roger Vergé, and Gaston Le Nôtre were pooling their considerable talents to open a restaurant in Epcot Center, Disney dining gained instant respectability. San Angel Inn—Modeled after one of Mexico City's premier restaurants, this spot in Epcot's Meso-American pyramid serves authentic regional fare. California Grill—The latest addition to Disney's American regional lineup, this restaurant brings the farm-fresh California concept to a colorful, modern setting in the contemporary resort.

GRILLED POMPANO WITH GINGERED STICKY RICE, RED CURRY—COCONUT SAUCE, AND RUM GLAZE

Serves 4

Pompano is so popular in Florida, they named a beach after it. Here it is prepared with a full palette of Floribbean ingredients.

• 1 tablespoon peanut oil	• 1 cinnamon stick
• 3 tablespoons minced fresh ginger	• 1 star anise pod
• 2 shallots, minced	• 1½ cups water
• 2 cloves garlic, minced	• ¾ cup Asian short-grained rice, uncooked
• 2 teaspoons red curry paste	• Salt
• 1 tablespoon sugar	• 4 (6-ounce) pompano fillets
• 1 (14-ounce) can coconut milk	• Freshly ground black pepper
• ¼ cup dark rum	• 4 teaspoons chopped fresh cilantro
• 2 tablespoons molasses	• 1 tablespoon black sesame seeds

To make the sauce: Heat the oil in a medium saucepan over medium heat. Add 1 tablespoon of the ginger, the shallots, garlic, and curry paste. Sauté, stirring, for 3 minutes. Stir in the sugar and cook for 30 seconds. Add the coconut milk. Bring to a boil, reduce the heat, and simmer for 15 minutes or until thickened. Pour the sauce into a blender and purée. Strain the sauce back into the saucepan. Set aside and keep warm until ready to serve.

To make the glaze: Place the rum, molasses, cinnamon stick, anise pod, and 1 tablespoon of the ginger in a small saucepan over low heat. Cook until reduced by half. Remove from the heat, strain, and reserve, covered, until ready to serve.

To make the rice: Bring the water to a boil in a medium saucepan. Add the rice, the remaining 1 tablespoon of ginger, and season with salt. Reduce the heat to low, cover, and simmer for 15 minutes or until the rice is tender and all the water has been absorbed. Remove from the heat and keep covered until ready to serve.

Prepare the grill. Season the pompano with salt and pepper. Grill until just opaque throughout, about 5 minutes, turning once.

To serve, portion the rice onto 4 warm dinner plates and top with the fish fillets. Pour the sauce around the rice and fish. Drizzle with the glaze and sprinkle with the cilantro and sesame seeds.

YUCCA CON MOJO
ADAPTED FROM A RECIPE BY EFRAIN VEIGA AND GUILLERMO VELOSO, YUCA RESTAURANT, MIAMI

Serves 6

Yucca is related to the agave, the century plant from which tequila is made. It has a starchy, potato-like texture and a mild flavor. In this simple recipe, it is augmented, not overshadowed, by a "mojo" made from herbs and fruit juice.

• 2 pounds fresh yucca, peeled and cut into 1-inch chunks	• 2½ cups orange juice
• ¼ cup olive oil	• 1 bunch fresh parsley, chopped
• 1 onion, sliced	• 1 bunch fresh oregano, chopped
• 8 cloves garlic, minced	• Salt and freshly ground pepper

Bring a large pot of water to a boil over high heat. Add the yucca and cook until tender, about 20 minutes. Drain the yucca, return it to the pot, and set aside.

To make the mojo: In a large saucepan, heat the oil over medium heat and sauté the onion, stirring occasionally, 8 minutes. Add the garlic and sauté, stirring, 2 minutes. Stir in the orange juice, parsley, and oregano. Bring to a boil. Add the mojo to the yucca pot and cook over low heat, uncovered, for 15 minutes. Season with salt and pepper.

PAN-SEARED FLORIDA SHRIMP ON HOPPIN' JOHN RISOTTO

ADAPTED FROM A RECIPE BY ROBIN HAAS, BANG, MIAMI

Serves 4

This is the kind of recipe that demonstrates the resilience and potential of modern American cooking. The very talented Chef Haas mixes Florida, the South, and Italy in this dish and comes out a winner.

- 20 jumbo shrimp in the shell
- ¼ cup (4 tablespoons) peanut oil
- 1 onion, diced
- 1 head fennel, diced
- 1 carrot, diced
- 8 tomatoes, seeded, and diced
- 3 cups chicken stock
- 3 tablespoons chopped fresh thyme
- 1 bay leaf
- Salt and freshly ground black pepper
- 2 tablespoons unsalted butter
- ½ cup Arborio rice
- ½ cup thawed frozen black-eyed peas (if you can use fresh, do so)
- ¼ cup grated Manchego *or* Parmesan cheese
- 2 tablespoons chopped fresh basil
- 2 tablespoons chopped fresh parsley
- 2 tablespoons snipped fresh chives
- Lemon wedges

Peel and devein the shrimp. Reserve both the shrimp and their shells.

Pour 2 tablespoons of the oil into a large saucepan and place over medium heat. Add the shrimp shells and sauté for 2 minutes. Add the onion, fennel, and carrot. Sauté, stirring occasionally, until the vegetables are golden brown, about 15 minutes. Stir in the tomatoes, 2 cups of the stock, 2 teaspoons of the thyme, and the bay leaf. Bring to a boil, reduce the heat, cover and simmer for 30 minutes. Strain and discard the solids. Season with salt and pepper. Set aside.

Melt 1 tablespoon of the butter in a medium saucepan over medium heat. Add the rice and sauté for 1 minute. Add ½ cup of the remaining 1 cup of stock and stir constantly until all the liquid is absorbed. Stir in the remaining ½ cup stock, again stirring until all is absorbed. Add the reserved tomato-shrimp sauce ½ cup at a time in the same way as the stock, adding more only when the previous addition has been absorbed. When all the liquid has been absorbed, remove the pan from the heat. The rice should be tender. Stir in the black-eyed peas, cheese, 1 teaspoon of the remaining thyme, and the remaining 1 tablespoon butter. Season with salt and pepper. Set the risotto aside and keep warm.

In a small bowl, combine the basil, parsley, chives, and the remaining 2 tablespoons of thyme. Season the shrimp with salt, pepper, and the herbs, making sure the herbs are pressed onto the shrimp to adhere well.

Heat the remaining 2 tablespoons of oil in a large skillet over medium-high heat. Add the shrimp and sear on both sides until crisp, golden brown, and opaque throughout, about 1½ to 2 minutes.

To serve, divide and mound the hot risotto on 4 warm dinner plates. Top with the shrimp and accompany with the lemon wedges.

Chef Mark Militello

If there is one chef responsible for putting South Florida on America's culinary map, it is Mark Militello of Mark's Place in North Miami. This highly talented, Texas-born chef weaves tropical Caribbean ingredients and California and Mediterranean cooking techniques into a cuisine that is uniquely his own.

Chef Militello was a premed student at Marquette University when he decided to pursue his love of cooking. He studied cooking and restaurants at Florida International University and at the State University of New York Hotel and Culinary Program.

In 1988, Chef Militello became owner and executive chef of Mark's Place, gaining immediate popular and critical acclaim. In 1992 the James Beard Foundation named him the "Best Regional Chef in the American Southeast." He has been profiled in Time, Esquire, Bon Appetit, Condé Nast Traveler, *and* The New York Times. *In 1994, he launched his second restaurant, Mark's Las Olas in Ft. Lauderdale.*

Icky Sticky Coconut Pudding

ADAPTED FROM A RECIPE BY MARK MILITELLO, MARK'S PLACE, NORTH MIAMI

Serves 6

Chef Militello uses Caribbean coconut and rum in this fanciful dessert. Don't be misled by the name of the dish; actually it is much more like the best sticky bun you've ever had.

- 5 tablespoons butter, at room temperature
- ¾ cup sugar, plus 3 tablespoons (for sugaring the molds)
- ½ cup finely chopped pitted dates
- 1 cup finely grated fresh coconut
- 1 cup water
- 1 teaspoon baking soda
- 2 eggs
- 1½ cups unbleached all-purpose flour
- 2 teaspoons baking powder
- ½ teaspoon salt
- 1 teaspoon vanilla extract
- Warm Rum Toffee Sauce (see below)
- ¼ cup toasted, chopped macadamia nuts

Preheat the oven to 400°F. Butter six 6-ounce ramekins (or one 9-inch cake pan) using 1 tablespoon of the butter. Lightly sugar the molds with the 3 tablespoons of sugar.

Combine the dates, coconut, and water in a saucepan over high heat. Bring to a boil. Remove from the heat, stir in the baking soda, and set aside.

Cream the remaining 4 tablespoons of butter in a bowl. Beat in the remaining ¾ cup of sugar, little by little, and continue beating until light and fluffy. Beat in the eggs one at a time. Sift the flour with the baking powder and salt onto the egg mixture, then fold in gently. Stir in the coconut mixture and the vanilla.

Spoon the pudding mixture into the molds and cover with a sheet of buttered aluminum foil. Bake the puddings on a baking sheet until set and a cake tester or toothpick inserted into the center comes out clean, 20 to 25 minutes. Uncover the molds and prick the puddings with a skewer. Pour 1 tablespoon of the Warm Rum Toffee Sauce over each pudding. Return the puddings to the oven and bake, uncovered, for 1 minute.

Let the puddings cool for 5 minutes. Unmold the puddings onto individual plates or a platter. Spoon the remaining sauce over the puddings and sprinkle them with the toasted nuts.

Warm Rum Toffee Sauce

Makes 1½ cups

- ¾ cup plus 2 tablespoons packed light brown sugar
- 6 tablespoons heavy cream
- ½ cup (1 stick) butter
- ½ teaspoon vanilla extract
- 3 tablespoons dark rum

Combine all the ingredients in a heavy saucepan over medium heat. Boil until thick and well blended, about 3 minutes. Serve warm.

KEY LIME PIE

Makes one 9-inch pie

Key limes, planted in the Florida Keys in the early 1800s, are golfball-sized, yellowish fruits with a bitter, spicy flavor. When the Borden Company developed sweetened condensed evaporated milk in 1856, the recipe combining this canned product (there were no cows in the Keys) and key limes was developed soon afterward. Key lime juice may be somewhat difficult to find in your local market. (Steven Raichlen makes a half-and-half mixture of lemon juice and regular lime juice as a substitute.)

- 1½ cups graham cracker crumbs
- ¼ cup granulated sugar
- ½ teaspoon cinnamon
- ¼ teaspoon freshly ground nutmeg
- ½ cup (1 stick) unsalted butter, melted
- 1 (14-ounce) can sweetened condensed evaporated milk
- ½ cup key lime juice, fresh *or* bottled
- 4 egg yolks
- ½ cup heavy cream
- 1 tablespoon powdered sugar
- ¼ teaspoon vanilla extract

Preheat the oven to 375°F. In a medium bowl, combine the crumbs, granulated sugar, cinnamon, and nutmeg. Stir in the butter to coat the crumbs completely. Press the crumb mixture onto the bottom and up the sides of a 9-inch pie plate. Bake 8 minutes. Remove to a rack to cool completely, about 1 hour.

Place the condensed milk, juice, and egg yolks in a medium bowl. Beat with an electric hand mixer until smooth. Pour into the cooled pie shell and chill until firm, about 4 hours.

In a small bowl, beat the cream with an electric hand mixer to form soft peaks. Gently fold in the powdered sugar and vanilla. Spread over the pie or place in a pastry bag fitted with a star tip and pipe decorative rosettes on top.

FLOATING ISLANDS WITH MANGO-GINGER SAUCE AND FRESH SUMMER FRUITS
ADAPTED FROM A RECIPE BY ALLEN SUSSER, CHEF ALLEN'S, NORTH MIAMI

Serves 8

Here is a clever adaptation of a classic French dessert which was popular in American upper-crust kitchens in the nineteenth and early twentieth centuries. Chef Allen has turned the islands tropical with his addition of colorful fruit.

- 4 egg whites, at room temperature
- ⅛ teaspoon cream of tartar
- 1 cup superfine sugar
- 1 cup powdered sugar, sifted
- 1 quart water
- 1 cup milk
- 2 large ripe mangos, peeled and seeded
- 2 tablespoons lemon juice
- 1 teaspoon minced fresh ginger
- Pinch of salt
- Assortment of fresh summer fruits such as peaches, apricots, lychees, blueberries, papaya, raspberries, pineapple, *and/or* cherries
- Mint leaves

To make the meringues: In an electric mixer bowl, beat the egg whites to a froth and add the cream of tartar. Whip until peaks form and add ½ cup of the superfine sugar little by little. When firm and stiff peaks form, fold in the powdered sugar. In a large saucepan, warm the water and milk together and bring to a simmer. Using a large ice cream scoop, scoop the meringue into the milky water to make 8 meringues. Cover and simmer for 2 minutes or until firm. With a slotted spatula, remove the meringues to a baking sheet lined with waxed paper. Place in the refrigerator to cool completely.

To make the sauce: In a food processor fitted with a metal blade, purée the mangos with the lemon juice, ginger, salt, and the remaining ½ cup of superfine sugar. Chill until ready to serve.

To serve: Clean and slice your choice of summer fruits and arrange them on each plate with the sauce as a base and the floating island in the center. Garnish with mint leaves.

PLANTAIN CAKE
ADAPTED FROM A RECIPE BY EFRAIN VEIGA AND GUILLERMO VELOSO, YUCA RESTAURANT, MIAMI

Makes one 9-inch cake

If banana cake works, why not a cake made from plantains, a less sweet member of the banana family?

- 1¾ cups granulated sugar
- ¾ cup (1½ sticks) unsalted butter, at room temperature
- 3 eggs
- ½ cup sour cream
- 3 ripe plantains, mashed
- 2¼ cups all-purpose flour
- 1½ teaspoons baking powder
- ¼ teaspoon salt
- ¼ cup dark rum
- 2 teaspoons vanilla extract
- 1 pound cream cheese, at room temperature
- 1 pound powdered sugar
- 2 tablespoons grated lemon zest

Preheat the oven to 350°F. Lightly grease two 9-inch round cake pans. In the bowl of an electric mixer, cream together the granulated sugar and butter.

Slowly beat in the eggs, one at a time, scraping the bowl frequently. Mix in ¼ cup of the sour cream, scraping the edges of the bowl occasionally. Add the plantains and mix well.

Add the flour, baking powder, and salt. Mix until combined. Mix in the rum and 1 teaspoon of the vanilla.

Scrape the batter into the prepared cake pans, dividing it equally. Bake 35 minutes or until a toothpick or cake tester inserted into each cake's center comes out clean. Remove to racks to cool 15 minutes. Remove from the pans and cool completely.

To make the icing, in the bowl of an electric mixer beat together the cream cheese, powdered sugar, lemon zest, and the remaining ¼ cup sour cream and 1 teaspoon vanilla. Set aside until ready to use.

Frost cake with the cream cheese icing.

New Orleans

South Louisiana is its own wonderful universe, and food is at its center. Whether you are gobbling crawfish at a roadside stand along a bayou or dining lavishly at one of the legendary restaurants in New Orleans, one thing becomes abundantly clear: Food is not an accessory here, nor merely a basic necessity, it's the life of the party. Everyone here loves to talk about food and lives to eat. Cooking is part of the regional fiber, and even the name of the local music, zydeco, is derived from the French word for beans, *haricots*.

South Louisiana cooking is dominated by the Creoles and the Cajuns, two ethnic groups with separate heritages. Cajun, a corruption of Acadia, originally referred specifically to those French Canadians who emigrated to Louisiana from what is now Nova Scotia, and were immortalized in Henry Wadsworth Longfellow's "Evangelina." Creole is a more general term for people of mixed heritage, usually including French, Spanish, and African. Over the years, though, the distinction between the two cultures has become blurred, and restaurants around the country often use Creole and Cajun interchangeably.

To some degree, this is justified because the two traditions share many dishes, ingredients, and techniques. Rice, shellfish, and pork are vital to each cuisine. Both the Creole and Cajun cooks often begin with a roux (see box page 119), and both can be found fixing a pot of gumbo. They also share a common spirit of culinary individuality and experimentation. Try the jambalaya from five homes within a mile of each other, and you'll find five different recipes. If one ingredient is scarce, there is no hesitation to substitute another. If you're out of filé, thicken the stew with okra. A Louisiana proverb neatly sums up the freewheeling approach: "Each cook knows his own pot best."

So how do we separate Cajun from Creole? In simplest terms, Creole is the fancy city cuisine born in the stately homes of New Orleans, while Cajun is country cooking, practiced on the bayous of southwestern Louisiana. A look at their histories provides further distinctions.

Creole

Creole cuisine boasts a most unusual beginning. The first French settlers had arrived in southern Louisiana by 1700, clustering along a swampy bend of the Mississippi River in an area that would later become the Crescent City of New Orleans. Unfortunately, the area's settlers were slow to adopt native ingredients. As a result, they fed their families a dreary diet of cornmeal mush. In 1722, unable to stomach another bowl of the bland food, about fifty young women marched on Governor Jean Baptiste Bienville's mansion in the growing city, banging pots and pans, demanding something be done to add spice to their food.

The savvy Bienville, eager to avoid insurrection, commissioned his house-keeper, Madame Langlois, to introduce the women to local ingredients. She passed along cooking secrets she had learned from the Choctaws —how to use ground sassafras leaves for flavor and thickening in gumbo, how to make hominy grits, and how to best use the abundant wild game and shellfish. The essence of Creole cooking was formed by this convergence of French tradition with Native American know-how and would evolve considerably in the ensuing years.

In the second half of the eighteenth century, the territory came under Spanish rule, and a new wave of colonists added spice to the regional cuisine, as they adapted such Spanish specialties as paella—a rice dish made with meats, seafood, and vegetables—into flavorful jambalaya. The Spaniards called the early French settlers *criollo,* from which the French derived "creole." The word has come to describe both the food and the people. In both cases, it is a loose-fitting label that originally referred to a person of French or Spanish heritage who was born in the colonies. It soon came to denote a person of mixed parentage. Their ethnic background may be open to debate, but one thing is beyond doubt: Creoles certainly know how to cook.

The sophistication that separates Creole cooking from Cajun was encouraged by the Spanish colonists who, along with a second wave of French settlers—in the late eighteenth century—had fled revolution in their homeland and come to America. The Europeans brought with them classically trained chefs who further refined the dishes of the Creole kitchen in an attempt to create a delicate, subtle cuisine similar to what they already knew. The European style of dining—with aperitifs, several courses, and plenty of wine—was firmly established in the grand maisons of New Orleans during this time. It was fine dining in all its glory, with elegant place settings, formal service, and food that was at once refined and full of surprises.

Later groups of immigrants would further expand Creole cooking. Italians added the Muffaletta (see page 112), a staple sandwich among workers on the river's edge, made with green olives, ham, salami, and provolone cheese. German immigrants introduced new types of sausage, while West Indians added mirlitons, sugar cane, and bananas.

But perhaps the most enduring contributions have come from the African community. Louisiana had a plantation-based economy, with blacks working the cotton and rice fields both before and after the Civil War. Black women ran almost every private kitchen, and black men worked in most professional ones. With each new flag that flew over Louisiana, the chefs catered their cooking styles to whoever was in power. In this way, the black chefs nurtured the Creole tradition, shaping and defining it as they went along and adding hard work and soul. Today, as in the past, many of New Orleans' top restaurants owe their success to the skill and imagination of black chefs.

Settlers from Acadia

The lineage of Cajuns is easier to trace. In the early seventeenth century, a hardy corps of French farmers and fishing families emigrated to Canada and settled the area now known as Nova Scotia. They named the settlement Acadia and quietly went about living off the land and sea. When the British assumed control of Canada, the Acadians refused to speak English or renounce Catholicism. As a result, in 1755, the English began driving them out of Nova Scotia, in the process scattering the French families throughout North America.

The Acadian castaways wandered the continent, hoping to reunite with their families while searching for a place in the New World that would accept them. A large contingent eventually reached southern Louisiana, where they settled in the swampy bayous west of New Orleans. Acadian was soon corrupted into "Cajun."

Life on the bayous was dangerous and unforgiving. Poisonous snakes, malarial mosquitoes, alligators, quicksand, and hurricanes were some of the hazards that made the landscape more treacherous than it appeared. The Cajuns had to survive on what they could grow, catch, or trap. The Choctaws helped them make the most of the wild foods, and the Cajuns applied country French techniques to the preparation. They used the carefully browned roux of fat and flour to thicken and add flavor to sauces and gravies for meat, fowl, and fish.

Compared to the elaborate presentations and multiple courses of Creole dining, a Cajun meal is downright simple. Often the ingredients are combined in one black iron pot and slow cooked to bring out the subtle flavors of each ingredient. It is not unlike the French tradition of *potager* or the fireplace kettle common to early New England cooking. And while the classic Creole meal is a formal affair, there's always room for another place at the Cajun table.

German settlers had a great impact on Cajun cooking, particularly with their emphasis on pork. Andouille, a garlicky, pecan-smoked sausage, is just one of the many meats to be found at a local boudin, or sausage maker. And it was the German influence that inspired the Cajun tradition of boucherie, a communal feast that centers around the slaughter of a pig. In the days before refrigeration, these gatherings were held in the fall or winter, when cooler temperatures allowed time to cure meats before they spoiled. The cooks never wasted any part of the animal, turning out cracklings from the skin, head-cheese, blood sausage, white sausage, tasso, and backbone stew.

Bringing Home Dinner

Hunters have always put dinner on Louisiana tables. The season starts in the early fall with Louisiana alligator, and moves on to less fearsome fare such as rabbit, deer, duck, and quail. Cajun and Creole cooking have relied on these foods from the beginning, along with farm-raised chicken, which appear in such popular dishes as Chicken Rochambeau and Chicken Bienville (a dish that memorializes the early governor).

To get to the heart of Louisiana cooking, though, you have to take to the waterways, and at the top of any local list of preferred seafood are crawfish. By the way, although the more formal name is crayfish (pronounced with a long a), you will usually see references to crawfish, crawdads, or crawdaddys in bayou country. During the crawfish season, which runs from late December to the beginning of summer, lakes, ponds, rivers, and flooded fields teem with these small crustaceans. Trappers need only drop their baited cages in the water, to haul in a feast. A decent pond can yield a thousand pounds of the succulent shellfish in a season. The demand is so great that rice farmers will frequently flood their fields to breed crawfish after the rice harvest. In 1959, the Louisiana legislature allocated funds for crawfish farming, and today the bulk of the crop comes from artificial ponds. The total annual crawfish harvest measures in the millions of pounds, most of which never leave Louisiana.

Cajuns and Creoles adore crawfish. Festivals, like those at Breaux Bridge and Eunice, reflect the enthusiasm and reverence felt for these "Louisiana lobsters." During the height of the season, many locals consume little else. And you can always identify people who come from south Louisiana by watching them eat boiled crawfish. Their deft fingers are a blur, effortlessly removing flesh from shell. If you can count the empty shells on a plate, you've spotted the out-of-towners.

Louisiana's Gulf coast also provides a wealth of other shellfish. Oysters flourish in the marshy "prairies" along the shore, and the firm meat of these large, juicy bivalves finds its way into many roux-based sauces. They are also enjoyed on the half shell in such Creole favorites as Oysters Bienville (see page 113) and Oysters Rockefeller—a dish named appropriately for its richness.

The brackish waters where the Mississippi joins the Gulf of Mexico provide one of the most fertile shrimping grounds in the country. An experienced trawler can net several tons a year. River shrimp are considerably smaller than their offshore cousins and are subtler in flavor. Don't expect to find them in stores, however, since commercial river shrimping is no longer allowed.

The Gulf also is home to blue crabs. Their sweet and delicate meat has become popular around the country. Farther out, boats catch redfish, pompano, and speckled trout, a saltwater trout popular for fish soups or cooked on its own.

Many of the peppers that give Cajun cooking its kick are grown on the marshy islands southwest of New Orleans. The most famous of these is Avery Island, where red peppers are harvested to make Tabasco sauce (see box page 124). Rice is the staple starch of Louisiana cuisine, finding its way into jambalaya and gumbo and traditionally served with red beans as part of Monday leftovers.

New Orleans Cuisine

You can still experience the pomp of New Orleans's legendary restaurants like Brennan's or Commander's Palace. But there are also new establishments that offer a fresh interpretation of the classics. One of the leaders of the new New Orleans cuisine is Emeril Lagasse. Born in Massachusetts, Lagasse cooked at restaurants in Boston, Philadelphia, and New York before being lured to New Orleans by Ella Brennan of Commander's Palace. Once he discovered the explosive flavors of Cajun and Creole cooking, the Big Apple could never pull him back from the Big Easy.

After seven years at Commander's, Lagasse opened his own restaurant, creating a bold menu that features imaginative variations on the region's cuisine. His recipes mix ingredients and techniques to great effect. Barbecued salmon with andouille sausage and potato hash, roast quail stuffed with grillades and served with creamy cheese grits, and the massive Emeril's New New Orleans Paellaya are a few of the dishes that have Creole origins with contemporary twists.

The New Orleans Pantry

ANDOUILLE
This most popular Cajun pure-pork sausage is made with meat taken from the neck and stomach, then stuffed into a large casing with onions, garlic, and cayenne. It is often smoked over pecan wood. The name (pronounced an-doo-ee), is a French word for sausage. Look for andouille mixed into jambalaya and gumbo. The town of La Place, Louisiana, is known as the "Andouille Capital of the World" and holds an annual festival.

BLUE CRAB
Blue-crab meat enhances some of the finest Creole dishes, though perhaps the most popular way to enjoy the sweet, delicious meat is boiled with peppery Creole spices. The meat turns bright red when cooked. Blue Crabs flourish in the brackish waters along the coast, especially from April to September. Periodically they shed their shells, and when they are taken before their new shell hardens, they become the sought-after delicacy called soft-shell crabs.

BROKEN RICE
A short-grain rice that produces stickier jambalaya than long grain. Many cooks pound short-grain rice to make it even starchier. Per capita rice consumption in Louisiana rivals that of Asia and is three times the national average.

CRAWFISH
The name is related to the French *écrevisse*. These freshwater crustaceans look like tiny lobsters and live naturally in rivers and lakes. The majority of the crawfish today come from farmed ponds, though locals swear the wild catch is tastier. Once you get the knack of cracking the tail and "sucking the head," you'll be rewarded with sweet, white meat that's moderately fatty. NOTE: Don't freeze crawfish, because the oils will turn rancid.

CREOLE CREAM CHEESE
A thick, white, smooth-textured fresh cheese, with the sweet flavor of whole cream. It's made from skim milk that is clabbered then ladled into perforated molds to drain overnight. The end result is a softer, more delicately flavored cream cheese than the Philadelphia style. It is typically eaten with sugar and fruit at breakfast. A true regional creation, Creole cream cheese can be difficult to make elsewhere because of the lack of unidentified but essential bacteria in the milk or air.

CREOLE MUSTARD
Pungent mustard made from spicy brown seeds that are steeped in distilled white vinegar, then coarsely ground and left to marinate before packing. A specialty of Creoles of Austrian and German heritage.

CREOLE TOMATOES
Tomatoes grown along the reclaimed areas in the Mississippi delta, where the soil characteristics are ideal, with a high salt content and proper mineral profile. Creole tomatoes are always vine-ripened, and have a lower acid content and smoother texture than typical tomatoes. You can substitute a local vine-ripened tomato for the Creole version.

FILÉ
An herb of ground young sassafras leaves often used as a flavoring and thickener in gumbo and other soups and stews. It is pronounced "FEE-lay" and was another seasoning the settlers learned about from the Choctaws. It imparts a delicate flavor similar to thyme, and should be added after the pot is removed from the fire.

MIRLITON
A white to green pear-shaped vegetable from a West Indian vine of the cucumber family. Technically a tropical squash known in this country as chayote, it is popular in the Caribbean and Latin America where it is also called *christophene* or *chocho*. The flesh is firm, crisp, and white, with a flavor even more delicate than a summer squash. In U.S. groceries outside of Creole country, the mirliton may go by the name vegetable pear or custard marrow.

OKRA

A vegetable that grows on tall (up to eight or nine feet) treelike stalks that produce tapered green pods. Okra is prized in Africa and was called "gumbo" by the slaves who introduced it to Louisiana, a name later adopted for the stew in which it was used. Okra imparts an earthy, acidic flavor and acts as a thickening agent, thanks to a gummy substance from the pod.

OYSTERS

Louisiana gulf oysters are the local choice, but since freshness is so important, cooks should always use oysters from their closest source. The Louisiana variety is a big, plump, flabby oyster that's among the juiciest and briniest anywhere. Because of coastal water pollution, oysters should generally not be eaten raw unless you are certain they come from a "safe" bed. Cooking, in stews or on the half shell in baked dishes such as Oysters Bienville and Oysters Rockefeller, make them quite safe to enjoy.

PECANS

The second most popular nut in the United States after the peanut. Pecans come from the native American hickory tree, which was introduced east of the Appalachians by Thomas Jefferson. When the nuts are roasted, their sugar and oil come to the surface.

RABBIT

This meat, hunted in season or available at the butcher year-round, is low in calories and fat. Loyalists claim you can eat nothing else for six months and not gain a pound. Rabbit can be substituted for chicken in many recipes. The front legs, hind legs, and loin area are the basic cuts. Cajun cooks will often prepare each part separately, usually by smothering, frying, or stewing.

REDFISH

A member of the croaker and drum family, this copper- or bronze-colored saltwater fish has religious significance among the Cajun fleets of south Louisiana. According to legend, redfish was what Christ fed the masses, and the distinctive black spot on its tail marks where Jesus touched the fish. Sometimes called channel bass or red drum, the fish can run as large as thirty pounds, but smaller specimens have better flavor. Actually, the redfish wasn't too widely known until chef Paul Prudhomme used it to make his famous Blackened Redfish (see recipe page 123). Now it is so popular that it is nearly endangered.

SCALLIONS

Everywhere else in the United States the term "scallion" refers to a long, green, bulbless onion also called "green onion" or "spring onion." In Louisiana, the term denotes a small greenish-brown bulb known elsewhere as a "shallot." These pungent onions add a special texture and flavor to the basic roux for gumbo and stews.

SHRIMP

White, brown, red, and pink shrimp are culled by the ton from the Gulf Coast and the mouth of the Mississippi River during a season that runs from May to December. They're best fresh, with heads and shells intact, especially since the heads give richness to a broth.

SPECKLED TROUT

This spotted, blue-gray game fish found in the Gulf is not a trout at all. It's a member of the weakfish family and a relative of redfish, croakers, and drum. "Specks" are a mainstay of Louisiana markets.

TURTLE

An important ingredient in the Creole soup kitchen. The native diamondback terrapin, found in the marshes and waters along the coast, is the best for soup. The green sea turtle or loggerhead is the second choice. Some chefs insist on freshwater turtles for their thick, creamy soups.

The Recipes

PAIN PERDU

Serves 4

Pain perdu means "lost bread" in French, but is better known as "French toast." Most New Orleans breakfasts include this lovely, sweet confection.

- 1 cup milk
- 3 eggs
- 2 tablespoons granulated sugar
- 1 teaspoon cinnamon
- 1 teaspoon vanilla
- 8 (¾-inch thick) slices of French bread
- 6 tablespoons (¾ stick) unsalted butter
- Powdered sugar, for dusting
- Assorted fresh berries

In a medium bowl, beat the milk, eggs, granulated sugar, cinnamon, and vanilla. Pour the mixture into a large, shallow pan. Add the bread slices and allow them to soak for 20 minutes, turning after 10 minutes.

Melt 3 tablespoons of butter in each of 2 large skillets over medium heat. Add the soaked bread slices. Cook for 3 to 5 minutes, or until lightly browned. Turn and cook for 3 to 5 minutes on the other side. Serve on warm plates, dusted with the powdered sugar and topped with berries.

RAMOS GIN FIZZ

Serves 1

Cocktails for breakfast, or any other time of day, is encouraged in hedonistic New Orleans. Invented around the turn of the century by a bar owner named Henry C. Ramos, this drink became so popular that thirty-five bartenders mixed it up at the 1915 Mardi Gras.

- 2 tablespoons (1 ounce) gin
- 2 teaspoons sugar
- ¼ cup half-and-half (light cream)
- 1 splash orange juice
- 2 squirts orange flower water
- 1 egg white
- 6 ice cubes
- 1 teaspoon vanilla extract
- Club soda
- Freshly ground nutmeg
- Orange slice

Blend the first 8 ingredients on low speed. Pour the blend into a tall collins glass with a splash of club soda in the bottom of the glass. Sprinkle the freshly ground nutmeg on top and garnish with the slice of orange.

BEIGNETS

Makes about 2 dozen

These are the New Orleans version of doughnuts, eaten for breakfast and nibbled with chickory-laced coffee in the afternoon.

- 1½ cups all-purpose flour
- 1½ teaspoons baking powder
- ½ teaspoon cinnamon
- ½ teaspoon salt
- ¼ teaspoon ground mace
- ½ cup milk
- 1 egg
- 1 tablespoon granulated sugar
- 1 teaspoon vanilla extract
- 1 teaspoon grated lemon zest
- Vegetable oil, for frying
- Powdered sugar, for dusting

In a medium bowl, mix together the flour, baking powder, cinnamon, salt, and mace.

In a small bowl, whisk together the milk, egg, granulated sugar, vanilla, and lemon zest. Add to the flour mixture, stirring just until a soft dough forms.

On a lightly floured surface, knead the dough for 15 seconds or just until soft. Roll out the dough to form a 10 x 12 inch rectangle, about ½ inch thick. With a floured knife, cut the dough into 2 dozen 2 x 1½ inch squares.

In a large heavy skillet, heat ½ inch of oil over medium heat to 350°F. Carefully drop half of the squares of dough into the hot oil. Cook, turning once or twice with 2 forks, for 2 minutes or until puffed and golden brown. Remove with a slotted spoon to a paper towel—lined baking sheet. While still hot, sprinkle with powdered sugar. Repeat with the remaining dough. Serve warm.

CAJUN POPCORN

ADAPTED FROM A RECIPE BY PAUL PRUDHOMME,
K-PAUL'S LOUISIANA KITCHEN, NEW ORLEANS

Serves 4-6

This dish of batter-fried crawfish tails was popularized by Chef Prudhomme in the mid-1980s. It is still one of the most popular appetizers in Cajun restaurants around the country.

- 1 cup all-purpose flour
- 1 tablespoon cayenne pepper
- 2 teaspoons black pepper
- 2 teaspoons white pepper
- 1 teaspoon chili powder
- 1 teaspoon salt
- 1 teaspoon sugar
- 1 teaspoon paprika
- 1 teaspoon garlic powder
- Vegetable oil, for frying
- 1 pound peeled crawfish tails or small shrimp
- Lemon wedges and prepared tartar sauce (page 23)

In a pie plate, combine the flour and all of the seasonings. Set aside.

In a large heavy skillet, heat ¾ inch of vegetable oil until hot but not smoking. Dredge the crawfish in the flour mixture, shaking off the excess. Fry the crawfish, about ⅓ of them at a time, in the hot oil for about 3 to 4 minutes or until golden brown. Drain on a paper bag–lined baking sheet. Repeat with the remaining crawfish. Serve hot with the lemon wedges and tartar sauce, for dipping.

Crawfish Capital of the World

During the first full weekend in May each year, the official "Crawfish Capital of the World" honors its favorite crustacean with a lavish festival. People from around the country descend upon Breaux Bridge, Louisiana, a normally quiet Cajun town of five thousand.

Local Cajun chefs cook thousands of pounds of crawfish any and every way imaginable. Revelers can enjoy boiled crawfish, fried crawfish, crawfish étouffée, crawfish dogs, crawfish jambalaya, crawfish pies, crawfish gumbo, and more.

The Breaux Bridge Crawfish Festival celebrates all of Cajun culture, including music, dancing, and folk arts. There are crawfish races, a crawfish étouffée cook-off, and the obligatory crawfish-eating contest. This last event tests both appetite and dexterity in extracting meat from the shells. Andrew Thevenet of Breaux Bridge holds the record, downing 33⅓ pounds in one hour!

OYSTER PO'BOY

Serves 4

The "poor boy" sandwich was created in the 1920s by Benny and Clovis Martin of the Martin Brothers Grocery in New Orleans, who served them free of charge to striking streetcar workers. It is similar to a "hero" and can be made with ham, beef, cheese, and other ingredients.

- 1 cup mayonnaise
- ¼ cup chopped fresh parsley
- ¼ cup snipped fresh chives
- 2 tablespoons lemon juice
- 1 tablespoon grated lemon zest
- Dash hot pepper sauce
- Vegetable oil, for frying
- ⅔ cup yellow cornmeal
- ½ teaspoon dried oregano
- ½ teaspoon salt
- ½ teaspoon cayenne pepper
- ½ teaspoon freshly ground black pepper
- 2 (10-ounce) jars shucked oysters, drained and patted dry
- 4 (6- to 7-inch long) French bread rolls
- 3 cups shredded romaine or iceberg lettuce
- 2 large tomatoes, thinly sliced

In a small bowl, whisk together the mayonnaise, parsley, chives, lemon juice, and zest; season with the hot pepper sauce. Cover and refrigerate until ready to use.

In a large heavy skillet, heat ½ inch of oil over medium heat until hot but not smoking. Meanwhile, in a pie plate, combine the cornmeal, oregano, salt, cayenne, and black pepper. Dredge the oysters in the cornmeal mixture to coat completely. Add half of the oysters to the skillet and fry, turning carefully with tongs, for about 3 minutes or until the coating is golden brown. Remove with a slotted spoon to a paper bag–lined baking sheet. Repeat with the remaining oysters.

To serve, cut the rolls in half horizontally and pull out some of the inner bread to make a pocket for the oysters. Spread the cut sides of the rolls with the mayonnaise mixture. Spoon the oysters into the bottom halves of the rolls and add the lettuce and tomatoes. Cover with roll tops, cut-sides down. Serve immediately.

SHRIMP RÉMOULADE

Serves 6 for lunch

Rémoulade sauce is the New Orleans version of the French rémoulade, *a mayonnaise flavored with mustard. The Big Easy version is usually much spicier than the French. The combination of this sauce with fresh shrimp is heavenly.*

- 1½ cups dry white wine
- 1 (8-ounce) bottle clam juice
- 1 bag crab, shrimp, and crayfish boil (such as Rex brand)
- 2 pounds medium shrimp, peeled and deveined
- 1 cup mayonnaise
- 2 stalks celery, finely chopped
- 1 small red onion, grated
- ⅓ cup chopped fresh parsley
- ⅓ cup Creole mustard
- 3 tablespoons prepared horseradish
- 1 tablespoon paprika
- 1 teaspoon cayenne pepper
- Freshly ground black pepper
- 4 cups shredded romaine lettuce
- 4 cups shredded radicchio
- Lemon wedges

In a medium saucepan, combine the wine, clam juice, and crab boil bag and set over medium heat. Simmer 5 minutes. Add the shrimp. Poach until just opaque throughout, about 3 to 5 minutes. Drain shrimp. Discard poaching liquid and seasoning bag. Set the shrimp aside to cool completely.

To make the sauce: In a medium bowl, combine the mayonnaise, celery, onion, parsley, mustard, horseradish, paprika, and cayenne pepper.

In a large bowl, gently toss the shrimp with about 1½ cups of the sauce. Season with the black pepper. Cover with plastic wrap and chill for at least 1 hour or overnight. Chill the remaining sauce, covered, as well.

To serve, toss together the romaine and radicchio and distribute among 6 plates. Spoon the shrimp over the greens and accompany with the lemon wedges and additional sauce.

MUFFALETTA

Serves 4-6

*This overstuffed sandwich is based on a Sicilian idea. It was invented in
New Orleans by Salvatore Lupo in 1906.*

- 1 (5-ounce) jar pimiento-stuffed green olives, drained and sliced
- 1 tomato, seeded and chopped
- 1 stalk celery, thinly sliced
- 3 tablespoons chopped fresh Italian parsley
- 1 clove garlic, minced
- 1 teaspoon dried oregano
- 3 tablespoons olive oil
- 2 tablespoons balsamic vinegar
- ¼ teaspoon freshly ground pepper

- Dash hot pepper sauce
- 1 (9- to 10-inch) round loaf Italian *or* French bread with sesame seeds
- ½ cup mayonnaise
- 3 ounces thinly sliced salami
- 3 ounces thinly sliced provolone cheese
- 3 ounces thinly sliced baked ham
- 3 ounces thinly sliced mozzarella cheese

In a medium bowl, combine the olives, tomato, celery, parsley, garlic, and oregano. Toss gently. Add the oil, vinegar, and pepper. Season with the hot pepper sauce. Set aside.

To assemble the Muffaletta, cut the loaf in half horizontally and pull out some of the inner bread to make a pocket for the sandwich ingredients. Spread both cut sides of the loaf with the mayonnaise. Layer the bottom half of the loaf with the salami, provolone, ham, and mozzarella. Spoon the olive mixture over the cheese and cover with the loaf top, cut-side down. Wrap tightly in plastic wrap. Place in the refrigerator and weight with a large dinner plate that is loaded with cans of food. Refrigerate 2 to 4 hours. Cut into quarters or wedges to serve.

OYSTERS BIENVILLE

Makes 2 dozen

Oysters are an important part of New Orleans cuisine, and this preparation featuring mushrooms, peppers, white wine, and bread crumbs is one of the triumphs of this cooking style. The dish is named after the man who was Louisiana's governor at the beginning of the eighteenth century.

- ¼ cup (½ stick) unsalted butter
- 8 green onions (scallions), finely chopped
- ½ cup finely chopped mushrooms
- ½ cup finely chopped red *or* green bell pepper
- 1 clove garlic, minced
- 2 tablespoons all-purpose flour
- ½ cup dry white wine
- ¼ cup oyster liquor *or* bottled clam juice

- 1 egg yolk
- 2 tablespoons hot pepper sauce
- 2½ teaspoons lemon juice
- Salt, hot pepper sauce, and cayenne pepper
- ¼ cup fine bread crumbs
- ¼ cup (¾ ounce) grated Parmesan cheese
- 2 dozen oysters
- Rock salt

In a medium saucepan, melt the butter over medium heat. Add the onions, mushrooms, bell pepper, and garlic. Sauté, stirring occasionally, for 10 minutes or until the vegetables are soft. Sprinkle the flour over the vegetables and cook, stirring, for 2 minutes. Add the wine and oyster liquor. Cook, stirring, until the sauce is smooth and bubbly, about 2 minutes.

In a small bowl, lightly beat the egg yolk. Whisk ¼ cup of the hot pepper sauce into the yolk to temper it. Return this mixture to the saucepan. Cook over low heat, stirring, for 5 minutes or until thickened slightly. Do not boil. Stir in the lemon juice and season with salt, hot pepper sauce, and cayenne pepper. Remove the pan from the heat; set aside.

In another small bowl, combine the bread crumbs and cheese. Set aside.

Preheat the oven to 400°F.

Shuck each oyster by holding the side of the shell in a kitchen towel to prevent slippage. Insert the point of an oyster shucker into the hinge of the shell, push it in and twist to pop open. Slide the shucker under the flesh to loosen it from the bottom muscle. Discard the upper shells.

In a large shallow baking pan, make a bed of rock salt 1½ inches deep. Nestle the oysters on their shells into the rock salt. Spoon the sauce over the oysters, dividing equally. Sprinkle each with the breadcrumb mixture. Bake for 10 to 15 minutes or until the crumbs are brown and the sauce bubbly. Serve hot.

A Journey Back in Time for the Best Gumbo in Town

Most cities had stores like the Krauss Department Store at one point in their history. Located on Canal Street at Basin in downtown New Orleans, this glorious relic exudes the charm of an earlier era. It still sells fabric by the yard and has an in-house beauty salon, a millinery department, and a 1940s-style luncheonette.

The five floors of merchandise feature a range of ultra-luxury goods and low cost items. There is something for everyone here. And you won't find modern marketing tactics like escalators that make you walk around the store each time you want to change levels. Charge slips are still delivered by a 1930s-era pneumatic tube system. Krauss is truly a museum of American retailing.

While other great mercantile establishments fell victim to suburban sprawl, Krauss managed to survive thanks to its proximity to the French Quarter and to major employers like Charity Hospital that provide a strong customer base. It remains a wonderful antidote to the shopping malls that have taken over much of America.

A trip to the store is never complete without a stop at Eddie's. In addition to the classic, hearty luncheonette fare, Eddie's offers superb Creole food, including what might be the best bowl of gumbo in town. The style—complete with padded red stools and walnut formica counters—is pure 1940s, and the prices are modest.

EGGS SARDOU

Serves 6

This rich dish was invented in the late nineteenth century by Antoine Alciatore, the owner of Antoine's Restaurant. He made it in honor of the visit of French playwright Victorien Sardou. This dish is traditionally made on artichoke hearts, but this version avoids the intensive work necessary by using English muffins instead.

- 2½ cups plus 6 tablespoons (5¾ sticks) unsalted butter
- 3 shallots, minced
- ½ cup all-purpose flour
- 2 cups milk
- Pinch ground nutmeg
- 4 (10-ounce) bags fresh spinach, washed, steamed, thoroughly squeezed dry, and puréed
- ½ cup heavy cream
- 8 egg yolks, at room temperature
- 1½ tablespoons water
- 3 tablespoons lemon juice
- Dash hot pepper sauce
- Salt and freshly ground white pepper
- 3 tablespoons distilled white vinegar
- 12 eggs, at room temperature
- 12 English muffins, split and toasted
- Snipped fresh chives

To make the creamed spinach: Melt 6 tablespoons of the butter in a medium saucepan over medium heat. Add the shallots; sauté, stirring occasionally, for 3 minutes. Sprinkle in the flour. Cook, stirring, for 2 minutes. Stir in the milk and nutmeg. Cook, stirring constantly until thick, about 4 minutes. Stir in the spinach and cream; season with the salt and white pepper. Set aside and keep warm.

To make the hollandaise sauce: Melt the remaining 2½ cups of butter. Place the egg yolks and water in a blender. Process until the color lightens and they are well blended. With the machine running, gradually incorporate the hot butter drop by drop into the yolk mixture. After 2 or 3 tablespoons have been added, pour in the remaining butter in a very thin stream, with the machine still running. A thick emulsion will result. Add the lemon juice and hot pepper sauce. Process briefly just to mix. Season with salt and white pepper. To hold until ready to serve, transfer the sauce to a covered saucepan placed in a pan of hot water and whisk frequently.

Bring 1½ inches of water with the vinegar to a boil in a large skillet. Reduce the heat to medium-low so that the water just simmers. Gently break in the eggs; reduce the heat to low and poach the eggs, uncovered, for about 3 minutes. The whites should be firm and yolks still soft. Remove each egg with a slotted spoon and drain briefly on paper towels.

For each serving, place 2 muffin halves on a warm plate and cover each with creamed spinach, a poached egg, and hollandaise sauce. Sprinkle with chives and serve immediately.

CREOLE SALAD DRESSING
ADAPTED FROM A RECIPE BY FRANK BRIGTSEN, BRIGTSEN'S, NEW ORLEANS

Makes 1½ cups

A New Orleans salad dressing—as you might imagine—is a little zestier than your average vinaigrette.

- ¼ cup thinly sliced green onions (scallions)
- ¼ cup finely diced celery
- ½ cup red wine vinegar
- 2 tablespoons Creole mustard (if necessary, you may substitute Pommery-style whole-grain mustard)
- 1 teaspoon sweet Hungarian paprika
- 1 teaspoon hot Hungarian paprika
- 1 clove garlic, minced
- ½ teaspoon salt
- ¼ teaspoon dried oregano
- ¼ teaspoon sugar
- ½ cup plus 2 tablespoons vegetable oil

In a mixing bowl, combine all the ingredients except the oil. Blend well. Whisking constantly, slowly add the oil in a thin stream until it is thoroughly incorporated. This dressing can be used on a variety of salads. Here is a suggested composed salad:

Serves 4

- 4 medium tomatoes, sliced
- 4 medium new red potatoes, boiled until tender, cooled, and sliced
- 4 stalks celery, sliced
- 1 red bell pepper, seeded and julienned
- 6 green onions (scallions), three sliced and three whole
- 1 head of Bibb *or* butter lettuce, washed, dried, and torn

ANDOUILLE AND CHICKEN GUMBO

Serves 8 with leftovers

*Gumbo is a thick Louisiana soup that normally contains okra. This version is okra-less,
but it has some of the characteristic seasonings. Andouille is a spicy
smoked pork sausage that is typical of Cajun cooking.*

- 2 tablespoons vegetable oil
- 1 pound andouille sausage, cut into ½-inch slices
- 1 (3- to 3½-pound) chicken, cut into 8 pieces
- ½ teaspoon freshly ground black pepper
- ⅓ cup all-purpose flour
- 8 green onions (scallions), sliced
- 1 large yellow onion, chopped
- 1 large green bell pepper, seeded and chopped
- 3 stalks celery, chopped
- 1 quart chicken stock
- 2 tablespoons filé powder
- 1 teaspoon dried thyme leaves
- ½ teaspoon cayenne pepper
- 2 bay leaves
- Hot pepper sauce
- Salt
- 6 cups hot cooked white rice

In a large, heavy, deep saucepan, heat the oil over medium heat. Add the sausage and cook, stirring often, until browned, about 5 minutes. Remove to a paper towel–lined plate.

Season the chicken with the black pepper and add to the pan. Cook about 10 minutes until browned, turning once. Remove from the pan and set aside.

Pour off and measure the fat in the pan. Put 6 tablespoons of the fat back into the pan and discard the remainder. Sprinkle the flour over the fat and cook, stirring constantly, until the mixture (roux) turns a deep reddish color, about 6 minutes. Add the green onions, yellow onion, bell pepper, and celery. Cook, stirring frequently, for 5 minutes. Stir in the stock, filé powder, thyme, cayenne pepper, and bay leaves. Return the sausage and chicken to the pan. Cook over low heat, partially covered, for 30 minutes or until chicken juices run clear.

With a slotted spoon, remove the chicken pieces to a plate. When cool enough to handle, remove the meat, discarding the skin and bones. Cut the chicken into bite-size pieces and return it to the gumbo. Cook the gumbo over medium heat, uncovered, about 10 to 15 minutes, to reduce the liquid slightly. (The gumbo should be the consistency of a moderately thick soup.) Season to taste with the hot pepper sauce and salt.

To serve, spoon the rice into deep soup plates and top with the hot gumbo.

BARBECUED SALMON WITH ANDOUILLE SAUSAGE AND POTATO HASH

ADAPTED FROM A RECIPE BY EMERIL LAGASSE, EMERIL'S, NEW ORLEANS

Serves 4

This is an amazing dish that blends many strong flavors successfully. Chef Lagasse has a special gift for making apparently incompatible elements completely harmonious. This dish is assertive and complex but not jarring in its flavors.

- ¾ cup ketchup
- 1 tablespoon dark brown sugar, packed
- 1 tablespoon water
- 3 cloves garlic, minced
- 2 teaspoons molasses
- 1½ teaspoons sesame oil
- ½ teaspoon grated fresh ginger
- ½ teaspoon chili powder
- ¼ cup (½ stick) unsalted butter
- 1 pound russet potatoes, cut into ½-inch cubes and blanched until tender

- ½ pound andouille sausage, coarsely chopped
- 2 green onions (scallions), thinly sliced
- 1 shallot, minced
- 2 tablespoons chicken stock
- 4 (6-ounce) skinned salmon fillets
- 1 tablespoon olive oil
- 1½ teaspoons commercially available Creole seasoning

To make the barbecue sauce: In a small bowl, combine the ketchup, sugar, water, 1 clove of the garlic, the molasses, sesame oil, ginger, and chili powder. Set aside.

To make the hash, melt the butter in a large nonstick skillet over medium heat. Add the potatoes and sausage and sauté about 12 minutes, until the potatoes are golden brown, tossing occasionally. Stir in the green onions, shallot, stock, and the remaining 2 cloves of garlic. Sauté 3 minutes. Stir in ⅓ cup of the barbecue sauce and heat through. Set aside and keep warm.

Prepare the grill. Brush the salmon fillets with the olive oil and rub with the Creole seasoning. Grill about 6 to 8 minutes or until just opaque throughout, turning once and brushing with some of the reserved barbecue sauce.

To serve, place each salmon fillet on top of a generous serving of hash. Drizzle the salmon with additional barbecue sauce.

Chef Emeril Lagasse

Emeril Lagasse worked as executive chef at the legendary Commander's Palace in New Orleans before opening his own restaurant, Emeril's, in 1990. Chef Lagasse is devoted to using the freshest Louisiana ingredients, and he tirelessly explores local food sourcces for new flavor experiences.

Trained at Johnson & Wales University, Chef Lagasse traveled to Paris and Lyon to polish his culinary skills. He practiced his art in fine New York, Boston, and Philadelphia restaurants before being lured to New Orleans by Ella and Dick Brennan of Commander's Palace.

Chef Lagasse's creative interpretation of south Louisiana cooking has earned him national attention. In 1991 Chef Lagasse won the James Beard Award for "Best Southeast Regional Chef." He recently opened Nola restaurant in New Orleans' French Quarter, which was named "Best New Restaurant" by Esquire *magazine. His first cookbook,* Emeril's New New Orleans Cookbook, *was published in 1994.*

ROCK SHRIMP ÉTOUFÉE

Serves 6

The term étoufée was borrowed from French cooking where it means "braised." In New Orleans, étoufée refers to a stewed dish served over rice. It is often prepared with crayfish.

- ¼ cup vegetable oil
- 6 tablespoons all-purpose flour
- 3 stalks celery, sliced
- 1 large onion, chopped
- 1 green bell pepper, chopped
- 4 cloves garlic, minced
- 2 (8-ounce) bottles clam juice
- 1½ teaspoons dried basil
- 1½ teaspoons dried oregano
- 1½ teaspoons hot pepper sauce
- ½ cup (1 stick) unsalted butter
- 4 leeks, white part only, halved lengthwise, cleaned, and thinly sliced
- 1½ pounds rock shrimp
- 2 tablespoons lemon juice
- 1 tablespoon Worcestershire sauce
- 2 teaspoons grated lemon zest
- ½ cup chopped fresh parsley
- Salt and freshly ground black pepper
- 6 cups hot cooked white rice

In a large heavy saucepan, heat the oil over medium heat. Add the flour and cook until the mixture (roux) is a deep mahogany color, about 6 to 10 minutes. Stir in the celery, onion, bell pepper, and garlic. Cook, stirring, for about 5 minutes or until the vegetables begin to soften. Stir in the clam juice, bring to a boil, and cook, stirring, for 1 minute. Reduce the heat to a simmer and stir in the basil, oregano, and hot pepper sauce. Cover and simmer 10 minutes, stirring occasionally. Remove from the heat.

In a large skillet, melt ¼ cup of the butter over medium heat. Add the leeks and cook, stirring occasionally, for 15 minutes. Add the shrimp and cook, stirring, for about 3 minutes or until they become opaque. Stir in the lemon juice, Worcestershire sauce, and lemon zest. Stir the shrimp mixture into the vegetable mixture.

Place the shrimp-vegetable mixture over medium heat. Stir in the remaining ¼ cup of the butter and cook until the mixture is hot and the butter is melted. Stir in the parsley and season with the salt and pepper.

To serve, spoon the rice into deep soup plates and top with the étoufée.

Preparing a Roux: The Secret of Louisiana Cooking

The starting point for many Creole and Cajun dishes, a roux is a thickening mixture made of flour and fat that is very similar to the French beurre manié. While it may seem simple enough, cooking a roux is a delicate procedure. Color comes to a roux quickly, and the roux can easily be burned if not carefully tended.

A deep, honey-colored roux made from butter and flour is best suited to sauces for dark, heavy meats like beef and game. A dark reddish-brown roux made with vegetable oil or animal fat yields thinner sauces and will enhance light, white meats such as pork, rabbit, and fish. The darker roux is best for gumbo as well.

A typical roux combines an equal amount of fat and flour over low heat. This mixture is then stirred constantly until it has turned the desired color. Be patient. This can take a long time.

GRILLADES AND GRITS

Serves 6

*When it comes to Sunday brunch in New Orleans, one of the essential
dishes is this combination of beef (or veal) braised in a spicy sauce.
Served with a mound of cheddar grits, this defines comfort food.*

- 2 pounds top round of beef
- Salt and freshly ground black pepper
- 3 tablespoons vegetable oil
- 2 tablespoons all-purpose flour
- 1 onion, chopped
- 1 red bell pepper, seeded and chopped
- 2 stalks celery, chopped
- 3 cloves garlic, minced
- 1 (14½-ounce) can beef stock
- 1 (14½-ounce) can chopped tomatoes, in juice
- 2 teaspoons dried thyme
- 1 teaspoon cayenne pepper
- 2 bay leaves
- 1 recipe Cheddar Grits (page 62)
- 4 green onions (scallions), sliced

Cut the beef into 1½-inch thick slices. Cut the slices into 2½-inch squares.
Between sheets of waxed paper, pound the chunks of beef into thin pieces about
twice their original size. Season the beef lightly with salt and black pepper.

Heat the oil in a large skillet over medium-high heat. Cook the beef, in
batches if necessary, until browned on both sides, about 2 to 3 minutes a side.
Remove the beef from the skillet. Reserve.

Reduce the heat to medium. Sprinkle the flour over the pan drippings.
Cook, stirring constantly, for 2 minutes. Add the onion, bell pepper, celery, and
garlic. Sauté, stirring often, for 5 minutes. Stir in the stock, tomatoes, thyme,
cayenne pepper, and bay leaves. Return the beef to the skillet. Bring to a boil,
reduce the heat, cover and simmer for 2 hours. Uncover the skillet during the
last 20 minutes of cooking to thicken the sauce. Remove and discard the bay
leaves. Season with salt and pepper. Set aside and keep warm.

Prepare the Cheddar Grits.

Serve the grillades sprinkled with the green onions and with the
grits on the side.

Two Chefs

The names Brennan and Prudhomme are
enough to excite the taste buds of anyone
familiar with south Louisiana cooking.
Chefs Ella Brennan and Paul Prudhomme
have introduced Creole and Cajun cooking to
countless food lovers around the world.

Ella Brennan started in the restaurant
business in 1934 at the age of nineteen, and
today, along with brother Dick, she runs New
Orleans' most influential restaurant, Commander's Palace. Like so many successful restaurateurs and chefs, Brennan found her
inspiration at home, in her mother's kitchen.
Meals were always prepared with the freshest
local ingredients, and classic French dishes
were often cooked with Creole seasonings.

At Brennan's, the family restaurant
owned by her father and older brother
Owen, she learned both the importance of
pleasing the customer and the need for total
commitment to the business. On Sundays,
when Brennan's was closed, young Ella
would eat breakfast with chef Paul Blange
and talk about food and study his techniques. She immersed herself in every cookbook she could get her hands on and was
fortunate to visit such noted New York
establishments as the "21" Club and Le
Pavillon when they were at their best. She
brought all collective food and business
savvy to bear when she and Dick took charge
of historic Commander's Palace in 1974.

They infused new life into this Garden
District landmark, which overlooks a pic-
turesque New Orleans cemetery. Brennan has
introduced her "haute Creole" menu, with its
healthful, modern interpretation of New
Orleans cuisine. Just as important is the

casually elegant atmosphere, learned from the cozy family meals of her childhood.

Ella Brennan has been awarded just about every honor in the industry, including Grande Dame of Les Dames d'Escoffier, Who's Who of Cooking in America, and the James Beard Service Award.

But Brennan is perhaps most proud of the prodigious talent that has emerged from her kitchen. Emeril Lagasse has moved on from Commander's Palace to open his acclaimed and innovative Emeril's restaurant and French Quarter Nola. Paul Prudhomme also stepped from Brennan's kitchen into the spotlight. Few chefs are so closely identified with a culinary region as is Prudhomme, who has brought Louisiana cooking before the national audience.

Born to a Cajun sharecropping family, Prudhomme learned firsthand the techniques of rural cooking. Freshness was never a concern, because the Prudhommes grew the ingredients themselves. The youngest of thirteen children, Paul was fortunate that his family had pulled itself from poverty by the time he was born. Material goods were still scarce, but there was at least enough food to go around. In the tradition of bayou country, meals took on a communal quality, with often as many as thirty people sitting down to the table. Prudhomme would never forget these flavors and smells throughout his many travels.

Chef Prudhomme particpates in innumerable culinary events throughout the year, and his K-Paul's food product line has brought the flavors of Louisiana to home kitchens around the country. (For a catalog call 800-457-2857.)

ROAST QUAIL STUFFED WITH NEW ORLEANS GRILLADES AND CREAMY CHEESE GRITS
ADAPTED FROM A RECIPE BY EMERIL LAGASSE, EMERIL'S, NEW ORLEANS

Serves 8

Grillades is a French word meaning "broiled meat," but in New Orleans it refers to meat that has been braised with seasonings. This recipe gives a contemporary spin to a traditional idea.

- 1 pound veal stew meat, cut into ½-inch cubes
- 1 small onion, chopped
- 1 carrot, chopped
- 1 tomato, chopped
- 2 tablespoons chopped fresh parsley
- 2 cups veal *or* chicken stock
- ¾ cup fresh bread crumbs
- 2 tablespoons commercially available Creole seasoning
- 2 teaspoons lemon juice
- Salt and freshly ground black pepper
- 8 (4-ounce) boneless quail, split down the back
- 1 tablespoon olive oil
- 1 quart water
- 1 cup grits
- ½ cup (1 stick) unsalted butter
- ¾ cup (2¼ ounces) grated Parmesan cheese
- ¼ cup heavy cream

In a medium saucepan, combine the meat, onion, carrot, tomato, and parsley. Pour in the stock. Bring to a boil, reduce heat and simmer for 20 minutes or until the meat is tender, adding more stock if necessary to keep the mixture moist. Remove from heat and strain, reserving the liquid.

Place the veal mixture in a food processor fitted with a metal blade. Process until smooth. Add the bread crumbs, 1 tablespoon of the Creole seasoning, and the lemon juice. Process until the mixture comes together. Season with salt and pepper. Cool completely.

Place the quail, skin-sides down, on a work surface. Season the inside of each quail with the remaining 1 tablespoon of Creole spice. Form the veal mixture into 8 equal balls and place 1 on each quail. Wrap the quail around the stuffing. Place the quail, split-sides down, on a baking sheet. Mold into nice round shapes. Rub with the olive oil. Place in the refrigerator for 15 minutes.

Preheat the oven to 425°F. Roast the quail for 25 minutes or until they reach an internal temperature of 180°F. Remove from the oven and let stand 5 minutes.

To make the grits, bring the water to a boil in a large saucepan. Add the grits and butter. Reduce the heat to medium-low and stir constantly until thickened. Remove from the heat and stir in ½ cup of the cheese and the cream. Season with salt and pepper. Keep warm.

Reheat the reserved liquid from the veal mixture.

To serve, divide the grits among eight warm dinner plates. Top each with a quail. Ladle over a spoonful of the veal broth and sprinkle with some of the remaining cheese.

Rabbit Jambalaya
Adapted from a recipe by Paul Prudhomme,
K-Paul's Louisiana Kitchen, New Orleans

Serves 4

Jambalaya, a highly seasoned dish of rice with meat or fish, has been a mainstay of Creole cooking since the eighteenth century. This version uses another New Orleans staple, rabbit. Also important to this dish is tasso—*smoked, spiced, pickled pork.*

- ½ cup (1 stick) unsalted butter
- 1 (3-pound) rabbit, cut up
- 2 yellow onions, finely chopped
- 2 red *and / or* green bell peppers, finely chopped
- 4 stalks celery, finely chopped
- ½ pound tasso *or* other smoked ham, diced
- 1 teaspoon dried oregano
- 1 teaspoon garlic powder
- 1 teaspoon dried thyme

- 1 teaspoon salt
- 1 teaspoon freshly ground white pepper
- ½ teaspoon cayenne pepper
- ½ teaspoon hot pepper sauce
- ¼ teaspoon freshly ground black pepper
- 2 bay leaves
- 1 (8-ounce) can tomato sauce
- 1 cup rice
- 2¼ cups chicken stock
- 3 green onions (scallions), finely chopped
- ¼ cup chopped fresh parsley

Melt the butter in a large skillet over medium heat. Add the rabbit and brown well on all sides, about 10 minutes. Remove the rabbit from the skillet and reserve.

Stir in 1 of the yellow onions, 1 of the bell peppers, and 2 of the celery stalks. Sauté, stirring, for 5 minutes. Add the tasso, oregano, garlic powder, thyme, salt, white and cayenne peppers, hot pepper sauce, black pepper, and bay leaves. Cook until the onion is dark brown, about 20 minutes, stirring frequently. Stir in the remaining yellow onion, bell pepper, and celery. Cook, stirring occasionally, for 5 minutes.

Stir in the tomato sauce. Cook, stirring, for 3 minutes. Return the rabbit to the skillet; simmer for 15 minutes, uncovered.

Stir in the rice and stock. Bring to a boil, reduce the heat, cover, and simmer for 17 to 20 minutes or until the rice and the rabbit are tender. Remove from the heat. Remove and discard the bay leaves. Stir in the green onions and sprinkle with the parsley.

Chef Paul Prudhomme

From his small K-Paul's Louisiana Kitchen in New Orleans' French Quarter, Chef Paul Prudhomme has left an indelible stamp on the food world as a chef, educator, entrepreneur, author, and ambassador for the cuisine of his native state.

Born and raised in Louisiana's Acadiana country, Chef Prudhomme began cooking with his mother, whom he proudly cites as his greatest influence. In 1979, he opened K-Paul's Louisiana Kitchen with his late wife Kay Hinrichs. In a city known for its food, Chef Prudhomme was soon the talk of the town.

As one of America's best known chefs, he has been featured on the Today Show, Good Morning America, CBS This Morning, Donahue, *and* Late Night with David Letterman. *He has produced numerous bestselling cookbooks and videos, and he runs the successful K-Paul's Mail Order business (see page 121).*

BLACKENED REDFISH
ADAPTED FROM A RECIPE BY PAUL PRUDHOMME, K-PAUL'S
LOUISIANA KITCHEN, NEW ORLEANS

Serves 4

More than any other dish, blackened redfish symbolizes the new interest in New Orleans food. In the mid-1980s nearly every contemporary restaurant in America featured a version of this classic that was popularized by Chef Prudhomme. Redfish became so popular that the species, also known as "red drum," started to become seriously depleted. To preserve it, the government banned commercial fishing of redfish in the Gulf of Mexico in 1987.

- 2 teaspoons paprika
- 1 teaspoon dried oregano
- 1 teaspoon salt
- 1 teaspoon freshly ground black pepper
- 1 teaspoon cayenne pepper
- ¾ teaspoon dried thyme
- ¾ teaspoon onion powder
- ¾ teaspoon garlic powder
- 4 (6-ounce) redfish fillets, about ½ inch thick (if redfish is unavailable substitute bluefish, catfish, *or* snapper)
- 8 teaspoons butter, melted
- Lemon wedges

In a pie plate, combine the paprika, oregano, salt, black and cayenne peppers, thyme, and onion and garlic powders.

Heat a large cast-iron skillet over medium-high heat until beyond the smoking stage, about 10 minutes. Completely coat the fillets with the spice mixture, shaking off the excess. Cook the fillets for 2 to 3 minutes or until the undersides are dark brown. Carefully spoon 1 teaspoon of the melted butter over each fillet, trying not to let it spill onto the pan as it may flare up. Turn the fillets over and spoon the remaining butter over the blackened sides of the fish. Cook for 2 to 3 minutes more or until the undersides are dark brown and the fish is opaque throughout. Serve immediately, with the lemon wedges.

CRISPY FRIED CATFISH

Serves 6

Catfish used to be a muddy tasting, bottom-feeding fish found in southern rivers. Now this whiskered fish is raised in scrupulously clean ponds on farms (mostly in Mississippi). This allows its lovely mild and sweet flavor to come through clear and unsullied.

- 1 cup corn flour
- 2 teaspoons cayenne pepper
- 1 teaspoon chili powder
- 1 teaspoon paprika
- 1 teaspoon salt
- ½ teaspoon freshly ground black pepper
- Vegetable oil, for frying
- 6 (6-ounce) catfish fillets
- Lemon wedges

In a pie plate, combine the corn flour, cayenne pepper, chili powder, paprika, salt, and black pepper. Set aside.

In a large, heavy skillet, heat ½ inch of oil until hot but not smoking. Dredge the fillets in the flour mixture, shaking off the excess. Carefully place the fillets, 3 at a time, in the hot oil and cook for about 5 minutes, turning once, until golden brown and crusty on both sides. Drain on a paper bag–lined baking sheet. Repeat with the remaining fillets. Serve hot with the lemon wedges.

Stewed Okra, Tomatoes, and Bell Peppers, Creole Style

Serves 6

Okra was brought to the southern part of the United States from Africa. It is an unusual vegetable that elicits strong opinions from people—some like it, some hate it. In this dish, after long cooking, the unpleasant characteristics dissipate and lovely flavors triumph.

- ¼ cup (½ stick) unsalted butter
- 1 (1-pound) bag frozen sliced okra (or use fresh, if you can get it)
- 1 onion, sliced
- 1 yellow bell pepper, seeded and coarsely chopped
- 4 cloves garlic, minced
- 3 tomatoes, coarsely chopped
- 1½ cups chicken stock
- 1 bay leaf
- 4 teaspoons Worcestershire sauce
- 1 teaspoon sugar
- ½ teaspoon hot pepper sauce
- Salt and freshly ground black pepper

In a large skillet, melt the butter over medium heat. Add the okra, onion, bell pepper, and garlic. Sauté, stirring occasionally, for 8 minutes.

Stir in the tomatoes. Cook, stirring, for 1 minute. Add the stock and bay leaf. Cook over low heat, covered, for 30 minutes, stirring occasionally. If the sauce is too watery, cook uncovered over medium heat for 2 to 3 minutes to thicken slightly. Remove and discard the bay leaf.

Stir in the Worcestershire sauce, sugar, and hot pepper sauce. Season with salt and pepper. Serve hot.

Tabasco: New Orleans's Own Fire Island

Edmund McIlhenny and his wife, Mary Avery, returned to their Avery Island plantation after the Civil War to find that not much had survived. The salt works on this Gulf Coast island were inoperable. The sugarcane fields had been destroyed. But McIlhenny was delighted to find that the Capiscum peppers he had planted in his garden before the war had survived. A friend had brought the pepper seeds from Mexico, and the piquant flavor of the hardy peppers helped sustain the food-loving bon vivant through the era of monotonous food during Reconstruction.

McIlhenny began to experiment with making pepper sauce and eventually hit upon a formula. He crushed the ripest, reddest peppers, mixed half a cup of local salt with each gallon, and then aged the mixture for thirty days. He added fine French wine vinegar and aged the sauce for another thirty days before straining and bottling it. Friends who tasted "That Famous Sauce Mr. McIlhenny Makes" encouraged him to sell it commercially.

He chose a native Central American name for the product, "Tabasco," and shipped the first fiery batch of 350 bottles in 1868. Orders came in faster than they could be filled. The company had its greatest expansion under the aegis of Edmund's son, John Avery McIlhenny. Throughout the 1890s, he aggressively marketed his father's Tabasco sauce, posting signs, canvassing house-to-house, and even sponsoring a light opera ("The Burlesque Opera of Tabasco").

Tabasco has since become the definitive seasoning sauce, offering people around the world a taste of south Louisiana. Just a few drops accentuate the flavor in foods. "It pushes the natural flavor of the food. There's an afterglow in your mouth," beams Chef Paul Prudhomme. The uses seem endless, and Tobasco sauce is a vital additive to many recipes, including Bloody Marys.

Avery Island is well worth a detour on a visit to south Louisiana. In addition to touring the Tabasco factory, you can enjoy the island's two-hundred-acre Jungle Gardens, filled with azaleas, camellias, and bamboo. You might even spy some alligators, deer, raccoons, and bear that live in the surrounding hills and marshes. The McIlhenny family has established a unique refuge for the nearly extinct migratory Snowy Egret. Today, some twenty-thousand egrets and other water birds nest here each year at the specially built "Bird City." (For more information, call 318-369-6243.)

LOUISIANA DIRTY RICE

ADAPTED FROM A RECIPE BY FRANK BRIGTSEN, BRIGTSEN'S
RESTAURANT, NEW ORLEANS

Makes 8 side-dish servings

*Rice with chicken giblets, known euphemistically as "dirty rice,"
is a standard element of basic south Louisiana cooking. Here
is a classic version by one of New Orleans' top chefs.*

- 3 tablespoons unsalted butter
- ½ pound chicken gizzards, ground
- ½ pound ground pork
- 1 small yellow onion, finely chopped
- 1 small red *or* green bell pepper, seeded and finely chopped
- 1 stalk celery, finely chopped
- ¾ cup diced eggplant, unpeeled
- 2 cloves garlic, minced
- 2 teaspoons salt
- 1 teaspoon ground cumin
- 1 teaspoon dried oregano
- 1 teaspoon cayenne pepper
- ½ teaspoon freshly ground black pepper
- ¼ teaspoon freshly ground white pepper
- 1 bay leaf
- 3 cups chicken stock
- ½ pound chicken livers, ground
- 1½ cups rice
- 4 green onions (scallions), thinly sliced

Melt the butter in a large saucepan over medium heat.
Add the chicken gizzards and pork. Cook, stirring occasionally, until brown, about 5 minutes.

Add the yellow onion, bell pepper, celery, and eggplant. Cook until the vegetables are soft, about 4 minutes.

Stir in the garlic, salt, cumin, oregano, cayenne pepper,
black and white peppers, and the bay leaf. Cook, stirring,
2 minutes.

Stir in ½ cup of the chicken stock. Cook for 4 to 5
minutes, scraping the bottom and sides of the pan with
a wooden spoon. Add the chicken livers and the remaining 2½ cups stock; bring to a boil. Stir in the rice,
reduce the heat, cover, and simmer for 17 to 20 minutes
or until the rice is just tender. Remove and discard the
bay leaf. Remove from the heat, uncover, and stir in the
green onions.

CRÈME BRULÉE

Makes 8 servings

*"Burnt cream" originated in England, but it quickly became part of
the Creole culinary lexicon. Versions of crème brulée have been
made in New Orleans since the nineteenth century. After being
reintroduced at New York's Le Cirque restaurant, this rich dessert
has become a common item on restaurant menus across the country.*

- 1 quart heavy cream
- 1 vanilla bean, split lengthwise
- Pinch of salt
- 8 egg yolks
- ¾ cup plus 2 tablespoons granulated sugar
- ½ cup golden brown sugar, packed

Preheat the oven to 300°F.

Combine the cream, vanilla bean, and salt in a medium saucepan over medium-low heat. Simmer for 5 minutes. Remove from the heat. Scrape the seeds out of the
vanilla bean into the cream with the tip of a paring knife;
discard the vanilla bean.

Into a mixer bowl, place the egg yolks and granulated
sugar. Beat on low speed just to combine. With the mixer
running on low speed, slowly pour in the hot cream.
Strain the custard into a large pitcher; skim any bubbles
off the top.

Place eight ¾-cup ramekins in a roasting pan. Pour
the custard into the ramekins, filling them to the rims.
Carefully pour warm water into the pan until it reaches
halfway up the sides of the ramekins. Cover the pan
loosely with aluminum foil. Bake until just set, about 1¼
hours.

Remove the ramekins from the water bath and allow
them to cool. Cover each ramekin individually and
refrigerate for at least 3 hours or up to 2 days.

When ready to serve, preheat the broiler. Uncover the
ramekins and place them on a baking sheet. Top each
with 1 tablespoon of the brown sugar and, using a knife,
spread the sugar evenly over the custard to cover the surface completely. Broil the custards, watching closely, until
the sugar caramelizes, from 30 seconds to 2 minutes.
Serve immediately or refrigerate for up to 4 hours.

BANANAS FOSTER

Serves 4

Created by chef Paul Blange of Brennan's Restaurant in the 1950s, this dessert has become a New Orleans classic.

- 4 firm but ripe bananas, peeled
- ⅓ cup unsalted butter
- 1 cup golden brown sugar, packed
- ¼ cup banana-flavored liqueur
- ½ teaspoon ground cinnamon
- ⅓ cup dark rum
- 4 large scoops vanilla ice cream

Cut bananas in half horizontally. Slice each half into 2-inch sections. Melt the butter in a large skillet over medium heat. Add the sugar, banana liqueur, and cinnamon. Cook, stirring, until the sauce is bubbly, about 2 minutes. Add the bananas to the skillet and cook, turning them over gently, until slightly softened and browned, about 3 minutes. Remove the skillet from the heat.

In a small saucepan, warm the rum over low heat. Remove from the heat and carefully light the rum with a match. Pour the flaming rum over the bananas and allow the sauce to flame until it dies out.

Spoon the warm bananas and sauce over the ice cream.

TOASTED PECAN ICE CREAM SAUCE

Makes 2 cups

There is nothing like the combination of pecans, butter, and plenty of sweetness. Here is an easy sauce that can dress up vanilla ice cream quite smartly.

- 1¼ cups toasted pecan halves
- ½ cup dark corn syrup
- ⅓ cup light corn syrup
- ¼ cup dark brown sugar, packed
- ½ cup (1 stick) unsalted butter, cut into small pieces
- Pinch of salt
- Ice cream

In a medium saucepan, combine the pecans, corn syrups, and brown sugar over medium-high heat; bring to a boil. Remove from the heat; add the butter and stir until melted. Stir in the salt. Serve warm over your favorite ice cream.

PRALINES

Makes about 2 dozen

The name of these crystalline confections comes from the French word that refers to almonds or hazelnuts that are caramelized and then pulverized into a powder. Creole cooks substituted pecans for the other nuts and didn't bother to do any pulverizing.

- 1½ cups granulated sugar
- 1½ cups golden brown sugar, packed
- 1 cup whole milk
- 2 tablespoons light corn syrup
- Pinch of salt
- 2 cups coarsely chopped pecans
- 6 tablespoons (¾ stick) unsalted butter
- 2 teaspoons vanilla

Line 2 baking sheets with greased waxed paper. Set aside.

In a medium saucepan, combine the sugars, milk, corn syrup, and salt and place over medium-high heat. Bring the mixture to a boil, stirring constantly. Add the pecans. Reduce the heat to medium-low and cook, stirring often, until the mixture reaches 238°F to 240°F on a candy thermometer. Immediately remove the pan from the heat.

Stir in the butter and vanilla. Beat vigorously until the mixture loses its glossy sheen and thickens. Working quickly, drop the mixture by spoonfuls onto the prepared baking sheets, spaced apart. Cool the pralines completely before removing them from the paper. Store in an airtight container, layered between waxed paper at room temperature, up to 2 weeks.

Creole Coffee

Individuality is the hallmark of coffee in New Orleans, where Latin American or Indonesian beans are preferred. Creole coffee is made more pungent by the addition of chicory.

Strong café noir (black coffee) starts the early riser and completes a typical meal—it helps the digestion, your Creole host will explain. Breakfast in New Orleans, however, usually is accompanied by café au lait (half coffee, half hot milk). Try coffee and beignets (Creole "doughnuts") at the classic Café Du Monde (813 Decatur Street) in the French Quarter, where there's nothing else on the menu, and both are prepared to perfection.

The Heartland

Food is big business in America's heartland. In many ways the Midwest is the nation's larder. Just look in any grocery store. Many of the most common brand names are from the Midwest: Post, Pillsbury, General Mills, Kraft, Green Giant, Proctor & Gamble, Land O' Lakes.

Almost everyone in the Heartland is tied to the food industry in one way or another, and the force of this concentrated energy pushes production to truly colossal numbers. Massive quantities of meats, grains, vegetables, and processed foods flow daily to every corner of the nation and fill market shelves. In Chicago apoplectic traders spend their days in noisy rooms enthusiastically buying and selling contracts for pork bellies, corn, wheat, and soybeans. Despite the decidedly corporate nature of the food business and the array of cities through which most of the finances are filtered, the "heart" of the Heartland is still found on the small farm. And the kitchens on those farms produce the Midwest's true comfort food—a cuisine that is uncomplicated, nourishing, and delicious.

Climate plays a significant role in what appears on the Heartland table. Fare that "sticks to the ribs" is necessary to fortify residents in the frigid winters, while simple, refreshing foods are in order for the hot summers. There are no surprises here. This is perhaps the most "American" of regional cuisines.

Northwest Territory

The first to explore the vast unsettled land north and west of the Ohio River were French trappers and missionaries who followed the rivers and lakes to the upper reaches of Michigan and Wisconsin. Known back East as the Northwest

Territory, today's Midwest was the wild frontier of the eighteenth century. After the Revolutionary War, many of the "new Americans" grew restless in increasingly populous and urbanized New England and migrated west. Around the Great Lakes, they found a forgiving landscape crisscrossed by waterways and populated with friendly Native American tribes including the Winnebago, Chippewa, and Ojibway.

From the Native Americans, the settlers learned lessons: how to prepare wild rice (Indian Oats), how to weave gill nets for fishing, and where the best hunting grounds were. They also learned local cultivation techniques for raising squash, pumpkin, beans, and, most importantly, corn.

In the northern forests, the pioneers feasted on venison, partridge, and wild pigeon, and word of this bountiful frontier quickly spread. When the Erie Canal opened in 1825, more New England settlers arrived in the region, eager to stake claim to the land. The canal also brought newly arrived European immigrants to this area, mostly Germans fleeing revolutions on their native soil. What began as a trickle would become a flood with the Homestead Act of 1862. Land speculators began to advertise in Europe, and Scandinavian, German, Eastern European, Dutch, Irish, Welsh, and Scottish families came by the thousands, dispersing throughout the region, seeking out landscapes that reminded them of home.

It was this immigration wave that shaped the cuisine and economy of the Heartland. The fertile soils of Illinois, Indiana, Ohio, and southern Michigan—black as gunpowder—were enthusiastically cultivated by farmers who planted corn, wheat, rye, and garden vegetables. Those who settled farther west in the Plains states of Nebraska, Kansas, and Missouri were challenged by dry, stubborn soils overgrown with prairie grasses. But thanks to a hardy, drought-resistant strain of winter wheat brought by Ukrainian and Czech settlers, determined farm families managed to reverse the region's agricultural fortunes.

Germans worked the land alongside Danes and Norwegians in Missouri and Iowa, while Czechs settled in eastern Nebraska and Russians in Kansas. The scale of food production was auspicious from the beginning. In addition to the development of grain crops, the Germans established a lasting tradition of animal husbandry in Iowa and the other Plains states, and when the railroad was completed in 1867, Iowa and her neighbors were ready to feed the nation.

Working the Mines and the Forests

Europeans were drawn to the Heartland by more than just farming opportunities. In the northern tier of states, lucrative mining and timber claims brought young workers from Norway, Finland, Germany, Ukraine, Yugoslavia, Poland, Hungary, and Ireland. The Scandinavians and northern Germans felt immediately at home in this cold, glacial landscape, which was filled with rich hunting grounds and rivers choked with fish.

Many young men lived in boarding houses. They were generously fed pancakes and thick-cut bacon for breakfast, hearty stews and meats in the evening. These comfort foods sustained them during their long workday. For lunch, many workers would heat a "pasty" on their shovels. These pastry turnovers filled with juicy meat and vegetables were first introduced by Cornish miners and are still popular in northern Michigan.

Rural Areas

While different ethnic groups converged in the mining towns and timber camps, most residents of rural farming communities formed ethnic enclaves which helped to preserve native recipes and foods. These were the hearty, indulgent foods of their homelands: pickled meats, sausages, and pungent cheeses. Quality standards were important in the farm kitchen, and not just for the family. Seasonal workers needed for such tasks as threshing grain often followed their stomachs and sought work at those farms that offered the best stews and pies.

Good eating was also found in the religious communities established throughout the region. The strictest and most famed of these sects are the Amish, who settled in eastern Pennsylvania and later in Iowa. An abundance of wholesome food is one of the rewards of their diligent lifestyle, and these families have brought a treasury of fruit, vegetable, and meat dishes to the Heartland table.

Dairy

Dairy is queen in Wisconsin, where there is one cow for every two people in the state. And the cows are kept very busy. In 1994 they produced an astonishing 23 billion pounds of milk, or roughly 15,000 pounds per cow. Wisconsin leads the U.S. in both milk and cheese production and accounts for a quarter of the country's butter output.

New England transplants formed the first dairy cooperatives in the mid-nineteenth century, followed shortly thereafter by Scandinavian, German, Swiss, Italian, and Eastern European settlers who must have found the lush pastureland, dotted with lakes carved out by glaciers, irresistible. Using milk that was pure and plentiful, the skilled dairy farmers produced butter and rich cheeses. They made the specialty cheeses of their homelands: Italian Parmesan, Asiago, Gorgonzola, and Provolone; French Brie and Camembert; Dutch Gouda; and German Muenster are just some of the popular varieties. Several midwestern originals emerged as well. Frederick Maytag developed a pungent blue cheese in Iowa, and Joseph Steinwand crafted his cheddar-inspired Colby cheese in Wisconsin. Colby, milkier than cheddar, remains one of the state's most popular cheeses.

Most Midwest dairy products found on supermarket shelves come from a handful of large companies. But a recent revival of consumer interest in smaller, craft-style cheeses—not to be confused with "Kraft"-style—has been a boon for specialty dairy farmers. Locally made goat's milk, sheep's milk, and raw milk cheeses can now be found in gourmet shops around the country.

The Corn and Wheat Belts

The tall corn fields that carpet much of the farmland in Illinois, Indiana, Iowa, and Ohio suggest the earlier landscape in which wild grasses grew to amazing heights. Back then, natural tall grasses ran roughly in a long, east-west belt across the prairie, with a belt of forests to the north and short grasses to the southwest. The pattern remains the same today, but the grasses have been replaced with corn and wheat. Wheat, a short grass, grows best in the drier states of the Great Plains, though there is considerable overlap between the two belts. The Plains area has known hard times, first with seemingly unworkable land, and later during the "Dust Bowl" years of the 1930s. That environmental calamity, which contributed to the Great Depression, was a result of drought; overplowing of impoverished, sandy lands; and the planting of soil-depleting crops like cotton. Crop rotation and proper irrigation have since helped farmers overcome such obstacles.

Early entrepreneurs like Charles Pillsbury and Cadwaller Washburn (founder of General Mills) relied on the knowledge of Hungarian millers to teach them how to mill tough wheat kernels into pure, white flour. From the earliest settlement days, this abundance of quality flour made baking a favorite pastime throughout the Heartland, and savory ethnic breads, pastries, and pies have always been common products of regional home kitchens. Of the many creative uses for corn developed by midwesterners, perhaps the most notable was an invention by Dr. John Harvey Kellogg—the cornflake, cornerstone of the cereal industry.

Beef & Pork

It's no coincidence that the all-American hamburger and hotdog were introduced at the 1904 World's Fair in St. Louis. Meat and the Midwest are practically synonymous. Nebraska is the country's leading supplier of beef with one out of every five steaks in the U.S. coming from the Cornhusker state.

Pigs were favored by pioneer farmers because they took up minimal space in the barnyard and were easily fed with leftovers and table scraps. Pork remains vital to the Midwest economy. Iowa leads the country in swine-production, and nine of the top ten swine-producing states nationwide are in the Heartland. (North Carolina is the only non-midwestern state on the list.)

Buffalo, the primary food of the Sioux and other Plains Native Americans, is making a small comeback as a specialty meat in restaurants around the country. Leaner than beef, buffalo can be substituted for beef in most recipes. It is raised in South Dakota, Colorado, and Montana.

Farmers of both cattle and pigs have responded to consumer demand for lighter and healthier meat by raising leaner animals. Of course, most midwesterners will hasten to point out that a hefty beefsteak or a fatty, flavorful Polish sausage topped with sauerkraut and grilled onions is a necessary indulgence.

Much of the meat produced in the Heartland stays in the region and is served in legendary steakhouses and barbecue pits in Kansas City and Chicago. For most of this century, the Chicago stockyards were the primary meat-processing centers in the world. Approximately 600 million cattle were butchered there until the stockyards closed in 1971.

Oceans of Lager

Another widely enjoyed product comes from the Heartland's vast supplies of grain: beer. Milwaukee and St. Louis are home to such national brewers as Anheuser-Busch, Miller, Pabst, and Heileman. There are also midsize regional brewers including Stroh's in Detroit, Falstaff in Indiana, Hudepohl-Schoenling in Cincinnati, and August Schell in Minnesota. As the names suggest, German influence is dominant here, and the favored brew is lager. Some smaller, microbreweries produce excellent ales.

Not Just Staples

In addition to the staples of dairy, grain, and meat, a variety of other ingredients are grown in this remarkably productive region. Apple orchards are plentiful in Missouri, Iowa, and Michigan. In northern Michigan, the temperate influence of Lake Michigan allows cherries to prosper near its shore. Indigenous ingredients such as fiddlehead ferns, wild leeks, and wild rice also appear on authentic Midwest menus.

As Chef Jimmy Schmidt of Detroit's Rattlesnake Club notes, "Foraged ingredients are quite popular, especially wild mushrooms. In summer, freshwater fish is enjoyed; during the cooler months, game birds have a big following."

Rightfully known as the nation's "breadbasket," the Midwest has come to symbolize what is quintessentially American, both in the rhythms of its small-town life and its satisfying, unpretentious specialties such as meatloaf, casseroles, and fruit pies. On tables throughout the region you will find warm and generous farm cooking—solid and reliable and intimately tied to our notion of home.

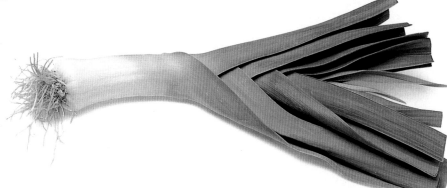

The Heartland Pantry

APPLES

Apples flourish in the Heartland. Red and Golden Delicious and Jonathans are popular in Iowa and Missouri. Michigan and the northern states grow McIntosh, Cortland, Northern Spy, and other varieties.

BLACK WALNUTS

If you've ever stained your hands struggling to pick the meat from the black walnut shell, you know the effort is well rewarded with a rich, strongly flavored nut that is wonderful in breads and cakes. Walnut trees are most numerous in Wisconsin, Iowa, and Minnesota.

CHERRIES

More than four million cherry trees dot the rolling hills alongside Lake Michigan, and when they blossom in mid-May, it is a sight to behold. The orchards in northern Michigan supply almost three-quarters of the nation's sour cherry crop, with Traverse City claiming the title of "The Cherry Capital of the World." These tangy fruits are most popular in pies, but midwesterners also use them in soups and salads, with meats, and in preserves.

CORN

A vital part of the early American diet, corn has since grown into a formidable industry. Corporate farms in the Midwest harvest over 85 percent of the nation's corn, selling it to cereal makers and as feed. Sweet corn for the table is picked when it is underripe, before the kernels harden. The varieties used for animal feed are left on the stalk until the kernels are hard and dry. When choosing sweet corn, look for tightly closed husks, clean, golden silk, and a stem that looks freshly cut. Old or "heirloom" varieties have more depth and complexity of flavor than the common types, and they are making a comeback. Multicolored Indian ears are grown mainly for show.

JUNIPER BERRIES

Most commonly known as the flavoring in gin, these round, bitter berries were popular among German and Scandinavian settlers. They are used as a seasoning in sauerkraut or in marinades for game and pork.

MOREL MUSHROOMS

Enthusiastic mushroom hunters forage for these spongy, cone-shaped fungi each spring. Their earthy, nutty flavor adds a wonderful note to cream sauces, sautés, and salads. Never gather wild mushrooms unless you have enough experience to properly identify them.

PERSIMMONS

These small, full-flavored fruits are traditionally used in puddings and desserts. The milder Asian persimmon is often substituted for the Midwest variety. Try to select ones that yield slightly to the touch when gently squeezed. To ripen persimmons quickly at home, place them stem side up in a plastic container. Put a few drops of brandy on the stems and close the container tightly. (You can also put them with a banana in a tightly sealed brown paper bag.) In three or four days the persimmons will be ripe.

SUNFLOWERS

A native crop that thrives in Kansas and the Dakotas, most of the harvested seeds go to the cereal industry or to the production of cooking oil. The tubers of sunflower roots are a delicious vegetable that can be sliced raw over salads or sautéed. These are called "sunchokes" or Jerusalem artichokes, because they have a flavor reminiscent of artichokes.

WHEAT

Wheat is a descendant of the short grasses that once carpeted the Great Plains. Whole-wheat flour is a popular base for healthy breads and pancakes. Baking is a passion in the Heartland, and wheat flour is vital for a host of cookies, pastries, breads, pies, and cakes. Popular wheat by-products include bran (the outer covering of the wheat kernel), bulgur (the ground whole kernel), and wheat germ (the wheat kernel's embryo).

WILD LEEKS

Also called ramps, these scallion-like vegetables were an important food for Native Americans in Minnesota and Wisconsin. Stronger in flavor than the cultivated leek, they make a nice addition to stews and meat dishes.

WILD RICE

The seed of aquatic grasses that grow in the lakes of Wisconsin and Minnesota was a staple of the Chippewa tribes. A high fiber fuel, wild rice should be cooked until it puffs and the light inner grain is visible. Wild rice expands considerably during cooking.

BEEF

With Nebraska leading, the Midwest supplies much of the country's favorite meats. Experiments with feed, grazing, and breeding have resulted in unsurpassed quality. Angus and Simmental breeds are the most popular varieties. Though health awareness has reduced the demand for certain cuts, prime aged beef remains the all-American protein.

BUFFALO

These animals have experienced a resurgence among specialty ranchers. Leaner and more nutritious than beef, buffalo can be substituted for beef in most recipes. Just remember to reduce cooking times because the meat cooks faster and can easily dry out.

DAIRY

Wisconsin lives up to its motto, "America's Dairyland," by producing a staggering amount of milk, cheese, sour cream, ice cream, and butter. Cheesemakers of Italian, German, Dutch, Scandinavian, and English descent prepare a wide variety of specialty cheeses, more than 250 different varieties in all.

FISH

A ready supply of fish inhabits lakes and rivers in the northern Heartland, and the sport of ice fishing proves the mettle of Midwest anglers. There are many popular varieties for the table.

Smelt: A small, silvery fish. Smelting season occurs during four weeks in early spring when the fish move toward the shore to spawn. To fish, one needs no poles or bait. All that's required is a net and a boat. Smelt (see page 140) is typically either deep fried or pan fried and served accompanied by French bread and washed down with beer.

Walleye: A member of the perch family, this popular fish is prized for its sweet white meat. It is caught commercially with gill nets under the winter ice, or sport-fished during the spring river migrations.

Sturgeon: The heavyweight of Great Lakes aquaculture, this long, slim fish has delicate, firm flesh.

Coho salmon: This Pacific transplant is often used to make Gravlax, the salt-and-sugar-cured Scandinavian treat. Exclusively a sport fish, commercial harvesting of Coho is prohibited.

Whitefish: Found in the frigid waters of the northern Great Lakes, this variety has a delicate, sweet flavor and snow-white meat that is excellent for smoking. Whitefish is a main ingredient in popular fish boils (see page 139).

Muskellunge: The state fish of Wisconsin is prized among expert anglers who have landed trophies weighing more than fifty pounds.

GAME BIRDS

The woods and fields of Michigan are thick with game, and wild quail, pheasant, partridge, and turkey glean the fields in the Corn Belt after grain harvest, particularly in Iowa. Squab (wild pigeon) features rich, dark meat. Wild turkey has an uncanny anticipation of danger that challenges the most skilled hunter. Farm-raised duck is popular in Indiana and Illinois. Wild and farm-raised game is growing in popularity in the Midwest.

PORK "THE OTHER WHITE MEAT"

Farmers now raise their hogs lean, with some cuts rivaling the low-fat content of chicken and turkey. Aggressive promotional campaigns have presented a more upscale image than the traditional bacon-and-sausage view. To control fat, choose lean cuts, trim any visible fat before cooking, and use low-fat cooking methods such as roasting, broiling, or grilling.

POULTRY

Chickens have long populated Midwest farmyards. Today, in addition to large-scale commercial producers, "free-range" chicken farmers have found eager buyers.

The Recipes

RUTABAGA-APPLE SOUP

Serves 6

Rutabaga is a root vegetable that grows well in Heartland soil. It is known in Europe as the Swedish turnip.
This delicious soup combines the rich, earthy flavors of the rutabaga with the tart sweetness of apple.

- ¼ cup (½ stick) unsalted butter
- 1 onion, chopped
- 1 quart chicken broth
- 2 (1-pound) rutabagas, peeled and cut into ½-inch chunks
- 2 Granny Smith apples, peeled, cored, and cut into ½-inch chunks
- 1 cup heavy cream
- 2 teaspoons lemon juice
- ½ teaspoon curry powder
- Salt and freshly ground pepper
- ¾ cup crème fraîche
- 1 cup peeled, cored, and diced Granny Smith apples
- Snipped fresh chives

Melt the butter in a 3-quart saucepan over medium heat. Add the onion and sauté, stirring occasionally, for 5 minutes. Add the chicken broth, rutabagas, and chunked apples. Bring to a boil, reduce the heat, cover, and simmer for about 40 minutes or until the rutabagas are tender. Remove the saucepan from the heat and purée contents in a blender (or with a hand blender) until smooth.

Return the contents of the blender to the saucepan. Stir in the heavy cream, lemon juice, and curry powder. Heat through. Season with the salt and pepper.

To serve, spoon the soup into individual bowls; top with a dollop of crème fraîche and sprinkle with the diced apples and snipped chives.

ASPEN MUSHROOM SOUP
ADAPTED FROM A RECIPE BY CHARLES DALE,
THE RENAISSANCE RESTAURANT, ASPEN, COLORADO

Serves 8

The wooded areas of the Rocky Mountain states are prime sources for wild mushrooms. Here is a luscious combination of several varieties.

- ¼ cup (4 tablespoons) olive oil
- 1 pound button mushrooms, sliced
- 1 medium white onion, chopped
- 5 peeled whole garlic cloves
- ½ cup dry sherry
- 5 cups chicken stock
- 1 branch each fresh rosemary and thyme, tied together with kitchen twine
- 1 cup heavy cream
- 1 cup milk
- 1 ounce dried porcini (cèpe) mushrooms
- 1 ounce dried morel mushrooms
- ¼ pound shiitake mushrooms, stemmed and sliced
- ¼ pound tree oyster mushrooms, foot removed and sliced
- Salt and freshly ground pepper
- ¼ cup snipped fresh chives

In a heavy stockpot heat 2 tablespoons of the oil over medium heat. Add the button mushrooms and sauté, stirring, for 3 minutes. Add the onion and sauté, stirring, for 3 more minutes. Add 3 of the garlic cloves and cook 2 more minutes. Stir in sherry and allow to reduce for 5 minutes. Add 4 cups of chicken stock and the herb bundle. Bring to a boil. Reduce the heat, cover, and simmer for 20 minutes.

Remove from the heat and discard the herb bundle. Purée the soup with a blender. Stir in the cream and milk. Set aside.

In a small saucepan, bring the remaining cup of stock to a boil. Add the porcini and morel mushrooms. Remove from the heat and let steep for 15 minutes. Drain the mushrooms, reserving the stock. Finely chop the mushrooms and add to the puréed soup along with the reserved stock.

Heat the remaining 2 tablespoons of oil in a medium skillet over medium heat. Add the shiitake and tree oyster mushrooms and the remaining 2 garlic cloves. Sauté, stirring, for 3 minutes. Remove and discard the garlic cloves. Stir the sautéed mushrooms into the puréed soup.

Simmer the soup over low heat to warm through. Season with salt and pepper. Stir in the chives. Serve immediately.

SWEET 'N' SOUR COLESLAW

Serves 6

The name of this traditional salad comes from the German kohl, *which means "cabbage." Although various versions of coleslaw are found across the country, the German settlers in the Midwest give this region the most convincing claim to it, especially for this tangy version.*

- 1 small green cabbage, cored and shredded
- ½ small red cabbage, cored and shredded
- 2 medium carrots, peeled and shredded
- 4 green onions (scallions), sliced
- ¾ cup apple cider vinegar
- ¼ cup (4 tablespoons) vegetable oil
- ¼ cup sugar
- 2 teaspoons dry mustard
- 1 teaspoon celery seeds
- Salt and freshly ground pepper

In a large bowl, toss the cabbages, carrots, and onions.

In another bowl, whisk vinegar, oil, sugar, mustard, and celery seeds.

Pour the dressing over the cabbage mixture and toss to coat completely. Season with salt and pepper. Cover and refrigerate at least 1 hour. Serve cold.

Wisconsin Fish Boil

To the uninitiated, a fish boil in Door County, Wisconsin, looks like a bonfire gone wild. A huge pot rests at a slightly tipped angle over a raging wood fire. The skilled cook first salts the water to raise the boiling point, then adds a large basket filled with small potatoes and sweet onions. After the vegetables have boiled for about half an hour, a second basket packed with fish steaks is dropped in. Originally trout was used, but since it is no longer fished commercially in the Midwest, fresh Lake Michigan whitefish has become the fish of choice. The succulent, sweet meat is ideally suited to the vegetables and butter combined in the boil.

The highlight of the boil comes when the fish is cooked. A bucket of kerosene is thrown on the fire, causing the flames to leap dramatically upward. This theatrical display causes the pot to boil over. Fish lovers will be surprised to find how delicious this simple creation tastes. Accompaniments typically include cole slaw and, for dessert, cherry pie.

CRISPY FRIED SMELTS
WITH LEMON, GARLIC, AND ROSEMARY
ADAPTED FROM A RECIPE BY JIMMY SCHMIDT,
THE RATTLESNAKE CLUB, DETROIT, MICHIGAN

Serves 6 as an appetizer

Despite their rather unappealing name, these slim, silvery fish make a crunchy, flavorful appetizer. If smelts are unavailable (because they are perishable, they are often found frozen), any small fish—such as "whitebait"—can be substituted.

- Canola oil, for frying
- 2 cups fresh Italian parsley leaves
- 12 cloves garlic, peeled and halved lengthwise
- 4 sprigs fresh rosemary
- 2 cups milk
- 2 eggs
- 2 cups all-purpose flour
- 2 teaspoons paprika
- 1 teaspoon salt
- ½ teaspoon cayenne pepper
- 2 pounds smelts (about 2 dozen)
- Freshly ground black pepper and additional salt
- Lemon wedges

Fill a large, deep skillet with the oil to a depth of 3 inches; heat to 375°F. Add the parsley leaves and cook until crisp, about 1 minute. Remove leaves with a slotted spoon and drain on a paper towel—lined plate. Transfer parsley to a large bowl. Add the garlic to the oil and cook until golden, about 1½ minutes. Drain, chop finely, and add to the parsley. Add the rosemary to the oil and cook until crisp, about 2½ minutes. Drain, remove the leaves from the stems, and add the leaves to the parsley and garlic, mixing well to combine. Run a dry, fine, small sieve through the oil to remove any remaining herb particles.

In a medium bowl, whisk the milk and eggs. Into another bowl, sift together the flour, paprika, salt, and cayenne pepper. Dip the smelts into the egg mixture, shaking off excess. Transfer the smelts to the flour mixture and shake to coat completely. Slip the smelts into the hot oil, stirring occasionally, and fry until crisp and golden brown. Drain well. Transfer to the bowl with the herbs and garlic and toss gently. Season with pepper and salt. Serve immediately on a warmed platter lined with lemon wedges.

PECAN TROUT WITH LEMON AND SAGE

Serves 4

Trout inhabit the freshwater streams and lakes of the Heartland. This recipe adds a few flavorful elements but doesn't interfere with the wonderful fresh flavor of the fish.

- 8 slices bacon
- 4 whole boneless trout
- Salt and freshly ground pepper
- 8 green onions (scallions)
- All-purpose flour, for dredging
- 6 tablespoons (¾ stick) unsalted butter
- 1 cup chopped toasted pecans
- 2 tablespoons lemon juice
- 2 tablespoons chopped fresh sage

In a large skillet over medium heat, cook the bacon until crisp, about 8 minutes. Remove the bacon to a paper towel—lined plate. Reserve the pan drippings.

Season the trout cavities lightly with salt and pepper; lay 2 green onions inside each trout. Dredge the trout in the flour, shaking off any excess, and sauté in the bacon drippings over medium heat. Cook until opaque throughout, about 12 minutes, turning once. Set aside; keep hot.

Chop the bacon slices. In a small saucepan melt the butter over medium heat. Stir in the pecans, lemon juice, sage, and bacon. Pour over the trout and serve.

Chef Jimmy Schmidt

A native midwesterner, Jimmy Schmidt has opened a group of restaurants in Michigan that showcase New American regional cooking. The flagship of these is the award-winning Rattlesnake Club in Detroit.

Chef Schmidt's formal training began at the Luberon College in Avignon, France, where he received a diploma in 1974. Two years later, he graduated First in Class from Modern Gourmet in Massachusetts, under the direction of Madeleine Kamman. He then moved to Detroit to become executive chef of the London Chop House.

In 1985, he opened the first Rattlesnake Club in Denver. The Detroit Rattlesnake Club followed in 1988.

In 1993, Chef Schmidt won the James Beard Award for "Best Chef in the Midwest." He has authored two cookbooks and writes a weekly column for the Detroit Free Press.

Roast Chicken with Wild Rice, Pecan, and Dried Fruit Stuffing

Serves 6

Stuffing is a European tradition. While stuffing with sausage or bread likely descended from Italian or French creators, stuffing with fruit is decidedly German in origin. Most German immigrants in the United States settled in the Heartland.

- ½ cup (1 stick) unsalted butter
- 4 leeks, halved lengthwise, cleaned, and sliced
- 1 onion, chopped
- 1 stalk celery, sliced
- 1 cup wild rice
- 3 cups apple cider
- 2 cups chicken stock
- ½ cup applejack brandy
- 1 Granny Smith apple, peeled, cored, and chopped
- ½ cup dried tart cherries
- ½ cup diced dried apples
- 1 cup chopped toasted pecans
- ¼ cup chopped fresh rosemary
- Salt and freshly ground black pepper
- 1 (6-pound) roasting chicken

Melt ¼ cup of the butter in a large skillet over medium heat. Add the leeks, onion, and celery; sauté, stirring, until tender, about 6 minutes. Stir in the rice and sauté for 2 minutes. Add 1 cup of the cider, the stock, and brandy. Bring to a boil. Reduce the heat, cover, and simmer for 30 minutes. Stir in the Granny Smith apple and the dried cherries and apples. Cover and cook another 15 minutes or until rice is tender. Stir in the pecans and 2 tablespoons of the rosemary. Season with salt and pepper. Cool stuffing completely before filling the chicken.

In a small bowl mix together the remaining ¼ cup butter, softened, and 2 tablespoons of rosemary. Set aside.

Preheat the oven to 325°F. Season the chicken on all sides with salt and pepper. Loosen the skin from the breasts of the bird, and spread the rosemary butter over the breast meat and under the skin. Spoon enough of the rice stuffing into the chicken to fill it, but do not pack it too tightly; reserve any extra stuffing in a covered casserole dish.

Set the chicken on a rack in a shallow roasting pan. Roast, basting with the remaining 2 cups of apple cider, until the juices run clear when a pick is inserted into the thickest part of the leg, about 2 hours. Remove the chicken from the roasting pan and place on a serving platter. Let it stand 10 minutes. (Place the extra stuffing in the oven during the last 20 minutes of roasting the chicken, to reheat it.)

Place the roasting pan with the chicken juices and cider over medium heat. With a wooden spoon, scrape the bottom of the pan to release the browned bits and reduce the liquid slightly.

Carve the chicken and serve it with the rice stuffing and pan juices.

CUMIN-ROASTED PHEASANT WITH BULGUR-CHILI STUFFING
ADAPTED FROM A RECIPE BY CHARLES DALE, THE RENAISSANCE RESTAURANT,
ASPEN, COLORADO

Serves 6

Wild pheasants can be found throughout most of the Heartland. These flavorful birds are also raised commercially, and they make a lean and lively tasting chicken substitute.

- ½ cup olive oil
- 8 cloves garlic, minced
- 1 tablespoon toasted ground cumin
- Salt and freshly ground black pepper
- 3 whole pheasants (about 1½ pounds each), livers removed, chopped, and reserved
- 6 tablespoons (¾ stick) unsalted butter
- 1 to 2 Anaheim chiles, roasted, peeled and diced
- 1 red onion, diced
- 2 cups chicken stock
- 1 cup bulgur wheat
- ⅓ pound chicken livers, chopped
- 1 tablespoon chopped fresh sage
- 1 tablespoon chopped fresh parsley

To make the marinade: In a large nonmetallic bowl whisk the olive oil, 6 cloves of the garlic, and the cumin; season with salt and pepper and set aside.

With each pheasant, cut down both sides of the backbone with poultry or kitchen shears, pull out the bone and discard it. With the tip of a knife, cut through the membrane covering the breastbone. Pick up the pheasant with both hands and press on the ribs to break them away from the breastbone, which will pop out. Pull out the breastbone, including cartilage, and discard it. You will now have 6 pheasant halves. Add the pheasants to the marinade, coating liberally. Cover and refrigerate 6 hours, turning occasionally.

To make the stuffing: In a large saucepan, melt 4 tablespoons of the butter over medium heat; add the chile, onion, and the remaining 2 cloves of garlic. Sauté, stirring occasionally, for 5 minutes. Add the stock, cover, and bring to a boil. Stir in the bulgur, cover, and return to a boil. Remove from heat and stir well. Cover and let stand 5 minutes. Meanwhile, melt the remaining 2 tablespoons of butter in a medium skillet over medium heat; add the pheasant livers and chicken livers and sauté, stirring, until brown on the outside but still pink on the inside, about 2 minutes. Add the livers to the bulgur mixture along with the sage and parsley; mix gently. Season with salt and pepper. Cool, cover, and refrigerate until ready to use.

Preheat the oven the 375°F. Lightly grease a roasting pan large enough to hold the pheasant halves in one layer (use two pans, if necessary). For each pheasant half, mound 1⅓ cups stuffing into the roasting pan; place a pheasant half over it, skin-side up, to cover stuffing completely. Roast about 30 minutes, until pheasant juices run clear. Remove from the oven and preheat the broiler; broil about 2 minutes to crisp the skins, watching closely so as not to burn them. Serve hot.

KC Barbecue

Barbecuing can hardly be called a skill in Kansas City—it's more of an instinct, a natural reflex. There are scores of barbecue restaurants in town, and a backyard here would seem barren without the requisite grill. Everyone has his or her own special sauce and most memorable barbecue experience.

The secrets, as prescribed by the Kansas City Barbecue Society, are long, slow cooking and smoking, not grilling. For proper technique, you need a barbecue unit that has a vented cover; an open grill won't do. Start with charcoal briquets, lit well in advance so they are white with ash when it is time to cook. Pile them to one side and sprinkle water-soaked hickory chips on top to create smoke. Place the meat high on the grill and away from the coals, cover the unit, and let the slow smoking begin. Depending on the meat, cooking times can range from fifteen minutes to fifteen hours. Pork spareribs and beef brisket are the most common meats on the Kansas City grill, but chicken, fish, and sausage appear as well. Generally, the meats are prepared with a rub, and any sauce used is spread on at the last moment or is served on the side.

CRISPY AND SPICY LAMB CHOPS
ADAPTED FROM A RECIPE BY KEVIN TAYLOR,
ZENITH AMERICAN GRILL, DENVER, COLORADO

Serves 4

Here's a hearty and savory way to prepare lamb chops without masking the flavors of the meat.

- 8 medium loin lamb chops
- ¾ cup plain bread crumbs
- ½ cup Dijon-style mustard
- 2 dry chipotle chiles, reconstituted in boiling water, drained, and minced (page 197)
- 2 cloves garlic, minced
- ¼ cup olive oil

Place the bread crumbs on a dinner plate. In a small bowl mix the mustard, chiles, and garlic. Spread a thin layer of the mustard mixture on 1 side of each chop. Put the chops, mustard-side down, in the bread crumbs. Repeat the process on the other side of the chops.

Heat the oil in a large skillet over medium heat. Add the chops and cook about 10 minutes for medium rare, turning once. Serve immediately with Garlic Mashed Potatoes (see page 247).

Chef Kevin Taylor

Born and raised in Denver, Colorado, Chef Kevin Taylor has built strong relationships with local farmers, whose produce he showcases at the Zenith American Grill. It is vital, he believes, to appreciate the integrity of ingredients.

Chef Taylor began working in professional kitchens as a high school student and honed his skills under the tutelage of classically trained European chefs. By the time he was a senior in high school, he had thirty-five cooks working under his supervision. At the age of twenty-one, he knew he wanted to create a restaurant of his own, and its identity had already begun to take shape.

The Zenith American Grill is the result of this vision. Chef Taylor's cuisine is firmly rooted in the spirit of the Heartland. The restaurant has been featured in Bon Appétit.

HEART OF WISCONSIN MACARONI AND CHEESE

Serves 8

Macaroni and cheese has become a quintessentially American dish. While most of its fans are under the age of fifteen, this recipe elevates this dish to its original status as a hearty, meatless meal for grownups.

- 3 cups (12 ounces) elbow macaroni
- 1 tablespoon olive oil
- 1 cup heavy cream
- 1 cup half-and-half (light cream)
- 2 egg yolks
- ½ teaspoon ground nutmeg
- 2 cups (8 ounces) shredded Wisconsin extra-sharp Cheddar cheese
- 2 cups (8 ounces) shredded Wisconsin Fontina cheese
- 2 cups (6 ounces) grated Wisconsin Parmesan cheese
- 2 teaspoons Worcestershire sauce
- ½ teaspoon freshly ground white pepper
- 6 tablespoons (¾ stick) butter
- 3 cups fresh bread crumbs

Preheat the oven to 400°F. Grease a 12-inch round baking dish (or large gratin dish) and set aside.

Bring a large pot of lightly salted water to a boil. Add the macaroni and cook until tender but still firm to the bite. Drain well and transfer to the prepared baking dish. Toss the macaroni with the oil to prevent it from sticking together; set aside.

Place the cream, half-and-half, egg yolks, and nutmeg in a medium saucepan. Whisk to combine. Set over medium-low heat and add 1½ cups each of the cheddar, Fontina, and Parmesan cheeses. Cook until the cheeses are melted and the sauce is smooth, about 5 minutes. DO NOT BOIL. Season with the Worcestershire sauce and white pepper. Pour the sauce over the macaroni and stir until the pasta is completely coated. Bake until the sauce bubbles and the top is a light golden brown, about 15 minutes.

Meanwhile, place the butter in a large skillet and melt over medium heat. Stir in the bread crumbs and toss until coated with the butter and lightly toasted.

After baking, sprinkle the macaroni and cheese with the bread crumbs and preheat the broiler. Broil until the bread crumbs are golden brown, about 1 minute.

Pot Roast with Cornmeal Dumplings and Roasted Root Vegetables
Adapted from a recipe by Brad Ogden, Lark Creek Inn, Larkspur, California

Serves 8

Chef Ogden, who is best known for his San Francisco Bay Area restaurants (Lark Creek Inn, One Market), has strong roots in the Heartland. He grew up in Traverse City, Michigan, and many of his cooking ideas derive from there. Pot roast is an American tradition, and this version has strong midwestern and German influences.

- 1½ cups all-purpose flour
- 2 tablespoons dry mustard
- 1 tablespoon salt
- 1 teaspoon freshly ground pepper
- 1 (4-pound) boneless beef chuck roast
- ½ cup (8 tablespoons) olive oil
- 3 carrots, chopped
- 1 yellow onion, chopped
- 1 stalk celery, chopped
- 2 cups dry red wine
- 2 (14½-ounce) cans beef stock
- 2 tablespoons tomato paste
- 2 teaspoons dried thyme
- 2 teaspoons dried rosemary
- 24 white boiling onions, peeled
- 16 baby carrots
- 8 medium red new potatoes, quartered
- 1 medium rutabaga, peeled and cut into 1-inch chunks
- 1 medium turnip, peeled and cut into 1-inch chunks
- 1 cup yellow cornmeal
- 2 teaspoons baking powder
- 1 teaspoon sugar
- ¾ cup milk
- 1 egg
- 1 tablespoon vegetable oil
- Chopped fresh parsley, for garnish

In a shallow dish, combine ½ cup of the flour, the dry mustard, 1 teaspoon of the salt, and ½ teaspoon of the pepper. Dredge the beef in the flour mixture to coat completely, shaking off excess. Heat 2 tablespoons of the olive oil over medium-high heat in a large, deep pot; brown the roast well on all sides. Remove from the pot and set aside.

Reduce the heat to medium and add 2 more tablespoons of the olive oil to the pot. Add the carrots, yellow onion, and celery; sauté, stirring occasionally, for 10 minutes.

Return the roast to the pot and add the wine, beef stock, tomato paste, and 1 teaspoon each of the thyme and rosemary. Bring to a boil, reduce the heat, cover, and simmer for 2 hours or until the meat is very tender.

Meanwhile, prepare the roasted vegetables. Preheat the oven to 425°F. In a roasting pan toss the boiling onions, baby carrots, potatoes, rutabaga, and turnip with the remaining ¼ cup of olive oil, 1 teaspoon salt, and ½ teaspoon of pepper. Roast about 40 minutes or until tender,

tossing occasionally. Remove from the oven and set aside.

When the roast is cooked, remove it to a platter and tent it with aluminum foil to keep warm. Place the pot on top of the stove and simmer the liquid for 20 minutes to reduce it slightly. Using a handheld mixer, purée the mixture to achieve a nice, thick gravy. Set aside and keep hot.

Place the roasted vegetables over medium heat; deglaze with ¼ cup of the gravy. Set aside and keep hot.

To make the dumplings, in a medium bowl combine the remaining 1 cup flour, the cornmeal, baking powder, sugar, and the remaining 1 teaspoon each of thyme, rosemary, and salt. In another bowl, whisk together the milk, egg, and vegetable oil; add this to the flour mixture and stir just until combined. Spoon the mixture by tablespoonfuls into the gravy. Cover the pot and simmer for 25 minutes without lifting the lid.

Slice the roast. Serve it with the roasted vegetables and dumplings, all on top of a generous serving of gravy.

Pork Loin with Cider Sauce, Caramelized Apples, and Onions

Serves 6-8

The Heartland is home to the nation's biggest pork producers. Over the past two decades pork farmers have improved their product so that it is disease-free and lean. Today's pork loin has fewer than 200 calories per serving. In addition, pork is still about the most delicious meat around.

- ¾ cup (1½ sticks) unsalted butter
- 2 tablespoons vegetable oil
- 1 (3½-pound) boneless pork loin, rolled and tied
- Salt and freshly ground pepper
- 7 Pippin apples, peeled and cored
- 3 onions, sliced
- 3 carrots, chopped
- Peel of 1 orange
- Peel of 1 lemon
- 3 sprigs fresh thyme
- 2 bay leaves
- 10 peppercorns
- 3 cups apple cider
- 2 cups chicken stock
- ½ cup applejack brandy
- ¼ cup Dijon-style mustard

An Iowa Original

When Frederick Maytag II inherited his father's prize herd of Iowa Holsteins, he decided to produce a dairy product that could be shipped by mail order. He traveled to the University of Iowa and struck a deal to make blue cheese from a patented formula developed by the school. Maytag built a cheese plant and curing caves, and the first vat of cheese was made in 1941. Today, the family-run company makes 300,000 pounds annually, all of which is still handmade in small batches and carefully aged in caves. To order a piece of wonderfully pungent Maytag Blue, call 800-247-2458.

Melt ¼ cup butter with the oil in a large, ovenproof casserole over medium-high heat. Season the pork with salt and pepper and add it to the casserole to sear it on all sides. Remove the pan from the heat and remove the meat from the pan. Set the pork aside.

Preheat the oven to 350°F. Chop 4 of the apples. Return the casserole to medium heat and add the chopped apples, 1 of the onions, and the carrots. Sauté, stirring occasionally, until soft, about 10 minutes.

Place the peels, thyme, bay leaves, and peppercorns in a muslin bag. Add it to the vegetables along with the cider, stock, and brandy; bring to a boil. Return the pork to the casserole; cover and braise for about 2½ hours or until the internal temperature of the pork reaches 160°F on a meat thermometer.

While the pork is cooking, make the caramelized apples. Melt the remaining ½ cup of butter in a large skillet over medium heat. Slice the remaining 3 apples and add them to the skillet along with the remaining 2 onions. Sauté, stirring occasionally, until caramelized and golden brown, about 30 minutes. Season with salt and pepper. Set aside; keep warm.

When the pork is done, remove it from the casserole, set it on a platter and tent the meat with aluminum foil to keep it warm.

Remove and discard the seasoning bag from the casserole. Purée the vegetables with the pan juices in a blender; return the mixture to the casserole. Bring to a boil and reduce slightly. Whisk in the mustard and season with salt and pepper.

Slice the pork and serve it with the sauce and the caramelized apples and onions.

SHEPHERD'S PIE

Serves 12

This English dish easily made the move to America, where it has continued to be popular. Originally shepherds would heat some of it over an open fire while tending their flocks. Nowadays, it is the definitive "comfort food"—unpretentious, hearty, and incredibly delicious.

- 2 (14½-ounce) cans beef broth
- 2 ounces dried porcini mushrooms
- 3 pounds red new potatoes, cut into 1-inch chunks
- 8 cloves garlic
- 1 cup (2 sticks) unsalted butter
- ¾ cup crème fraîche
- ½ cup heavy cream
- 2 green onions (scallions), finely chopped
- 3 tablespoons chopped fresh parsley

- Salt and freshly ground black pepper
- 2 yellow onions, chopped
- 3 cups sliced button mushrooms
- 2 cups sliced shiitake mushrooms
- 3 pounds ground beef
- ½ cup all-purpose flour
- 1 cup dry sherry wine
- 2 tablespoons soy sauce
- 2 tablespoons dried thyme
- 6 fresh ears of corn, kernels cut from cobs

In a medium saucepan, bring the broth to a boil. Add the dried porcini mushrooms, turn off the heat and let stand at least ½ hour.

Place the potatoes and garlic in a large saucepan; cover with water and bring to a boil. Cook until the potatoes and garlic are soft when pierced with the tip of a knife. Drain well. Mash the potatoes and garlic. Stir in 6 tablespoons of the butter, the crème fraîche, heavy cream, green onions, and parsley. Season with salt and pepper. Set aside.

Preheat the oven to 350°F. Lightly grease a 3½- to 4-quart baking dish; set aside.

Melt 6 tablespoons of the butter in a large skillet. Add the yellow onions and button and shiitake mushrooms; sauté over medium heat, stirring, until the onions are soft, about 8 minutes. Add the ground beef; cook, stirring, until well browned, about 10 minutes.

Drain the porcini mushrooms, reserving the soaking liquid. Finely chop the mushrooms.

Sprinkle the flour over the beef mixture. Cook and stir for 3 minutes. Stir in the sherry, porcini mushrooms, and the reserved soaking liquid. Cook, stirring, until slightly thickened, about 3 minutes. Stir in the soy sauce and thyme. Season with salt and pepper.

Melt the remaining ¼ cup butter in a medium skillet. Stir in the corn and sauté for 5 minutes. Season with salt and pepper.

Spoon the beef mixture into the prepared dish; spread evenly. Spread the corn over the beef. Spoon the potatoes over the corn; spread evenly. Bake for 45 minutes or until hot throughout.

MINNESOTA MEATLOAF

Serves 6, with leftovers

Meatloaf's roots are in Italy or maybe Greece, but it is now a completely Americanized dish. This midwestern version, which uses beef, pork, and veal for texture and flavor, is a classic.

- 2 tablespoons olive oil
- 2 medium onions, chopped, *or* ¾ cup green onions (scallions), sliced
- 1 stalk celery, diced
- 1 carrot, diced
- ½ cup red bell pepper, diced
- 3 cloves garlic, minced
- ½ cup half-and-half (light cream)
- ¼ cup chili sauce
- 2 tablespoons Dijon-style mustard
- 1 tablespoon Worcestershire sauce
- ¼ teaspoon cayenne pepper
- ½ cup stale bread crumbs
- 1 pound lean ground beef (round)
- ½ pound ground veal
- ½ pound ground pork
- 2 eggs, lightly beaten
- ½ teaspoon freshly grated nutmeg
- ½ teaspoon dried thyme
- 2 teaspoons salt
- ½ teaspoon freshly ground black pepper
- ¼ cup finely chopped fresh parsley

Heat the olive oil in a medium skillet over medium heat. Sauté the onions, celery, carrot, bell pepper, and garlic for 5 minutes, stirring frequently, or until the vegetables are soft. Stir in the half-and-half, chili sauce, mustard, Worcestershire sauce, and cayenne pepper. Add the bread crumbs and stir to combine. Remove the mixture to a large glass or ceramic bowl and refrigerate for at least 20 minutes.

Preheat the oven to 350°F. Add the three ground meats to the bowl with the red pepper and onion mixture. Add the eggs and sprinkle the seasonings over the mixture.

Knead the mixture with your hands, being careful not to overmix. The mixture should remain fluffy and mottled in color. Put the meat mixture into a 9 x 5 x 3 inch loaf pan. Tap the pan on the work surface to eliminate air bubbles. Place the pan on a cookie sheet in the center of the oven. Bake for 1 hour or until a meat thermometer inserted into the loaf's center registers 150°F.

Remove the meatloaf from the oven and let cool for 5 minutes. Slice and serve with Basic Gravy (see page 152).

TWICE-BAKED IDAHO POTATOES

Serves 6

Baked potatoes have been elevated to a level of sophistication by American cooks that they have never achieved anywhere else. This version combines fresh Idahos with American cheeses.

- 3 (8-ounce) Idaho russet potatoes
- ¼ cup (½ stick) unsalted butter, melted
- 1½ cups (6 ounces) shredded Wisconsin extra-sharp cheddar cheese
- ½ cup (1½ ounces) grated Wisconsin Parmesan cheese
- 6 tablespoons heavy cream
- 2 green onions (scallions), minced
- 1 egg yolk, beaten
- ½ teaspoon salt
- ¼ teaspoon freshly ground white pepper
- Paprika
- Snipped fresh chives

Preheat the oven to 400°F. Pierce the potatoes with the tines of a fork and rub potatoes all over with 1 tablespoon of the melted butter. Bake until tender, about 45 minutes.

Reduce the oven to 350°F. When the potatoes are cool enough to handle, cut them in half lengthwise. Scoop out the potato pulp and place it in a medium bowl, leaving ¼-inch thick potato shells. Mash the pulp together with 1 cup of the cheddar cheese, the Parmesan cheese, cream, green onions, egg yolk, salt, white pepper, and the remaining 3 tablespoons of butter. Mound the mixture into the potato shells and place them in a 9 x 13 inch baking dish. Sprinkle with the remaining ½ cup of cheddar cheese. Bake about 15 minutes, until the potatoes are hot and the cheese is bubbly.

Preheat the broiler. Broil the potatoes until the cheese is light golden brown, about 45 seconds.

To serve, lightly dust the potatoes with paprika and sprinkle with chives.

POTATO PANCAKES WITH ARTICHOKE HEARTS
AND WISCONSIN GORGONZOLA CHEESE
ADAPTED FROM A RECIPE BY MICHAEL FOLEY, PRINTER'S ROW, CHICAGO, ILLINOIS

Serves 6 as an appetizer (18 pancakes)

Potatoes and cheese are standard ingredients in the northern Heartland.
This combination of the two is the brainchild of one of Chicago's most talented chefs.

- 4 (8- to 10-ounce) russet potatoes
- 1 cup all-purpose flour
- 1 cup heavy cream
- 4 eggs, lightly beaten
- 1 generous tablespoon chopped fresh oregano
- 2 cloves garlic, minced
- 1½ teaspoons salt (or more, if needed)
- 1 teaspoon white pepper
- Pinch freshly ground nutmeg
- ½ to 1 cup milk
- 2 (6-ounce) jars marinated artichoke hearts, drained and finely chopped
- Unsalted butter, as needed
- 1 cup plus 2 tablespoons crumbled Wisconsin Gorgonzola cheese

Preheat the oven to 400°F. Pierce potatoes with the tines of a fork. Bake about 45 minutes or until tender. Cool slightly, peel off the skins, and crumble potatoes into a medium bowl.

Add the flour, cream, eggs, oregano, garlic, salt, pepper, and nutmeg to the potatoes. Using an electric hand mixer, beat into a smooth batter. Beat in enough of the milk to achieve a semisoft batter. Gently fold in the artichoke hearts.

Over medium heat melt enough butter to coat the bottom of a 12-inch nonstick skillet. Drop in ¼ cup batter for each pancake and flatten slightly to form 3-inch pancakes. Cook about 3 minutes until golden brown on one side. Flip pancakes over and top each with one tablespoon of the cheese; cook another 3 minutes until bottom is browned and the cheese is slightly melted. Repeat with the remaining pancake batter.

BASIC GRAVY

Makes 2 cups

*Making good gravy can be an art form.
Here is a true all-American, from scratch gravy
that goes well with just about anything.*

- 2 tablespoons unsalted butter
- 2 medium onions, coarsely chopped
- 1 medium carrot, coarsely chopped
- ½ stalk celery, coarsely chopped
- ½ teaspoon dried thyme
- 1 cup red wine
- 1 cup chicken stock
- 1 cup beef stock
- 2 tablespoons tomato paste
- Salt and freshly ground black pepper

Melt the butter in a wide-bottomed, medium saucepan over medium heat. Add the onions, carrot, celery, and thyme. Sauté over medium heat until vegetables are soft and caramelized, about 30 minutes, stirring occasionally.

Add the wine and reduce over high heat until the liquid forms a glaze, about 7 minutes.

Deglaze as you add the stocks and the tomato paste and reduce by half. Season to taste with salt and pepper.

Using a hand blender, purée the gravy to a smooth consistency (or pour the gravy into a regular blender). If you wish an even smoother texture, pour the gravy into a medium-fine strainer and press the solids through using a wooden spoon.

BROWNIE PUDDING CAKE

Serves 8

America's love affair with chocolate continues unabated. Here is a good, old-fashioned chocolate feast—moist, gooey, and delicious.

- 1 cup all-purpose flour
- ⅔ cup unsweetened cocoa powder
- ¾ teaspoon baking powder
- ¾ teaspoon salt
- 1 cup granulated sugar
- 6 tablespoons (¾ stick) unsalted butter, melted and cooled
- ½ cup heavy cream
- 2 eggs
- 1 teaspoon vanilla
- 1⅓ cups boiling water
- ¾ cup golden brown sugar, packed

Preheat the oven to 350°F. Into a medium bowl, sift together the flour, ⅓ cup of the cocoa powder, the baking powder, and salt; set aside.

In a large bowl, using an electric hand mixer, beat together the granulated sugar, butter, cream, eggs, and vanilla. Add the flour mixture and beat on low speed until just combined. Spread the batter evenly in an ungreased 8-inch square baking pan; set aside.

In another bowl, whisk together the remaining ⅓ cup cocoa powder, the boiling water, and brown sugar; pour this mixture over the batter. Bake about 35 minutes or until a cake tester or toothpick inserted into the center comes out with crumbs adhering to it. Serve warm, topped with vanilla or coffee ice cream, if desired.

A Chicago Treat

In 1977, Eli Schulman decided he wanted to do something special for customers at his popular Eli's The Place for Steak restaurant in Chicago. He developed two rich cheesecakes, "original plain" and chocolate chip, which quickly became the restaurant's signature desserts. Word quickly spread among cheesecake-aholics, and by 1980 Eli's began shipping its prized desserts far and wide. Four years later, after Eli's death, his son, Mark Schulman, stepped in to start a separate cheesecake company. Production rose from two hundred cakes per day to the current nine thousand. "Original plain" remains the most popular for cheesecake purists (President Clinton and Frank Sinatra among them), but there are plenty of new, irresistible flavors to choose from, including white chocolate macadamia, cherry vanilla, southern mud pie, and raspberry swirl. Holiday favorites include eggnog, pumpkin, peppermint twist, and Irish mint. For a complete catalog, or to order Eli's Chicago's Finest Cheesecake, call 800-999-8300.

BAKED APPLES WITH CREAM CHEESE, WALNUTS AND CURRANTS, WITH AN APPLE CIDER GLAZE
ADAPTED FROM A RECIPE BY BRAD OGDEN, LARK CREEK INN, LARKSPUR, CALIFORNIA

Serves 4

Chef Ogden cooks in California but hails from Traverse City, Michigan. His roots give him 100 percent Heartland credentials. These are great for breakfast or as an autumn dessert.

- 1½ cups apple cider
- ⅓ cup orange juice
- 5 tablespoons light brown sugar, packed
- 2½ tablespoons lemon juice
- ⅛ teaspoon cinnamon
- 3 tablespoons cream cheese, softened
- 3 tablespoons chopped toasted walnuts

- 1 tablespoon currants
- 1½ teaspoons maple syrup
- 4 baking apples, such as Granny Smith or Winesap
- 2 teaspoons cold water
- 1 teaspoon cornstarch

Preheat the oven to 400°F. In a small saucepan, combine the cider, orange juice, 2 tablespoons of the sugar, the lemon juice, and the cinnamon over high heat. Bring to a boil and reduce the liquid by half, stirring frequently. Remove from the heat and set aside.

In a small bowl, combine the cream cheese, walnuts, currants, maple syrup, and the remaining 3 tablespoons of sugar. Mix well.

Peel each apple ⅓ of the way down from the top and core, leaving the bottom intact so that the cheese mixture does not seep out while baking. Fill the apples with the cheese mixture. Place the filled apples in an 8-inch square baking dish. Pour the cider mixture over the apples. Bake for about 30 minutes or until tender, basting occasionally with the cider mixture. Remove the dish from the oven. Place the apples on a warm platter, reserving the liquid in the dish. Cover the apples loosely with aluminum foil and set aside.

Meanwhile, in a small bowl, whisk together the water and cornstarch. Pour the cider mixture from the baking dish into a small saucepan and place over medium heat. Whisk in the cornstarch mixture and cook, whisking constantly, until thickened and glossy looking, about 1½ minutes.

To serve, place each apple on a small plate and drizzle with some of the glaze.

American Spoon Foods

American Spoon Foods opened its first store in Petoskey, Michigan, to showcase the regional foods of the area. The brainchild of Justin Rashid and Chef Larry Forgione (An American Place in New York), this delightful company has grown to include three more retail stores in Michigan, one in New York, and a successful mail-order catalog.

All the Spoon Foods products have a wonderful, homespun feel. Back in the old days, farm families would preserve summer fruits to add welcome flavor in the long, cold winter months. Chef Forgione has masterfully revived this tradition with a collection of jams, jellies, preserves, and butters. Sample the sour cherry, Damson plum, or wild blackberry preserves and his cherry, pumpkin, and apple butters. American Spoon Foods also features such regional favorites as black walnuts, wild rice, and dried Michigan morels. American Spoon Foods: 1668 Clarion Ave. / P.O. Box 566, Petoskey, Michigan, 49770. 800-222-5886. Fax: 800-647-2512.

PENNSYLVANIA DUTCH SOUR CREAM COFFEE CAKE

Makes one 9-inch cake (8-12 servings)

The idea of eating sweet cakes with coffee is an invention that was brought to America by immigrants from middle Europe. This version is lovely and very easy to make.

- 1½ cups sour cream
- 1 cup granulated sugar
- 1 egg
- ½ cup dried cranberries
- ½ cup chopped dried cherries
- ½ cup chopped dried apples
- 2 cups all-purpose flour
- 2 teaspoons baking powder
- ½ teaspoon salt
- 1 cup coarsely chopped black *or* regular walnuts
- ½ cup light brown sugar, packed
- 1 teaspoon cinnamon
- ⅓ cup unsalted butter

Preheat the oven to 350°F. Grease a 9-inch springform pan and set it aside.

In a large bowl, whisk together the sour cream, granulated sugar, and egg. Stir in the dried cranberries, cherries, and apples.

In a small bowl, combine the flour, baking powder, and salt. Add to the sour cream mixture and stir until thoroughly combined. Scrape batter into the prepared pan. Smooth the surface and sprinkle evenly with the walnuts, brown sugar, and cinnamon; dot with the butter. Bake about 1 hour or until a cake tester or toothpick inserted into the center comes out clean. Let cool in the pan for 10 minutes, then unmold and serve, cut into wedges. If desired, serve with butter and jam.

BAKED PERSIMMON AND BLACK WALNUT PUDDING

ADAPTED FROM A RECIPE BY LARRY FORGIONE, AN AMERICAN PLACE, NEW YORK

Serves 6

Persimmons became popular in the 1860s when Logan Martin, who eventually became known as "Persimmon" Martin, began to raise them commercially in southern Indiana. They have become a fall standard all over the country, and this Heartland dessert is a good choice for Thanksgiving.

- 1 cup persimmon purée (pulp of ripe persimmons puréed in a processor or blender)
- 1⅔ cups buttermilk
- 1 cup plus 1 tablespoon sugar
- 3 tablespoons unsalted butter, melted
- 2 eggs
- 1⅓ cups all-purpose flour
- 1 teaspoon baking soda
- 1 teaspoon baking powder
- ½ teaspoon cinnamon
- ½ teaspoon ground nutmeg
- ¼ teaspoon salt
- ½ cup toasted, finely chopped, black *or* regular walnuts

Preheat the oven to 350°F. Lightly grease a 2-quart soufflé dish and sprinkle in a little sugar to coat the bottom and sides. Set aside.

In a large bowl, beat together the persimmon purée and buttermilk until smooth. Stir in 1 cup of the sugar and 2 tablespoons of the melted butter. Add the eggs and beat until smooth.

Sift together the flour, baking soda, baking powder, cinnamon, nutmeg, and salt. Add to the persimmon mixture, a little at a time, beating well after each addition. Stir in the walnuts.

Pour the pudding mixture into the prepared dish and place in a larger pan. Fill the pan with enough water to reach halfway up the sides of the soufflé dish. Bake in the center of the oven for 55 minutes or until a cake tester or toothpick inserted into the pudding's center comes out clean. Remove from the oven and brush with the remaining 1 tablespoon of butter and sprinkle with the remaining 1 tablespoon of sugar. Serve warm, with sweetened whipped cream, if desired.

The Northwest

From crystal rivers splashing with silver fish to endless forests densely populated with game and carpeted with mushrooms, the Northwest offers a generous culinary landscape. Wild berries hang from brambles along quiet country roads. Clams and oysters cluster in the estuaries along the seashore, one low tide away from discovery. With all this bounty, the Pacific Northwest might be characterized as one of the world's largest open-air markets.

Native Americans were the first to appreciate the abundance of local ingredients. Location dictated diet, and those living along the coast depended heavily on seafood, especially salmon. The Skagit, Wishram, and Clackamas were just a few of the tribes that structured their life around the salmon. Many of their religious ceremonies centered on the spawning cycle of the fish—the remarkably heroic upriver journey the salmon take each year to lay thousands of eggs. Today in Seattle, Native Americans still organize an annual salmon homecoming that includes dancing, crafts, and storytelling.

Early Settlement

No one ethnic tradition dominates the culinary style of the Northwest. Around the beginning of the nineteenth century, Spanish and English attempts at settlement in the area failed. The first successful immigrant communities were established in the 1840s when wagon trains arrived from Independence, Missouri. Spurred on by the reports of explorers Lewis and Clark, as well as accounts from trappers and traders, the pioneers came along the Oregon trail expecting a frontier rich in natural resources.

Indeed, they found a plethora of raw ingredients, but they were ill-equipped to exploit them. Thanks to the kindness of native inhabitants, the settlers learned what was edible and how to pick berries, smoke fish, shuck oysters, and forage for mushrooms.

It didn't take long for the settlers to apply their culinary traditions to their new home. A German farm tradition developed in eastern Washington, where vast wheat fields were planted on the semiarid land between the Cascade and Rocky Mountains. Shipments of flour sent across the mountains supplied bread (often frozen so hard it was cut with a hatchet) to the Klondike miners in Alaska. Griddlecakes, often garnished with berries, remain a popular Northwest favorite.

Scandinavian dairy farmers cleared pastureland in the fertile inland valleys between the Coastal Ranges and the Cascades. Cows grazing on the hillside grass produced large amounts of exceedingly pure milk, and northwestern cheesemakers have earned national attention for Oregon blue, Yakima Valley Gouda, Cougar Gold, and Tillamook cheddar.

Basque sheepherders settled in Idaho, Oregon, and eastern Washington, tending their flocks and establishing scattered communities throughout the region. Unlike other lamb-producers who supplemented their animals' diets with corn, the lush pastures of the Northeast allowed the Basques to grass-feed their sheep. Today, lamb remains a more important ingredient than beef in Northwest cooking.

Asian Quality Standards

In the 1850s, Chinese immigrants arrived to work in the lumber and railroad camps, where they often served as cooks. While the cooks brought an Asian flavor to the food, their commitment to high quality standards was more significant. These standards raised the expectations of working men in the region, who not only demanded a lot of food, but expected it to be good. "There was plenty of work at the time," observes Christina Orchid of Christina's Restaurant on Orcas Island, "so if the food in one camp wasn't good, they would work down the street."

Japanese immigrants arrived not long after the Chinese. Over the ensuing years, the Japanese introduced their native Pacific oysters and Manila, or Japanese littleneck, clams. These foods have become staples of the region's cuisine. More recently, immigrants from Southeast Asia have begun to arrive. Their influence, like other Asian groups, is seen mainly in isolated dishes.

A Diverse Landscape

The geography in the Pacific Northwest is perhaps more varied than any other region in America. The central dividing feature is the Cascade mountain range, which runs north-south. To the east, the climate is arid and semiarid, irrigated for agriculture with snowmelt from the mountains and from dam projects on the Columbia River.

Along the edge of eastern Washington and western Idaho lies an area known as the Palouse (puh-LOOZ). Crops of wheat are rotated with peas and lentils, legumes that enrich the soil. Much of the nation's lentil crop comes from this fifty-mile stretch of land, and 90 percent of soft, white winter wheat comes from the Palouse and surrounding areas.

West across the massive Columbia River plateau is the Yakima Valley, an active agricultural area that is best known for its flavorful asparagus. Northwest cooks will tell you that the cool temperatures of the Yakima Valley produce asparagus that is superior to crops from Mexico and California. Each spring, hordes of asparagus enthusiasts arrive to gather wild shoots along the irrigation canals.

Across the Cascades are the fertile western lowlands, coursed by rivers descending from the mountains. For the best pears grown in the United States, you need look no further than the Hood River Valley. This brief river snakes its way from Oregon's snowy Mt. Hood toward the Washington border, where it intersects with the mighty Columbia River Gorge.

But the Hood River Valley is often overshadowed by the giant of Oregon agriculture: the Willamette Valley (pronounced wil-AAH-met, differentiating it from the New England WILL-a-met). Nestled between the Cascades and Coast Ranges south of Eugene, the Willamette Valley yields a wide variety of fruits, hazelnuts, dairy, vegetables, berries, and wine grapes.

Though the Coast Ranges rise no more than 2,000 feet at any point, this is enough to drain the clouds that come in from the Pacific, creating the area's characteristic rainy climate. Writing about the region, Tobias Wolff once remarked, "It's either raining, clearing, or about to rain," and his observation certainly seems true. The high precipitation supports coniferous forests along the coastal inlets, and many varieties of mushroom thrive in these conditions, as do elk, deer, and game birds.

Along the Pacific coastline, rivers and inlets lend their names to the region's trademark fish and shellfish. The Columbia, Rogue, Copper, and Yukon Rivers host phenomenal runs of steelhead and salmon, which are often sold or served under the name of where they were caught. Pacific oysters, are also known by their places of origin, such as Shoalwater, Quilcene, and Canterbury.

Perhaps the best known oyster bed is in Willapa Bay, a large estuary in southern Washington. The native Olympia was farmed nearly to extinction here in the nineteenth century. Today the Japanese Pacific oyster dominates Willapa Bay, though Olympia and another Japanese oyster, the Kumamoto, are becoming more available.

Mussels and crabs flourish, too, along the Washington and Oregon coast. Penn Cove Mussels on Whidbey Island in Puget Sound is the nation's oldest mussel farm. The nearby Whidbey Island Inn is so enamored of this blue-black delicacy, that it holds an annual mussel festival.

A hop across the Admiralty Inlet from Whidbey Island, on the Olympic Peninsula, is the town of Dungeness, home to the popular crab of the same name. Though the crustacean lives along much of the coast from Northern California to Alaska, Dungeness is where it was first commercially harvested.

A tour through the Northwest's culinary landscape continues offshore, where fisherman bring in shiny halibut, flounder, sturgeon, and salmon.

The Rediscovery of Regional Pride

Contemporary Northwest chefs are building their cuisine on foundations of the past. They are rediscovering traditions that have been ignored for a long time. In the 1970s and early 1980s, people looked to the outside for inspiration, largely reacting to trends from New York and California. With each steakhouse that opened, regional pride sank a little lower. But within the past decade, there has been a revival of interest in Northwest foods.

This rediscovery extends to both home cooks and professional chefs. Northwesterners are becoming more knowledgeable about local ingredients. They know the best river runs for fish, the best bays for clam digs, the difference between line and net caught fish. "There is regional pride," says Ms. Orchid, "particularly over where the food comes from."

So what can you expect in today's Northwest cooking? Most of the dishes adhere to the current trend toward lighter, more healthful creations. Presentation of the food is straightforward. You won't find towering spires of potatoes or precious arrangements of meats.

Freshness is an imperative. "We're not trying to do things out of season," notes Jerry Traunfeld of the Herbfarm. And despite the vast array of ingredients in the Northwest, the cooking is graced by a harmony of seasonal flavors. Whether it is Bartlett pears stuffed with cheese and hazelnuts, or chicken with asparagus and morels, the foods of the Northwest seem to come together in a natural, uncomplicated way. And in a quiet way, the chefs of the Northwest are building a memorable cuisine from an extensive natural bounty.

Oregon Wines

The Oregon wine industry has managed a rather extraordinary feat. Despite low production levels (about 6,000 total acres of vines, compared to California's 325,000 acres) the state has attracted investors from some of Europe's foremost estates and has consistently placed at the top of competition results. The reason is pinot noir—a notoriously temperamental grape that has an almost magical affinity for Oregon soils.

Pinot noir is the predominant red grape of Burgundy, where, at its best, it can yield wines of extraordinary richness and complexity. Unfortunately, pinot noir can fail just as magnificently as it succeeds. California vintners have long been puzzled by the grape, and only a few producers have achieved consistently first-rate results.

But Oregon wineries have had success with pinot noir from their earliest efforts. As in Burgundy, the cool Oregon climate allows the fruit to mature gradually. Oregon pinot noir is typically a medium-bodied wine, with bright cherry flavors and high acidity. These are wines that win you over with their charm, not their brawn.

Ironically, while the difficult pinot noir has come naturally to Oregon vintners, they have not achieved the same results with the usually more adaptable chardonnay grape. Chardonnay wines from Oregon tend to be firm and austere, lacking the explosive fruit and toasty, buttery depth that is California's trademark.

In terms of acreage the number three grape in Oregon is riesling, the noble grape of Germany. In the United States, riesling suffers from something of an image problem. First of all, there is some name confusion: Oregon vintners have adopted the name "white" riesling, which is the same variety that some people call "Johannisberg" riesling, and which is often called just plain "riesling." In addition, the grape is made in a range of sugar levels, from dry to honey sweet. When vinified dry, Oregon white riesling can have a steely, crisp flavor that is a nice match for shellfish.

A few other grapes have generated interest in Oregon, most notably pinot gris. This white grape (known as pinot grigio in Italy) is related to pinot noir, and succeeds in Oregon for many of the same reasons. It has the added marketing appeal of being somewhat rare and unique. This assertive, aromatic grape has the potential to surpass chardonnay as the state's leading white grape.

Apart from one large estate along the Columbia River, winegrowing in Oregon is confined primarily to the western part of the state, in the fertile river valleys that lie between the Coastal Ranges and the Cascades. Primary among these locations is the Willamette Valley, which stretches 170 miles from the Columbia River in the north to south of Eugene.

The modern history of Willamette Valley winemaking begins with a California-educated oenologist named David Lett. After careful studies, he determined the northern Willamette area was perfectly suited for the cultivation of pinot noir. At the time, most of the land was given to fruit orchards and hazelnut trees. Lett planted a vineyard in 1966 and built a winery near McMinnville in a converted turkey-processing plant.

His 1975 Eyrie Vineyards pinot noir gained notoriety when it beat many top burgundies in a pair of French-sponsored tastings. The event was a watershed for the Willamette Valley, and investors began to look seriously at this previously little-known region. Among those who took an interest was Robert Drouhin of the venerable Burgundian firm, Maison Joseph Drouhin. He is now producing pinot noir at Domaine Drouhin, situated near Lett's vineyard.

In the late 1970s and early 1980s, other vintners followed the lead of Eyrie Vineyards. Their goal was to produce premium wines in small quantities. The wineries established in the Willamette Valley during this time have set the quality standards for Oregon as a whole. Adelsheim Vineyards, Argyle, Amity Vineyards, Elk Cove Vineyards, Eola Hills Wine Cellars, Knudsen-Erath Winery, Montinore Vineyards, Panther Creek Cellars, Ponzi Vineyards, Rex Hill Vineyards, and Yamhill Vineyards are a few names to watch. The balance of these will not produce more than 10,000 cases a year.

Due south of the Willamette Valley is the Umpqua Valley, which extends a full seventy miles before ending at the Klamath Mountains. Though it contains only a handful of producers, the Umpqua is home to the first winery to feature European varietals after Prohibition. Hillcrest Vineyard was founded in 1961 by Richard Sommer, and from the outset, his emphasis has been riesling and cabernet. While other vintners cashed in on the pinot noir boom, Hillcrest's growth was limited by two grapes that never really took off. But the vineyard contains some of the most mature vines in the state, and it has the potential for yielding distinguished wines.

The climate in the Umpqua is similar to the Willamette, though with slightly less rain and more sunshine. The six wineries at latest count are clustered around the town of Roseburg. Scott Henry's Henry Estate has provided some of the finest Umpqua Valley wines, especially an aromatic gewürztraminer and a pleasant, if inconsistent, pinot noir.

Finally, tucked along the California border is the Rogue Valley where there are a few scattered winemaking outposts. The warm climate has shown potential for some interesting cabernet and merlot wines, but the isolated setting makes it unlikely that this area will ever develop into a major wine region. The best known producer is Valley View Vineyards.

The Northwest Pantry

APPLES

If there's one place on earth where it is easy to have an apple a day, it's Washington State. The apple growers in the Evergreen State produce the nation's largest supply of Red and Golden Delicious apples, America's most popular eating apple (although not its most flavorful). Other varieties, once rare in the state, have been added. Orchards now grow significant numbers of McIntosh, Rome Beauty, Spartan, Pippins, Gravenstein, and Jonathan apples.

BLUEBERRIES

The region's acidic soils and cool summers are ideal for blueberries, but farmers were reluctant to plant these bushes because it takes so long for a field to reach maximum productivity. Nevertheless, an industry begun in the 1960s has flourished, and today, the Northwest ranks second to New England in production.

CANEBERRIES

Each summer there is a berry explosion in the temperate climate and rolling hills of the Northwest. Caneberries are the many varieties that grow in clusters on cane-like branches. Some of the better known go by the following names.

Blackberries: Growing in wild tangles along roadsides, mountain paths, and coastal bluffs, native blackberries are the most outward sign of the region's gustatory generosity. The large Himalayan is the most prolific. Olallie blackberries are slightly smaller, with sweet, assertive flavors. Salmonberries, tayberries, and thimbleberries are a few other blackberry types.

Boysenberries: This blackberry-raspberry cross yields large, juicy, and tart fruit that's great for pies. Look for a deep maroon color.

Gooseberries: A round, green berry with tart fruit. Frequently used in Asian dishes.

Huckleberries: This sweet, musky, blue fruit grows at higher elevations. The red, tart variety is found in the Puget Sound lowlands.

Lingonberries: A tart, red berry used for Swedish pancakes. Lingonberries grow in alpine meadows and along tundra slopes.

Loganberries: A red raspberry–wild blackberry cross that is highly acidic. Balance the tart loganberries with sweeter berries in recipes or use lots of sugar.

Marionberries: Developed in Marion County, Oregon, this variety is a cross between wild and domestic blackberries. This aromatic berry has a nice balance of acid and sugar and is great for pies.

CLAMS

Who says there are no buried treasures anymore? The muddy tidelands of Oregon, Washington, and British Columbia are filled with dozens of clam varieties nestled beneath the surface. The most popular ones include: butter clams, razor, geoduck (GOOEY-duck, the largest of the American bivalves known as *mirugai* by Japanese sushi customers), Japanese little-neck (also called Manila), native littleneck, horseneck, surf, and steamer. Clams taste best when they're spawning, in the early summer. Look for tightly closed shells. They'll open after about six minutes of steaming. Be careful, clams toughen if overcooked.

DUNGENESS CRAB

Named after the town of Dungeness, on the Olympic Peninsula, where this popular hard-shell crab was first commercially harvested. Their usual weight ranges from 1½ to 3½ pounds. You'll have to venture to the West Coast (they are harvested from Northern California up into Canada) to taste fresh Dungeness; they're only shipped frozen to other parts of the United States. Expect a delicate, faintly sweet flavor, and succulent texture.

HALIBUT

The largest species in the flounder family, this flat, bug-eyed fish can grow to more than 200 pounds and live more than 150 years. The lean, white, firm meat breaks, when cooked, into big flakes. Usually available precut into steaks, halibut cheeks are a delicacy.

HAZELNUTS

High in calories, protein, and other

nutrients, the flavorful round nuts grown in Oregon's Willamette Valley, account for most of the U.S. crop. A versatile ingredient, hazelnuts go excellently with pears, apples, cheeses, chocolates, poultry, and port.

GAME BIRDS

These wild birds are more sinewy, more intensely flavored, and leaner than chicken. They exist in great numbers in the northwestern woods and on local farms:

Quail: The smallest wild or domesticated game bird has tender, mild-flavored meat.

Squab: Dark, gamey meat.

Poussin: A French hybrid chicken, similar to cornish game hen in size and intensity of flavor.

Chukar: Red-legged grouse, also sold as partridge.

Pheasant: Range birds have a leaner texture and wilder taste than pen-raised. They can be dry and stringy if overcooked.

Guinea hen: Sometimes called prairie chicken, this bird is dark-fleshed and gamey, similar to pheasant in taste.

Duck: Wild Northwest duck is much leaner than commercially raised birds.

Goose: Largest of the wild birds. The smaller the goose, the more likely it will tender.

MUSHROOMS

Mushroom hunting is popular in the Northwest, and the pickings are excellent in the fall. The bounty includes chanterelles, white oysters, morels, matsutake, shiitake, chicken of the woods, king boletes, and the white Oregon Truffle.

MUSSELS

Washington blue mussels have always gotten a raw deal when compared to their bivalve relatives, but they are among the best in the country. They are undoubtedly a delicacy—plump and tender with fine meat. Penn Cove in Puget Sound is a leading source of farmed mussels. Only within the last decade or two have mussels started appearing in Northwest fish markets and restaurants.

OYSTERS

The elegant, delicate, delicious oysters from America's west coast (particularly from Washington) are the best in the country. There are three basic types in the Northwest: Pacific (brought from Japan in the 1920s), native Olympia (sometimes called native Pacific), and the European flat type (belon). The only oyster indigenous to the West Coast, the Olympia is a tiny oyster with mild flavor and a slightly metallic aftertaste. The Pacific oyster is most common now and is often marketed under the name of the bay from which it came, reflecting distinct flavor nuances.

PEARS

Summer pears of the region include Bartlett (popular and versatile, the sweet and juicy flesh is suited to baking, canning, or eating raw) and Red Bartlett (less common than the golden variety, though plantings have increased in recent years). In winter the region produces: Comice (juiciest of all pears, bruises easily), Anjou (buttery flesh can be enjoyed as a fresh dessert pear), Bosc (sweetest pear, fragrant, with fine texture), Seckel (tiny, best when pickled or in preserves), and the Forelle (tart flavor, though its appealing yellow color with red freckling when ripe makes it a good decorative choice).

RAINBOW TROUT

The best of these bright, colorful fish come from the coldest waters. They should be bled and iced immediately. Don't scale trout, and always use simple flavorings that don't mask the delicate and distinctive flavor. Steelhead is a sea-dwelling rainbow trout that returns upriver to breed.

RHUBARB

Not many comestibles have as peculiar a history as rhubarb. Originally classified as a vegetable, its status was officially changed by the U.S. Department of Agriculture to fruit in 1954. The decision was based on usage, because this tart ingredient is perfect for pies, jams, and sweets. Look for firm, crisp stalks that are still thin. The thicker, more mature stalks tend to be too acidic. Much of the U.S. crop is grown in Washington's Puyallup Valley in the shadow of Mt. Rainier.

SALMON

The definitive Northwest ingredient. Line caught is the best, bled and gutted immediately. There are four varieties. King, or Chinook, is the largest of the Pacific salmon, weighing up to 120 pounds. A high oil content makes it good for smoking. King has the most intense flavor of all the salmon. Sockeye, or Red, with a deep red flesh and a firm texture, is best when ovenbroiled or baked. Coho, or Silver, has a pastel salmon color when cooked and is prone to rot so it must be gutted immediately. Larger fish have firmer flesh that tears, rather than flaking. On the bottom rung of the salmon hierarchy is Chum, a late-run salmon. Skin color reflects the oil level in the flesh. Look for silvery skin. Bright pink-colored flesh is the best; paler color indicates less flavor. Chum is often used for canning.

TILLAMOOK CHEESE

The green valleys of Tillamook County, Oregon, have been home to dairy herds for more than a hundred years. The pristine conditions led to an overabundance of milk, and farmers soon began converting the surfeit into butter. By the 1890s, they started experimenting with cheese production, and the industry took an immediate leap forward when Canadian cheesemaker Peter McIntosh came to the area in 1894 to teach the latest production techniques. Fifteen years later, ten dairies banded together to further the goals and quality standards established by McIntosh. They called their organization the Tillamook County Creamery Association, and from the beginning the name has stood among the country's finest cheeses.

Quality milk is the most important factor in cheesemaking, according to Tillamook cheesemaster Ed Yates. Free-range grazing, cool temperatures, and high quality standards in Tillamook ensure the best milk. The cheese is made at a centralized, modern facility built in the 1960s to compete with the major national producers.

Tillamook is best known for its sharp cheddars. Made from raw milk, the cheese ages smooth and soft and is ideally served at room temperature with Northwest fruits. Many chefs in the area bake with Tillamook because it melts more smoothly than other cheddars.

VENISON

Both wild and farmed, this dense, lean meat can be frozen for a year without losing its flavor. Wild venison is gamey and should be marinated in an acidic liquid such as red wine for a day or so.

WALLA WALLA ONIONS

Milder than most onions because they lack the sulfurous compounds that give others pungency and sharpness, Walla Wallas can be eaten raw on sandwiches or in salads. The onions have a high water content, and they don't keep well.

Washington Wines

Contrary to Washington's rain-soaked image, the early stumbling block to viticulture in the state was a lack of water. The vast plateau east of the Cascades, with its warm, dry climate and workable soils was perfect for growing grapes if irrigation could be provided. The Columbia River dam projects in the 1930s opened the necessary floodgates, and grape vines sprang up alongside a host of other crops.

The first grapes to be planted were the indigenous varieties (vitis labrusca), most notably concord. This musky, ink-dark grape is often used for juice and sacramental wine. In the 1930s and 1940s, the large Pomerelle and Nawico companies made sweet, fortified wines from concord grapes. These heady, coarse wines appealed to workers in the lumber and mining camps, along with residents of Seattle's famed Skid Row. Sales soared among the down and out.

It wasn't until the mid-1950s that Washington began to inch toward premium wine production. The Pomerelle and Nawico companies merged in 1954 to form American Wine Growers. Under this new banner, European varietals were planted and vinified as table wine.

A few years later, a group of amateur winemakers from the University of Washington formed Associated Vintners to promote quality wines. They planted a vineyard in the Yakima Valley with chardonnay, pinot noir, gewürztraminer, and cabernet sauvignon grapes. By 1967, the members began producing commercial wines. The early efforts showed mixed results, with gewürztraminers holding the most promise.

It was a homemade gewürztraminer that caught the attention of André Tchelistcheff, the elder statesman of California winemaking. Sufficiently impressed, he agreed to act as a consultant for the burgeoning American Wine Company. The firm mounted an aggressive planting program, focused on a large site in the Columbia Valley near Richland. All the wines were made under the Chateau Ste. Michelle label.

After erratic initial vintages, Chateau Ste. Michelle received a huge boost in 1974, when it was bought out by Stimson Lane, the wine and spirits division of the U.S. Tobacco Company. The influx of capital brought a surge in production and quality, along with marketing savvy that would bring the wines to a national audience.

Chateau Ste. Michelle remains the giant in Washington winemaking, producing an excellent line of riesling, cabernet, merlot, and chardonnay. Their sister-operation, Columbia Crest, was originally intended as a jug-wine facility but has become a legitimate varietal producer in its own right. The Stimson Lane properties opened the way for other Northwest wineries to venture beyond their local markets, and ambitious, midsize wineries began to spring up in the 1970s and 1980s.

Most of these companies built their programs around riesling, a late-ripening grape that thrives in the cool fall months of the Yakima and Columbia Valleys. The early wines, whether vinified dry or sweet, displayed a lot of forward fruit and crisp acid. Riesling often succumbs to either a flabby or a thin style, but Washington manages to yield wines that are fresh and full. Unfortunately, when riesling simply failed to capture a wide market, many vintners switched to chardonnay or reverted to dull, uninspired rieslings, though there are still a few vintners who have stuck by the grape. The best examples currently are from the Hogue Cellars, Chateau Ste. Michelle, and Columbia Crest.

Cabernet sauvignon grows well through most of eastern Washington, though fans of California cabernet may not recognize it as the same grape. While Napa and Sonoma are known for explosive, plummy fruit, the Washington style is closer to a Bordeaux claret—herby and angular in youth though capable of great complexity. Washington cabernet invariably suffers from comparisons to California, a problem compounded by a few inconsistent producers.

Merlot may ultimately be the grape of the future in Washington. Initially planted for blending with cabernet, merlot has become a popular varietal choice because of its soft texture and pleasant fruity taste. Washington vintners have managed a lush, appealing style that is immediately approachable. Plantings are on the rise.

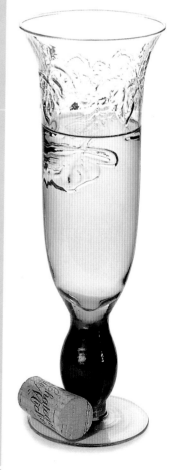

The Recipes

WILLAPA BAY KUMAMOTO OYSTERS WITH FRESH SALSA

ADAPTED FROM A RECIPE BY ANN KISCHNER, THE SHOALWATER, SEAVIEW, WASHINGTON

Makes 2 cups

Salsa has replaced ketchup as the American condiment of choice. Although it derives from the Sunbelt, salsa has become popular in every region of the country. In the Northwest, where the nation's best oysters are farmed, salsa is used instead of heavy cocktail sauce. Here is a superb version from one of the Seattle area's best restaurants.

- 2 tomatoes, peeled, seeded and finely chopped
- ¼ large red bell pepper, minced
- ¼ large red onion, finely chopped
- 1 green onion (scallion), sliced
- 2 tablespoons finely chopped fresh cilantro
- 4 teaspoons tomato paste
- 4 teaspoons white wine vinegar
- 2 cloves garlic, minced
- ½ jalapeño pepper, minced
- 2 teaspoons fresh squeezed lemon juice
- ½ teaspoon ground cumin
- ½ teaspoon sugar
- ½ teaspoon freshly ground pepper
- ¼ teaspoon ground coriander
- ¼ teaspoon salt
- Dash of hot pepper sauce
- 3 dozen Kumamoto oysters, on the half shell

In a small bowl, mix all the ingredients except the oysters. Spoon ½ teaspoon of salsa on top of each oyster. This salsa will keep in the refrigerator for two weeks. It is also great with chips and on salads.

CAULIFLOWER SOUP WITH COUGAR GOLD CHEDDAR AND TOASTED HAZELNUTS

Serves 8

This hearty, extremely lovely soup combines three Northwest ingredients: cauliflower, hazelnuts, and Cougar Gold, a rich, sharp cheddar cheese similar to Tillamook that was developed and is sold by Washington State University. It melts beautifully.

- 2 tablespoons unsalted butter
- 2 leeks, halved lengthwise, cleaned, and chopped
- 1 onion, chopped
- 1 (1-pound) head cauliflower, cut into florets
- 2 carrots, chopped
- 1 quart chicken stock
- 1 cup half-and-half (light cream)
- Salt and freshly ground black pepper
- 1 cup (4 ounces) shredded Cougar Gold *or* Tillamook cheddar cheese
- ½ cup chopped toasted hazelnuts

Melt the butter in a medium skillet over medium heat. Add the leeks and onion and sauté, stirring occasionally, for 8 minutes.

Place the leek-onion mixture, cauliflower, carrots, and stock in a Dutch oven. Bring to a boil, reduce the heat, cover, and simmer for 20 minutes or until the vegetables are tender. In batches, purée the vegetable mixture in a blender. Return the puréed soup to the Dutch oven. Stir in the half-and-half. Season with salt and pepper.

Serve hot, sprinkled with the cheese and hazelnuts.

SMOKED TROUT AND DILL SPREAD

Makes 1 quart

The crisp, cold streams, rivers and lakes that are fed by the Cascade Mountains are full of fresh trout. There are also a number of trout farms that keep them well stocked. Smoking is a method of preservation that has been used in the Northwest for generations. It works particularly well with the delicate flavor of trout. This spread is always a big success at parties.

- 1 small red onion, quartered
- 4 smoked trout, skinned and crumbled
- 2 hard-cooked eggs, peeled
- 1 cup mayonnaise
- ¼ cup lemon juice
- 3 tablespoons chopped fresh dill
- 2 tablespoons prepared horseradish
- 1 tablespoon rinsed and drained capers
- 1 tablespoon Dijon-style mustard
- 1 tablespoon Worcestershire sauce
- 2 teaspoons grated lemon zest
- Hot pepper sauce
- Salt and freshly ground black pepper

Place the onion in the bowl of a food processor fitted with a metal blade. Pulse until finely chopped. Add all the remaining ingredients except the hot sauce, salt, and pepper. Process until the ingredients form a smooth spread. Season to taste with the hot sauce, salt, and pepper. Cover and refrigerate until ready to use. This spread will keep up to a week, covered and refrigerated.

James Beard

James Beard, whose epicurean teachings have changed the way thousands of Americans eat, was a product of the Pacific Northwest. Born in Portland, Oregon, he was deeply influenced by the ingredients of the region and the cooking style of his parents and their Chinese cook. His father, a skilled cook, brought Olympia oysters, Dungeness crab, Columbia River salmon, blackberries, and game to the Beard table.

James Beard's mother was English, and she ran a hotel in Portland that was well known for its dining rooms. Her tastes favored the traditional dishes of her upbringing. After several Italian and French chefs disappeared in search of Yukon gold, Mrs. Beard hired a Chinese cook named Let. Let was equally adept at preparing his native specialties and proper English dishes like crumpets and scones.

James Beard was blessed with remarkable taste memory. At age four, his father began taking him once a week to Portland restaurants, and a year later his mother took him to Paris, where he was introduced to French cuisine.

Though his culinary travels would later introduce him to a wide array of cuisines, Beard's palate would always remember the vibrant flavors of his youth in the Northwest, and he would immortalize many of the recipes in his famous cookbooks. Wild morels, huckleberries, Oregon cheddar, Gravenstein apples, razor clams—these were the foods that inspired America's foremost gourmet.

OREGON SPOT PRAWNS WITH LENTIL SALAD
ADAPTED FROM A RECIPE BY PHILIPPE BOULOT,
THE HEATHMAN HOTEL, PORTLAND, OREGON

Makes 6 appetizer servings

This lovely combination of local ingredients is pure comfort food.

- 1 ½ dozen Oregon spot prawns
- 6 tablespoons olive oil
- 5 tablespoons balsamic vinegar
- 2 tablespoons lemon juice
- 2 cloves garlic, minced
- Salt and freshly ground black pepper
- 1 cup French lentils

- 1 yellow onion, quartered
- 1 bay leaf
- ½ bunch of parsley, tops only
- 2 tomatoes, peeled, seeded, and diced
- 1 small red onion, finely diced
- 3 tablespoons chopped fresh basil

With kitchen shears, cut down the backs and through the shells of the prawns; place them in a shallow dish. Add 3 tablespoons of the olive oil, 1 tablespoon of the balsamic vinegar, the lemon juice, and garlic; season with salt and pepper. Toss to coat the prawns. Marinate at room temperature 1 hour.

Meanwhile, place the lentils, yellow onion, and bay leaf in a 2-quart saucepan. Add enough water to cover the lentils. Bring to a boil over high heat, reduce the heat, cover, and simmer about 20 minutes or until tender. Drain lentils and allow them to cool. Remove and discard the onion and bay leaf. Set aside.

In a blender or food processor, purée the parsley with the remaining 3 tablespoons of the olive oil and 2 tablespoons of the balsamic vinegar. Season with salt and pepper. Set aside.

In a medium bowl, combine the cooked lentils, the tomatoes, red onion, basil, ¼ cup of the parsley oil, and the remaining 2 tablespoons of balsamic vinegar. Correct seasoning with salt and pepper if needed and toss well. Cover and chill until ready to serve.

Prepare the grill. Remove the prawns from the marinade. Grill or broil the prawns until just opaque throughout, about 1½ minutes a side, basting occasionally with the marinade. Discard any remaining marinade.

For each serving, spoon ⅔ cup of the lentil salad onto a plate. Stand 3 prawns up against the lentils. Drizzle some of the remaining parsley oil over the prawns and lentils and serve immediately. NOTE: Reserve any remaining parsley oil for another use, such as in salad dressings or marinades.

SAUTÉED HALIBUT WITH WARM APPLE AND CRANBERRY COMPOTE

Serves 6

Halibut, the largest member of the flounder family, abounds in the cold Pacific waters off Washington and Alaska. This combination of fresh fish fillet and Northwest fruit is one of the best ways to serve this elegantly flavored, tender fish.

- ⅔ cup dried cranberries
- ½ cup Oregon apple brandy
- ½ cup (1 stick) unsalted butter
- 2 medium Walla Walla onions, cut into thin wedges
- 2 large Granny Smith apples, peeled, cored and sliced
- 4 large cloves garlic, minced
- 1 tablespoon lemon juice
- ½ teaspoon salt
- ½ teaspoon freshly ground black pepper
- 6 halibut fillets (6 ounces each)
- 1 egg, beaten with 1 tablespoon water
- All-purpose flour, for dredging
- 2 tablespoons olive oil

Place the cranberries and brandy in a small saucepan; bring to a boil. Remove from the heat and set aside.

Melt 6 tablespoons of the butter in a medium skillet over medium heat. Add the onions and sauté, stirring occasionally, for 10 minutes. Stir in the apples and garlic. Continue to sauté, stirring occasionally, for 10 more minutes or until the apples are soft and the onions are golden brown.

Stir in the cranberries with the brandy, and the lemon juice. Warm through. Season with about half of the salt and pepper. Remove from heat but keep warm.

Dip the fillets into the egg mixture and dredge in flour, shaking off any excess. Season lightly with the remaining salt and pepper.

Heat the oil and the remaining 2 tablespoons of butter in a large skillet (preferably nonstick) over medium-high heat. Add the fillets and sauté about 6 minutes or until golden brown and opaque. Turn them once during the process. Serve the fillets topped with the warm compote.

GRILLED SALMON WITH HAZELNUT BUTTER

Serves 4

This easy recipe combines two characteristic and complimentary Northwest ingredients. Flavored butters are an excellent way to add moisture and additional interest to foods that have been grilled.

- 4 (1-inch thick) salmon steaks (about ¾ pound each)
- Vegetable oil
- ½ cup (1 stick) unsalted butter, softened
- 6 tablespoons peeled, chopped, and toasted hazelnuts
- 2 tablespoons fresh lime juice
- 2 tablespoons snipped fresh chives
- ½ teaspoon salt
- A few grindings of black pepper

Prepare the grill. If you are using charcoal briquettes, they should be 3 to 4 inches from the grill surface.

Without damaging the steaks, remove as many bones as possible using tweezers or long-nosed pliers. Coat the steaks lightly with vegetable oil to prevent them from sticking to the grill.

Mix the butter, nuts, lime juice, chives, and seasonings well and place on a sheet of waxed paper. Roll into a log shape (about 1½ inches in diameter) and refrigerate.

When the fire is at its hottest, place the steaks on the grill. Cook for 5 minutes on each side. The salmon should be moist and rare on the inside.

Remove to warm plates and top with a ½-inch round slice of the hazelnut butter. Serve immediately.

GINGER-MARINATED DUCK BREASTS
WITH LINGONBERRY-CRANBERRY SAUCE

Serves 4

*The idea of combining game or other meat with local fruits is a Northwest specialty.
Here duck breast is combined with two of the region's famous berries.*

- 2 whole ducks, about 4½ pounds each
- 1½ cups dry red wine
- 6 tablespoons grated, peeled fresh ginger
- 3 tablespoons rice wine vinegar
- 2 tablespoons reduced-sodium soy sauce
- 2 tablespoons honey
- 3 tablespoons olive oil
- 2 shallots, minced
- 2 cloves garlic, minced
- 1 cup fresh *or* frozen cranberries
- ½ cup lingonberry preserves
- ¼ cup red currant jelly
- 3 tablespoons minced candied ginger
- Salt and freshly ground pepper

Wash the ducks and pat them dry. Remove the innards. Bone the ducks so that the breasts are removed with the skin attached. Reserve the duck carcasses for stock and the legs for another use. (Freeze if desired.)

Split the duck breasts to make 4 half breasts. Remove all visible fat from the undersides of the skin. Place the duck breasts in a shallow dish. Into the dish, add ½ cup of the wine, 4 tablespoons of the fresh ginger, 2 tablespoons of the rice wine vinegar, the soy sauce, and honey. Toss to coat and let marinate in refrigerator 2 hours.

To make the sauce: Heat the oil in a 2-quart saucepan over medium heat. Add the shallots and garlic. Sauté, stirring, for 2 minutes. Stir in the cranberries, lingonberry preserves, currant jelly, candied ginger, and the remaining 1 cup of wine and 1 tablespoon of rice wine vinegar. Bring to a boil, reduce the heat, and simmer until the sauce thickens slightly. Season with salt and pepper. Keep warm.

Preheat the broiler. Remove the duck breasts from the marinade, discarding the marinade. Broil the breast halves, skin-side down, 6 inches from the heat source for 6 minutes. Turn and broil 2 to 3 minutes more until medium-rare and the duck skin is crisp. Be careful not to burn the duck. (If necessary, lower the rack to slow the cooking process.)

To serve, cut the duck breasts into slices about ¼ inch thick on the diagonal. Place the slices in a fan shape on each plate and spoon the warm sauce over the duck.

ROAST DUCK WITH RED CURRANT SAUCE
ADAPTED FROM A RECIPE BY TOM DOUGLAS,
THE DAHLIA LOUNGE, SEATTLE, WASHINGTON

Serves 6

Considering how many chickens are consumed in the United States, ducks are seriously underutilized. They have so much more flavor than chicken. This combination of duck and fruit sauce is typically northwestern.

- 2 fresh or thawed frozen ducks, 4½ to 5 pounds each
- Salt and freshly ground black pepper
- 2 lemons, quartered
- 8 cloves garlic
- 2 tablespoons low-sodium soy sauce
- 2 tablespoons molasses
- 1½ quarts duck or chicken stock

- 1 pint fresh red currants (raspberries *or* blackberries may be substituted), puréed and strained
- 2 shallots, minced
- ¾ cup red currant jelly
- ½ cup (1 stick) unsalted butter
- 2 tablespoons crème de cassis

To prepare each duck for roasting: With poultry shears, cut off the wing tips, 2 joints from the end. Unfold the flap of skin at the neck opening and trim it so it is 1 inch long. (The skin shrinks as it cooks, so if you trim it too closely, the breast meat will be exposed. Too much neck skin, however, will make the duck fatty.) Pull out any visible lumps of fat from around the cavity opening. Retrieve all the parts from inside the cavity of the duck and reserve them for another use.

Season the ducks inside and out with salt and pepper. Stuff the cavities with the lemons and garlic. Let the birds sit for 30 minutes. (The salt dehydrates the skin a little bit and makes for crispier birds.)

Preheat the oven to 500°F. Place the ducks on a rack in a roasting pan. Mix together the soy sauce and molasses; brush this glaze evenly over the ducks. Roast the ducks for 30 minutes, brushing occasionally with the remainder of the glaze. Reduce the oven to 350°F and roast for 35 to 45 minutes more, or until the juices run clear. Let the ducks sit for 30 minutes before serving.

Meanwhile, make the sauce. Place the stock in a large saucepan over high heat and boil until reduced to 2 cups. Stir in the puréed fruit and shallots. Simmer for 30 minutes. Stir in the jelly, butter, and cassis. Whisk until butter is melted. Season with salt and pepper. Set aside and keep warm.

After the ducks have rested, carve each duck into 2 boneless breasts with wings attached and 2 legs with thighs, being careful not to tear the skin. Place 2 large skillets over medium-high heat. Add the duck pieces, skin-sides down, and cook until the skin is golden brown and crispy and more fat has been rendered. Serve on warm plates with the sauce on the side.

Chef Tom Douglas

Beginning with his work at the acclaimed Cafe Sport in Seattle, Chef Tom Douglas has helped to define the Northwest style of cooking. His regional menu at the Dahlia Lounge incorporates influences from Asia, Alaska, and Canada, drawing on local, seasonal ingredients.

Douglas began cooking at the Hotel DuPont in Wilmington, Delaware, in 1977. Moving west to Seattle, he worked at several jobs before getting back into the restaurant business at Cafe Sport in 1984. Five years later, he decided to open his own restaurant, The Dahlia Lounge, in the heart of downtown Seattle. It has quickly become a leading destination for Northwest cooking, earning recognition from The New York Times, *the* Los Angeles Times, Money, *and the* James Beard Foundation.

CHANTERELLE AND PORCINI BREAD PUDDING
ADAPTED FROM A RECIPE BY CHRISTINA ORCHID, CHRISTINA'S,
EASTSOUND, WASHINGTON

Serves 6-8

Chef Christina Orchid

Seattle native Christina Orchid spent childhood summers on the family farm on Orcas Island, where she gained an appreciation for many of the foods native to the Pacific Northwest. Later, while an art student, she worked on the family cattle ranch in eastern Washington in the cookhouse, preparing meals for forty-five family members, ranch hands, and visiting dignitaries.

After working in several restaurants, Chef Orchid returned to Orcas Island where she opened Christina's in 1980. Dedicated to creating a small regional restaurant, she persuaded local farmers and fishermen to supply her kitchen.

When not in the kitchen, Chef Orchid donates her time to countless culinary events and programs, including the Save Our Strength coalition to fight hunger. Christina's has been featured in Bon Appétit, *and Chef Orchid was named "Best of the Best" top chef of the region by* Pacific Northwest.

The moist woods of the Northwest are ripe harvesting grounds for wild mushrooms. Foraging in the autumn can net enough fungi to last the year. Those that are not consumed fresh can be dried and stored in airtight containers for later use.

- 1 cup chicken stock
- ½ cup heavy cream
- 1 ounce dried porcini mushrooms
- 4 cups cubed challah (egg bread) *or* brioche
- 2 tablespoon chopped fresh parsley
- 1 tablespoon dried chervil
- 2 teaspoons chopped fresh rosemary
- 1 teaspoon dried thyme
- ½ cup (1 stick) unsalted butter
- 1 small red onion, minced
- 2 cups sliced fresh chanterelle mushrooms
- 2 cloves garlic, minced
- 2 eggs, lightly beaten
- ½ teaspoon salt
- ¼ teaspoon freshly ground pepper

In a small saucepan over medium heat, bring the stock and cream just to a simmer. Remove from the heat and add the porcini mushrooms. Set aside for 15 minutes.

Meanwhile, in a large bowl, toss the bread cubes with the parsley, chervil, rosemary, and thyme. Set aside.

In a medium saucepan, melt the butter over medium heat. Add the onion and cook, stirring occasionally, for 5 minutes. Stir in the chanterelle mushrooms and the garlic. Cook, stirring occasionally, until the mushrooms are soft, about 5 minutes. Add this mixture to the bread cubes, tossing gently.

Drain the porcini mushrooms, reserving the liquid. Mince the mushrooms and add them to the bread mixture along with the reserved liquid. Fold well until the bread cubes are thoroughly moistened. Cover and let sit for 1 hour.

Preheat the oven to 350°F. Add the eggs, salt, and pepper to the bread mixture; fold well. Place the mixture in a well-buttered 8½ x 4½ inch loaf pan and cover with a buttered piece of foil. Set the pan in a larger baking dish and fill with enough hot water to reach halfway up the sides of the loaf pan. Bake until just firm, about 1 hour. Remove from the oven and the water bath. Let rest 5 minutes. Cut into slices to serve.

BUTTERNUT SQUASH RISOTTO
ADAPTED FROM A RECIPE BY TOM DOUGLAS, THE DAHLIA LOUNGE,
SEATTLE, WASHINGTON

Serves 6-8

*Risotto, a northern Italian staple, became part of the American culinary landscape in the
1980s. Here is a Northwest version of this labor-intensive but delectable dish.*

- 1 small butternut squash
- 1 tablespoon olive oil
- ¼ cup (½ stick) unsalted butter
- 1 onion, finely chopped
- 2 cloves garlic, minced
- 1½ cups Arborio rice
- 4½ to 5 cups warm chicken stock
- 2 cups (6 ounces) grated Parmesan cheese
- 2 tablespoons chopped fresh Italian parsley
- Salt and freshly ground black pepper

Preheat the oven to 400°F. Cut the squash in half length-wise and remove the seeds. Brush the cut surfaces with the olive oil and place, cut sides down, on a baking sheet. Bake about 45 minutes or until very soft. Cool slightly. Scoop the flesh from the skins. Chop the flesh and set it aside.

Melt 2 tablespoons of the butter in a large saucepan over medium heat. Add the onion and garlic and sauté, stirring, for 3 minutes. Add the rice and stir to coat the grains with butter. Stirring constantly, add the chicken stock, ½ cup at a time, adding more stock only when the previous amount has been absorbed. When the rice has cooked to an *al dente* stage, stir in the remaining 2 tablespoons of butter, the squash, cheese, and parsley. Add enough of the remaining stock to cook until the rice is tender and the risotto is creamy in consistency. Season with salt and pepper.

BAKED WALLA WALLA ONIONS AND APPLES WITH ROSEMARY AND YAKIMA GOUDA

Serves 8

Walla Walla is a city in the eastern part of Washington near the Idaho border. The onions grown nearby are mild and sweet and cook very nicely.

- ¼ cup (½ stick) unsalted butter
- 4 Walla Walla onions, sliced
- 2 Granny Smith apples, peeled, cored, and sliced
- 1 tablespoon sugar
- 1 (9-ounce) container crème fraîche *or* 1 cup plus 2 tablespoons sour cream
- 4 teaspoons chopped fresh rosemary
- Salt and freshly ground black pepper
- 1 cup (4 ounces) shredded Yakima Gouda cheese

Melt the butter in a large skillet over medium-low heat. Add the onions, apples, and sugar. Sauté, stirring occasionally, until golden brown and caramelized, about 30 minutes.

Preheat the oven to 350°F. Transfer the onion-apple mixture into a greased 12-inch round or oval gratin dish. Mix in the crème fraîche and rosemary. Season with salt and pepper. Sprinkle with the cheese. Bake for 30 minutes or until hot and the cheese is bubbly.

Preheat the broiler. Broil the gratin, watching carefully, until the cheese is lightly browned. Serve hot.

AUTUMN APPLE AND OREGON BLUE CHEESE SALAD WITH HAZELNUT VINAIGRETTE

Serves 6

Fruit and cheese is a recurring Northwest theme. Here it is in a lovely salad dressed with the essence of hazelnut.

- ⅓ cup hazelnut oil
- 2 tablespoons raspberry vinegar
- 1 tablespoon apple juice
- 1 tablespoon hot-sweet mustard
- Salt and pepper
- 3 cups washed, dried, and torn butter lettuce leaves
- 2 cups washed and dried spinach leaves
- 2 cups washed and dried watercress
- 2 Gala *or* Braeburn apples, cored and thinly sliced
- 1 cup chopped toasted hazelnuts
- ¾ cup (3 ounces) crumbled Oregon blue cheese
- 1 small red onion, thinly sliced

To make the vinaigrette: In a small bowl, whisk together the oil, vinegar, apple juice, and mustard. Season with salt and pepper. Set aside.

Place all the remaining ingredients in a large salad bowl. Pour the vinaigrette over and toss well. Serve immediately.

ASIAN VEGETABLE STIR-FRY

Serves 6

The Asian influence in the Northwest has always been strong, and recent immigrants from southeast Asia and Hong Kong have brought new ideas and ingredients to the regional table.

- 1 cup chicken stock
- 1½ pounds baby bok choy, halved lengthwise
- ½ pound snap peas, trimmed
- ½ red bell pepper, seeded and julienned
- ½ yellow bell pepper, seeded and julienned
- 6 chanterelle mushrooms, sliced
- ¼ cup fermented black beans
- 2 cloves garlic, minced
- 2 tablespoons cornstarch mixed with 2 tablespoons water
- 1 tablespoon soy sauce
- 1 tablespoon sesame oil

Place the stock in a wok or large skillet over medium-high heat and bring to a boil. Add the bok choy. Cover and steam for 1 minute. Add the snap peas, bell peppers, mushrooms, black beans, and garlic. Cover and steam for 1 minute, tossing occasionally.

Stir in the cornstarch mixture, soy sauce, and sesame oil. Cook for about 30 seconds, tossing constantly, until the sauce thickens and the vegetables are nicely glazed. Serve immediately.

Three Appellations

Unlike California's intricate winegrowing map, where every hillside seems to have its own designated appellation, Washington contains only three growing areas. The massive Columbia Valley is an umbrella appellation that encompasses both the Yakima Valley and the Walla Walla Valley. It sprawls across a semiarid plateau that covers nearly 20,000 square miles. While the climate varies over this great expanse, much of the area experiences warm, dry summers, cool harvest months, and cold winters. Early fall frosts present the greatest threat to an otherwise bountiful landscape.

The Yakima Valley, situated close to the Cascades, is the coolest district in the Columbia Valley. It is also the most concentrated winemaking area in the appellation. The original Associated Vintners site—now called Columbia Winery—and the other midsize producers—such as Hogue Cellars, Covey Run Vintners, and Staton Hills Winery—have made the Yakima Valley the center of Washington viticulture.

If Yakima is the oldest and most active, then the Walla Walla Valley qualifies as the state's most curious growing area. Better known for its onions than its wine, this small region that skirts the Oregon border is home to a few scattered vintners. Many have had to supplement their Walla Walla grapes with batches from the Yakima and Columbia Valleys, and the story would end here, if not for Gary Figgins's tiny Leonetti Cellars. This red-wine-only winery produces handcrafted, atypical Washington cabernets and merlots. The wines are massive and intense, steeped in oak and noted for a lush fruitiness. They have attracted a near cult following in wine circles.

Figgins's friend and neighbor, Rick Small, cultivates a tiny parcel of family land for his Woodward Canyon Winery. He makes fine cabernets and merlots and stupendous chardonnays. Small is a strong advocate of Walla Walla wines, but it will be tough to convince farmers in the region to uproot their onion and wheat fields to make way for grapes.

RASPBERRY AND RIESLING SABAYON GRATIN
ADAPTED FROM A RECIPE BY JERRY TRAUNFELD, THE HERBFARM, SEATTLE, WASHINGTON

Serves 6

A glorious way to showcase northwestern raspberries and late-harvest riesling.

- 8 egg yolks
- ½ cup granulated sugar
- ¾ cup late-harvest riesling wine
- ½ cup well-chilled heavy cream
- 1 quart raspberries
- Superfine sugar, as needed
- Powdered sugar, as needed

Prepare a double boiler or select a medium stainless steel bowl and a saucepan in which the bowl will sit comfortably. Fill the saucepan with a few inches of water and bring it to a boil. Place the yolks and granulated sugar in the bowl and whisk until smooth. Whisk in the wine. Place the bowl into the saucepan and continue to whisk constantly and rapidly until the mixture becomes thick and fluffy and there is no trace of liquid left in the bottom of the bowl. This will take less than 5 minutes.

Immediately remove the bowl from the saucepan and set it in a large bowl filled with ice water. Continue to whisk the mixture until it has cooled completely.

In another bowl, whip the cream to form soft peaks and gently fold into the cooled mixture.

Preheat the broiler. Taste the raspberries and sweeten with the superfine sugar, if necessary. Divide the berries among 6 (6-ounce) ramekins and spoon the sabayon mixture on top of the berries, dividing equally. Place the dishes under the broiler and broil until browned, watching closely so as not to burn. This will only take 15 seconds or so. Remove from the broiler and dust with the powdered sugar. Serve immediately.

CARAMELIZED APPLE PIE WITH APPLE CIDER SAUCE

Makes one 9-inch pie

This is a Northwest version of the classic apple pie that uses some of the techniques of the traditional French tarte tatin.

- Double recipe of Super Flaky Pie Crust (page 34), substituting thawed apple juice concentrate for the amount of water called for in the recipe
- 9 tablespoons unsalted butter
- ¾ cup plus 2 teaspoons granulated sugar
- ¼ cup golden brown sugar, packed
- 6 Pippin apples, peeled, cored, and thinly sliced
- 2 tablespoons cornstarch
- 1 teaspoon vanilla extract
- 1 teaspoon grated lemon zest
- ¾ teaspoon plus a pinch cinnamon
- ⅛ teaspoon ground cloves
- 1 egg yolk
- 2 tablespoons heavy cream
- 4 cups apple cider
- Vanilla ice cream

Prepare a double recipe of the Super Flaky Pie Crust, substituting thawed apple juice concentrate for the amount of water called for in the recipe. Chill dough as directed.

Melt 6 tablespoons of the butter in a 12-inch skillet over medium heat. Add ¾ cup of the granulated sugar and the brown sugar. Cook, stirring, 5 minutes. Add the apples; cook, stirring occasionally, until soft and lightly caramelized, about 15 minutes. Remove from the heat and let cool 15 minutes.

Preheat the oven to 425°F. Remove the dough from the refrigerator and cut in half. On a lightly floured surface, roll one half of the dough to about 1½ inches larger than a 9-inch pie plate. Place the dough into the pie plate and press down lightly into the pan with your fingertips. Cut the edge of the pastry with kitchen shears so it hangs evenly about 1 inch past the outer edge of the pan. Set the pie plate aside.

Transfer the apples to a medium bowl. Add the cornstarch, vanilla, lemon zest, ¾ teaspoon of the cinnamon, and the cloves. Toss to combine. Spoon the mixture into the prepared pie plate and dot with the remaining 3 tablespoons of butter. Set aside.

Roll out the remaining half of the dough for the top crust. Moisten the rim of the bottom crust with water and cover with the top crust. Press the edges of the two crusts together to seal. Fold the dough edge under itself so it is even with the edge of the pie plate. Crimp the edge and freeze 15 minutes.

Cut 4 vents in the top crust so that steam can escape during baking. In a small bowl, beat the egg yolk with the cream. Brush this mixture lightly over the top of the pie. Combine the remaining 2 teaspoons of granulated sugar and the pinch of cinnamon. Sprinkle over the pie.

Bake in the middle of the oven for 10 minutes. Reduce the heat to 350°F and continue baking 30 to 40 minutes until the crust is crisp and golden brown and the apple juices are bubbling. (If the pie is browning too quickly during the baking process, cover loosely with aluminum foil.) Remove to a rack.

Meanwhile, to make the sauce, pour the apple cider into a large saucepan and bring to a boil over medium-high heat. Cook, uncovered, until reduced to 1 cup, about 20 minutes. The sauce should have a light syrupy consistency. Serve the pie warm, topped with the ice cream and warm sauce.

WARM CARAMELIZED PEARS WITH OREGON BLUE CHEESE AND CHAMPAGNE VINEGAR GLAZE

Serves 4

America's favorite pear, the Bartlett, was named after Enoch Bartlett of Dorchester, Massachusetts. This variety accounts for three-quarters of the nation's pear production, much of which comes from Washington and Oregon. This recipe showcases the Bartletts nicely and creates wonderful sweet and sour flavors.

- ¾ cup sugar
- 2 ripe red Bartlett pears, cored and cut into 6 wedges
- 2 ripe green Bartlett pears, cored and cut into 6 wedges
- ¾ cup Champagne vinegar
- 1½ teaspoons freshly cracked black pepper
- 2 tablespoons unsalted butter, at room temperature
- Salt
- 6 ounces Oregon blue cheese

Preheat a heavy nonstick skillet over medium-high heat until a bit of smoke rises from the pan. Place the sugar on a plate. Dip 1 side of each pear wedge into the sugar and place wedges, sugared sides down, in the skillet. Cook until the pears and sugar are golden brown and caramelized. Do not turn pears. Watch carefully and adjust the heat so the sugar does not burn. Set aside and keep warm.

To make the glaze: Add the sugar remaining on the plate to a small saucepan. Cook over medium-low heat until the sugar caramelizes to a light golden brown. Quickly add the vinegar and pepper and reduce by half, stirring constantly to keep the sugar from hardening. Add the butter and stir until melted. Season with salt.

Arrange the pear wedges, sugar sides up, in a star pattern on each of 4 salad plates. Cut the cheese into 4 wedges and stand 1 in the center of each plate. Spoon the glaze over the pears and serve immediately.

WILD MOUNTAIN BLACKBERRY COBBLER

ADAPTED FROM A RECIPE BY ANN KISCHNER, THE SHOALWATER, SEAVIEW, WASHINGTON

Serves 8

This is a pure and lovely expression of ripe, fresh blackberries.

- 2 quarts wild mountain blackberries (about 6 baskets)
- 1½ cups granulated sugar
- 2 tablespoons lemon juice, if the berries lack tartness (not too likely)
- 3 cups all-purpose flour
- 1 cup golden brown sugar, packed
- 1 cup (2 sticks) unsalted butter, melted and cooled slightly

Preheat the oven to 400°F. In a large bowl, toss the berries with the granulated sugar (and the lemon juice, if needed). Place in a 9 x 13 inch baking dish and set aside.

Place the flour and brown sugar in a medium bowl. Mix well. Add the melted butter, mixing with a wooden spoon, and leaving the mixture well mixed yet crumbly. Spoon the cobbler topping over the berries. (Do not press down.) Bake about 25 minutes or until the berry juices are bubbling around the edges and the topping is a rich golden brown. Cool 5 minutes and serve with generous scoops of your favorite vanilla ice cream.

BING CHERRY SAUCE

Makes 4½ cups

The orchards of Washington State produce America's finest cherries. In the late spring these plump, tangy fruits are at their best. This sauce is lovely spooned over vanilla ice cream.

- 3 cups pitted fresh bing cherries, halved
- 1 cup dried Rainier cherries
- ½ cup currant jelly
- ½ to ¾ cup sugar, depending on the sweetness of the cherries

In a nonreactive saucepan, simmer all the ingredients until soft, stirring often, for about 30 minutes. Serve over ice cream in wide-bowled red wine goblets.

WALNUT CAKE WITH CHOCOLATE BUTTER CREAM

Serves 8

*One of the Northwest's most prized products is the tender walnut.
This versatile nut not only produces oil, but also is wonderful in bread and produces
a superb cake whose brilliance is greatly enhanced by rich chocolate butter cream.*

Walnut Cake
- ½ cup (1 stick) unsalted butter
- 1 cup sugar
- 1½ cups sifted cake flour plus ½ tablespoon unsifted
- 1½ teaspoons baking powder
- ⅛ teaspoon salt
- 1 cup broken walnuts, toasted
- 2 eggs
- ½ cup milk
- ½ teaspoon vanilla extract
- ½ teaspoon almond extract
- Toasted walnut halves, for garnish

Chocolate Butter Cream
- 2 ounces semisweet chocolate, chopped
- 1 tablespoon very strong coffee
- 2 egg yolks
- ¼ cup sugar
- ⅛ teaspoon salt
- ½ cup (1 stick) unsalted butter, cut into ½-inch pieces

For the cake, preheat the oven to 350°F.

Place the butter and sugar in the bowl of an electric mixer. Beat on medium speed for 5 minutes.

Mix together the 1½ cups of sifted flour, the baking powder, and salt. Set aside.

Toss together the broken walnuts with the remaining ½ tablespoon of flour. Set aside.

Add the eggs to the butter mixture. Beat on medium speed for 2 minutes.

Combine the milk and extracts. Alternately, add the flour and milk mixtures to the butter mixture, beating well after each addition. Add the floured walnuts and continue beating on low speed until well blended.

Lightly grease one 9 x 5 inch loaf pan. Spoon cake batter into pan. Bake 1 hour, or until a cake tester or toothpick inserted into the cake's center comes out clean. Cool in the pan on a rack for 10 minutes. Turn the cake out onto the rack to cool completely.

To make the butter cream: Place the chocolate and coffee in a bowl over a saucepan of simmering water. Heat, stirring often, until the chocolate is melted and blended. Set aside.

Combine the yolks, sugar, and salt in another bowl. Set over a saucepan of simmering water. Beat the mixture rapidly with a whisk or a portable electric mixer until it forms a "ribbon" (the mixture is thickened and falls in a smooth ribbon when the whisk or beater is held up).

Scrape the chocolate mixture into the yolk mixture. Return the bowl to the simmering water and continue beating. Gradually beat in the butter, piece by piece.

Remove the bowl from the heat. Continue beating in a cool place until the mixture thickens slightly. Continue beating with a wooden spoon until the butter cream lightens in color. Let cool until spreadable.

Frost the top and sides of the cake with the butter cream. Garnish as desired with walnut halves.

RHUBARB-STRAWBERRY LATTICE PIE

Makes one 9-inch deep-dish pie

Rhubarb is a long-stalked plant that comes from Asia. It actually became popular among Alaskan Eskimos who ate it raw. Rhubarb grows in the Northwest and is at its best in pies. This combination with strawberries is classic.

• Double recipe of Super Flaky Pie Crust (page 34)	• ¾ teaspoon vanilla
• 4½ cups sliced rhubarb	• ⅛ teaspoon salt
• 3 cups sliced strawberries	• 3 tablespoons unsalted butter
• 2¼ cups sugar	• 1 egg
• ¾ cup all-purpose flour	• 1 tablespoon heavy cream
• 1 tablespoon grated orange zest	• Additional sugar, for sprinkling on top of pie

Prepare the pastry, roll out half of it and line a 9-inch deep-dish pie plate. Crimp the edge. Chill for 15 minutes. Refrigerate the remaining pastry for the top crust.

Preheat the oven to 450°F.

In a large bowl, combine the rhubarb, strawberries, 2¼ cups sugar, flour, orange zest, vanilla, and salt. Toss to blend well. Pour into the pie shell. Dot the fruit filling with the butter.

Roll out the remaining pastry to a circle about ¹⁄₁₆-inch thick. Using a ruler as a straight edge, cut the pastry with a sharp knife or rolling pastry cutter into twelve ½-inch wide strips. In a small bowl, beat the egg with the cream; moisten the edge of the pie shell with this mixture. Criss-cross the dough strips to form a lattice design over the fruit filling. Press the ends of the strips onto the bottom crust. Pinch off any excess dough and crimp the edge to seal it. Brush the pastry with the egg glaze and sprinkle with the additional sugar.

Place the pie on a rimmed baking sheet and bake for 15 minutes. Reduce the heat to 350°F and bake until the crust is golden brown and the juices are bubbly, about 40 minutes. Cover the edge of the crust with strips of aluminum foil, if necessary, to prevent excess browning. Remove the pie to a rack to cool slightly. Serve warm, with vanilla ice cream, if desired.

FRESH APPLE WAFFLES WITH CINNAMON-CIDER SYRUP

Serves 6

Breakfast is an important meal for the outdoors-oriented residents of the Northwest. This dish is so good that you can serve it as dessert if you choose.

• 1 quart apple cider or juice	• 2 eggs, separated
• ¼ cup light brown sugar, packed	• 1½ cups buttermilk
• 1 (3- to 4-inch) cinnamon stick	• 3 tablespoons vegetable oil
• 1¼ cups all-purpose flour	• 1 red apple (such as Braeburn or Jonathan), cored and finely chopped
• ¼ cup whole-wheat flour	• Vegetable cooking spray, for coating the waffle iron
• 1½ teaspoons baking powder	• Red apples, cored and sliced for garnish
• ½ teaspoon baking soda	
• ½ teaspoon salt	

To make the Cinnamon-Cider Syrup: In a heavy medium saucepan, combine the cider, 2 tablespoons of the sugar, and the cinnamon stick. Place over medium heat and cook at a slow boil for about 1 hour or until reduced to 1 cup. Discard the cinnamon stick. Set aside and keep warm.

To make the waffles: In a medium bowl, combine the flours, baking powder, baking soda, salt, and the remaining 2 tablespoons of the sugar. Mix well and set aside.

Beat the egg whites in the bowl of an electric mixer at high speed until stiff and peaks form. Transfer to another bowl and set aside.

In the same mixer bowl, combine the egg yolks, buttermilk, and oil. Mix well. On low speed, gradually beat in the flour mixture until just blended. Stir in the apple and fold in the egg whites. Set the waffle mixture aside.

Preheat the waffle iron and spray with the vegetable cooking spray. Spoon about ¾ cup batter per waffle onto the hot waffle iron. Bake about 5 minutes or until the steaming stops. Serve the waffles hot with the Cinnamon-Cider Syrup. Garnish with apple slices, if desired.

The Southwest

The mystical grandeur of the Southwest deserves to be matched with an equally distinctive cuisine, and it is. This is a region of snowcapped mountains, solitary deserts, flat-topped mesas, high blue skies, and otherworldly natural wonders. The Southwest table perfectly evokes the varied landscape. The food is boldly flavored, surprising, and dramatic. The colors of the food—bright red, yellow, and green chiles, slate-blue corn, brownish-beige beans—echo the hues that paint the horizon.

The flavors are in perfect harmony. Meats grilled over mesquite and pecan wood absorb the aromas of the desert. Likewise, the earthy taste of black bean chili, the rugged texture of corn tortillas, the pungent aroma of pine nuts, and the searing heat of chiles describe the environments of Arizona, New Mexico, and Texas better than words ever could.

It is no surprise that the designs and foods of the American Southwest have been embraced by people across the country. On a wintry day in downtown Minneapolis, you can feast on Stephan Pyles's stylish Texan fare, and Mark Miller's popular Red Sage in Washington, D.C., rumbles with simulated New Mexico thunderstorms.

What is it about these foods that has captivated our taste buds? Certainly, the seductive heat of superhot chiles are a large part of the appeal. But more important, there is something uplifting and spiritual in the rough, pure flavors. The elements of Southwest cooking are not complicated, but the end result is at once vast and enchanting.

History

As many as 10,000 years ago, ancient arrivals entered North America by way of a land bridge across the Bering Strait. Those that reached the Southwest settled into a pattern of hunting deer and elk on the highlands, bison on the plains, and jack rabbits and other small animals in the deserts. They also gathered pinion nuts, beans, and the fruit and pulp of prickly pear and saguaro cacti. In time, some groups abandoned the nomadic life and learned to cultivate corn, beans, and squash. This holy trinity of ingredients would become central to both religious ceremony and daily sustenance.

Three civilizations emerged from the early tribes and flourished until about the year 1300. The Mogollon culture developed a sedentary life in the mountain country that stretches from central Arizona to south central New Mexico. They crafted stone tools and pottery and constructed permanent buildings.

Farther south and west, along the drainage of the Gila River, the Hohokam culture developed a similar, but distinct lifestyle. These desert farmers survived their unforgiving environment with sheer ingenuity. They were master irrigators, steering local stream water through an extensive canal network to feed their crops of squashes, lima and tepary beans, and corn. These canals are still evident today, running parallel to the modern canal that supplies downtown Phoenix.

But these accomplishments were soon overshadowed by the Anasazi culture, which developed on the high plateaus where the states of Utah, Arizona, New Mexico, and Colorado now neatly join to form the "Four Corners." The early Anasazi were a seminomadic people, identified by their skills at basket weaving. But during the eighth century, they began to build on a massive scale, constructing complex, stone cities on mesa tops and clinging precipitously to sheer canyon walls, building techniques that earned them the name Pueblo.

These ingenious people also showed remarkable sophistication in pottery design and agriculture. They developed a complex and mystical religion. Food was revered by the Anasazi, and it was common to find ears of corn and piles of beans arranged around grave sites.

By the time of their mysterious decline at the beginning of the fourteenth century (some say this cataclysmic change was brought about by drought, others blame conflict with warring tribes), the Anasazi culture had spread through much of the Southwest. Over the next hundred years or so, many splinter tribes formed from Pueblo traditions, the Hopi and Zuni among them. Nomadic forebears of the Navajo culture also arrived from the Great Plains during this time.

Franciscan monk Fray Marcos de Niza led an expedition north from New Spain (now Mexico) into Arizona in 1539 in search of the Seven Cities of Cibola, the mythic cities of gold that spurred the Spanish imagination. Marcos de Niza retreated after the death of his guide, but not before he mistook a distant pueblo for a golden edifice. This sighting prompted a journey the following year by the Conquistador Coronado, who found no gold and took out his frustrations by destroying several Pueblo villages.

With no riches in sight, the conquistadors left the territory to the missionaries, who set about converting people to Christianity. The friars established Santa Fe as a *villa real*, a royal city, in 1609, with a band of missions stretching outward across the territory. The conversions, however, did not come easily. When the people resisted, the friars called in force. The Pueblo tribes waged a valiant revolt in 1680, but ultimately were no match for the Spanish cavalry with its steel weaponry.

Birth of a Cuisine

Following the suppression of the Pueblo Revolt, the Spanish and Native Americans lived together in the region for nearly two hundred years without outside interference, and though the relationship was mostly a hostile one, a natural blending of culinary traditions took place. This interaction formed Southwest cooking as we know it today. During this time, the unique varieties of native corn, such as Platinum Lady and blue corn, and the stunning array of indigenous beans were incorporated into Spanish dishes. So too were squashes, cacti, pine nuts, and local game.

The Spanish considerably broadened the native diet, bringing new foodstuffs with them to plant in the soil stained with Pueblo blood. They introduced peaches, plums, apricots, and grapevines in the dry southern climes, and apples in the north. They grew wheat to make flour for breads and tortillas, which they preferred to those made from corn. The missionaries also led herds of cattle and sheep up from Mexico, adding beef, milk, and cheese to the local diet.

Most important, the Spanish began to cultivate chile peppers on a large scale, and their fiery flavors became a signature of Southwest cooking. Chiltepin peppers grew wild in the region and had long been used to spice foods, but the Spanish introduced many more varieties, and they integrated the chile more closely into the cuisine. Today, chiles—with temperatures ranging from mild to incendiary on the Scoville scale—are the leading cash crop in New Mexico.

The native tribes worked many Spanish ingredients and techniques into their culinary repertoire. Navajo fry breads were made with flour from the newly planted wheat. And adobe ovens, called *hornos,* which were used by the Pueblos for baking, were adapted from a Spanish design.

The Spanish colonists influenced not only what was eaten, but how it was eaten as well. Their custom of serving appetizers *(antojitos)* has made the Southwest a grazer's paradise of small dishes such as nachos, quesadillas, and ceviche.

When Mexico won its independence from Spain in 1821, it inherited control of *Nuevo Mexico* as well. In the very same year the Santa Fe trail opened, connecting the Southwest to Independence, Missouri. Anglo settlers and traders began to trickle in, and when the region became a U.S. territory after the Mexican-American war in 1848, their numbers increased markedly. These were the rough-and-tumble times of frontier legend.

The new arrivals brought with them a taste for steaks, hearty stews, and sausages. But the American pioneers also came to appreciate the Southwest cooking that was already in place, and once their taste buds acclimated to the volatile seasonings, there was no turning back. Food scarcity continued to be a problem for many settlers and some ate little more than tortillas and beans.

Meanwhile, Texas had already earned its statehood in 1845. The process was not an easy one. Once liberated from Mexico, Texas still had to overcome resistance from northern states that did not want another slave state in the Union. Even after admission, the new state's disputes with Mexico lasted another decade until the Gadsden Purchase was signed, which added a portion of Arizona and New Mexico.

After the American Civil War, the new western lifestyle on the Texas ranges meant cattle drives. The animals were descendants of the original Spanish herds, many of which had been crossbred with other cows that had roamed in from the north and east. The classic Texas longhorn was raised more for its hide than meat, which tended to be tough.

Millions of animals were moved across the state, and the most crucial person on these journeys was the chuckwagon "cookie." Usually an older man, he prepared the hearty meals that sustained the cowboys through their long days in the saddle. The most famous chuckwagon dish was "son of a gun stew," a thick beef stew bolstered with the innards of a freshly slaughtered cow. Other foods prepared over the open fire included sour-dough biscuits, strong cowboy coffee, cooked pinto beans, and chili con carne—made in its traditional form with only beef and chile powder. Savvy cooks would even plant chiles and vegetables at strategic points along the route.

The cowboy tradition remains vital to the identity of Texas cuisine, and many of the early dishes are still popular on local menus. The chuckwagon penchant for cooking over an open fire has inspired a thriving barbecue tradition in the state. As Chef Stephan Pyles of Star Canyon restaurant in Dallas notes, "grilling, smoking, and roasting are our most enduring regional cooking techniques."

New Mexico and Arizona earned their statehood in 1912, but despite this newly incorporated status, the land remained starkly desolate. Artists and writers were naturally drawn to the Southwest, with its majestic landscapes and unique desert lighting. The paintings of Georgia O'Keefe did much to capture the mystic, solitary beauty of the region. This romantic vision of the Southwest attracted a new wave of settlers into New Mexico and Arizona.

During the 1950s, as southwestern cities grew and retirees flooded into the Sun Belt, authentic native fare went into a tailspin. It was viewed by many people as second-rate cooking, appropriate only for the poor who knew nothing else. The closest many residents got to Southwest cooking during this unfortunate time was a green chile laid atop a hamburger.

In later years, the proliferation of Tex-Mex dealt another blow to the regional fare. Authentic Tex-Mex is a blend of Mexican techniques and ingredients with the Texas chuckwagon tradition of grilled and smoked meats. But across the country, Tex-Mex sadly came to represent a bland version of the cuisine, neatly tempered for the Anglo palate. Many Southwest dishes, like tacos and chili, had become culinary clichés that bore little resemblance to the originals.

But the tide began to turn in the 1980s. Southwestern jewelry, art, and interior design came into vogue across the country, and this in turn generated interest in the culture and foods. It was not long before eager, young chefs became culinary scholars, researching the authentic ingredients and historical traditions introduced during the crucial years of Spanish rule. Stephan Pyles and Dean Fearing arrived on the Dallas scene. Robert Del Grande surfaced in Houston. Mark Miller came to Santa Fe from California to open the Coyote Cafe in 1987. His commitment to fresh, locally grown ingredients and traditional Pueblo and Spanish techniques have placed him at the forefront of the modern Southwest cooking revival.

Other chefs during this fervent time further expanded the Southwest concept, adding contemporary interpretations of the classic ingredients. Each variation offers a new thrill for the taste buds, and only one thing is guaranteed: As soon as the hot flavors cool off, you'll find yourself wanting more.

The Southwest Pantry

ANISEED

Excellent in desserts and breads, the small, curved seeds of the anise plant add a sweet licorice flavor when roasted and ground.

APPLES

Apples may take a back seat to chiles in northern New Mexico around Chimayo, but the Gravensteins, Pippins, and Winesap varieties grown there are surprisingly good. The fruit from Chimayo seems to have a natural affinity with the local chiles when combined in salsas or tarts.

AVOCADO

Not native to the area, but southwesterners have adopted this luscious green vegetable as one of their own. Look for the Haas avocado with its black-purplish bumpy skin and buttery green flesh. Buy them a few days before you expect to use them to allow time for ripening.

BEANS

One of the three holy ingredients of the ancient tribes (along with corn and squash), a great diversity of beans has been cultivated in the Southwest. Dried beans should generally be soaked overnight, then cooked slowly in unsalted water. Addition of the Mexican herb epazote is reputed to reduce the gaseous effects.

Black Beans: Also called turtle beans, these small, dark purple beans are popular throughout the Caribbean and Latin America for their strong, earthy flavors.

Bollito Beans: A wild bean, related to the pinto. This beige-colored bean has a stronger, more distinct flavor than the pinto.

Pinto Beans: The most common and most nutritious bean in the country. A Southwest native, the pinto is beige with brownish streaks that becomes entirely pink upon cooking.

Tepary Beans: Important in the ceremonies of the Zuni, this earthy bean is rarely cultivated because of a mold spore it can harbor that destroys other beans.

BEEF

Texas has the largest cattle inventory of any state in the nation, with more than five million head. Some of the animals are shipped to Nebraska or Kansas for processing. Crossbreeding is common in Texas, and Herefords were crossed with Angus, Charollais, Brahman, and other exotic breeds to mature rapidly and grow lean. New Mexico corn-fed Angus is a popular choice in the Southwest.

CACTUS (nopales)

The oval "paddles" of the Opuntia cactus can be grilled or used in salsas. The cactus has a flavor similar to that of green beans and is available pre-cut in cans under the name nopalitos. The prickly pear is the greenish-yellow fruit of the cactus, with bright red flesh. Cut the fruit in half and scoop out the flesh. Best in salsas, sauces, or desserts.

CHEESE

Many Mexican-style cheeses are produced in the Southwest, including: Asadero (mild, soft, melts well), Cotija (hard, dry, aged), Manchego (rich, mellow-flavored table cheese), Oaxaca (melts easily, sold in braids, as a snack or used in quesadillas), Queso Fresco (fresh, unripened, moist cheese with sharp, tangy flavor). Anglo-style dishes will most commonly substitute Monterey Jack, a smooth-melting cheese that approximates the flavor of some Southwestern cheeses. Tex-Mex cooking might also use a cheddar-style cheese.

CHILES

The premier seasoning of the Southwest, chile peppers interbreed easily and have given rise to hundreds of varieties over the years. All chiles start growing in a green state and ripen through yellow, orange, then red stages. In general, when picked green, the chile will be pickled and canned or eaten fresh, and when left to ripen red the chile will be dried or powdered. Over 150 varieties of chiles have been identified.

Here are a few of the more popular fresh ones and the color when most often used:

Anaheim: Bright green color, closely related to the New Mexican green. A mild, medium- to thick-fleshed chile, it is often used for rellenos and stews.

Ancho: see poblano.

Chiltepin: Grows wild in the Southwest, this red, round chili is extremely hot and should be used sparingly. The cultivated Pequin variety is an appropriate substitute.

Guero: Also called a cera or wax pepper, this small, hot chile is yellow in color; used primarily as a garnish.

Habanero: Caution! Small green, yellow, or orange, this variety is the hottest of all chiles and should be handled carefully. The perfect incendiary ingredient for salsas, when used in moderation.

Jalapeño: The most common hot chile in the U.S., finding its way atop numerous nacho plates and in countless quesadillas. Often pickled.

New Mexico Green/Red: New Mexican Green is hotter than the Anaheim, with a distinctive sweet, earthy flavor. It is roasted and used in rellenos, stews, and salsas. The New Mexican red, a ripened version of the green, is sweeter and can be used in many of the same recipes. Many are dried and tied in bunches, called ristas, which decorate Southwest kitchens.

Poblano: Dark green, thick-fleshed chile that works well for rellenos. Roasting brings out its smoky, earthy flavor. Also called ancho in its fresh or dried forms. In some areas, particularly California, the poblano is erroneously called the pasilla, which is an entirely different variety.

Serrano: Dark green to bright red, this small, cylindrical chile is hotter than the jalapeño, and is commonly used in sauces and salsas.

Dried chiles have an intense flavor, and may be stored indefinitely in sealed containers. White spots may indicate improper drying. A strong aroma that's not too dusty or dirty is ideal.

Ancho: A dried poblano chile, deep red to brown in color. Sweeter than most other dried chiles.

Cayenne: Usually dried and powdered, bright red in color, with pungent heat.

Chipotle: A dried and smoked jalapeño, brownish in color with a sweet, smoky flavor. Most often stewed in a seasoned broth called adobo sauce. This is available already prepared in most Latin markets or by mail order (see page 197).

Pasilla: Dark purplish-black, with wrinkled texture. Intense, smoky flavors. Often added to mole sauces.

Pequin: Related to the wild tepin, this small orange-red chile has a light, sweet, smoky flavor.

CORIANDER
The dried seed of the cilantro plant, used as a seasoning, ground or whole.

CORN
Sacred to the Native Americans, who grew it in a dazzling array of colors. Blue corn is more nutritious, with a high protein content. It is less starchy than most varieties, so handle it with care. The local tribes used every part of the corn, including the husks which were used as the wrapping for tamales. The cornmeal dough, called masa, is used to fill tamales and is also the base for corn tortillas.

CUMIN (comino)
When ground, the seeds release a strong, earthy flavor that combines nicely with chiles. For maximum flavor, grind the seeds yourself rather than purchasing them already ground.

GOAT
Meat from young goats—stronger in flavor than that of baby lamb—is commonly used in Southwest feasts. Older animals are relied upon for milk and cheese. Goat's milk adds a distinct flavor note to Mexican cajeta, a rich caramel dessert topping.

JICAMA

An edible tuber, also known as the Mexican potato, with thick brown skin and white flesh that's sweet, crispy, refreshing, and cool; similar in flavor and texture to a water chestnut. Often eaten raw in salads, though it will retain its texture when cooked. Look for young jicama, with smooth skin and a heavy feel.

OREGANO

Mexican oregano is more pungent than the domestic variety and is commonly used in stews and chile powders. Can be overpowering in its powdered version, so select dried flakes.

PECANS

Native to the Southwest, the pecan nut was foraged by the Indians, and it remains a popular ingredient for breads and desserts. Pecan wood may be used for grilling in place of mesquite.

PINE NUTS (pinons)

An important foraged food for the Native Americans, especially during years of drought. Can be added to breads, salads, and soups or ground into flour for desserts. Excellent eaten raw or roasted.

PORK

Used more than any other meat in Mexican cooking, pork is now bred to be leaner than before. Carnitas are small, tender pieces of pork that have been slowly cooked and are often served in tacos and enchiladas. So too is chorizo, a highly seasoned fresh sausage that combines pork, garlic, chili powder, and other spices.

POULTRY

Chicken is an important meat in the Southwest larder, with free-range birds strongly favored for their assertive, gamier flavor that stands up well to salsas and seasonings. Quail is native to the Southwest and remains a popular choice for roasting or frying, though the subtle flavor is easily overwhelmed. Squab is much darker and richer. Larger birds, like duck, turkey, and pheasant, are also popular on Southwest menus.

SAGE

Grows wild throughout New Mexico and parts of Texas. Wild sage is stronger than the garden version and, used sparingly, is a nice addition to meat and fowl dishes.

SQUASH

Available in both winter and summer varieties, this ancient food has been hybridized into a wide assortment of colors, shapes, and flavors. The centers of winter squash are mostly seeds, which are excellent when cleaned and roasted. Look for smooth, unblemished skin. Winter squash will keep for several months if kept dry and cool. Summer squash is more perishable. Zucchini is by far the most popular and versatile of the summer varieties. Buy them firm with unblemished skin.

Acorn: Generally dark green on the outside with golden orange flesh, this lusciously sweet winter squash was a favorite of the Native Americans who baked them whole in their adobe ovens.

Butternut: Tan, shaped like a bowling pin, it is creamy and sweet.

Chayote: Pear-shaped squash that's pale green to cream in color, with smooth skin and crisp flesh. Flavor is similar to zucchini. It's also called a vegetable pear.

Hubbard: Oversized squash with yellow flesh and gray to orange exterior.

Pumpkin: Familiar orange-colored squash, available in baseball-sized Jack Be Littles to oversized versions.

Turban: As the name suggests, this multicolored squash wears a bulbous cap. Rich in flavor, it is a good substitute for pumpkin or butternut.

Zucchini: Cucumber-shaped squash with a light to dark green skin. The smaller forms have a sweeter, more intense flavor.

SQUASH BLOSSOMS

Popular in Mexican and Southwest cooking, these fragrant flowers can be sautéed as a vegetable, deep fried, added to soups and quesadillas, or used as a garnish. Almost any squash produces a blossom, but those of the zucchini are preferred.

VENISON

As the many cave paintings suggest, venison was vital to the early native tribes. Black-buck antelope is prized for its meat and is featured in fine restaurants throughout the region. Pueblo dwellers hunted deer, elk, and rabbit, which they stewed or spit-roasted with minimal seasoning.

Mail Order Heat

For those of you who prefer to get your heat in a jar, there are several excellent mail-order sources that supply every hot sauce available. Mark Miller's Coyote Cocina is a treasury of Southwest supplies. Coyote's own sauces range from the top-rated Fire Roasted Salsa to the searing Howlin' Hot Sauce. The catalog also features a wonderful collection of Southwest spices, red chile ristas, Santa Fe dinnerware, and locally produced foodstuffs. There are gift packs for the chile fanatic, including a salsa-of-the-month club. To order a catalog, call 1-800-866-HOWL.

Another excellent mail-order source is Don Alphonso from Austin, Texas. The company makes a stunning mole poblano. This dense sauce is made from three different chiles—ancho, mulato, and pasilla—along with peanuts, Mexican chocolate, sesame seeds, herbs, and spices. It is incredible with chicken. Don Alphonso makes chipotle and habanero salsas, and they sell a complete range of dried chiles. There is also a selection of cooking utensils, such as the mocajete, a lava rock mortar and pestle that is used to prepare and serve guacamole. The charming catalog costs $1, which will be applied to your first purchase. To order one, call 1-800-456-6100.

For pure eye-watering, sinus-clearing thrills, it's hard to beat the sauces and salsas offered in the Mo-Hotta Mo-Betta catalog. This lively catalog features exotic products from around the world that are bound by a common temperature range. Whether you want Satan's Revenge from Indonesia, Vernon's Jamaican Jerk Sauce, or Widow of Sanchez from Mexico, this is the place to find it. There are plenty of scorching Southwest specialties as well. Operating out of San Luis Obispo, California, Tim and Wendy Eidson have produced an ebullient, homestyle catalog that includes sauces, spices, salsas, and snacks. All the products have wonderful, humorous descriptions and delightful line drawings. Everything is rated from mild to hot. Admittedly, these ratings are subjective, and they are based on the assumption that the customer likes relatively spicy food. The Mo Hotta-Mo Betta catalog can be ordered by calling 1-800-462-3220.

Finally, for a southwestern pit stop on the information superhighway, check out Chile Today, a company that offers the Hot Sauce of the Month Club and The Hottest Gift Boxes in the World. This company can be found at: emall.com/chile/chile1.html. Even more impressive is HOT HOT HOT a catalog of hot sauces complete with pictures of the labels of all the products being offered. HOT HOT HOT can be found at WWW.hot.presence.com/g/p/h3/. If you would rather call this company on the phone, they are in Pasadena at 1-800-626-6100.

The Recipes

HUEVOS RANCHEROS

Serves 6

"Ranch eggs" are the centerpiece of many southwestern breakfasts.

- ¼ cup vegetable oil
- 2 onions, chopped
- 6 cloves garlic, minced
- 1½ cups dried black beans, picked over to remove any stones, soaked in water overnight and drained
- 3 cups chicken stock
- 2 tablespoons chopped fresh oregano
- 2 tablespoons chopped fresh cilantro
- 2 teaspoons ground cumin
- ½ teaspoon red pepper flakes
- 1 bay leaf
- Salt and freshly ground black pepper
- 3 large tomatoes, coarsely chopped and puréed
- 2 fresh ears of corn, kernels cut from the cob
- 1 tablespoon tomato paste
- 1 jalapeño pepper, seeded and minced
- ½ teaspoon cayenne pepper
- 2 tablespoons distilled white vinegar
- 12 eggs
- 12 warm (6-inch) corn tortillas
- ¾ cup (3 ounces) shredded Monterey Jack cheese
- Sour cream, avocado, and orange slices, for garnish

In a large saucepan, heat 2 tablespoons of the oil over medium heat; add 1 of the onions and sauté, stirring, for 3 minutes. Add 4 of the garlic cloves; sauté, stirring, 2 minutes. Stir in the beans, chicken stock, 1 tablespoon of the oregano, 1 tablespoon of the cilantro, the cumin, pepper flakes, and bay leaf. Bring to a boil, reduce the heat, cover, and simmer about 40 minutes until the beans are tender. Remove and discard the bay leaf; season with salt and black pepper. Keep hot.

Meanwhile, to make the ranchero sauce, heat the remaining 2 tablespoons of oil in a large skillet over medium heat; add the remaining onion and sauté, stirring, for 3 minutes. Add the remaining 2 cloves of the garlic; sauté, stirring, 2 minutes. Stir in the puréed tomatoes, corn kernels, tomato paste, jalapeño, cayenne pepper, and the remaining 1 tablespoon each of oregano and cilantro; cook, stirring occasionally, until the sauce is slightly thickened, about 15 minutes. Season with salt and black pepper. Keep hot.

Pour water into a large skillet to a depth of 2 inches; place over medium heat and warm until barely simmering. Stir in the vinegar. Working in 2 batches, carefully break the eggs into the water and cook for 3 to 4 minutes or until the whites are just set. Remove with a slotted spoon and drain well.

For each serving, overlap 2 warm tortillas on a dinner plate. Top with 1 cup of the black beans, 2 eggs, ⅓ cup of the ranchero sauce, and 2 tablespoons of the cheese. Garnish with sour cream, avocado, and orange slices, if desired.

GREEN CHILE SCRAMBLE WITH CHORIZO IN WARM FLOUR TORTILLAS

ADAPTED FROM A RECIPE BY STEPHAN PYLES, STAR CANYON, DALLAS, TEXAS

Serves 4

Here is a delightful wake-up call.

- ¼ cup (½ stick) unsalted butter
- 1 onion, diced
- ½ pound Chorizo sausage, thinly sliced
- 2 Anaheim chiles, roasted, peeled, and chopped
- 1 tomato, seeded and diced
- 1 serrano chile, seeded and minced
- 2 cloves garlic, minced
- 8 eggs
- 2 tablespoons chopped fresh basil
- 2 tablespoons chopped fresh cilantro
- ¾ teaspoon salt
- ½ teaspoon freshly ground black pepper
- 4 warm (7-inch) flour tortillas
- ¼ cup sour cream
- 1 cup prepared fresh salsa (page 168)

Melt the butter in a large skillet over medium heat; add the onion and sauté, stirring occasionally, for 8 minutes. Add the sausage; cook, stirring, for 6 minutes. Stir in the Anaheim chiles, tomato, serrano chile, and garlic; sauté for 2 minutes. Remove from the heat.

Crack the eggs into a large bowl. Add the basil, cilantro, salt, and pepper; beat the eggs thoroughly. Return the skillet to medium heat and pour in the eggs. Scramble the eggs to desired consistency.

To serve, roll the eggs up in the warm tortillas and place 1 tablespoon sour cream on each tortilla. Serve with the salsa.

POTATO, POBLANO CHILE, AND CORN SOUP

Serves 8

The poblano chile is a large, thick-skinned chile that is often mistakenly called a pasilla, especially in California. (A true pasilla is a dried chilaca chile.) This soup is thick and warming.

- 6 slices bacon, diced
- 6 poblano chiles, roasted, peeled, and diced
- 1 onion, chopped
- 4 cloves garlic, minced
- 6 cups chicken stock
- 2½ pounds Yukon Gold potatoes, cut into ¾-inch cubes
- 4 fresh ears of corn, kernels cut from the cobs
- 1 cup crème fraîche *or* sour cream
- 3 tablespoons chopped fresh cilantro
- 1 tablespoon ground cumin
- Salt and freshly ground black pepper

In a stockpot or Dutch oven, cook the bacon over medium heat, stirring occasionally, until crisp. With a slotted spoon, remove the bacon to a paper towel–lined plate; reserve.

Add half of the chiles and the onion to the stockpot; sauté, stirring, for 8 minutes. Stir in the garlic; sauté, stirring, for 1 minute.

Add the stock and potatoes to the pot. Bring to a boil, reduce the heat, partially cover, and simmer for 20 minutes or until the potatoes are tender. In batches, purée the soup until smooth. Return the soup to the stockpot. Stir in the corn, crème fraîche, cilantro, cumin, and the reserved chiles and bacon; heat through and simmer for 5 minutes. Season with salt and pepper. Serve hot.

TORTILLA, LIME, AND CHICKEN SOUP

Serves 6-8

Most modern Southwest menus seem to offer a version of tortilla soup. The combinations of textures are lovely, the flavors are rousing, and the dish is a fitting beginning to a true Southwestern meal.

- 7 (6-inch) corn tortillas
- 2 tablespoons vegetable oil
- 1 onion, finely chopped
- 4 cloves garlic, minced
- 1 jalapeño pepper, seeded and minced
- 8 Roma tomatoes, seeded and diced
- 4 Anaheim chiles, roasted, peeled, and chopped
- 1 (6-ounce) can tomato paste
- 6 cups chicken stock
- 1 (15-ounce) can golden hominy, drained
- 1 tablespoon minced chipotle in adobo (page 197)
- 2 teaspoons ground cumin
- 2 teaspoons dried oregano leaves
- ½ teaspoon cayenne pepper
- ¾ pound cooked chicken, shredded
- 1 ripe avocado, pitted, peeled, and diced
- ½ cup lime juice
- ⅓ cup chopped fresh cilantro
- Salt and freshly ground black pepper
- 1 cup (4 ounces) shredded Monterey Jack cheese

Cut 3 of the tortillas into 1-inch pieces. Heat the oil in a stockpot or Dutch oven over medium heat. Add the tortilla pieces and cook until they are golden brown and slightly crisp. Add the onion; sauté, stirring occasionally, for 5 minutes. Add the garlic and jalapeño; sauté for 2 more minutes. Stir in the tomatoes, Anaheim chiles, and tomato paste; cook for 10 minutes on low heat, stirring occasionally. Stir in the stock, hominy, chipotle in adobo, cumin, oregano, and cayenne pepper. Bring to a boil, reduce the heat, partially cover, and simmer for 20 minutes or until slightly reduced. Stir in the shredded chicken, avocado, lime juice, and cilantro; heat through. Season with salt and black pepper. Keep warm until ready to serve.

Preheat the oven to 350°F. Cut the remaining 4 tortillas into thin strips. Place the strips on a baking sheet and bake for 10 to 15 minutes or until crisp.

To serve, ladle the soup into bowls and sprinkle with the cheese and crispy tortilla strips.

VEGETARIAN BLACK BEAN CHILI

Serves 4

The term "comfort food" in the Southwest must have had this dish in mind. This is a classic chili with intense, tummy warming flavors. In Texas chili is usually "con carne," with meat. In New Mexico it is more likely to be meatless like this one.

- 1½ cups dry black beans
- 2 tablespoons chili powder
- 1 tablespoon whole cumin seeds
- 1 tablespoon dried oregano leaves
- 1 tablespoon paprika
- 1 teaspoon cayenne pepper
- ½ cup olive oil
- 3 onions, chopped
- 5 cloves garlic, minced
- 3 (14½-ounce) cans vegetable broth
- 3 tomatoes, seeded and chopped
- 2 teaspoons rice wine vinegar
- 1 teaspoon minced chipotle in adobo (page 197)
- 2 bay leaves
- Salt and freshly ground black pepper
- ¾ cup shredded smoked cheddar cheese
- ½ cup crème fraîche *or* sour cream
- ¼ cup chopped fresh cilantro

To presoak the beans: Place them in a medium saucepan and cover with plenty of water. Bring to a boil and cook for 2 minutes. Remove from the heat, cover and let stand for 1 hour. Drain and discard the water; reserve the beans.

Place the chili powder, cumin seeds, oregano leaves, paprika, and cayenne pepper in a small dry skillet set over medium heat. Toast the spices for about 2 minutes, swirling the pan occasionally, until they are aromatic. Finely grind the spices in an electric spice grinder. Set aside.

Heat the oil in a large saucepan over medium heat. Add the onions and sauté, stirring occasionally, for 8 minutes. Add the garlic and sauté for 2 minutes. Stir in the broth, tomatoes, vinegar, chipotle in adobo, bay leaves, and the reserved beans and spices. Bring to a boil, reduce the heat, cover, and simmer for 1 to 1½ hours until the beans are cooked and the chili is thick. Remove and discard the bay leaves. Season with salt and black pepper.

To serve, sprinkle the cheese into 4 deep soup plates. Top with the chili, crème fraîche, and cilantro.

FIELD GREENS WITH FIRE-ROASTED POBLANO CHILES IN BALSAMIC VINAIGRETTE

ADAPTED FROM A RECIPE FROM KATHARINE KAGEL'S CAFÉ PASQUAL'S, SANTA FE, NEW MEXICO

Serves 6

Salad is not typical in the American Southwest because succulent lettuce has a difficult time growing in the dry soils of the region. One of the Native American groups from Arizona was actually named the Sinagua, meaning "without water." In modern times the greens can be transported quickly from California and other better irrigated areas.

- ⅓ cup olive oil
- ¼ cup balsamic vinegar
- 1 teaspoon ground cumin
- 1 teaspoon ground coriander
- Salt and freshly ground black pepper
- 6 poblano chiles, roasted, peeled, and coarsely chopped
- 6 cups spring salad mix of field greens (mesclun)
- 1 cup diced, peeled jicama
- 1 cup red *and/or* yellow pear tomatoes

In a small bowl, whisk together the oil, vinegar, cumin, and coriander; season with salt and pepper. Mix in the poblanos. Set aside.

Place the field greens, jicama, and tomatoes in a large salad bowl. Pour the dressing over and toss to coat completely. Serve immediately.

SOUTHWESTERN COBB SALAD
ADAPTED FROM A RECIPE BY STEPHAN PYLES, STAR CANYON, DALLAS, TEXAS

Serves 6-8

The original Cobb salad was created in 1926 by Bob Cobb, owner of the Brown Derby Restaurant in Los Angeles. It is a chopped salad that includes bacon, chicken, avocado, lettuce, cheese, and a number of other ingredients. Here this California concept becomes a Southwest original.

- 1½ cups chicken stock
- ½ cup dry white wine
- 1 small yellow onion, chopped
- 1 serrano chile, seeded and minced
- 2 cloves garlic, minced
- ½ teaspoon dried tarragon leaves
- 1 pound boneless, skinless chicken breasts
- 8 cloves roasted garlic (page 236)
- 2 tablespoons balsamic vinegar
- 2 tablespoons red wine vinegar
- 1 tablespoon honey mustard
- 1½ teaspoons ground cumin
- 1 teaspoon *each* chopped fresh cilantro, thyme, sage, and basil
- ½ teaspoon cayenne pepper

- 1⅓ cups olive oil
- Salt and freshly ground black pepper
- 1 heart romaine lettuce, sliced crosswise
- 2 heads Belgian endive, sliced crosswise
- 1 bunch watercress, stems removed
- ½ cup packed fresh cilantro leaves
- 4 hard-cooked eggs, peeled and chopped
- 2 medium tomatoes, diced
- 1 avocado, peeled, pitted, and diced
- 1 cup (4 ounces) shredded jalapeño Monterey Jack cheese
- 8 slices bacon, diced, cooked crisp, and drained
- 4 green onions (scallions), sliced

Place the stock, wine, yellow onion, serrano chile, minced garlic, and tarragon in a large saucepan. Bring to a boil, reduce the heat to simmer and add the chicken breasts. Cover and poach for about 20 minutes or until firm. Remove the chicken from the saucepan and allow it to cool. Meanwhile, return the saucepan to medium heat and reduce the stock mixture to 2 tablespoons. Strain the mixture, cool, and reserve. When the chicken is cool enough to handle, cut it into ½-inch chunks. Set aside.

To make the vinaigrette: Place the roasted garlic, vinegars, mustard, cumin, chopped cilantro, thyme, sage, basil, cayenne pepper, and reduced stock in a food processor fitted with the metal blade. Purée. With the motor running, slowly pour the oil through the feed tube and process until the vinaigrette is thoroughly emulsified. Season with salt and black pepper. Set aside.

Place the romaine, endive, watercress, and cilantro leaves in a large bowl; toss gently to combine. Transfer the greens to a large platter. In rows or circles, arrange the chicken, eggs, tomatoes, avocado and cheese over the greens. Sprinkle the bacon and green onions over the salad.

To serve, bring the salad platter to the table, pour the vinaigrette over the salad and toss well. Serve immediately.

SOUTHWEST CAESAR SALAD WITH
SPICY POLENTA CROUTONS
ADAPTED FROM A RECIPE BY STEPHAN PYLES, STAR CANYON, DALLAS, TEXAS

Serves 8

Chef Stephan Pyles

Stephan Pyles is one of the founding fathers of contemporary Southwest Cuisine. He was chef/owner of the Routh Street Cafe in Dallas and its more casual spin-off, Baby Routh. In 1994, he opened Star Canyon, featuring his estimable New Texas Cuisine.

Chef Pyles began cooking at age eight in his family's Truck-Stop Cafe in West Texas. After college, he traveled to France and then worked in several Dallas-area restaurants before signing on as Chef's Assistant at the Robert Mondavi Winery cooking school. There, he worked with such masters as Michel Guerard, George Blanc, and the Troisgros brothers.

In 1985, he became the first Texan named to the Who's Who of Cooking in America, and in 1991, he was given the James Beard Award for "Best Chef in the Southwest Region." His first book, The New Texas Cuisine was published in 1994.

Here is an eye-opening variation on Caesar salad from one of the most creative and talented cooks in the southwest. The croutons take a little time to make, but the result is breathtaking.

- 2¾ cups milk
- 4 serrano chiles, seeded and minced
- 2 teaspoons salt
- ¾ teaspoon cayenne pepper
- 1½ cups yellow cornmeal
- Peanut oil, for frying
- 1 shallot, coarsely chopped
- 4 anchovy fillets
- 4 cloves roasted garlic (page 236)
- 3 egg yolks
- ¼ cup lemon juice
- 4 teaspoons Dijon-style mustard
- 1 tablespoon balsamic vinegar
- 2 teaspoons chopped chipotle in adobo (page 197)
- ¼ teaspoon ground cumin
- 1 cup extra virgin olive oil
- 4 to 6 hearts of romaine lettuce, washed, dried, and torn
- 1½ cups shaved Parmesan cheese

To make the croutons: Bring the milk, serranos, 1½ teaspoons of the salt and ½ teaspoon of the cayenne pepper to a boil in a medium saucepan. Slowly add 1 cup of the cornmeal, stirring constantly. Reduce the heat to medium and cook for 3 minutes or until the mixture pulls away from the side of the pan and forms a ball. Press the mixture into a 9-inch pie plate that is lined with plastic wrap. Refrigerate, uncovered, until cooled. Remove from the pie plate and cut into ½-inch cubes. Heat 1 inch of peanut oil in a large heavy skillet to 350°F. Dredge the polenta cubes in the remaining ½ cup cornmeal. Fry the croutons until crisp and golden brown, 1 to 2 minutes. Remove from the oil with a slotted spoon to a paper towel–lined baking sheet. Keep warm until ready to serve.

To make the dressing: Place the shallot, anchovies, and garlic in a food processor fitted with the metal blade; process until finely chopped. Add the egg yolks, lemon juice, mustard, vinegar, chipotle, cumin, and the remaining ½ teaspoon salt and ¼ teaspoon cayenne pepper; blend until smooth. With the machine running, slowly pour the olive oil through the feed tube and process until emulsified and thoroughly incorporated. Set aside.

In a large salad bowl, toss the lettuce with the dressing, croutons, and ¾ cup of the cheese. Divide the tossed greens among 8 plates and top with the remaining ¾ cup cheese. Serve immediately.

CHIPOTLE SHRIMP WITH CORN CAKES
ADAPTED FROM A RECIPE BY MARK MILLER, COYOTE CAFE, SANTA FE, NEW MEXICO

Serves 6

The combination of spiced shrimps and corn cakes is a perfect meshing of flavors. Chef Miller is tremendously inventive, but his ideas always make sense. This recipe is a modern Southwest classic.

- ¾ cup all-purpose flour
- ½ cup yellow cornmeal
- 1 teaspoon sugar
- 1 teaspoon salt
- ½ teaspoon baking powder
- ½ teaspoon baking soda
- 1¼ cups buttermilk
- 10 tablespoons melted unsalted butter
- 1 egg, beaten
- 1 cup fresh corn kernels
- 4 green onions (scallions), chopped
- 2 tablespoons chipotle in adobo (page 197)
- ¼ cup unsalted butter
- 1½ pounds medium shrimp, peeled and deveined (about 30)
- Freshly ground black pepper
- 1 cup prepared fresh salsa (page 168)

To make the corn cakes: Place the flour, cornmeal, sugar, salt, baking powder, and baking soda in a bowl. In a large bowl, whisk together the buttermilk and 2 tablespoons of the melted butter, then whisk in the egg. Gradually add the dry ingredients to the liquid and stir until thoroughly combined. Purée ½ cup of the corn kernels and fold into the batter with the whole kernels and 2 of the green onions. If the batter is too thick, add a little bit more buttermilk.

Into a nonstick skillet over medium heat, ladle the batter to form 3-inch corn cakes. Cook until golden brown, about 2½ minutes on each side. Repeat until all the batter is used (you should have 18 corn cakes). Set aside; keep warm.

In a small bowl, mix together the remaining ½ cup melted butter with the chipotle in adobo. Set aside; keep warm.

Melt the solid butter in a large skillet over medium heat. Season the shrimp with pepper and additional salt. Cook the shrimp until opaque throughout, about 3 to 4 minutes.

Place 3 corn cakes on each plate. Arrange 5 shrimp on top of the cakes. Drizzle with the chipotle butter and sprinkle with the remaining 2 green onions. Serve the salsa on the side.

MIXED SEAFOOD TACOS WITH CUCUMBER SALSA

Makes 8 tacos (4–8 servings)

Tacos are tortillas that have been fried and formed into a pocket to hold various foods. In this case the taco is filled with a delectable mixture of shrimp, crabmeat, and scallops.

- 2 tomatoes, seeded and diced
- 1 cup diced English cucumber
- 1 small red onion, diced
- 1 jalapeño pepper, seeded and minced
- ¼ cup chopped fresh cilantro
- ¼ cup lime juice
- 2 tablespoons orange juice
- 1 tablespoon grated orange zest
- Salt and freshly ground black pepper
- 3 avocados, peeled, seeded and mashed
- ½ pound crabmeat
- ½ pound medium shrimp, peeled, deveined, and cut in half crosswise
- ½ pound bay scallops
- 1 teaspoon ground cumin
- 1 teaspoon dried oregano leaves
- 1 teaspoon cayenne pepper
- ¼ cup olive oil
- 4 romaine lettuce leaves, shredded
- 8 prepared super-size taco shells
- Hot pepper sauce

To make the salsa: In a small bowl, combine the tomatoes, cucumber, onion, jalapeño, 2 tablespoons of the cilantro, 2 tablespoons of the lime juice, the orange zest, and orange juice; toss gently. Season with salt and black pepper. Cover and refrigerate until ready to serve.

Place the avocados in another bowl. Add the remaining 2 tablespoons of cilantro and 2 tablespoons of lime juice; mix well. Season with salt and black pepper. Cover and set aside until ready to serve.

Place the crab, shrimp, and scallops in a medium bowl. Add the cumin, oregano, and cayenne pepper; toss gently to coat the seafood completely. Season with salt and black pepper. Heat the oil in a large skillet over medium-high heat. Add the seafood; sauté, tossing constantly, until opaque throughout, about 2 minutes.

To serve, line each taco shell with lettuce. Top with the seafood mixture, salsa, and avocado. Drizzle with hot pepper sauce.

PAN-FRIED SWORDFISH WITH TEQUILA-TOMATILLO VINAIGRETTE AND JICAMA SALAD

ADAPTED FROM A RECIPE BY DEAN FEARING, THE MANSION ON TURTLE CREEK, DALLAS, TEXAS

Serves 6

Tomatillos look like little green tomatoes, but actually they are members of the Cape Gooseberry family. Here they provide a tangy counterpoint to the richness of the swordfish.

- ½ cup 100% agave tequila
- ¼ cup white wine vinegar
- 1 shallot, minced
- 1 clove garlic, minced
- ¼ cup olive oil
- 4 tomatillos, diced
- 1 tomato, seeded and diced
- ¼ cup chopped fresh cilantro
- Salt and freshly ground black pepper
- 1 small jicama, peeled and cut into julienne strips
- 3 tablespoons lime juice
- Cayenne pepper
- 6 (8-ounce) swordfish steaks, trimmed of any fat, skin, and dark membrane
- ½ cup peanut oil
- 6 fresh cilantro sprigs, for garnish

To make the vinaigrette: Combine the tequila, vinegar, shallot, and garlic in a small saucepan over medium heat. Bring to a boil and cook until reduced by half, about 10 minutes. Remove from the heat and whisk in the olive oil, pouring in a thin stream. Add the tomatillos, tomato, and 2 tablespoons of the chopped cilantro. Season with salt and black pepper. Cover and set aside.

To make the salad: Combine the jicama, lime juice, and the remaining 2 tablespoons chopped cilantro. Toss lightly. Season with salt and cayenne pepper. Cover and set aside.

Season the swordfish with salt. Heat the peanut oil in a large skillet over high heat. Pan fry the swordfish for 3 minutes. Reduce the heat to medium, turn the fish over, and cook for 2 more minutes or until no longer translucent. Allow no more than 5 minutes of total cooking time for each ½ inch of thickness at thickest part. Do not overcook. The fish should be very moist.

To serve, ladle the vinaigrette over the bottom of each of 6 dinner plates. Place 1 swordfish steak in the center of each plate. Mound the salad on top of the fish; garnish with the cilantro sprigs. Serve immediately.

MARINATED CHICKEN BREASTS WITH CILANTRO-PEANUT PESTO SAUCE

Serves 4

Here is living proof that a dish can be loaded with flavor and still be virtually cholesterol-free.

½ cup olive oil	¼ teaspoon ground allspice
5 tablespoons lemon juice	4 boned and skinned chicken
¼ cup chopped fresh cilantro	breast halves, about
1 tablespoon *achiote* powder	4 ounces each
(available in Hispanic markets)	1 clove garlic
1 teaspoon dried	½ of 1 serrano *or* jalapeño
oregano leaves	pepper, seeded
1 teaspoon ground cumin	¼ cup roasted peanuts
½ teaspoon freshly ground	1 teaspoon Dijon-style mustard
pepper	Salt

To make the marinade: In a shallow dish, whisk together 2 tablespoons of the oil, ¼ cup of the lemon juice, 2 tablespoons of the cilantro, and the achiote powder, oregano, cumin, pepper, and allspice. Add the chicken; cover and refrigerate for 1 hour.

To make the sauce: Place the garlic and the serrano into a food processor fitted with the metal blade; process until finely chopped. Add the peanuts, mustard, and the remaining 6 tablespoons of oil, 2 tablespoons of cilantro, and 1 tablespoon of lemon juice. Process until well blended. Season with salt. Set aside.

Prepare the grill. Remove the chicken from the marinade. Grill the chicken, basting with the marinade, for 6 to 8 minutes, until the juices run clear, turning once. Discard any remaining marinade.

To serve, place the chicken breasts on 4 warmed plates and spoon the sauce over them.

COUNTRY-STYLE PORK RIBS IN GREEN CHILE SAUCE WITH STEAMED CABBAGE

ADAPTED FROM A RECIPE BY ROBERT DEL GRANDE, CAFÉ ANNIE, HOUSTON, TEXAS

Serves 4

These ribs are not the traditional cut. Instead they are cut from the rib end of the pork loin, the shoulder blade bone is chined (cracked), and then they are butterflied. They are particularly meaty. The green chiles give this hearty dish lively flavor.

4 pounds country-style pork	2 (6-inch) corn tortillas, toasted
ribs, cut as described above	in a dry skillet and torn into
6½ cups water	small pieces
2 white onions, coarsely	½ cup chopped fresh
chopped	cilantro
4 cloves garlic	2 to 4 tablespoons lime juice
2 teaspoons salt	Freshly ground black pepper
2 poblano *or* Anaheim chiles,	1 small head green cabbage,
roasted and peeled	coarsely chopped
	2 tablespoons olive oil

Place the pork ribs, 6 cups of the water, the onions, garlic, and salt in a stockpot or Dutch oven. Bring to a boil, reduce the heat, and simmer, covered, for 1½ hours.

When the ribs are tender, remove them from the pot. Bring the liquid back to a boil and reduce to 3 cups, about 10 to 15 minutes. Transfer the liquid with the solids to a blender. Add the chiles and tortillas; blend to a coarse purée. Transfer the purée back to the pot. Bring to a boil, then reduce to a simmer. Add the ribs to the pot and simmer, covered, for 15 minutes. If the sauce is too thick, add a little water. Stir in the cilantro. Season with the lime juice, pepper, and additional salt, if necessary. Keep hot.

In a large skillet, combine the cabbage, olive oil and the remaining ½ cup water. Bring to a boil, reduce the heat, cover, and steam until tender, 3 to 5 minutes. Season with salt and pepper.

To serve, cut the ribs into serving pieces. Place the cabbage on each of 4 dinner plates. Top with the ribs and spoon the sauce over them.

BLUE CORN TORTILLA–CRUSTED CHICKEN BREASTS WITH ANNATTO RICE

ADAPTED FROM A RECIPE BY STEPHAN PYLES, STAR CANYON, DALLAS, TEXAS

Serves 4

One of the best uses for blue corn flour is in this dazzling recipe by one of the Southwest's young geniuses.

- ½ cup olive oil
- 2 tablespoons annatto seeds
- 1 small onion, finely diced
- 1 small carrot, finely diced
- 1 stalk celery, finely diced
- 2 cloves garlic, minced
- 2 cups sliced wild mushrooms
- 1 fresh ear of corn, kernels cut from the cob
- 1 cup long-grain rice
- 1 teaspoon ground cinnamon
- 3½ cups chicken stock
- ½ crumbled *queso fresco*
- 6 tablespoons chopped fresh cilantro
- Salt and freshly ground black pepper
- 1 cup finely ground blue tortilla chips
- ⅓ cup yellow cornmeal
- ⅓ cup all-purpose flour
- 1 teaspoon ground cumin
- 1 teaspoon cayenne pepper
- 1 teaspoon chili powder
- 2 eggs
- 2 tablespoons milk
- 4 skinless, boneless chicken breast halves
- ¼ cup vegetable oil
- 1 cup dry white wine
- ⅔ cup sour cream
- 4 teaspoons puréed chipotle in adobo (page 197)

To make the rice: Heat the olive oil and annatto seeds in a small saucepan until the oil becomes very hot. Remove from the heat and let stand 3 hours. Carefully skim off the colored oil, leaving the bottom layer undisturbed.

In a large saucepan, heat the annatto oil over medium heat. Add the onion, carrot, celery, and garlic; sauté, stirring, for 2 minutes. Add the mushrooms and corn; cook for 2 minutes longer. Add the rice and cinnamon; stir for 1 minute. Add 2½ cups of the stock; bring to a boil, reduce the heat, and simmer for 15 minutes, uncovered. Cover the pan and continue cooking for 5 minutes more. Remove the pan from the heat and let stand, covered, for 5 minutes. Mix in the queso fresco and cilantro; season with salt and pepper. Set aside and keep warm.

In a medium bowl, combine the ground chips, cornmeal, flour, cumin, cayenne pepper, and chili powder. In another bowl, whisk together eggs and milk. Dip the chicken breasts into this mixture, then dredge in the tortilla mixture to coat completely. Season with salt and black pepper. Heat the vegetable oil in a large skillet over medium heat; add the chicken breasts and sauté about 10 minutes until the juices run clear, turning once. Remove the chicken from the skillet and set aside.

Pour off the oil from the skillet. Deglaze the skillet with the wine and reduce to 2 tablespoons. Add the remaining 1 cup of stock, bring to a boil, and reduce to ¼ cup. Whisk in the sour cream and chipotle purée; season with salt and black pepper. Serve the chicken drizzled with the sauce and accompanied by the rice.

RED CHILE-CHORIZO SAUCE

ADAPTED FROM A RECIPE FROM KATHARINE KAGEL'S CAFÉ PASQUAL'S, SANTA FE, NEW MEXICO

Makes 3 cups

This multipurpose sauce can turn the blandest things into exciting Southwest dishes. A combination of chiles and spicy sausage, it adds zing to omelets, scrambled eggs, griddle polenta, enchiladas, burritos, rice, or even pasta.

- 6 ounces dried red New Mexico chiles
- 1 white onion, coarsely chopped
- 4 cloves garlic
- 1 teaspoon dried oregano leaves
- ½ teaspoon ground cumin
- ½ pound cooked crumbled Chorizo sausage
- Pinch of sugar
- Salt

To rehydrate the chiles: Place them in a large saucepan and cover with hot tap water. The chiles will float, so cover them with a plate slightly smaller than the circumference of the pot to keep them submerged. Let soak until soft and pliable, about 20 minutes.

When the chiles are fully rehydrated, remove the plate and add the onion, garlic, oregano, and cumin. Bring to a boil, reduce the heat, and simmer, uncovered, for 20 minutes.

Drain the chile mixture, reserving the liquid. Place the chile mixture in a blender and purée with enough of the liquid to reach a ketchup-like consistency. When the sauce is thoroughly blended, pass it through a fine-mesh sieve over the saucepan. Stir in the sausage. Heat through and season with the sugar and salt.

ROAST PORK ADOBO STYLE

Serves 6

Pork en adobo *is pork served with a red chile sauce. Here is a delicious and memorable recipe for this classic Southwest dish.*

- 1 (3-pound) boned and tied pork loin roast
- 4 cloves garlic
- 2 dried ancho chiles, stems removed and discarded
- ¼ cup chili powder
- 1 tablespoon cayenne pepper
- 1 tablespoon dried oregano leaves
- 1 tablespoon dried thyme leaves
- 1 tablespoon ground cumin
- 1 tablespoon garlic powder
- 1 tablespoon ground coriander
- 1 tablespoon celery salt
- 1 tablespoon onion powder
- 1 tablespoon paprika
- 6 thick slices bacon, diced
- 4 tomatoes, seeded and diced
- 2 red bell peppers, roasted, peeled, seeded, and diced
- 2 Anaheim chiles, roasted, peeled, seeded, and diced
- 1 red onion, diced
- 1 tablespoon minced chipotle in adobo (page 197)
- 1 cup dry red wine
- 2 cups veal stock
- 1 tablespoon honey
- Salt and freshly ground black pepper

Preheat the oven to 475°F. Cut small slits in the pork and set it on a rack in a roasting pan. Thinly slice 1 of the garlic cloves and stud the slices into the slits in the pork. Set aside.

Place the ancho chiles in a blender and grind to a fine powder; transfer to a small bowl. Stir in the chili powder, cayenne pepper, oregano, thyme, cumin, garlic powder, coriander, celery salt, onion powder, and paprika; mix well. Remove ½ cup of the mixture and set it aside for the sauce. Rub the remainder of the mixture all over the pork to coat completely.

Place the pork in the oven and roast for 30 minutes. Remove the meat from the oven and let cool for 30 minutes. It will still be raw in the center, but the cooking will be finished later. This cooling period will guarantee even cooking and very tender meat. Reduce the oven temperature to 375°F.

While the roast is cooking, make the sauce. Cook the bacon in a large skillet over medium heat until crisp; remove with a slotted spoon and allow to drain on a paper towel–lined plate. Reserve. Drain all but 2 tablespoons of the fat from the skillet. Add the tomatoes, bell peppers, Anaheim chiles, and onion; sauté, stirring occasionally, for 10 minutes. Mince the remaining 3 cloves of garlic; add them to the skillet along with the chipotle in adobo and sauté, stirring occasionally, for 5 minutes. Pour in the wine and cook until reduced to a glaze. Pour in the stock and continue to cook until reduced by half, about 10 minutes. Stir in the honey and the reserved bacon; season with salt and black pepper. Set aside; keep warm.

Return the pork to the oven; continue to roast for 20 to 25 minutes longer or until a meat thermometer registers 140°F. Remove from the oven; transfer to a platter and let rest 15 minutes before slicing. Slice and serve with the sauce.

CINNAMON-ROASTED CHICKEN WITH RUSTIC PAN SAUCE
ADAPTED FROM A RECIPE BY ROBERT DEL GRANDE,
CAFÉ ANNIE, HOUSTON, TEXAS

Serves 4

Anyone who ever doubted that there is authentic American food which is not derivative of European cooking should taste this extraordinary dish. The flavors here are unique, distinctive, and completely seductive.

- 1 (3½ to 4-pound) whole chicken
- 1 teaspoon ground cinnamon
- ½ teaspoon chili powder
- ½ teaspoon salt
- ¼ teaspoon freshly ground black pepper
- 1½ cups assorted wild mushrooms, stemmed and chopped
- 3 Roma tomatoes, cut into quarters
- 2 poblano chiles, seeded and chopped
- 1 small white onion, coarsely chopped
- 1 (6-inch) corn tortilla, cut into quarters
- ⅓ cup pumpkin seeds
- 5 cloves garlic
- 2 tablespoons olive oil
- 2 cups chicken stock
- 1 tablespoon dark brown sugar
- Additional salt and freshly ground black pepper

Preheat the oven to 325°F. With poultry shears or a sharp knife, split the chicken through the back. Pull the chicken open, place the bone-side down on your work surface and press firmly to flatten the bird. To secure the legs in place, make 2 slits through the skin on each side of the chicken near the tail. Insert the ends of the legs through the holes.

In a small bowl, combine the cinnamon, chili powder, ½ teaspoon salt, and ¼ teaspoon pepper. Rub the chicken all over with the spice mixture; reserve.

In an ovenproof skillet large enough to hold the chicken, evenly spread the mushrooms, tomatoes, chiles, onion, tortillas, pumpkin seeds, and garlic. Drizzle 1 tablespoon of the oil over the mixture. Place the chicken, skin-side up, on top of the mixture. Brush the chicken with the remaining 1 tablespoon oil. Roast in the oven for 1 hour or until the chicken juices run clear.

When cooked, remove the chicken from the skillet; keep warm. Add the stock to the pan; stir the ingredients and scrape the bottom of the pan to loosen any caramelized pieces that might be stuck to the surface. Transfer the ingredients with the stock to a blender. Purée until smooth. Return the sauce to the skillet; bring it to a boil, reduce the heat, and simmer for about 15 to 20 minutes until thick. Stir in the brown sugar; season with salt and pepper.

Cut the chicken into serving pieces. Return them to the pan and warm through. Serve the chicken with a generous helping of the sauce.

Sauces and Salsas

Hot is hot! The latest rage around the country is hot food, food seasoned with hot chiles. A few years ago, salsa surpassed ketchup as the national condiment of choice. Not only are these sauces fiery and flavorful, but they are healthy too (chiles are loaded with vitamin C). Salsa is easy to make fresh at home, and the variations are almost endless.

Salsa is Spanish for sauce, but in the Southwest, not every sauce is a salsa. Salsas are typically made from raw ingredients, and are usually served condiment-style at the table. Sauces, generally, are cooked mixtures that are a fundamental part of a dish. An adobo sauce, for instance, might be used as a marinade for meat or seafood and is applied before or during the cooking.

The basic tomato-onion-chile salsa remains the bestseller, a natural partner for dipping with tortilla chips. But even this simple version can be chunky or smooth, hot or mild, and the flavor can be altered by choice of chiles. Chefs around the country have taken the basic concept and let their creativity run wild, coming up with salsas made with tropical fruits, seafood, and exotic nuts. These inventive condiments are a great way to spice up chicken, steak, or fish entrees.

If you want to learn more about the art of salsa, then Reed Hearon's Salsa (Chronicle Books) and Mark Miller's The Great Salsa Book (Ten Speed Press) are required reading. The recipes by these two leading chefs are certain to warm up family and friends.

Marinated Rack of Lamb with Rosemary-Serrano Aioli
Adapted from a recipe by Mark Miller, Coyote Café, Santa Fe, New Mexico

Serves 4

Here is a modern Southwest treatment of the classic Provençal combination of garlicky aioli and lamb. Chef Miller suggests adding sliced black olives and orange zest to the aioli if desired.

- 1¾ cups olive oil
- ½ cup lime juice
- 3 tablespoons chopped fresh rosemary
- 3 tablespoons chopped fresh cilantro
- 4 serrano chiles, seeded and minced
- 4 cloves garlic, minced
- Salt and freshly ground black pepper
- 2 half-racks of lamb (each with 4 double-rib chops, serving 2 double-rib chops per person)
- 3 egg yolks

To make the marinade: In a large, shallow dish whisk together ½ cup of the oil, ¼ cup of the lime juice, 2 tablespoons of the rosemary, 1 tablespoon of cilantro, 2 of the serrano chiles, and 2 of the garlic cloves. Season with salt and pepper. Add the lamb and coat with the marinade. Cover, refrigerate, and marinate for 4 hours or overnight.

To make the aioli: Place the egg yolks and the remaining ¼ cup of lime juice, 2 tablespoons of cilantro, 2 serranos, 2 cloves of garlic, and 1 tablespoon of rosemary in a food processor fitted with the metal blade; purée. With the motor running, slowly drizzle 1 cup of the oil through the feed tube and process until thickened and emulsified. Season with salt and pepper. Chill for 30 minutes. Serve cool, but not cold.

Preheat the oven to 400°F. Drain the lamb; discard the marinade. In a large ovenproof skillet (use two if necessary) set over high heat, bring the remaining ¼ cup of oil to almost smoking and then reduce the heat to medium. Sear the lamb until browned, 1 to 2 minutes per side. Place the skillet in the oven and cook until medium-rare, or until the internal temperature reaches 130°F, about 12 minutes.

Cut the racks into double-rib chops. Serve topped with the aioli.

Chef Mark Miller

Mark Miller is nationally recognized for his innovative and robust modern Southwest Cuisine. His restaurants include the Coyote Cafe in Santa Fe, the Coyote Cafe in Las Vegas, and Red Sage in Washington, D.C.

Chef Miller began his culinary training with Alice Waters at Chez Panisse in Berkeley. In 1979 he opened the Fourth Street Grill in Berkeley. One year later, he opened the Santa Fe Bar and Grill, also in Berkeley. As the next logical step, he moved to Santa Fe to open the first Coyote Cafe in 1987. Chef Miller was named "one of the most influential chefs of the decade" by Life. *He has authored several bestselling cookbooks and has produced the popular Great Chile Posters. His Coyote Cocina products are available in gourmet stores and through mail order (see page 197).*

Southwest Barbecue

Unlike Kansas City barbecue where sauce is often placed on the meat during cooking, Texas barbecue is a slow method in which meat, often brisket, is dry cooked for three days. Sauce, if used at all, is added at the table. At Clark's Outpost Bar-B-Q in Tioga, fifty miles north of Dallas, various cuts of beef and pork are cooked, as well as quail and "mountain oysters."

COWBOY STEAKS WITH RED CHILE ONION RINGS
ADAPTED FROM A RECIPE BY MARK MILLER, THE COYOTE CAFÉ, SANTA FE, NEW MEXICO

Serves 4

The Southwest is cattle country, and this is steak at its best. Add the seasoned onion rings for a memorable feast.

- 4 white onions, cut into thin rings
- 3 cups milk
- 3 cups all-purpose flour, sifted
- ¼ cup chili powder
- 3 tablespoons cornstarch
- 1 tablespoon ground cumin
- 1 tablespoon paprika
- 1 tablespoon salt
- 2 teaspoons sugar
- Vegetable oil, for frying
- 4 bone-in rib-eye steaks (*or* T-bone or porterhouse steaks), 1½ inches thick
- Freshly ground black pepper
- Pico de Gallo Salsa (recipe below)

Soak the onions in the milk in a large bowl for 1 hour. Drain well. Mix together the flour, chili powder, cornstarch, cumin, paprika, salt, and sugar in another large bowl. Dredge the onions in the flour mixture; shake off any excess. Pour enough oil into a large heavy saucepan to reach a level of 2 inches; heat to 360°F. Add the onions in batches and cook until golden brown, about 45 seconds each batch. Transfer to a paper towel–lined baking sheet; drain well. Keep hot.

Prepare the grill. Season the steaks with pepper and additional salt. Grill or broil to desired doneness, turning once. Serve immediately with the onion rings and salsa.

Pico de Gallo Salsa: In a medium bowl combine 2 chopped large tomatoes, ¼ cup minced onion, 2 tablespoons chopped fresh cilantro, 2 tablespoons lime juice, 2 seeded, minced serrano chiles, 2 teaspoons sugar, and 1 teaspoon salt. Cover and refrigerate until ready to use.

BARBECUED FLANK STEAK WITH GRILLED ONION GUACAMOLE

ADAPTED FROM A RECIPE BY DEAN FEARING, THE MANSION ON TURTLE CREEK, DALLAS, TEXAS

Serves 4

Flank steak grills nicely and has lots of flavor. Its lean meat can be tough if it isn't cut across the grain.

- ½ cup plus 2 tablespoons olive oil
- ½ cup plus 2 tablespoons lime juice
- ½ cup plus 2 tablespoons chopped fresh cilantro
- 1 yellow onion, thinly sliced
- 8 cloves garlic, minced
- 5 jalapeño peppers, seeded and minced
- Salt and freshly ground black pepper
- 1½ pounds flank steak
- 2 tablespoons lemon juice
- 1 tablespoon red wine vinegar
- 1 teaspoon ground cumin
- 1 large red onion, cut into ¼-inch thick slices
- 2 avocados, peeled, pitted, and diced
- 1 tomato, diced
- 8 (7-inch) warm flour tortillas
- Sour cream
- Sliced, pitted ripe olives

Combine ½ cup of the oil, ½ cup of the lime juice, ½ cup of the cilantro, the yellow onion, 6 cloves of the garlic, and 4 of the jalapeños in a large shallow dish. Season with salt and pepper. Add the flank steak; cover and marinate in the refrigerator for 8 hours or overnight, turning from time to time.

Meanwhile, in another shallow dish, combine the lemon juice, vinegar, cumin, and the remaining 2 tablespoons of oil. Season with salt and pepper. Add the red onion; marinate at room temperature for 1 hour.

Prepare the grill. Remove the flank steak and onion from their marinades; discard the marinades. Grill the steak to desired doneness, turning once, and grill the onion until soft, turning once. Set the steak aside, tented with aluminum foil. Chop the grilled onion.

Place the grilled onion in a medium bowl. Add the avocados, tomato, and the remaining 2 tablespoons of lime juice, 2 tablespoons of cilantro, 2 cloves of garlic and 1 jalapeño. Mix gently. Season with salt and pepper. Set aside.

Slice the meat across the grain into thin strips. Serve with the guacamole, tortillas, sour cream, and olives.

VEGETABLE CORNBREAD

Makes one 9-inch square cornbread

Corn is an essential ingredient in the development of American cuisine. In the Southwest cornbread can be made into a flavorful vegetable accompaniment.

- 1⅓ cups yellow cornmeal
- 1 tablespoon sugar
- 1½ teaspoons cayenne pepper
- 1 teaspoon baking powder
- 1 teaspoon salt
- ¾ cup buttermilk
- 2 eggs, lightly beaten
- ¼ cup melted bacon fat *or* vegetable oil
- 3 fresh ears of corn, kernels cut from cobs
- 2 poblano chiles, roasted, peeled, and diced
- 1 tomato, seeded and diced
- 1 tablespoon chopped fresh cilantro

Preheat the oven to 350°F. Grease a 9-inch square baking pan; set aside.

In a large bowl, combine the cornmeal, sugar, cayenne pepper, baking powder, and salt. In another bowl, beat together the buttermilk and eggs. Add to the dry ingredients with the bacon fat, corn, chiles, tomato, and cilantro; mix well. Scrape the batter into the prepared baking pan. Bake for 35 minutes or until a cake tester or toothpick inserted into the center comes out clean. Remove to a rack to cool slightly. Cut into squares and serve warm with lots of sweet butter.

SOUTHWEST APPLE-JALAPEÑO JACK CHEESE CRUMB TART

ADAPTED FROM A RECIPE BY DEAN FEARING, THE MANSION ON TURTLE CREEK,
DALLAS, TEXAS

Makes one 12-inch tart

*Monterey Jack cheese was first made in California by David Jacks in the mid-1800s.
It is mild and similar in style to the cheese made by the mission padres. As a result it
has become a staple in the pantry of California and the Southwest.*

- ½ cup plus 2 tablespoons granulated sugar
- ½ cup plus 1 tablespoon milk
- ¼ teaspoon vanilla extract
- 2 eggs
- 1 tablespoon cornstarch
- ¾ cup all-purpose flour
- ¼ cup (½ stick) unsalted butter, at room temperature
- 2 tablespoons golden brown sugar, packed

- 2 tablespoons toasted slivered almonds, finely chopped
- ¾ teaspoon cinnamon
- ½ of a (17¼-ounce) package frozen puff pastry dough, thawed
- 1 cup (4 ounces) shredded jalapeño Monterey Jack cheese
- 3 large Granny Smith apples, peeled, cored, and thinly sliced
- 2 tablespoons powdered sugar

To make the pastry cream: Combine 2 tablespoons of granulated sugar, ½ cup of milk, and the vanilla in a small saucepan over medium heat. Bring to a boil. Remove from the heat. Combine the eggs, cornstarch, 2 tablespoons of the granulated sugar, and the remaining 1 tablespoon of milk in a small bowl. Add a bit of the hot liquid to the eggs, stirring vigorously. Slowly whisk the egg mixture into the hot milk. Return the pan to medium heat and cook, stirring constantly, until the mixture thickens, about 2 minutes. DO NOT BOIL. Remove from the heat immediately, still stirring. Stir for a few minutes longer, then let cool. Cover and chill.

To make the crumb topping: In a small bowl combine the flour, butter, brown sugar, almonds, 2 tablespoons of the granulated sugar, and ¼ teaspoon of the cinnamon. Using your hands, mix the ingredients together until small crumbs form. Set aside.

To make the cinnamon sugar: In a bowl, combine the remaining ¼ cup granulated sugar and ½ teaspoon cinnamon. Set aside.

Preheat the oven to 400°F. Roll the puff pastry into a 12-inch circle; place on a baking sheet. Spread the pastry cream on the dough, leaving 1 inch clear around the edge. Sprinkle the cheese over the pastry cream. Leaving the edge clear, overlap the apple slices to form an outer circle. Continue to form inner circles of apple slices which partially cover the previous or outer circle. Sprinkle with the cinnamon sugar. Cover with the crumb topping, still leaving the edge clear. The puff pastry will form its own edge this way.

Bake for 30 minutes or until the puff pastry is flaky and golden brown. Remove to a rack to cool slightly. Dust with the powdered sugar. Serve warm with scoops of vanilla ice cream, if desired.

RED CHILI AND CINNAMON-CHOCOLATE CAKE

ADAPTED FROM A RECIPE BY KEVIN TAYLOR,
THE ZENITH AMERICAN GRILL, DENVER, COLORADO

Makes one 9-inch cake (8 servings)

Chef Taylor's restaurant straddles the imaginary border between the Heartland and the Southwest, so his recipes appear in both sections. This incredible cake is a must for chocolate lovers.

1 cup heavy cream	1 teaspoon red chili powder
¼ cup (½ stick) unsalted butter	5 eggs
	⅓ cup granulated sugar
10 ounces bittersweet chocolate, chopped	1 teaspoon vanilla
1½ teaspoons cinnamon	Powdered sugar, for dusting

Preheat the oven to 350°F. Grease and flour a 9-inch round cake pan; set aside.

Place the cream and butter in a large saucepan and bring just to a boil over medium-high heat. Remove from the heat and add the chocolate, cinnamon, and chili powder; stir until the chocolate is melted and the mixture is smooth. Set aside.

Place the eggs, granulated sugar, and vanilla in a mixer bowl and set over simmering water. Whisk briefly until the mixture is just warm to the touch. Remove from the heat and beat at high speed until the mixture triples in volume. Whisk ¼ of the egg mixture into the chocolate mixture until well blended. Then gently fold in the remaining egg mixture just until blended. Pour the mixture into the prepared cake pan. Place the cake pan in a larger baking dish and fill with enough hot water to reach halfway up the sides of the pan. Bake about 50 minutes or until a cake tester or toothpick inserted into the center comes out clean. Remove from the water bath and place on a rack to cool completely. Turn the cake out onto a serving plate and dust with powdered sugar.

CARAMEL FLAN WITH ORANGES

Serves 10

In southern Spain crème caramel is known as flan. The tradition of serving this elegantly simple dessert was brought to the Southwest in the seventeenth century by the Spanish.

2 quarts milk	1 teaspoon vanilla extract
2 cups sugar	⅓ cup water
6 eggs	5 large oranges, peeled and cut into segments
6 egg yolks	

Bring the milk and 1 cup of the sugar to a boil in a large saucepan. Regulate the heat so the mixture simmers rapidly without boiling over and let reduce to 1 quart, about 45 minutes.

In a large bowl, beat the eggs, yolks, and vanilla; slowly whisk in the hot milk. Strain through a fine-mesh sieve. Set aside.

Place the remaining 1 cup of sugar in a small saucepan over medium heat and dribble in the water, first around the sides and then over the sugar, stirring often. Bring to a boil, wash down the sides of the pan with a brush dipped in water, then simmer over medium heat, without stirring, until the syrup begins to color. Swirl the pan over the heat until the syrup is a deep amber color. Whisk 2 tablespoons of the syrup into the milk mixture. Working very quickly, pour the remaining syrup into 10 (6-ounce) custard cups, tilting the cups to distribute it over their bottoms and sides.

Preheat the oven to 350°F. Place the custard cups in a large roasting pan. Fill the cups with the milk mixture. Pour enough hot water into the pan so it comes halfway up the sides of the cups. Cover with aluminum foil and bake until the flans are just set, about 25 minutes. Remove from the oven and the water bath. Let cool completely. Cover and chill well.

Run a thin knife around the edge of each flan. Invert a dessert plate over the top of each flan, reverse the two and listen for the flan to drop. Remove the custard cups. Serve the flans accompanied by the orange segments.

MARGARITA ROULADE

Serves 10-12

There is considerable controversy as to who actually invented the margarita, which is a combination of tequila, Triple Sec, lime juice, and a bit of salt. This fanciful dessert uses the same ingredients in a slightly different way.

- 4 eggs, separated
- ¼ cup granulated sugar
- ¼ cup lime juice
- 5 teaspoons grated lime zest
- ¼ teaspoon salt
- ½ cup sifted all-purpose flour
- 3 tablespoons Triple Sec
- 4 teaspoons 100% agave tequila
- ½ cup lime marmalade
- 1½ cups heavy cream
- ¼ cup powdered sugar plus more for dusting the roulade

Preheat the oven to 375°F. Grease a 10 x 15 inch jelly roll pan. Line the bottom with waxed paper and grease the paper. Dust the pan lightly with flour and tap out any excess.

In a medium bowl, beat the egg yolks with an electric mixer. Gradually add the granulated sugar, then 1 tablespoon of the lime juice, 2 teaspoons of the lime zest, and the salt. Beat until the mixture is pale and thick. In a large bowl, beat the egg whites until stiff but not dry. Fold in ⅓ of the whites into the yolk mixture. Sift ⅓ of the flour over the batter and gently fold in until blended. Repeat with another ⅓ of the whites, then flour. Finish folding in the remaining whites and flour. Fill the prepared pan with the batter and spread evenly. Bake for 15 minutes, or until golden brown and the edges have started to pull away from the sides of the pan. Let cool for 5 minutes.

Meanwhile, combine 2 tablespoons of the Triple Sec, 1 tablespoon of the tequila, and 1 tablespoon of the lime juice in a small bowl. Set aside.

Place a damp kitchen towel on 2 wire racks placed side by side and turn the cake out onto the towel. Remove the waxed paper. Sprinkle the Triple Sec mixture over the cake. Starting with a long side of the cake, fold this edge up about 2 inches. Continue to roll up the cake in the towel, with the towel between the layers. Let sit until cool, at least 15 minutes but no longer than 1 hour.

In a small bowl mix together the marmalade and the remaining 1 tablespoon of Triple Sec. Set aside.

In a large bowl, beat the cream to soft peaks. Gently stir in the ¼ cup powdered sugar and the remaining 2 tablespoons of lime juice, 1 tablespoon of lime zest, and 1 teaspoon of tequila. Set aside.

To assemble, unroll the cake. Spread the jam evenly over the cake, then spread with the whipped cream mixture. Roll up the cake again without the towel. Wrap in plastic wrap and refrigerate for at least 3 hours or overnight. Just before serving, dust with powdered sugar and cut into slices.

California

What is new—That is what is California. There is a rich history, however, and California's contemporaneous quality is actually a product of that history. Isolated from the settlements along the Atlantic by the vast continent, accessible by sea only after a dangerous voyage between the tip of South America and the icy unknown of Antarctica, California was the most isolated place in America. Geography encouraged those who developed this varied land to use indigenous and nearby influences as the basis of local cuisine, helping instill an independent, adventurous spirit. After the Gold Rush of the mid-1800s, a mix of cultural influences gave California cooking depth and complexity. Then, in the 1970s, a determined group of talented young cooks set the stage for a unique and modern cuisine based on the rich California heritage and the ready availability of fresh ingredients.

The Beginnings

The Native Americans who lived in California before Europeans finally settled there were nomadic, dependent on game, fish, and wild berries for sustenance. They also used acorns, which were ground into flour and cooked into a simple mush. This elementary fare was what the first Spanish missionaries found when they crossed from Baja (lower) to Alta (upper) California in 1769.

Despite the forbidding nature of this new territory, the Spanish resolved to bring "civilization" to the region. They built a series of self-sustaining missions up the California coast, bringing with them cuttings and seeds to plant olive trees, apple trees, pear trees, date palms, fig trees, nut trees, and grape vines.

By 1823 the Franciscans had twenty-one missions stretching from San Diego to Sonoma, each with farms, orchards, and vineyards. (Actually there were two that did not have vineyards, Santa Cruz and San Francisco. In both places the summers were much too foggy to allow grapes to mature.) Wine was incidental but essential to the life of the missions, and the man most responsible for introducing viticulture to California was Father Junipero Serra, who established the first mission at San Diego de Alcal.

The food of the missions was Spanish in style, quite similar to today's "Mexican food." Tamales, tortillas, and chile con carne were standard fare. The Spanish introduced beef and pork, as well as beans, corn, chiles, avocados, and tomatoes they brought with them from New Spain (now Mexico). Some ingredients were adapted from the Native Americans of the region—berries, nuts, fruits, fish, and game—but the Indian influence was relatively small.

In the 1830s the missions were secularized, and their influence was replaced by enormous land-grant ranchos that raised tens of thousands of cattle and sold their hides to traders on the east coast. The local vaqueros (cowboys) lived on a diet built around beef. For eighty years from the time when the first missionary set foot in California, the region was completely Spanish in style. But just before the midpoint of the nineteenth century, the nature of California changed dramatically and forever.

The Gold Rush

Upon the discovery of gold in 1848 at John A. Sutter's mill on the American River, the region abruptly went from being the most isolated place on the continent to becoming the most desirable destination for many people. From 1848 to 1860, the population exploded, growing from 26,000 to 380,000.

The other dramatic change for California also took place in 1848 when the Guadalupe Hidalgo Treaty was signed at the end of the Mexican War. In this document Mexico surrendered its claim to California and ceded the province to the United States. Two years later California became the thirty-first state.

The Gold Rush brought a flood of immigrants seeking instant riches in the foothills and rivers of the Sierra Nevada. Some found what they were looking for, most didn't. Many of the fortune hunters were people with experience as farmers, orchardists, cheesemakers, winemakers, and fishermen. These recent arrivals were surprised and delighted at the potential of their new homeland. The large new population required many goods and services, and the most successful "49ers" were entrepreneurs like Levi Strauss, who provided work pants for the miners, and Domingo Ghirardelli, who made chocolate candies for them.

The Gold Rush participants were not just from other parts of the United States and its territories. They came from as far away as England, France, Germany, and Italy and brought with them their culinary preferences and skills.

The rise of the entrepreneur stimulated ideas for development of the region. The way to overcome California's geographic isolation from "back East" was to build a transcontinental railroad. At least, this was how San Francisco moguls—Leland Stanford, Charles Crocker, Mark Hopkins, and Collis P. Huntington—saw things. And they needed cheap labor to lay the tracks.

Thousands of Chinese workers were imported to work on the railroads, and they brought with them the culinary skills of their homeland. When the railroad was completed, many Chinese stayed to become one of California's most productive and industrious ethnic groups. Most settled in northern California, specifically in San Francisco, and because of their prodigious kitchen skills, many found employment in the homes of the rapidly growing bourgeoisie. Naturally, a substantial number of Chinese techniques, ingredients, and styles crept into the local cuisine.

Meanwhile, in southern California, the Latin American influence held sway. Many Mexicans and Central Americans could be found in the kitchens of upwardly mobile Angelinos.

The population of the state continued to grow rapidly, boosted by a second big wave of immigration in the 1880s. Different groups founded enclaves in different parts of the state. Basques settled in northern California. A large Italian population moved to San Francisco's North Beach region as well as to the wine valleys of Napa and Sonoma and the artichoke farms of Castroville. Fresno attracted a large Armenian population, many of whom became successful in the raisin business. Add Portuguese, French, Finnish, Swedish, Dutch, Japanese, Korean, and Filipino settlers, and you begin to understand the complexity and diversity of the Golden State.

The Big Farms

Many of the disappointed gold seekers settled in the enormous central valley of California. There they found an ideal growing area for walnuts, peppers, tomatoes, almonds, pistachios, peaches, plums, pears, nectarines, cherries, apricots, rice, broccoli, carrots, asparagus, and—most of all—grapes. Agriculture became California's biggest industry, a position it holds to this day.

A vast network of aqueducts and canals was constructed to bring precious water from the mountain lakes of the Sierra Nevada in the north to the thirsty fields. With the resulting bounty and the advent of refrigerated railcars, California became the nation's garden.

The Modern California Revolution

The modern food revolution took place in California after the end of World War II. First the automobile ascended to its position as the state's most potent icon. Then the fast-food restaurant was born, as was the drive-in restaurant.

In the 1950s, America was on a binge of TV dinners and frozen peas. California's harvest was being flash frozen in little boxes, pasteurized and put into jars, and steamed and put into cans. The great farms were servicing one of the greatest food delivery systems ever developed. The only problem was that wonderfully fresh produce became bland and overprocessed.

In Berkeley, across the bay from San Francisco, a young woman named Alice Waters started a restaurant in 1971 that revolutionized American cooking and renewed our indigenous regional cuisines. The fresh ingredients in the food at her restaurant, Chez Panisse, were organically grown on small, nearby farms.

A whole cottage industry sprang up around the new California food. The superb goat cheeses of Laura Chenel, ranch-raised lambs and goose liver from Sonoma, designer sausages from Bruce Aidells and others, organic vegetables from Chino Ranch, Tassajara's Green Gulch and many other family farms, all became part of the California food experience. The kitchen at Chez Panisse was a training center for the new culinary luminaries. Joyce Goldstein and Jeremiah Tower are two of the best-known graduates.

Meanwhile, in southern California a talented Austrian-born and French-trained chef opened a casual Italian restaurant that changed eating habits. Wolfgang Puck's Spago popularized the open kitchen, where customers could watch their dinners being prepared. Chefs emerged from the kitchen to take their rightful place in the limelight. The era of the superstar chef had arrived.

Wolfgang Puck reinvented the pizza, using the new California ingredients (see page 236). He reinvented pasta, adding all sorts of unusual elements (see page 243). He mounted main dishes on top of unusual salad greens and shook the food world with his skillful inventions. The tireless Mr. Puck then took on and redefined California's Asian influence, opening Chinois on Main in Santa Monica. He dazzled northern California with Postrio.

One of the most interesting aspects of the new California food is the number of women who have become important chefs in the creation of this exciting cuisine. Alice Waters and Joyce Goldstein have been joined by Nancy Oakes, Elka Gilmore, Barbara Tropp, Kimberly Schor, Annie Sommerville, Annie Gingrass, Tricia Tracy, Judy Rogers, Lissa Doumani, Traci des Jardins, Susan Feniger, and Mary Sue Milliken.

Because it was one of the last regional cuisines to evolve and because it evolved in America's most populous state, California cuisine has absorbed more influences than any of the others. And although it has grown into a respected, world-renowned cuisine, it continues to transform, because in addition to all the obvious characteristics of this wonderful food—the freshness, the seasonings, the emphasis on vegetables and fruits, the purity of flavors, the colors—its main elements are still change and invention, its main element is still what is new.

Napa Valley Wines

The Napa Valley begins at the top edge of San Francisco Bay and extends northward for thirty miles or so until it is pinched off by mountains. It is a wide, flat valley edged by the Mayacamus Mountains on both sides. The valley floor is blanketed entirely with verdant, well-maintained vineyards. Vines are planted on the sloping sides of the surrounding mountains as well. This is California's most valuable agricultural soil. One acre of prime cabernet sauvignon vineyard can bring more than $50,000.

There are nearly thirty thousand acres of vines in Napa, with the greatest area being devoted to cabernet sauvignon, the state's most popular red variety, and Chardonnay, the most popular white variety. Other premium varieties that flourish in the Napa Valley are sauvignon blanc and riesling, among whites, and merlot and pinot noir, among reds. There are about two hundred wineries in Napa County.

The coolest vineyards in Napa are in the southern part of the region, close to the bay, where the famous fog often covers the vines until late in the morning and returns in the afternoon. This part of Napa is called Los Carneros and it extends westward into the lower part of Sonoma County also. Varieties that do best in this region are chardonnay and pinot noir, the traditional grapes of Burgundy. Los Carneros is also an excellent place to grow the grapes used in sparkling wine.

Farther north, from the small city of Napa to the town of St. Helena, the climate is warmer and other varieties thrive. In this central part of the Napa Valley, which also encompasses the towns of Yountville, Oakville, and Rutherford, sauvignon blanc and cabernet sauvignon flourish. The northernmost part of the valley, around the spa town of Calistoga, is the warmest part of the region, but cool pockets—called microclimates—allow fine cabernet sauvignons, merlots, and sauvignon blancs to be made there.

Within the Napa Valley are several smaller appellations that produce wines of distinctive character. Besides Carneros, there is the Stag's Leap District, a region in the southeastern part of the valley that is famous for velvety and rich cabernet sauvignons, and Howell Mountain, a small region on the slopes at the eastern edge of the valley that grows dense, well-structured cabernet sauvignon, zinfandel, and chardonnay.

The Napa Valley is bisected by Highway 29. Visitors to the area can drive this road and stop at wineries along the way. There are large, modern wineries such as Robert Mondavi in Oakville and Beringer in St. Helena, that offer informative guided tours and impressive tasting rooms, and smaller, more intimate wineries such as Sequoia Grove or Cakebread, both in Rutherford, and Far Niente in Oakville. Wine lovers are welcome to visit most wineries, but calling ahead for an appointment is always a good idea, especially where small wineries are concerned.

To the east of the main highway is another, less busy road called the Silverado Trail. It passes through the Stag's Leap District and continues to Calistoga. Visitors have the opportunity to stop at a string of attractive, high-quality, small wineries such as Stag's Leap Wine Cellars, Pine Ridge, Mumm—Napa Valley, and Joseph Phelps.

The California Pantry

ABALONE

This univalve mollusk is not well known outside California because a conservation law prevents its shipment across state lines. The Chinese were the first to harvest abalone, and in post–Gold Rush days the meat was most often chopped, canned, or dried, and exported to the Orient. Soon the succulent, delicate abalone meat grew rapidly in popularity, which, combined with the boundless appetites of the state's sea otter population, brought the mollusk to near extinction. Thanks to export laws and recent aquaculture technology, the abalone is making a slow but steady comeback. The most common preparation involves giving an abalone steak several tenderizing whacks, dredging it in flour or bread crumbs, and panfrying it briefly.

APRICOTS

Wild apricots have grown in California for hundreds of years. Native Americans used them, and the mission priests domesticated the trees, using the early-ripening, juicy fruit in stews, sauces, and marinades. Along the way, people noticed that dried apricots are often better tasting than fresh. Today's consumers agree: only 5 percent of apricots are eaten when fresh. Dried apricots are used in both sweet and savory dishes.

ARTICHOKES

First planted in California by Italian settlers after the Gold Rush, the artichoke is a form of thistle and is considered an aphrodisiac. California produces virtually all of the artichokes in the United States, and most of those come from the thirty-seven growers and seven packing houses around Castroville. As popular as artichokes have become in this country, our per capita consumption is still only 0.5 percent that of Italy and France.

Tackling a whole artichoke requires commitment. Once the vegetable is steamed, each leaf should be pulled off, dunked in butter or some other sauce, and the meaty portion of the leaf stripped off with your teeth. Just when you are about to give up, the succulent heart is revealed. Artichoke hearts are a welcome reward at the end of the eating process. They can also be used in pasta sauces, vegetable dishes, or in soups or stews.

ASPARAGUS

Asparagus is a member of the lily family and comes in white, purple, and green varieties. This graceful and unique vegetable reaches the height of its short season in the spring. Many prefer pencil-thin stalks, but you can also find "jumbo" stalks, which may require some peeling. The debate continues over whether asparagus should be served hot or cold. Both ways are delicious, just don't overcook them or you'll end up with a slimy mess.

BEEF

Cattle ranches in nineteenth-century California existed primarily for the leather and tallow trade; beef was essentially considered a by-product. Ranch cooks dried the beef for jerky, shredded it into chiles, and rubbed it with garlic and spices for roasting. Today beef is still California's second largest agricultural business (after grapes), although Californians eat less beef than most Americans. Ground beef is the basis for San Francisco Joe's Special, sliced beef is used for stir-fries and sukiyaki, and the meat is still used in Mexican dishes from carne asada burritos to tacos and enchiladas.

CHILES

Capsaicin is the substance in chiles that burns your tongue, and it can also irritate your eyes and skin. There are too many varieties of chile peppers to enumerate here (see page 195), but the varieties found most often in California's Mexican and mission-style cuisines are the Anaheim (pale green and fairly mild), jalapeño (dark green and hot), and Serrano (small, green, and very hot). A handy rule of thumb states that the smaller the chile, the hotter it will be. The seeds and veins contain 94 percent of the heat, so remove them if you want a milder flavor. Dried chiles and chile powder add smoky, rich flavors to dishes.

DATES

Most U.S. dates are grown in the irrigated oasis of southern California's Coachella Valley. Dates were introduced to California at the turn of the century, and Americans can now enjoy domestically grown Khadrawi, Golden Saidy, Deglet Noor, as well as many other varieties. Dates go well with butter, cream, cheese, and yogurt. Indio, California, is famous for its "date shakes." In Indian and Middle Eastern dishes, dates are paired with nuts or rice to accompany roasted meats.

DUNGENESS CRAB

Although this meaty, red-shelled crab is named after a place in Oregon, it is San Francisco that has made it famous. The meat of this seasonal (November through April) delicacy is sweet and very adaptable to spicy sauces.

FIGS

Franciscan monks brought figs to California, planting the trees along the King's Highway, El Camino Real. Although Utah, Hawaii, and some southern states grow figs, the majority are grown in California's central valley. Varieties include the mission figs planted by the monks, Kadotas, Calimyrnas, and whites. Figs are a lovely accompaniment to cheese and smoked meats, especially ham. They can be used in stuffing or, of course, in desserts.

GARLIC

Also known as "the stinking rose," garlic, another member of the lily family, has been enjoyed in California since pre-Colombian times. The pungent crop now flavors French, Italian, Mexican, and Asian dishes across the state and the country.

Most of the U.S. supply of garlic is grown in five California counties: Monterey, San Benito and, especially, Santa Clara, the home of Gilroy, the self-proclaimed garlic capital of the world. These three coastal counties are in the north-central part of California. Also part of garlic country are Fresno and Kern Counties in the big San Joaquin Valley. The five counties produce more than 130 million pounds of garlic annually on more than ten thousand acres.

When garlic grows, it sends up slender green stalks which produce pretty white flowers. After the flowers wilt and the stalks die back, the underground garlic is ready to harvest. The bulbs are pulled up and left on the ground to "cure." The garlic bulb is considered well cured when its sheathing is dry enough to allow the cloves to be separated with ease. When shopping for garlic try to buy it loose. Look for firm, plump bulbs with clean, unbroken skins. Store garlic in a cool, dry place in an open container. Do not refrigerate.

Use fresh garlic in stir-fries, pestos, salad dressings, marinades, or in any other dish that will benefit from the sharp, heady aroma. Roasted garlic is mellower and sweeter and has a nutlike smoothness that works well in soups and spreads or with vegetables or meats. Elephant garlic—where each clove is nearly the size of a head of regular garlic—is milder.

If you are afraid of garlic's strong taste, just cook the cloves longer and they lose their pungency. For a mild, subtle taste, keep the cloves whole or cut them in large pieces and cook with long-cooking roasts, soups, or casseroles. If you like the strong taste of garlic, use it puréed, minced, or crushed. If you have trouble peeling garlic cloves, rinse them in hot water —the skin will loosen with the heat.

GOAT CHEESE

This intense cheese made from acidic goat's milk is called *chèvre* in France. California produces some of the best goat cheese in the world. Laura Chenel was the first to make a high-quality product in the state, but several others have followed, and goat cheese has become a key part of California cuisine.

GRAPES, RAISINS

Grapes were one of the many foods brought to the Golden West by the Spanish missionaries in the late-eighteenth century. Almost every mission planted vineyards, and today California boasts world-renowned wines from many areas of the state, including: Napa, Sonoma, Monterey, Santa Barbara and the big San Joaquin Valley (see pages 223 and 233 for more on California wines). California's vast grape industry is supported by researchers, growers, and enologists at the University of California at Davis and Fresno State Universities. In the big central valley, Thompson Seedless grapes are the major dessert grape grown. Raisins are the mainstay of the area near Fresno.

KIWI

Hardly a traditional or native crop, kiwis were brought to the U.S. from New Zealand quite recently but are now an important California crop. The Central Valley produces 95 percent of U.S.-grown kiwi. Whether you think they taste like melon or like strawberries, the real punch they pack is visual, with their brilliant green interior featuring a white starburst and dots of black seeds. The kiwi's interior is especially gratifying after the somewhat drab, furry exterior (the French term for kiwi translates as "mice vegetables"). Use kiwis to brighten fruit salads, or simply cut them in half and spoon out the flesh.

LETTUCE

Salinas is the undisputed salad bowl of the country, producing tons of greens that are consumed locally and shipped around the country. The Salinas lettuce industry pioneered the technology by which fresh greens are washed, dried, shredded, and packed in plastic bags ready to fill your salad bowl. America's salad craze started in California, and the year-round availability of a wide range of greens makes it easy to see why. Recently, growers across the state have responded to chefs' demands for mesclun, a mix of several varieties of baby lettuces and other greens like chicory and arugula.

NUTS

California claims the almond tree as a native plant, and the Central Valley produces about half of the world's supply of the nut. Pistachios, a member of the cashew family, require a temperate but very dry climate, preferring rocky hillsides to easily tended fields. Pistachio trees require almost twenty years of cultivation before they produce nuts, which explains their high price. Almonds and pistachios appear in ice creams and baked goods, as well as in many Asian and Middle Eastern dishes.

OLIVES, OLIVE OIL

Another by-product of Spanish mission work, olive trees were brought to California in the late-eighteenth century. Originally used primarily for oil, the olives themselves found a market at the turn of this century when lye-curing was developed. The four main types are: Spanish greens, Sicilian, the black-purple Kalamata, and the California pitted olive (officially known as the Lindsay, for the town that considers itself the olive capital of the country). California produces 99 percent of domestic olives, and because olive trees flourish in the same conditions as do grapevines, many vineyards and wineries are now producing outstanding premium olive oils.

OYSTERS

California oysters compete with those from the East Coast and the Pacific Northwest in quality, variety, and abundance. Tomales Bay and Drake's Estero, north of San Francisco, claim some of the purest waters for oyster cultivation in the country. San Francisco has its selection of oyster bars, where the freshly shucked shellfish need only a squirt of lemon juice or perhaps a bit of mignonette sauce before sliding down your throat. Or, you can enjoy historic Hangtown Fry (an oyster omelette), oysters Kirkpatrick (with cheese, bacon, and ketchup), or an oyster loaf.

POULTRY AND GAME BIRDS

Wander through the Chinese districts of San Francisco or Los Angeles, and you will see many examples of California poultry. Roasted ducks hanging by their hind legs and live chickens awaiting their fate greet you at every corner. The Sonoma town of Petaluma is a well-known poultry center, raising chickens, geese, and ducks (many of whose livers will end up as foie gras in upscale San Francisco restaurants) on small organic farms and in huge commercial ventures. Chicken plays a role

in all of California's cooking traditions, including elegant preparations using wine, dried fruits, and Asian spices so typical of contemporary chefs. Quail, squab, and other domestically raised game birds are also commonplace on menus across the state.

RICE

It may surprise you that California grows more rice than any other state except Arkansas. Californians have been rice farming since the mid-1700s, but the commercial industry did not begin until the turn of the twentieth century. Short-, medium-, and long-grain rices are grown, both brown and white, and are a staple of Asian, Mexican, and northern Italian cuisines. California is also the only state besides Minnesota to grow wild rice, which is not actually a rice but the seed of a wild grass.

SEAFOOD

With twelve hundred miles of seacoast and many additional miles of rivers, California is blessed with outstanding seafood. Dungeness crabs, shrimp, calamari, rex sole, salmon, sand dabs, scallops, and red snapper are often served simply grilled with lemon, butter, and herbs; or they are turned into ceviche, Cioppino (see page 240), or Asian dumplings. Mountain trout are grilled or panfried. The varied treatment of seafood in California is another example of the happy marriage between the state's natural bounty and its wealth of cultures and cuisines.

The Recipes

SALAD OF GRILLED CORN AND ARUGULA WITH A TOMATO VINAIGRETTE AND SHAVED PARMIGIANO-REGGIANO
ADAPTED FROM A RECIPE BY GARY DANKO, THE DINING ROOM, THE RITZ-CARLTON HOTEL, SAN FRANCISCO

Serves 6

It was California cuisine that moved the salad from the position of afterthought, following the main course and before the dessert, to a primary spot at the beginning of the meal. The fresh salads of California deserve such an important position. Now, fresh picked greens are available from markets and farm stands in almost every state in the nation. Here is a dramatic and flavorful presentation that gives salad its due.

- 6 ears unhusked sweet, tender corn
- 2 red bell peppers
- 1 large tomato, coarsely chopped
- 1 clove garlic
- ½ cup extra virgin olive oil
- 3 tablespoons tarragon vinegar
- Salt and freshly ground black pepper
- 3 bunches tender arugula, washed and dried
- Shaved Parmigiano-Reggiano, as needed
- Snipped fresh chives

To grill the corn: Place it over glowing embers and grill until the husks are black and the corn is cooked and shows signs of light browning. Remove from the grill and let cool. Husk the corn and cut the kernels from the cobs. Reserve until ready to serve.

To make the vinaigrette: Roast the bell peppers over an open flame or under the broiler until black on all sides. Place in a paper bag and let steam 5 minutes. Remove from the bag and peel off the skins. Stem, seed, and coarsely chop the peppers. Place the peppers, tomato, and garlic in a food processor fitted with a metal blade. Purée. Add the oil and vinegar; purée until emulsified. Season with salt and pepper.

To serve, ladle 2 tablespoons of the vinaigrette onto each of 6 large plates. In a large bowl, toss the arugula and corn with a generous ½ cup of the vinaigrette. (Reserve the remaining vinaigrette for another use.) Divide the salad among the plates. Sprinkle with the shaved cheese and the chives.

Chef Gary Danko

Chef Gary Danko of the Ritz-Carlton Dining Room in San Francisco has, at a young age, become one of the leading lights of California cuisine. His menu showcases strictly seasonal ingredients, prepared with classic technique.

Chef Danko's formal training began at the Culinary Institute of America. He went on to study with the legendary Madeleine Kamman in New York, and later traveled with Mme. Kamman throughout France.

With this solid foundation in French cooking, he returned to California where he worked at Beringer Winery and the Chateau Souverain Winery restaurant, transforming it into one of the premier destinations in wine country. He was appointed Chef of the Ritz-Carlton Dining Room in 1992 and named Best West Coast Chef by the James Beard Awards in 1995.

GOAT CHEESE, PANCETTA, DATE, AND GARLIC SALAD

Serves 8

The fresh produce grown in the farms of the Salinas and San Joachin Valleys have made California into the salad state. This version combines some of the Golden State's definitive ingredients.

- ½ pound pancetta, diced
- 6 tablespoons olive oil
- 12 dried dates, halved and pitted
- 4 cloves garlic, minced
- ¾ cup sherry vinegar
- ½ pound California goat cheese, crumbled
- 1 tablespoon minced fresh thyme
- 8 cups finely shredded red *and/or* green cabbage
- Salt and freshly ground pepper black

Place the pancetta in a large skillet over medium heat; sauté, stirring occasionally, until crisp. Add the oil, dates and garlic; sauté until the dates and garlic have softened, about 2 minutes. Stir in the vinegar, reduce the heat and simmer 5 minutes. Remove from the heat; stir in the cheese and thyme.

Place the cabbage in a large salad bowl; immediately toss with the pancetta mixture. Season with the salt and pepper. Serve immediately.

ROASTED EGGPLANT, RED BELL PEPPER, AND GARLIC SOUP WITH CHIPOTLE CRÈME FRAÎCHE

ADAPTED FROM A RECIPE BY KIMBALL JONES, WENTE BROS., LIVERMORE

Serves 8

Rich and velvety smooth, this soup features an unusual combination of roasted vegetables. Finish it with a swirl of the smoky-flavored Chipotle Crème Fraîche.

- 2 large globe eggplants, cut into ½-inch thick slices
- 2 red onions, quartered
- Extra virgin olive oil, for roasting the vegetables
- Balsamic vinegar, for roasting the vegetables
- Salt and freshly ground black pepper
- 2 heads garlic, tops cut off to expose cloves
- 2 large red bell peppers
- 1 bouquet garni (herb bundle of 2 sprigs each of fresh parsley, sage, rosemary, and thyme tied together with kitchen twine)
- 1 quart chicken stock
- 1 cup crème fraîche *or* sour cream
- 2 tablespoons chopped prepared chipotle in adobo (page 197)

Preheat the oven to 350°F. In a large roasting pan, toss the eggplants and onions with oil and vinegar to coat completely. Season with salt and pepper. Set aside. In an 8-inch square baking pan, toss the heads of garlic with additional oil and vinegar to coat completely; season with salt and pepper and pour ¼ inch of water into the bottom of the pan. Place both pans in the oven and roast about 45 minutes or until the vegetables are soft and tender.

Meanwhile, place the bell peppers over an open flame or under a preheated broiler until the peppers are charred and black on all sides. Place the peppers in a paper bag and close to seal. Let rest 10 minutes. When cool enough to handle, peel off the skins of the peppers and remove their seeds and ribs. Set aside.

When the eggplants, onions, and garlic are cooked, remove them from the oven. Place the eggplants and onions in a large saucepan or Dutch oven. Squeeze the garlic cloves from their skins into the saucepan with the eggplants and onions. Add the skinned and seeded peppers, the bouquet garni, and stock. Bring to a boil, reduce heat, cover and simmer for 45 minutes. Remove and discard the bouquet garni. In a food processor or blender, working in batches, purée the soup. Strain the soup and return it to the saucepan. Adjust the seasoning with salt and pepper, if necessary. Keep the soup hot while preparing the Chipotle Crème Fraîche.

To prepare the Chipotle Crème Fraîche: In a small bowl, whisk together the creme fraîche and the chipotle in adobo. Season with salt and pepper.

To serve, spoon the soup into bowls and drizzle with the Chipotle Crème Fraîche.

Sonoma and Other Wine Regions

Over the mountains to the west of Napa is Sonoma County, a sprawling area that is considerably larger and much more varied than Napa. Compared to the Napa Valley's pristine orderliness, Sonoma presents a crazy quilt of vineyards, orchards, cattle ranches, and thick woodland. Its landscape is constantly fractured by unexpected hills, valleys, bluffs, and streams. From its rocky coast and winding Russian River area to the burgeoning city of Santa Rosa and the lush Alexander Valley, Sonoma offers a patchwork of scenic delights.

In the south near Petaluma, eggs, chickens, and ducks are the cash commodities. Sebastopol, in the western part of the county, revolves around apples. In several regions, cattle graze on gently sloping meadows and trees groan under the weight of peaches, walnuts, and succulent Santa Rosa plums.

Sonoma's variegated topography creates small, cool microclimates where the moist fog from the county's Pacific coast creates an assortment of temperatures and growing conditions, allowing production of a full range of varietal wines. Most successful are sauvignon blanc, gewürztraminer, chardonnay, pinot noir, cabernet sauvignon, and zinfandel.

The southern part of the county, on the north side of San Francisco Bay, is an extension of the cool Los Carneros region. Buena Vista, California's oldest winery, is located in this area. North of this is the charming town of Sonoma and the Sonoma Valley, an important producing region. A drive north and west from the town of Sonoma allows the traveler to see a number of important wineries, including St. Francis, Kenwood, and Château St. Jean on Highway 12, and Matanzas Creek Winery on Bennett Valley Road near Glen Ellen.

Other important Sonoma appellations include: the Russian River Valley, a cool region that produces excellent pinot noir; the Dry Creek Valley, where some of California's best zinfandels are grown; and the Alexander Valley, a source of excellent cabernet sauvignon. Château Souverain and Geyser Peak Winery are both large wineries located in the Alexander Valley. Another premium region north of Sonoma is Mendocino County, a cool coastal area where good chardonnay and sparkling wines are produced. Recently the cool Anderson Valley has been developed by Roederer Estate and Scharffenberger as a prime region for sparkling wine production. The large and highly successful Fetzer winery is located in the central part of the county.

Next to Mendocino is Lake County, which provides good sauvignon blanc and zinfandel. The best known wineries from this region are Kendall-Jackson and Guenoc. East of San Francisco, in the Livermore Valley, lovely chardonnays and sauvignon blancs are made. The most important producer in this area is Wente Bros., a historic family-owned winery. South of San Francisco there are fine wines made in Santa Clara and Santa Cruz Counties, the most celebrated of which come from the Ridge winery in Cupertino.

Farther south, in Monterey, excellent chardonnays and rieslings are grown, and in the Central Coast region, two hundred miles south of San Francisco, rich zinfandels and syrahs are made. In Santa Barbara County, just one hundred miles north of Los Angeles, the specialties are pinot noir, chardonnay, and sauvignon blanc.

GUACAMOLE SALSA
ADAPTED FROM A RECIPE BY DIANE ROSSEN WORTHINGTON, LOS ANGELES

Makes 4 cups

Guacamole, the celebrated avocado dip, has convincingly trounced onion dip as America's favorite use for chips. Diane Worthington has neatly combined the top dip with the top condiment, salsa.

- 2 large tomatoes (about 1 pound), peeled, seeded, and finely diced
- ½ medium yellow bell pepper, seeded and finely diced
- ½ medium red bell pepper, seeded and finely diced
- 1 large carrot, peeled and finely diced
- 1 medium ear of corn, kernels cut from the cob
- 2 tablespoons finely chopped fresh Italian parsley
- 2 tablespoons finely chopped fresh cilantro
- 1 jalapeño pepper, seeded and finely chopped
- 1 teaspoon salt
- ¼ teaspoon freshly ground black pepper
- 2 tablespoons fresh squeezed lemon juice
- 1 medium avocado, peeled and cut into ½-inch cubes
- Fresh cilantro leaves

Combine all the ingredients except the avocado and the cilantro leaves in a medium mixing bowl. Refrigerate for 1 hour.

Spoon the mixture into a serving bowl. Just before serving, add the avocado and taste for seasoning. Garnish with cilantro leaves and serve with fresh tortilla chips.

GRILLED MISO-MARINATED BEEF SALAD
WITH GINGER-MUSTARD VINAIGRETTE
ADAPTED FROM A RECIPE BY HIRO SONE, TERRA, ST. HELENA

Serves 6

This Wolfgang Puck protegé combines Asian ingredients with typically intense California flavors in this lively salad. Mesclun is a blend of wild salad greens.

- ½ cup rice wine vinegar
- 2 tablespoons vegetable oil
- 2 tablespoons plus 1 teaspoon soy sauce
- 2 tablespoons golden brown sugar, packed
- 2 tablespoons sesame oil
- 5 teaspoons Dijon-style mustard
- 5 cloves garlic, minced
- 1 tablespoon plus 1 teaspoon minced fresh ginger
- ¼ teaspoon red pepper flakes
- 3 tablespoons red (inaka) miso, a soy-based paste available in Asian markets
- 5 teaspoons granulated sugar
- 1 tablespoon mirin (sweet Japanese cooking wine)
- 1½ pounds beef top loin
- 4 cups spring salad mix (mesclun)
- 2 carrots, thinly sliced on the diagonal
- 1 Japanese cucumber, thinly sliced on the diagonal
- 4 Roma tomatoes, cut into wedges
- ⅓ cup chopped roasted peanuts
- ¼ cup thinly sliced red onion
- 2 tablespoons packed cilantro leaves
- 6 large whole radicchio leaves
- 1 cup fried rice noodles
- 1 tablespoon black sesame seeds
- 1 tablespoon white sesame seeds

To make the vinaigrette: Place the vinegar, vegetable oil, 2 tablespoons of the soy sauce, the brown sugar, 1 tablespoon of the sesame oil, the mustard, 3 cloves of the garlic, 1 tablespoon of the ginger, and the red pepper flakes in a blender. Purée. Set aside until ready to use.

In a shallow dish, whisk together the miso, granulated sugar, mirin, the remaining 1 tablespoon of sesame oil, 2 cloves garlic, 1 teaspoon soy sauce, and 1 teaspoon ginger. Add the beef; marinate at room temperature for 1 hour.

Prepare the grill. Remove the beef from the marinade; discard the marinade. Grill the beef to desired doneness, turning once. Thinly slice the beef across the grain.

In a large salad bowl, combine the mesclun, carrots, cucumber, tomatoes, peanuts, onion and cilantro. Add the vinaigrette; toss well.

To serve, place a radicchio leaf in the center of each of 6 plates. Fill each leaf with the salad mixture. Top with the beef strips and noodles. Sprinkle with the sesame seeds. Serve immediately.

SWEET CORN SOUP WITH SHRIMP AND CHILES
ADAPTED FROM A RECIPE BY JEREMIAH TOWER,
STARS, SAN FRANCISCO

Serves 4

Here is a dramatic glorification of farm fresh California ingredients by the "father of California cuisine."

- ¼ cup (½ stick) unsalted butter
- 8 fresh ears of sweet, young corn, kernels cut from cobs
- 1 teaspoon dried marjoram leaves
- 3 cups water
- 1 pound medium shrimp, shells on
- 1 cup heavy cream
- 2 roasted poblano chiles, chopped
- 1 teaspoon ground cumin
- Salt and freshly ground white pepper

Melt the butter in a large saucepan over medium heat. Add the corn and marjoram; sauté, stirring, for 2 minutes. Remove from the heat; reserve.

In another saucepan, bring the water to a boil; add the shrimp and boil for 2 minutes. Remove the shrimp from the cooking liquid, reserving the liquid. Let the shrimp cool slightly, then peel them. Place the shrimp shells in the cooking liquid; boil for 5 minutes. Strain the liquid and pour over the corn. Bring to a boil again; remove from the heat. Purée the corn with the liquid in a blender; put through a food mill and return to the saucepan.

Coarsely chop all but 4 of the shrimp. Place the corn mixture over medium heat. Stir in the chopped shrimp, cream, chiles, and cumin. Heat through; season with salt and white pepper. Serve each portion of the soup garnished with a whole shrimp.

GRILLED FILLET OF PACIFIC SALMON WITH THAI RED CURRY SAUCE
ADAPTED FROM A RECIPE BY HIRO SONE AND LISSA DOUMANI, TERRA, ST. HELENA

Serves 6

There is a profound Asian influence in modern California cooking. This superb dish brings together the fresh ingredients of the Golden State and the spices and herbs of Thailand.

For the sauce:
- 1½ tablespoons peanut oil
- 3 cloves garlic, minced
- 2½ teaspoons fresh ginger, minced
- 1½ teaspoons coriander seeds, cracked or ground using a mortar and pestle
- 1 tablespoon curry powder
- 1 tablespoon Thai red curry paste
- 1 tablespoon paprika
- 1½ teaspoons ground cumin
- 20 ounces coconut milk
- 6 tablespoons tomato purée
- 2 tablespoons soy sauce
- 3 tablespoons dark brown sugar, packed

For the salmon:
- 6 (6-ounce) salmon fillets, ¾-inch thick
- 1 tablespoon olive oil
- Salt and freshly ground black pepper

To prepare the sauce: Heat the oil in a medium saucepan, over medium heat. Sauté the garlic and ginger until light brown in color. Add the coriander seeds, curry powder, curry paste, paprika, and cumin. Stir continuously over low heat for about 2 minutes. Add the remaining ingredients and raise the heat to medium. Bring to just below the boil, remove from the heat and cover. Set aside.

To prepare the salmon: Brush the salmon with oil and season with salt and pepper. Bring a charcoal or gas grill to high heat and grill the salmon for 3 minutes on each side or until just cooked through. Serve immediately, topped with the curry sauce.

SEARED TUNA BURGERS
WITH SESAME MAYONNAISE
ADAPTED FROM A RECIPE BY MICHEL RICHARD,
CITRUS, LOS ANGELES

Serves 4

Although meatless, these burgers are too richly flavored to remind anyone of health food. They are fresh, lively California food.

- 1¾ pounds fresh, well-chilled tuna fillets
- 6 tablespoons olive oil
- ¼ cup chopped fresh basil
- 4 cloves garlic, minced
- 4 anchovy fillets, minced
- 1 teaspoon salt
- ½ teaspoon freshly ground black pepper
- ½ cup mayonnaise
- 1½ teaspoons toasted sesame seeds
- ½ teaspoon sesame oil
- ½ teaspoon Champagne vinegar *or* white wine vinegar
- ¼ teaspoon ground cumin
- Dash hot pepper sauce
- 4 brioche *or* other soft hamburger buns, toasted
- 4 greenleaf lettuce leaves
- 1 large tomato, thinly sliced
- 4 thin slices red onion

Trim off any dark oily portions from the tuna. Thinly slice the tuna, then chop it until the fish is the texture of hamburger and presses together into a compact ball. Place the tuna in a medium bowl and gently mix in the ¼ cup (4 tablespoons) of the olive oil, the basil, garlic, anchovies, salt and pepper. Divide the mixture into 4 balls and form into 1-inch-thick patties. Place on a waxed paper–lined baking sheet. Cover and refrigerate for 30 minutes.

To prepare the mayonnaise: In a small bowl stir together the mayonnaise, sesame seeds, sesame oil, vinegar, and cumin; season with the hot pepper sauce. Cover and refrigerate until ready to use.

Heat the remaining 2 tablespoons of olive oil in a large nonstick skillet over medium-high heat until almost smoking. Add the tuna patties and cook for about 1 minute on each side for rare or 1½ minutes for medium-rare.

To serve, place the lettuce leaves on the bottoms of the buns. Top with the burgers, tomato, and onion; dollop with the mayonnaise. Cover with the bun tops.

CALIFORNIA HARVEST PIZZA

Makes one 12-inch pizza

The pizza has had a rebirth in California. This Italian oven-roasted bread, which originated on the back streets of Naples, has been transformed into an upscale confection by Wolfgang Puck and a coterie of California cooks. This fairly traditional version teams several ingredients that are regularly part of the new California cuisine.

- 1 head garlic
- ¼ cup (4 tablespoons) olive oil
- 6 baby artichokes
- 2 tablespoons balsamic vinegar
- 1 red bell pepper
- 1 (12-inch) thin-crust Italian bread shell, such as Boboli
- 1 (5-ounce) package California goat cheese, crumbled
- ½ cup (1½ ounces) grated Parmesan cheese
- 2 teaspoons fresh thyme leaves

Preheat the oven to 400°F. Cut the top off the head of garlic to expose the cloves. Rub with 1 tablespoon of the oil and loosely wrap in aluminum foil. Roast for about 1 hour or until the cloves are soft and slightly caramelized. Cool.

Meanwhile, cut the stem and top third off of each artichoke. Snap off the tough outer leaves until only the tender greenish-yellow leaves remain. Cut the hearts vertically into ¼-inch thick slices or wedges. Heat the remaining 3 tablespoons of oil in a medium skillet; add the artichoke slices and sauté, stirring occasionally, until the artichokes are tender, about 10 minutes. Deglaze the pan with the vinegar; set aside.

Place the bell pepper over an open flame or under the broiler and cook until charred and blackened on all sides. Place in a paper bag and set aside 10 minutes. Remove the pepper from the bag and peel off the charred skin. Seed the pepper and cut it into thin slices.

Raise the oven temperature to 450°F. Squeeze the roasted garlic cloves out of their skins and onto the bread shell. With a thin metal spatula, spread the cloves over the bread shell to cover it completely (they will now be in a paste-like form). Distribute the artichokes, bell pepper, and cheeses evenly over the bread shell. Bake about 8 minutes until hot and the cheese is melted. Sprinkle with the thyme.

CALIFORNIA CLUB SANDWICH WITH SUN-DRIED TOMATO AIOLI
ADAPTED FROM A RECIPE BY JEREMIAH TOWER, STARS, SAN FRANCISCO

Serves 4

One of the best aspects of the new California cuisine is its sense of fun. This tongue-in-cheek
approach to the traditional club sandwich is a clever invigoration of a tired concept.

- 1 (8-ounce) jar marinated sun-dried tomatoes, drained and marinating oil reserved
- 3 cloves garlic
- 1 cup mayonnaise
- 2 tablespoons Dijon-style mustard
- Salt and freshly ground black pepper
- 12 slices sourdough bread
- 2 cups arugula
- 2 tomatoes, sliced
- 4 poached chicken breasts, sliced on the diagonal
- 8 slices crisply cooked bacon
- 1 small red onion, sliced

To make the aioli: Place the sun-dried tomatoes and 2 cloves of the garlic in the bowl of a food processor fitted with a metal blade. Process until puréed. Add the mayonnaise and mustard and process until smooth. Season with salt and pepper. Set aside.

Preheat the oven to 400°F. Brush both sides of each bread slice with the reserved tomato marinating oil. Cut the remaining garlic clove in half lengthwise. Rub both sides of each bread slice with the cut sides of the garlic clove. Place the bread slices on baking sheets and toast for 10 minutes, turning once.

To assemble each sandwich, spread 1 bread slice with 3 tablespoons of the aioli. Top with ½ cup of the arugula, ½ of a sliced tomato, and 1 sliced chicken breast. Cover with another bread slice. Spread with another 3 tablespoons aioli and top with 2 slices of the bacon and ¼ of the sliced onion. Cover with another bread slice. Repeat with the remaining ingredients to make 4 sandwiches.

GRILLED BEEF AND VEGETABLE FAJITAS
WITH CHIPOTLE-HONEY SAUCE

Serves 6

The Mexican and Latin American influence on California cooking has been important since the eighteenth century. The new ascendancy of fajitas, which are traditionally made with beef, began in Texas. They are extremely popular in the Golden State, and the definition has been expanded to include chicken, pork, and other meats.

- 4 green onions (scallions), coarsely chopped
- ½ cup plus 2 tablespoons chopped fresh cilantro
- 8 cloves garlic, minced
- 1 cup lime juice
- ¾ cup olive oil
- 3½ teaspoons ground cumin
- 2 teaspoons cayenne pepper
- 2 teaspoons chili powder
- Salt and freshly ground black pepper
- 1½ pounds flank steak
- ¼ cup honey
- 2 tablespoons peanut oil

- 2 tablespoons balsamic vinegar
- 2 tablespoons brown mustard
- 1 tablespoon minced chipotle in adobo (page 197)
- 1 red bell pepper, cut into ¼-inch-thick slices
- 1 yellow bell pepper, cut into ¼-inch-thick slices
- 1 green bell pepper, cut into ¼-inch-thick slices
- 1 red onion, cut into ¼-inch-thick slices
- 12 (7-inch) flour tortillas, warmed
- ¾ cup sour cream

To make the marinade: Place the green onions, ½ cup of the cilantro, and 6 cloves of the garlic in a food processor fitted with a metal blade. Process until finely chopped. Add ½ cup of the lime juice, the olive oil, 2½ teaspoons of the cumin, the cayenne pepper, and chili powder. Process until combined. Pour the marinade into a shallow dish; season with salt and black pepper. Add the flank steak; marinate at room temperature for 1 hour.

To make the sauce: In a small bowl, whisk together the honey, peanut oil, balsamic vinegar, mustard, chipotle in adobo, and the remaining ½ cup of lime juice, 2 tablespoons cilantro, 2 cloves garlic and 1 teaspoon cumin. Season with salt and pepper. Set aside.

Prepare the grill. Remove the beef from the marinade. Grill the beef, bell peppers, and red onion, brushing with the marinade, until the beef is cooked to desired doneness and the vegetables are soft, turning once. Discard any remaining marinade. Thinly slice the beef across the grain.

To assemble, lay some of the beef and vegetables down the center of each tortilla; drizzle with some of the sauce and dollop with sour cream. Roll up to enclose the filling. Serve hot.

Chef Jeremiah Tower

Jeremiah Tower is one of America's most influential chefs and restaurateurs, and in 1993 he was honored as "California's Best Regional Chef" by the James Beard Foundation. His Stars Restaurant in San Francisco has been an overwhelming success since its inception and is a mandatory dining spot for visitors and locals alike.

Starting as co-owner and chef of Chez Panisse in the early 1970s, Jeremiah Tower conceived and prepared the first "California Regional Dinner," which initiated his reputation as the "Father of California Cuisine." After Chez Panisse, he moved on to the Santa Fe Bar & Grill before opening the legendary Stars restaurant. Chef Tower has appeared on the PBS series Cooking with the Master Chefs and on Good Morning America. His cookbook Jeremiah Tower's New American Classics was published in 1986.

CIOPPINO

Serves 8

This rich and flavorful fish stew is a fixture in San Francisco. It was introduced to the Bay Area by the Italian and Portuguese fishing communities who settled there.

- ½ cup olive oil
- 2 stalks celery, finely chopped
- 2 medium leeks, white part only, halved lengthwise, cleaned and sliced
- 1 medium onion, finely chopped
- 1 medium red bell pepper, seeded and finely chopped
- 1 medium carrot, finely chopped
- 2 pounds fresh tomatoes, peeled and coarsely chopped, *or* a 28-ounce can of diced Italian plum tomatoes
- 3 cups fish stock *or* clam juice
- 2 cups California zinfandel wine
- 6 tablespoons tomato paste
- ¼ cup California zinfandel port
- 3 tablespoons lemon juice
- 4 cloves garlic, minced
- ½ teaspoon saffron threads, crumbled
- Bouquet garni (see note)
- Pinch of sugar
- Salt and freshly ground black pepper
- 16 mussels, scrubbed and debearded
- 8 clams, scrubbed
- 1 pound red snapper, cut into bite-size chunks
- 1 pound shrimp, shelled and deveined
- 1 pound sea scallops, cut into bite-size chunks
- 1 cooked Dungeness crab, cracked (optional)
- ¼ cup finely chopped fresh parsley

Heat the oil over medium heat in a 6-quart nonreactive stockpot or Dutch oven. Add celery, leeks, onion, bell pepper, and carrot; sauté, stirring occasionally, for 5 minutes.

Add tomatoes, stock, zinfandel, tomato paste, port, lemon juice, garlic, saffron, bouquet garni, and sugar. Simmer 40 minutes, partially covered. Season with salt and pepper.

Add mussels and clams; cover and cook 5 minutes. Add snapper, shrimp, scallops, and crab; cook about 3 to 4 more minutes or until mussels and clams are open and other seafood is opaque throughout. Remove and discard bouquet garni.

Serve in deep bowls. Sprinkle with parsley.

NOTE: To make bouquet garni, wrap one bay leaf and 1 sprig each of oregano, basil, thyme, and rosemary in cheesecloth and tie with string.

PAN-STEAMED SHELLFISH WITH SUN-DRIED TOMATOES AND ANCHOVIES ON SOFT POLENTA

ADAPTED FROM A RECIPE BY GARY DANKO, THE DINING ROOM, THE RITZ-CARLTON HOTEL, SAN FRANCISCO

Serves 4

This robust dish is easy to prepare and makes a perfect cool-weather dish.

- ¼ cup olive oil
- 1 small onion, finely chopped
- 1 cup coarsely cracked polenta
- 6 cups boiling water, measured after the boil
- Salt
- 2 pounds green lip mussels (*or* clams)
- 2 tablespoons tomato marinating oil drained from 12 sun-dried tomatoes in oil
- 1 large shallot, minced
- 2 cloves garlic, minced
- 2 anchovy fillets, minced
- 1 cup dry white wine
- 1 (8-ounce) bottle clam juice
- 2 teaspoons minced fresh thyme
- ¼ cup heavy cream
- Freshly ground white pepper
- Snipped fresh chives

To make the polenta: Preheat the oven to 350°F. Heat the olive oil in a 2-quart ovenproof saucepan over medium heat; add the onion and cook, stirring occasionally, until translucent, about 5 minutes. Add the polenta and stir to coat with the oil. Remove from the heat and stir in the water. Return to the heat and bring to a boil. Place in the oven and bake for about 35 minutes until the water is absorbed and the polenta mounds slightly. The polenta should be soft and moist. Remove from the oven and season with salt. Keep warm.

Meanwhile, soak the mussels in cold water for 15 minutes. Drain, scrub, and debeard the mussels. Set aside.

In a large stockpot, heat the tomato marinating oil over medium heat. Add the shallot, garlic, and anchovies. Sauté for 1 minute. Mince the tomatoes. Add them to the pot with the wine, clam juice and thyme. Cover and cook for 5 minutes. Add the mussels and cream; cover and steam until the mussels open, about 8 minutes. Remove the mussels and keep them warm. Reduce the sauce until it coats the back of a spoon. Season with salt and pepper.

To serve, mound the polenta in individual bowls; top with opened mussels and sauce. Sprinkle with chives.

PEPPERED RIB-EYE STEAKS WITH CREAMY RAJAS

ADAPTED FROM A RECIPE BY MARY SUE MILLIKEN AND SUSAN FENIGER, BORDER GRILL, SANTA MONICA

Serves 6

Some critics say California food isn't hearty enough—too many salads, too many pastas. Here is a dish that certainly puts that idea to rout. One of the most refreshing aspects of cooking in the Golden State is the plethora of women chefs. Here are two whose approach to cooking is obviously on the hearty side.

- 6 rib-eye steaks, about 10 ounces each
- 6 tablespoons black peppercorns, crushed
- 6 tablespoons olive oil
- 2 onions, sliced
- 4 roasted red bell peppers, peeled, seeded and julienned
- 4 roasted poblano chiles, peeled, seeded and julienned
- 1 cup heavy cream
- ¾ cup (3 ounces) shredded Monterey Jack cheese
- ⅔ cup (2 ounces) grated Parmesan *or* Romano cheese
- Salt and freshly ground white pepper

Coat both sides of the steaks with the crushed black pepper, pressing firmly into the meat. Let stand at room temperature for 30 minutes.

Heat ¼ cup (4 tablespoons) of the oil in a large skillet over medium heat. Add the onions and sauté, stirring occasionally, for 10 minutes. Stir in the bell peppers and chiles; sauté for 2 minutes. Pour in the cream. Bring to a boil. Reduce the heat and simmer for 4 minutes or until the cream begins to thicken. Remove the rajas from the heat. Reserve.

Heat the remaining 2 tablespoons of oil in another large skillet. Add the steaks, working in batches if necessary, and cook until desired doneness, turning once. Remove the steaks to a serving platter. Keep warm.

Return the rajas mixture to medium heat; heat through. Blend in the cheeses and stir until melted. Season with salt and white pepper. Serve the steaks accompanied by the rajas.

ANGEL HAIR PASTA WITH SMOKED SALMON
AND GOLDEN CAVIAR

ADAPTED FROM A RECIPE BY WOLFGANG PUCK, SPAGO, WEST HOLLYWOOD

Serves 4

*One of the strongest influences on the cooking of California is the fresh, assertive flavors
and simple techniques of Italy. This glorious creation, one of Wolfgang Puck's signature
dishes, provides a dramatic combination of ingredients and lots of rich flavor.*

- Extra virgin olive oil
- 1 cup heavy cream
- Salt
- ½ pound angel hair pasta
- ½ pound smoked salmon, cut into thin strips
- 1 (2-ounce) jar golden caviar
- Freshly ground white pepper
- Snipped fresh chives

Bring a large pot of water to a boil with a little olive oil.

Pour the cream into a large skillet. Just before cooking the pasta, bring the cream to a boil and remove the skillet from the heat.

Add a pinch of salt to the boiling water, then add the pasta and cook until *al dente*. Drain the pasta quickly. Toss the pasta and the smoked salmon with the hot cream and heat the mixture through. Stir in half of the caviar, and season with salt and white pepper.

To serve, divide the pasta among 4 warm plates and garnish each serving with the remaining caviar and a light sprinkling of chives.

ROAST CHICKEN WITH ALMOND BUTTER, BRAISED ARTICHOKES, AND ARUGULA

ADAPTED FROM A RECIPE BY JEREMIAH TOWER, STARS, SAN FRANCISCO

Serves 4

New California cuisine is defined by strong flavors, fresh, top quality ingredients, and attractive but unfussy presentation. The use of salad greens in association with cooked food is also a hallmark.

- ½ cup (1 stick) unsalted butter, at room temperature
- ⅓ cup toasted whole blanched almonds
- 6 anchovy fillets
- 2 teaspoons chopped fresh tarragon
- 1 lemon, halved
- 1 (4-pound) roasting chicken, giblets removed, rinsed, and patted dry

- Salt and freshly ground black pepper
- 12 cloves garlic
- 2 pounds baby artichokes
- ½ cup olive oil
- 1 cup chicken stock
- 2 tablespoons lemon juice
- 4 cups tender arugula, washed and dried

Place the butter, almonds, anchovies, and tarragon in a food processor fitted with a metal blade. Process until smooth. Set aside.

Preheat the oven to 400°F. Squeeze the lemon over and in the chicken, rubbing well. Gently lift up the skin on the breast, then spread the almond butter over the breast and under the skin. Season the chicken inside and out with salt and pepper. Put the halved lemon and 6 cloves of the garlic inside the chicken cavity. Place the chicken on a rack in a roasting pan; cover it loosely with aluminum foil and roast for 20 minutes. Remove the foil, reduce the heat to 350°F, and continue to roast for another 30 minutes until the chicken juices run clear when pierced at the thigh. Let rest in a warm place for 15 minutes before serving.

While the chicken is roasting, prepare the artichokes. Slice off the tips and stems of the artichokes. Peel off the outer leaves until the tender greenish-yellow leaves are exposed. Thinly slice the artichokes and store in a bowl of acidulated water until all are sliced. Heat ¼ cup of the oil in a large skillet over medium heat. Drain the artichokes and add them to the skillet. Sauté, stirring, for 3 minutes. Mince the remaining 6 cloves of garlic and add them to the skillet with the stock. Cover and braise until tender, about 15 minutes. Uncover and reduce the liquid slightly. Season with salt and pepper. Set aside. Keep warm.

When the chicken is cooked, strain the roasting juices from the pan, remove the fat, and add the juices to the artichokes.

In a medium bowl, whisk together the remaining ¼ cup oil and the lemon juice; season with salt and pepper. Add the arugula and toss well.

Carve the chicken into 4 serving pieces. To serve, place a nest of the arugula in the center of each of 4 warm dinner plates. Place a ring of the warm artichokes around each nest and a piece of chicken on top, napped with the artichoke juices.

VEAL MEDALLIONS WITH ONION MARMALADE
ADAPTED FROM A RECIPE BY WOLFGANG PUCK,
SPAGO, NORTH HOLLYWOOD

Serves 6

*This Spago classic has definite French roots, but the purity
and flavor amplification of the onions is true California.*

- 3 onions, each cut into 8 wedges
- 3 cups chicken stock
- 2 tablespoons sherry wine vinegar
- 1½ cup heavy cream
- Salt and freshly ground black pepper
- 12 (3-ounce) veal tenderloin medallions
- All-purpose flour, for dusting
- ¼ cup (½ stick) unsalted butter
- 1 tablespoon olive oil
- ¾ cup port
- Watercress, for garnish

Place the onions, 2 cups of the stock, and the vinegar in a medium saucepan. Cook, partially covered, over medium heat for 15 minutes, until the liquid is evaporated. Remove from the heat.

In a small saucepan, bring the cream to a boil and reduce it to 4 or 5 tablespoons. Add the cream to the onions and bring back to a boil; season with salt and pepper. Remove from the heat. Keep warm.

Season the veal with salt and pepper and dust lightly with flour, shaking off any excess. Melt 2 tablespoons of the butter and the oil in a large skillet over medium heat. Sauté the veal in 2 batches for 3 to 4 minutes on each side, until golden brown but still pink inside. Transfer to a platter and keep warm.

Pour off all the fat in the skillet and add the port. Over medium heat, deglaze the pan by scraping up the brown bits on the bottom with a wooden spoon. Add the remaining 1 cup of stock. Bring to a boil and reduce to 4 or 5 tablespoons. Slowly whisk in the remaining 2 tablespoons butter.

To serve, spoon some of the onions onto each dinner plate. Top with 2 veal medallions and spoon on some of the sauce. Garnish with watercress.

Chef Wolfgang Puck

Austrian-born Wolfgang Puck is America's premier superstar chef. He is a brilliantly talented technician whose ability to combine culinary styles has made him the most influential chef of the twentieth century.

After learning classic French cooking in France, Chef Puck came to America, where he starred at Ma Maison in Los Angeles. Escaping the confines of French cuisine, he opened Spago, an Italian restaurant on the Sunset Strip. Spago's casual, chic interior, trendsetting open kitchen, and trademark gourmet pizza revolutionized California cooking.

After Spago, Mr. Puck went on to reinvent Chinese cooking at Chinois on Main. His empire now includes restaurants all over the world. He has authored The Wolfgang Puck Cookbook and Adventures in the Kitchen with Wolfgang Puck. Mr. Puck is a regular on Good Morning America and a frequent guest on The Late Show with David Letterman.

LAMB SHANKS BRAISED WITH RED WINE AND FIGLETS
ADAPTED FROM A RECIPE BY HIRO SONE,
TERRA, ST. HELENA

Serves 6

This robust and incredibly delicious recipe calls for figlets, which are available in most markets in dried—but not hard— form. If you cannot find them, pitted, halved figs or bite-size, pitted prunes, may be used.

- ¼ cup (4 tablespoons) olive oil
- 6 lamb shanks, 1 pound each
- Salt and freshly ground black pepper
- All-purpose flour, for dusting
- 2 carrots, chopped
- 1 onion, chopped
- 1 celery stalk, chopped
- 3 tablespoons chopped fresh basil
- 2 tablespoons chopped fresh thyme
- 3 cloves garlic, minced
- 5 cups chicken stock
- 1 (750-ml) bottle dry red wine
- 1 (12-ounce) package pitted whole Mission figlets
- 1 cup canned crushed tomatoes
- 1 (6-ounce) can tomato paste

Preheat the oven to 325°F. Heat 2 tablespoons of the oil in a Dutch oven over high heat. Season the lamb with salt and pepper and dust lightly with flour. Working in batches, add the lamb to the Dutch oven and brown on all sides, about 8 minutes per batch. Transfer to a platter.

Reduce the heat to medium; add the remaining 2 tablespoons of oil to the Dutch oven. Add the carrots, onion, celery, basil, thyme, and garlic and sauté, stirring occasionally, until the vegetables are tender, about 7 minutes.

Return the lamb to the pot. Stir in the stock, wine, figlets, crushed tomatoes, and tomato paste. Bring to a boil. Cover and place in the oven. Cook until the lamb is very tender, stirring occasionally, about 1 hour 45 minutes.

Transfer the lamb to a platter. Tent with foil to keep warm. Boil the cooking liquid in the pot until reduced to a thick sauce consistency, about 35 minutes. Skim off any fat from the surface. Season with salt and pepper.

Return the lamb to the sauce. Simmer until heated through. Arrange the lamb on a platter; spoon sauce over and serve. NOTE: This is an excellent choice for a prepare-ahead dinner party.

ARTICHOKE AND POTATO TRUFFADE
ADAPTED FROM A RECIPE BY NANCY OAKES,
BOULEVARD, SAN FRANCISCO

Serves 8

A truffade is a potato dish from the Auvergne in France, the region that produces the heartiest food in that great culinary nation. Chef Oakes adds artichokes to give this delicious vegetable side dish a California spin.

- 2 pounds baby artichokes
- Lemon juice
- 4 tablespoons olive oil
- 4 ounces slab bacon, diced
- 2 pounds Yukon Gold potatoes, peeled and thinly sliced
- 2 garlic cloves, minced
- Salt and freshly ground black pepper
- 1 cup (4 ounces) Gruyère cheese, shredded

Cut off the stems of the artichokes, slice off the leaf tips and peel off the leaves until the light greenish-yellow leaves are revealed. Slice thinly. Put the cut artichokes into cold water containing a few squeezes of fresh lemon juice until all have been sliced. Drain the artichokes. Heat 2 tablespoons of oil in a large, nonstick skillet and sauté the artichokes until tender, about 10 minutes. Set aside.

Render the bacon in another large, heavy ovenproof skillet until crisp and golden brown. Remove the bacon from the pan with a slotted spoon and drain on a paper towel–lined plate. Set aside. Add the remaining 2 tablespoons of olive oil to the skillet and cook the potatoes over medium heat, covered, for 10 minutes. Turn the potatoes. Add the bacon, artichokes, and garlic. Cover and cook for 10 more minutes. Turn the mixture again, crushing the potatoes. Cover and cook for 20 minutes, or until the potatoes are tender, adding the garlic during the last 10 minutes of cooking. Season with salt and pepper.

Preheat the oven to 500°F.

Turn the mixture again, crushing the potatoes. Sprinkle the cheese over the top and let melt. Put the skillet into the preheated oven until the cheese browns, about 5 minutes. Serve immediately.

GARLIC FLAN
ADAPTED FROM A RECIPE BY HANS RÖCKENWAGNER,
RÖCKENWAGNER, SANTA MONICA

Serves 8

You can't beat this creation by one of Southern California's most talented young chefs for sheer luxurious texture and lovely flavor.

- 2 cups milk
- 2 cups chopped parsnips
- 1½ cups garlic cloves
- 2 cups heavy cream
- 3 eggs
- Salt, freshly ground black pepper, and hot pepper sauce

Preheat the oven to 325°F. Lightly grease eight ¾-cup ramekins; set aside.

Place the milk, parsnips, and garlic in a large saucepan; bring to a boil, reduce the heat and simmer for 10 minutes or until the vegetables are tender. Drain, reserving 1 cup of the liquid.

Purée the vegetables and reserved liquid in a blender. Add the cream and eggs; purée once again. Season with salt, pepper, and hot pepper sauce.

Place the prepared ramekins in a roasting pan. Pour the custard into the ramekins, filling them to the rims. Carefully pour warm water into the pan until it reaches halfway up the sides of the ramekins. Bake until just set, about 1 hour. Remove the ramekins from the water bath and allow to sit for 10 minutes. Serve while still warm.

GARLIC MASHED POTATOES
ADAPTED FROM A RECIPE BY KIMBALL JONES,
WENTE BROS., LIVERMORE

Serves 6

Garlic is a California treat, and most of "the stinking rose" grown in the United States comes from Gilroy, not far from Livermore.

- 2 pounds medium-sized red new potatoes, with skins
- 6 whole garlic cloves, peeled
- Salt
- ½ cup crème fraîche
- ¼ cup heavy cream
- ¼ cup (½ stick) unsalted butter
- 1 green onion (scallion), finely chopped
- 2 tablespoons finely chopped, fresh Italian parsley
- Freshly ground black pepper

Place the potatoes and the whole garlic cloves in a heavy, medium stockpot. Add water to cover. Season with salt. Bring to a boil, reduce heat, cover and simmer until a knife passes through the potatoes with ease, about 30 minutes. Drain. Put through a ricer or mash with a potato masher. Stir in the crème fraîche, cream, butter, green onion, and parsley. Season with salt and pepper. Keep warm in the top of a double boiler until ready to serve.

BEET RISOTTO
ADAPTED FROM A RECIPE BY DAVID AND ANNIE GINGRASS,
HAWTHORNE LANE, SAN FRANCISCO

Serves 4

*Here is a delightful and colorful California version of risotto,
a northern Italian dish that has gotten a new lease
on life in American kitchens. This works best with
the plump Italian-style rice called Arborio.*

- 2 tablespoons olive oil
- 1 onion, diced
- 2 cloves garlic, minced
- 1 cup Arborio rice
- 2 cups dry white wine
- 1½ pounds trimmed beets, boiled until soft, peeled, and grated
- 1 (14½-ounce) can chicken broth
- ¼ cup crème fraîche
- 2 tablespoons unsalted butter
- Salt and freshly ground black pepper

Place the oil in a 2-quart saucepan over medium heat. Add the onion and sauté, stirring occasionally, for 6 minutes. Add the garlic and sauté for 2 minutes, stirring occasionally. Add the rice and stir until all the grains are coated with oil.

Add ½ cup of the wine. Stir constantly until all the wine is absorbed. Keep adding more wine, ½ cup at a time, stirring constantly and adding more only when the previous addition has been absorbed. Stir in the grated beets. Add the chicken broth in the same way as the wine. When all the liquid has been absorbed, remove the pan from the heat. The rice should be tender.

Add the crème fraîche and butter. Stir until the butter melts. Season with salt and pepper. Serve immediately.

SLOW-ROASTED OVEN TOMATOES

Serves 6

*California produces superb tomatoes from May until October.
This is an excellent way to concentrate their rich, sweet flavor.
It is best in late summer when tomatoes are sweetest.*

- 6 ripe, meaty medium tomatoes, halved horizontally
- 1 tablespoon extra virgin olive oil
- 1 teaspoon superfine sugar
- ½ teaspoon salt
- ¼ teaspoon freshly ground black pepper
- Snipped fresh chives

Preheat the oven to 325°F. Place the tomato halves, cut-sides up, in an 8 x 11 inch ceramic oval baking dish. They should fit tightly in the dish. Drizzle with the oil and sprinkle with the sugar, salt, and pepper. Roast in the oven 2½ hours until soft and sweet-smelling. After 1 hour of cooking, poke the tomatoes lightly with the tines of a fork to release their juices. Repeat after the second hour. Check the tomatoes during the last ½ hour of cooking to make sure that the tomato juices are not burning; if they are, cover loosely with foil. Sprinkle with the chives. Serve.

ROASTED ASPARAGUS WITH PARMESAN

Serves 4

Of all the ways to prepare asparagus, this modern California method works best. The spears stay bright green, become tender, and retain all their fresh, delicious flavor.

- 1 pound medium asparagus, ends trimmed
- 2 tablespoons olive oil
- ¼ teaspoon salt
- 3 grindings of black pepper
- 1 tablespoon freshly squeezed lemon juice
- ¼ cup freshly shaved Parmesan cheese

Preheat the oven to 500°F. Rinse the asparagus, pat dry with paper towels and, with a vegetable peeler, peel the bottom three inches of each stalk.

Put the olive oil into an ovenproof dish or skillet and add the asparagus spears. Sprinkle with the salt, pepper, and lemon juice and place, uncovered, into the preheated oven. Bake for ten minutes, shaking the pan two times during the process.

Remove the asparagus spears from the oven and sprinkle with the cheese. Serve immediately.

CALIFORNIA RATATOUILLE
ADAPTED FROM A RECIPE BY MICHEL RICHARD, CITRUS, LOS ANGELES

Serves 6

Here is a California slant on a French classic by French-born California star Michel Richard.

- 5 tablespoons olive oil
- 1 red onion, diced
- 1 red bell pepper, seeded and julienned
- 1 yellow bell pepper, seeded and julienned
- 1 fresh ear of corn, kernels cut from the cob
- 1 poblano *or* Anaheim chile, seeded and minced
- 1 jalapeño pepper, seeded and minced
- 2 tomatoes, seeded and diced
- 1 zucchini, coarsely chopped
- 1 yellow crookneck squash, coarsely chopped
- 4 green onions (scallions), coarsely chopped
- ½ cup tomato juice
- 2 tablespoons chopped fresh cilantro
- 1 tablespoon Champagne vinegar *or* white wine vinegar
- 1 tablespoon chili powder
- Salt and freshly ground black pepper

Heat 2 tablespoons of the oil in a large, nonstick skillet over medium-low heat. Add the red onion, cover, and cook until translucent, stirring occasionally, about 10 minutes.

Add the bell peppers, corn, poblano chile and jalapeño pepper. Increase the heat to medium and cook for 5 minutes, stirring occasionally.

Stir in the remaining 3 tablespoons oil, the tomatoes, zucchini, squash, green onions, tomato juice, cilantro, vinegar, and chili powder. Increase the heat to medium-high and cook until the vegetables are crisp and tender, stirring occasionally, about 5 to 7 minutes. Season with salt and pepper. Serve immediately or cool for 15 to 30 minutes to lukewarm.

GOAT CHEESE TART WITH GLAZED FRESH FIGS

Serves 10

In this delicious cheesecake dessert, the tanginess of the cheese is a perfect foil for the rich sweetness of the figs.

- 1 cup graham cracker crumbs
- ½ cup (1 stick) unsalted butter, melted
- ⅓ cup toasted, blanched whole almonds, very finely ground
- 1 (5-ounce) package California goat cheese, softened
- 1 ounce cream cheese (⅓ of a 3-ounce package), softened
- 1¼ cups sugar
- ⅔ cup sour cream
- 1 egg
- 2 tablespoons grated lemon zest
- 1 tablespoon lemon juice
- ½ cup water
- 2 dozen ripe, fresh figs, halved horizontally

Preheat the oven to 400°F. In a small bowl, mix the crumbs, butter, and ground almonds. Press onto the bottom and up the sides of a 10-inch tart pan with a removable bottom. Bake 6 minutes. Remove to a rack to cool. The bottom of the tart will puff up slightly during the baking process. After cooling for a couple of minutes, press it down onto the bottom of the pan.

Reduce the oven temperature to 250°F. In a medium bowl, beat the cheeses together with an electric hand mixer. Add ¼ cup of the sugar, the sour cream, egg, 1 teaspoon of the lemon zest, and the lemon juice. Beat until smooth. Pour the cheese mixture into the crust and spread evenly. Bake about 20 minutes until just set. Remove to a rack to cool slightly. Chill completely, about 1 hour.

To make the glazed figs: In a medium saucepan, combine the remaining 1 cup sugar, 5 teaspoons lemon zest, and the water. Set over medium heat and bring to a boil. Cook 5 minutes. Reduce the heat to medium-low and add the figs. Cook, watching constantly, until the figs are glazed and the sugar mixture is syrupy, about 10 minutes. Cool.

To serve, cut the tart into wedges and top with the glazed figs.

STRAWBERRY DUMPLINGS WITH LEMON CURD

ADAPTED FROM A RECIPE BY GARY DANKO, THE DINING ROOM, THE RITZ-CARLTON HOTEL, SAN FRANCISCO

Serves 4

California strawberries are so good, it seems almost unnecessary to do any more than serve them whole with powdered sugar and whipped cream. They are perfect in this festive dessert, which completely captures the essence of the luscious berries.

- 5 egg yolks
- 1 cup sugar
- 6 tablespoons plus 1½ teaspoons lemon juice
- 5 tablespoons unsalted butter, softened
- Salt
- 5 cups sliced strawberries
- ½ cup water
- 1 cup all-purpose flour
- 2 tablespoons baking powder
- 1½ teaspoons grated lemon zest
- ½ cup milk

To make the lemon curd: In a heavy-bottomed, stainless steel saucepan, whisk together the egg yolks, ½ cup of the sugar, and 6 tablespoons of the lemon juice. Cook over low heat, whisking constantly, until the mixture thickens. DO NOT BOIL. Remove from the heat and whisk in ¼ cup (4 tablespoons) of the butter and a pinch of salt. Immediately scrape the curd into a small bowl. Cover with plastic wrap, pressing it down directly onto the curd to prevent a skin from forming. Refrigerate until completely chilled.

Place 4 cups of the strawberries, the water, 6 tablespoons of the sugar, the remaining 1½ teaspoons of lemon juice, and a pinch of salt in a 12-inch skillet. Bring to a boil, reduce heat, cover, and simmer 5 minutes.

Meanwhile, in a food processor combine the flour, the remaining 2 tablespoons of sugar, the baking powder, the remaining 1 tablespoon of butter, the lemon zest, and ¼ teaspoon of salt. Pulse on and off until sandy looking. Through the feed tube, pour in the milk and process just until combined. DO NOT OVERPROCESS.

Drop the dumpling mixture by rounded tablespoonfuls into the simmering strawberry mixture to make 8 dumplings. Cover and simmer over low heat for 10 minutes without lifting the lid. Serve hot, topped with the lemon curd and sprinkled with the remaining cup of strawberries.

PRUNE TART WITH ALMONDS AND TEA
ADAPTED FROM A RECIPE BY MICHEL RICHARD,
CITRUS, LOS ANGELES

Makes one 10-inch tart

*Here is a lovely and unusual confection by a man who began his
career in the kitchen of legendary pastry chef Gaston LeNôtre.*

- 3 orange pekoe tea bags
- 2 cups boiling water
- 1 (12-ounce) package pitted prunes
- 1¼ cups toasted, slivered almonds
- 1 cup powdered sugar
- 3 eggs, at room temperature
- 1 cup (2 sticks) unsalted butter, at room temperature
- ¼ cup granulated sugar
- Pinch of salt
- 1¼ cups all-purpose flour
- 2 tablespoons Armagnac *or* other brandy
- Additional powdered sugar, for dusting
- Lightly sweetened whipped cream *or* vanilla ice cream

Place the tea bags in a medium bowl. Pour the boiling water over them and let steep for 5 minutes. Add the prunes and soak until plump and tender, about 1½ hours. Drain. Reserve the prunes and discard the tea bags.

Finely grind 1 cup of the almonds with the powdered sugar in a food processor fitted with a metal blade. Add 14 of the drained prunes and 2 of the eggs and process, pulsing on and off until the prunes are finely chopped. Add ½ cup of the butter and process until smooth. Cover and set aside at room temperature.

To make the dough: Process the remaining ¼ cup of almonds until finely chopped, with the granulated sugar and salt in a food processor fitted with a metal blade. Add the remaining ½ cup butter and process until smooth. Add the remaining egg and process until incorporated. Add ⅓ cup of the flour and mix until just incorporated. Add the remaining flour in 2 batches, processing until just barely incorporated. The dough will be soft. Scrape the dough out onto a piece of waxed paper. Shape into a disk. Wrap and refrigerate for at least 1 hour. (This can be prepared one day ahead of time.)

Preheat the oven to 350°F. Roll the dough out between 2 large sheets of plastic wrap into an 11-inch circle. Remove the top sheet of plastic. Invert the dough into a 10-inch tart pan with a removable bottom. Trim and finish the edge. Freeze for 15 minutes. Line the tart with parchment paper or aluminum foil and fill with pie weights or beans. Bake until the crust is firm and set, about 15 minutes. Remove the beans and paper. Prick the bottom of the crust with the tines of a fork. Continue to bake until well browned, 10 to 15 minutes.

Fill the tart with the prune-almond filling and smooth the top with a spatula. Arrange the remaining prunes evenly in concentric circles, pressing gently into the filling. Return the tart to the oven and bake until the filling is puffed and set, about 40 minutes. Immediately drizzle the Armagnac over the tart. Cool in the tart pan on a rack for 3 to 4 hours.

To serve, dust the tart with additional powdered sugar. Remove the tart ring. Cut into wedges and accompany with whipped cream or ice cream. Serve immediately.

ORANGE, ALMOND, AND OLIVE OIL CAKE
ADAPTED FROM A RECIPE BY DIANE ROSSEN WORTHINGTON,
LOS ANGELES

Makes one 9-inch cake

Using olive oil instead of butter or shortening in a cake may seem like an odd idea at first, but it actually makes good sense. It doesn't burn as butter can, and while it is not much different from vegetable shortening, it is much healthier. This cake combines typical California ingredients in a new and appealing way.

- 6 ounces blanched whole almonds
- 1 cup all-purpose flour
- 1 tablespoon baking powder
- 4 eggs, at room temperature
- 1½ cups sugar
- Zest of one medium orange, finely chopped
- Juice of one medium orange (about ½ cup)
- ½ cup extra virgin olive oil (pick an aromatic and fruity one)
- Powdered sugar, for dusting
- Thinly sliced oranges (blood oranges, if you can find them)
- Fresh mint leaves
- Lightly sweetened whipped cream

Preheat the oven to 350°F. Oil a 9-inch springform pan with olive oil. In a food processor fitted with a metal blade, process the almonds until finely ground, almost like bread crumbs. In a medium mixing bowl, combine the ground almonds, flour, and baking powder; set aside.

With an electric mixer on medium speed, in a large mixing bowl beat the eggs until frothy. Slowly add the sugar and beat the mixture until it is light, thick, and lemony in color. Slowly add the flour mixture and then add the orange zest, juice, and olive oil, stirring just to combine.

Pour the mixture into the prepared pan and bake for 50 to 60 minutes or until a cake tester or a toothpick inserted in the center comes out clean. Cool, then remove the sides of the pan. Place the cake on a serving platter and sprinkle powdered sugar in a decorative pattern on top. To serve, place a piece of cake on a dessert plate and arrange the orange slices, mint leaves, and a dollop of whipped cream on the side.

BLOOD ORANGE GRANITA

Serves 4

The blood orange, which was brought to America by Spanish and Italian settlers, is grown commercially in California. It produces a deep red juice that is as delicious as it is decorative. Granita is an Italian ice dessert that is usually made with coffee. In this case, blood orange juice is used instead, and the result is striking to look at as well as refreshing.

- ¼ cup sugar
- ½ cup freshly squeezed blood orange juice
- 1½ cups water
- Blood orange slices

Combine the ingredients in a stainless steel saucepan. Bring to a boil over medium heat. Stir until the sugar is dissolved. Remove from the heat and allow the syrup to cool completely.

Transfer the mixture to a shallow stainless steel pan (a brownie pan should do). Place in the freezer. After 15 minutes, remove from the freezer and stir with a fork to break up any lumps. Run the fork along the sides of the pan to disengage ice crystals. Return the pan to the freezer for another 15 minutes. Stir the granita again. Repeat the procedure every 15 minutes or so, for up to 3 hours. Spoon the granita into chilled balloon glasses and serve immediately. Garnish each serving with a slice of blood orange.

Hawaii

Alone in the middle of the vast Pacific, Hawaii is at least 2,300 miles from its nearest neighbor. This seclusion is the biggest single factor in the creation of Hawaii's unique and fascinating culture as well as its singular cuisine.

These volcanic islands, jutting out of the deep waters of the Pacific Ocean, were settled by Polynesians who made the arduous journey across thousands of miles of uncharted seas in hollowed-out, double-hulled wooden sailing canoes. And this miraculous voyage was accomplished more than a thousand years before Columbus made his first discovery mission to America. These first arrivals to Hawaii brought with them a belief that all foods had their own aura and life force. They also came ashore with seeds and plants from their home islands of the South Pacific. The Polynesian settlers planted taro, bananas, and coconuts. Their diet was simple and healthy: they lived on taro, fruit and fish.

From the date the islands were discovered—believed to be some time in the fifth century—until the end of the fourteenth century, there was a surprising amount of travel between Hawaii and the Marquesas and Tahiti. The adventuresome Hawaiian-Polynesians apparently thought little of sailing and rowing for several weeks to visit relatives.

Those who settled the Hawaiian Islands found a dramatic subtropical world, rich and unspoiled. There were tall mountains, deep valleys accented by precipitous waterfalls, and massive cliffs rising from the sea, as well as fabulous vegetation, great forests, and abundant wildlife. The surrounding seas were teeming with an enormous variety of fish and shellfish in addition to an excellent selection of seaweeds. Early writings indicated that more than 125 varieties of edible sealife had been identified.

At the beginning of the fifteenth century the voyages to Polynesia stopped, and the Hawaiians lived in complete isolation until the latter half of the eighteenth century. They fished the waters and grew their crops in the dark, rich volcanic soil. They raised hogs and chickens. When celebrating an event they staged an elaborate communal meal called a luau (see pages 270–71).

The Hawaiian "staff of life" was (and for many natives, still is) a starchy, sour paste called poi. Islanders ate it with everything. Poi can be made from breadfruit, sweet potato, or banana, but most typically it is made from taro. The root must be washed and cooked, then peeled. It is then scraped and pounded into a paste, a laborious procedure requiring strength and perseverance. Poi is almost always a disappointment to the uninitiated. Its pasty texture and sour flavor is unappealing to most people who haven't learned from childhood to like it.

The isolated idyll of the Hawaiian islanders came to an abrupt end on January 18, 1778, when a British naval captain named James Cook spotted Oahu while sailing from Tahiti to the North Pacific. Cook came ashore and traded with the friendly natives. The era of "post-contact" Hawaii had begun. Captain Cook named the islands the Sandwich Islands, after the Earl of Sandwich, first lord of the British Admiralty.

After two weeks, Cook departed. He returned in November and one more time the following year. During that visit he anchored in Kealakakua Bay on the Big Island. A series of misunderstandings developed between Cook's crew and the islanders. The disagreement led to a violent confrontation during which Captain Cook himself was killed.

But the door had been opened, and it would never be closed again. Many traders and explorers sailed to the islands in the ensuing years, bringing with them livestock, manufactured goods, plants, food, and culinary influences from places far away. They brought other, less welcome things from the outside world to the isolated paradise, and during the early 1800s many Hawaiians died of diseases introduced to their unspoiled, natural habitat.

The early nineteenth century was dominated by the rule of King Kamehameha, a benevolent monarch and fierce warrior who united the islands in 1796. During his reign, settlers, sailors, and fortune hunters from around the world came to Hawaii to take advantage of its natural resources. British, Americans, French, Portuguese, and Russians, among many others, brought their cultures and cuisines to the islands.

Kamehameha was a strong champion of Hawaiian culture, but after his death in 1819, political struggles within the monarchy and with European powers weakened the native religious and social systems. American whalers and missionaries came in large numbers, bringing with them new gods and new economic structure. The monarchy ended in 1893 when Queen Liliuokalani, a descendant of King Kamehameha, was deposed in a bloodless coup staged by a small number of Americans and Europeans. The next year Hawaii established a republic with American Sanford Dole as president. In 1898, recognizing the strategic value of this 1,523-mile-long collection of 132 islands, President William McKinley annexed Hawaii to the United States. Two years after that, on June 14, 1900, the islands officially became a territory of the U.S.

In the mid- to late-nineteenth century, vast sugar plantations were established in Hawaii, and many Chinese, Polynesian, and Japanese laborers were imported to work in them. The plantation owners became Hawaii's shadow monarchy and eventually brought down the true monarchy. Big commercial farming and the society that came with it changed Hawaiian languages, economy, and agriculture forever.

Toward the end of the nineteenth century there was an influx of Portuguese, Filipinos, Koreans, and Puerto Ricans who brought their own cultures, adding further complexity to the Hawaiian melting pot.

Hawaiian Climate

Almost all types of climates can be found somewhere in the Hawaiian Islands. Though much of the land is warm, there are also mountains that are covered in snow all year, rain forests, volcanic desert, and acres and acres of ranch land. The Big Island, especially, boasts a staggering range of climates, often within a few hundred yards of each other. The island has a dry side and a wet side, with average annual rainfall for the two differing by almost sixty inches.

Most of the agricultural land in Hawaii enjoys moderate temperatures—between 60°F and 80°F—year-round, allowing a twelve-month growing season for many crops. Local farmers assert that the deep volcanic soil is unique in producing intensely flavorful produce.

The Hawaiian pineapple industry was started in 1885 when a thousand plants were imported from Jamaica. Soon pineapple became big business in the islands. Some areas, especially Lanai, were blanketed with plantations. Not surprisingly the name Dole, once prominent in government, became important in lucrative commercial pineapple growing.

For nearly eighty years the island economy was built on sugar cane and pineapple. But beginning in the 1970s, big agribusiness began pulling out of Hawaii in favor of places such as Southeast Asia, where crops could be grown just as effectively and much more cheaply. Suddenly more than sixty-thousand acres of superb farmland became available. In a state that has had a long history of importing such basic agricultural staples as tomatoes, potatoes, garden vegetables, and grains, truck farms have opened to support the needs of demanding young chefs in Hawaii's hotels and restaurants.

The Most Diverse Culture in the World

From the most isolated place on earth, Hawaii has become one of the most diverse. Because of its strategic location and seductive climate, it has attracted immigrants from all over the world. Each group has added nuances and enriched the Hawaiian cultural experience.

Americans brought wheat and other grains, as well as garden vegetables and dairy products. Portuguese settlers contributed sausages, tomatoes, peppers, bean soups, and two favorite sweet starches, pao dolce and malasadas. When the sugar plantations brought Japanese and Chinese workers to the islands, rice became a staple starch. Chinese herbs and spices, plus stir-fry techniques, were assimilated. The Japanese introduced shoyu, sashimi, soybeans, tempura, noodle soup, and bento box lunches.

In the early twentieth century, Koreans brought fiery kim chee salad, pulgogi spice–marinated beef, and kalbi ribs. Soon after that, Filipinos brought adobo stews made of fresh meat or fish flavored with vinegar and garlic. The most recent influences are Southeast Asian, such as Laotian, Thai, and Vietnamese.

All these influences affected home kitchens and the restaurants frequented by locals, while the food in hotels and restaurants catering to visitors remained bland and dull. In the 1980s, however, perhaps the most exciting and rapid revolution in American culinary history took place. At that time, several young and gifted chefs, many of them trained in classic cooking in Europe and America, began to recognize the enormous untapped culinary resources that surrounded them.

There was Peter Merriman, who fished with local boats, climbed coconut trees, searched tirelessly for perfect fruit, and encouraged Hawaiian farmers to plant organic lettuce and herbs. Jean-Marie Josselin, a brilliant French-trained chef, adapted his classic techniques to a whole new palette of ingredients. Sam Choy, a native Hawaiian, transformed traditional Hawaiian cooking into a new style and form. Los Angeles–born Mark Ellman brings a sense of fun to his fanciful creations. Beverly Gannon is a Texas emigrant whose cooking retains a folksy, down-home style. Roger Dikon, an easterner, picks special herbs and exotic vegetables from his own home garden for his creative menus. George Mavrothalassitis, a Frenchman with a Greek name, has reinvented haute cuisine in Honolulu.

Alan Wong, another native who once cooked at Lutèce in New York, returned as one of Hawaii's most creative and luminous chefs. Japan-born Roy Yamaguchi's subtle and exquisitely imaginative cooking has illuminated dining rooms from Los Angeles to Guam to Honolulu to Tokyo. Amy Ferguson-Ota, a native Texan who married a Hawaiian fisherman, has also wed her southwestern cooking style with French training and a passion for local Hawaiian ingredients.

In 1991 these ten joined with two other talented cooks, Philippe Padovani and Gary Strehl, to form the Hawaii Regional Cuisine group. This organization promotes the new way of Hawaiian cooking, as opposed to the older, more traditional island cuisine featuring such classic dishes as lau lau, lomi lomi, poke, and poi.

Today, Hawaii is one of the most exciting places in the United States to eat. The twelve founding chefs of the Hawaiian Regional Cuisine group have spawned a new generation of cooks who are in the process of asserting their talents and styles. It has been a long and arduous road that took almost 2,000 years to traverse. It is safe to say, it was worth the trip.

The Hawaii Pantry

BANANAS AND PLANTAINS

Brought by Polynesian settlers, bananas, including the cooking variety called plantains, are grown on all the Hawaiian islands. Several varieties are popular, including the Valery, the Willimas, the Cuban Red, and the ice cream banana. The low price and wide availability of bananas make them a staple in Hawaiian cooking, especially in cakes, pies, and other baked sweets, as well as sweet sauces, curries, and salads.

BREADFRUIT

Called *ulu* by the Hawaiians, this starchy, somewhat bland vegetable has been a staple on the islands for centuries. It can be eaten slightly green or fully ripened, when it is more sweet and creamy. Roast breadfruit whole, like potatoes, or grate them into crab or fish cakes.

COCONUTS

The Polynesians brought coconuts to Hawaii and planted one at the birth of a child to bear fruit throughout the child's life. A large green drinking nut will have about a quart of fluid inside. This is not coconut milk, but coconut water. Coconut milk is the fluid squeezed from the grated, soaked coconut meat derived from a ripe coconut (which has a brown husk and thick meat.) A common Hawaiian dessert is haupia, a coconut pudding. Shredded coconut meat is used in many baked desserts; some Southeast Asian recipes, especially curries, call for coconut milk.

KONA COFFEE

Grown on the Kona side of the Big Island, this coffee is virtually the only coffee commercially grown in the United States (although there are some plantings on Kauai). Coffee was first brought to Hawaii in 1825 on a British warship that had picked the beans up in Brazil. Coffee lovers prize Kona coffee for its wonderful aroma and flavor, and many smaller growers in the Kona district grow and sun-dry the beans organically.

LIMU (seaweed)

These edible seaweeds—you'll also see them called "sea vegetables"—are regaining popularity in Hawaiian cooking. Limu ele'ele is a flat, green seaweed grown in freshwater streams. Limu lipoa is a flat, light-brown seaweed with a strong peppery perfume. Limu kohu, the most expensive seaweed, has a red color and strong flavor. The Japanese use the word ogo for several types of limu, much of which is aquacultured now. Limu and ogo are versatile vegetables, appearing in soups, noodle dishes, relishes, next to or wrapped around fish, or lightly dressed in a spicy salad.

MACADAMIA NUTS

Brought to the islands in the 1880s from Australia, macadamias are pale in color and have a rich, sweet, but not distinct flavor. Several growers in Hawaii rely on them as a staple cash crop. Most nuts are grown on the Big Island, but they are sold everywhere. Macadamia nuts are wonderful in ice creams, paired with chocolate in any kind of dessert, or used in baked goods (see pages 278 and 279). Ground nuts can be used to coat or stuff meat or fish, in pestos, rice pilaf or fried rice dishes, or to top noodle salads. They are also great to munch, roasted or not.

OTHER FRUITS AND VEGETABLES

Other important crops include lychee, guava, mango, papaya, ka'u oranges, sweet potatoes, pohole (fiddlehead ferns), mountain apples, and star fruit. The growth of Hawaii Regional Cuisine has also created a new market for much locally and organically grown produce, including tomatoes, cucumbers, watermelon, herbs, salad greens, and many Asian vegetables and herbs (bok choy, lemon grass, cilantro, etc.).

PASSION FRUIT

If you've never seen the inside of a lilikoi, it is exciting to slice it open and see the vivid colors and taste the tangy, seedy, pulp. Passion fruit was brought to Hawaii in the nineteenth century and was first planted on Maui, where it grows on forest vines. The fragrant fruit is perfect in juice, pies, marmalades, and even passion fruit butter, similar to apple butter. Today chefs use it for marinades, vinaigrettes, and savory sauces as well for sorbets and other sweets.

PINEAPPLE

Pineapple was probably brought to Hawaii from South America in the early 1800s by Spaniards, but the industry really boomed with the importation of plants from Jamaica in 1885. Once a very important industry in Hawaii, many pineapple plantations are now shutting down, unable to compete with fruit grown in countries with cheaper labor (such as Thailand and Malaysia). Always smell a pineapple before buying, because it will not ripen or sweeten after it is picked. You should be able to smell sweet pineapple at the non-stem end of the fruit. The fruit is often peeled, then sliced and grilled with meat and fish dishes. It is also used in Indian and Thai curries, added to salsas, and served as a refreshing dessert on its own. The pineapple also produces delicious juice.

SEAFOOD

Hawaii's coastal and offshore fisheries are an aquatic gold mine. All the ethnic cuisines rely heavily on seafood, and Hawaii Regional Cuisine chefs are masters at bringing out the best of each particular fish. The Ocean Resources Branch of the Hawaiian Department of Business, Economic Development and Tourism is constantly promoting awareness about Hawaiian fish, encouraging chefs, retailers, and consumers to explore what Hawaiian waters have to offer. The industry normally defines four categories—billfish, bottom fish, tuna, and other open ocean fish:

Billfish

Kajiki (Pacific blue marlin): Kajiki is also known as a'u, a generic term for all marlins. The flesh is firm, with a mild flavor somewhat more distinct than ahi. The amber flesh turns white when cooked, and because it has a very low fat content, kajiki should not be overcooked. Try using kajiki for grilling or for sashimi.

Shutome (broadbill swordfish): This incredibly popular billfish is shipped all over the continental U.S. The flesh is usually white to pinkish, and the meat is tender and mild to the taste. Shutome is high in fat but is not oily. Steaks are grilled, broiled, and often used in stir fry. Many shutome landed in Hawaii weigh from 100 to 300 pounds.

Bottomfish

Hapu'upu'u (grouper, sea bass): A bottom-dwelling fish, hapu'upu'u is noted for its clear white flesh and delicate taste. The fish is often steamed or used in Chinese restaurants for sweet-and-sour fish. A lean, relatively small fish, hapu'upu'u can be kept fresh for several days.

Onaga (ruby snapper): Small and highly prized, this delicately flavored fish is traditionally served as sashimi at Hawaiian ceremonies such as weddings or New Year's. Onaga is lovely when steamed, poached, or baked.

Opakapaka (pink snapper): Opakapaka has been a popular "catch of the day" fish in the islands since before World War II. The light pink flesh has a delicate flavor, and it is often steamed or baked and served with a light sauce. Its higher-fat content during the winter season makes opakapaka an excellent sashimi fish. The fish weighs from 1 to 12 pounds when caught.

Tuna

Ahi (yellowfin tuna, bigeye tuna): A rich, firm fish that ranges in color from pink to deep red. Widely prized for sashimi and other raw preparations, ahi is also excellent for grilling. Ahi is very perishable and will lose its color quickly when exposed to air, so it is important not to fillet or loin ahi until you're ready to eat it. "Longline" harvesting can yield fish weighing up to 200 pounds, which are redder and higher in fat than smaller fish.

Aku (skipjack tuna): Similar to ahi, aku has the same firm texture and rich flavor, with a slightly more pronounced taste. It is commonly used in poke, a spiced raw fish dish similar to ceviche. Aku commonly weigh from 4 to 15 pounds. Aku sashimi and other raw and dried dishes are favorite foods among the Japanese and other Asian groups in Hawaii.

Tombo (albacore tuna): Less prized for sashimi but excellent for cooking and grilling, this pink-fleshed tuna is the one most frequently canned. It cooks up into a firm and flaky white meat that is excellent in salads.

Open Ocean

Mahimahi (dolphin fish): Probably the best known of Hawaiian fish, since there is hardly a Hawaiian restaurant that doesn't have mahimahi on the menu. Surprisingly, much of the mahimahi eaten in Hawaii is imported frozen from outside the state, though connoisseurs strongly prefer the locally caught fresh fish. Mahimahi—typically weighing about 15 pounds—is an open ocean fish, landed mostly by commercial trollers. This moderately flavored, thin-skinned fish is almost sweet tasting, and many chefs will prepare a sweet sauce or salsa to accompany grilled or broiled mahimahi.

Ono (wahoo): Another open ocean fish, ono is whiter, flakier, and less sweet than mahimahi. Though it has less of the "blood meat" muscle used by marlin and tuna for long-distance migrations, the fish is lean and is often poached or steamed to avoid drying out. Ono works very well with marinades and sauces, and can be used for sashimi. Trollers land most of the ono sold commercially in Hawaii.

Opah (moonfish): This large, brightly colored fish has a nearly round profile that is the basis for its lunar name. It was looked upon as a good luck fish by old-time Hawaiian fishermen. Its large-grained flesh ranges from pink to red, and it is useful for broiling, smoking, and making sashimi.

TARO

Taro is still one the most important cultural and culinary crops in Hawaii, and forty-five different varieties of taro grow on the Islands. A highly nutritious plant with a brown skin and white, gray, or speckled flesh, it tastes like artichokes or chestnuts. Taro can be made into hash, fried into chips, or cooked, kneaded, and fermented into a sticky paste called poi. If eaten raw, taro and taro leaves are irritating to the skin and can cause stomach discomfort.

Hawaiian Vintage Chocolate

How many American chocolate companies use only cocoa beans that are grown in the United States? Just one, Hawaiian Vintage Chocolate of Honolulu. Inspired by Chef Philippe Padovani and his remarkable skill with pastry and desserts, Jim Walsh founded Hawaiian Vintage Chocolate on the premise that cocoa beans are like wine grapes: different varietals produce distinct flavors and textures, and subtle differences in soil and climate produce profound differences in the end product.

After circling the globe in search of special cocoa bean varieties, Walsh and Padovani planted their "vineyards," which today total one hundred acres on estates all over the islands. They planted criollo beans from Venezuela, which are considered to be the best flavored and most fragrant of the three types of cocoa beans. (The other two are forastero, the most common and highest-yielding, grown in West Africa and Brazil, and trinitario, similar to criollo, produced mostly in Central America.) All of Hawaiian Vintage Chocolate's crops are grown organically. Cocoa beans—and the resulting chocolate—are identified by year and estate.

Hawaiian Vintage Chocolate is sold mostly to hotels, restaurants, and pastry chefs. Many top American chefs outside of Hawaii, Larry Forgione and Robert Del Grande among them, use the chocolate exclusively for desserts. There is, however, a small mail-order business (see page 275), and the chocolates are now available at retail in select gourmet stores. Hawaiian Vintage Chocolate is not only America's sole domestically produced chocolate, it is its best.

The Recipes

SAIMIN

ADAPTED FROM A RECIPE BY SAM CHOY, SAM CHOY'S, KONA, BIG ISLAND

Serves 4

*This is a typical Hawaiian dish—a wonderful quick meal and a complete lunch
for many islanders. The influences here are pan-Asian: Japanese noodles, soup,
fish cake and Chinese pork, mixed with the Hawaiian penchant for improvisation.
All the ingredients can be found in any good Asian market.*

- 1 pound fresh saimin noodles
- 4 cups dashi (make this Japanese soup stock from a dry powder)
- 6 green onions (scallions), sliced
- 2 cups chopped fresh spinach
- ¼ pound kamaboko (Japanese fish cake), thinly sliced into crescents
- ½ pound char sui (Chinese glazed roast pork), thinly sliced
- Soy sauce

Add the noodles to a pot of boiling water and cook for 3 minutes. Drain the noodles and divide among 4 soup bowls.

Meanwhile, stir 2 teaspoons of dried dashi powder into 4 cups of water set over medium heat. Do not boil. Pour a cup of dashi over the noodles in each soup bowl.

Divide and add the remaining ingredients to each bowl (1 teaspoon of soy sauce is usually about right). Serve hot.

THAI RED CURRY SOUP

Serves 6-8

Lemongrass is a stalky, fragrant grass that grows in tropical climates and lends its perfume to the cooking of Thailand, Malaysia, and Indonesia. The flavors of Southeast Asia came to Hawaii with the arrival of Thai and Vietnamese immigrants after the Vietnam War. This delicious soup can be an appetizer or, in a larger serving, a main course.

- 2 cups dry white wine
- 4 stalks lemongrass (bottom 4 inches only), thinly sliced
- 1 tablespoon minced fresh ginger
- 3 cloves garlic, minced
- 4 (8-ounce) bottles clam juice
- 1 quart canned, unsweetened coconut milk
- 2 tablespoons red curry base (available in Asian markets)
- 1 teaspoon grated lime zest
- 3 tablespoons cornstarch
- 3 tablespoons water
- 1 pound medium shrimp, peeled, deveined, and halved lengthwise
- 1 pound red snapper fillets, cut into ½-inch cubes
- 6 tablespoons fresh basil leaves, julienned
- 3 tablespoons sugar
- 2 tablespoons lemon juice
- Salt and freshly ground black pepper

Combine the wine, lemongrass, ginger, and garlic in a stockpot or Dutch oven; bring to a boil over medium-high heat. Add the clam juice and coconut milk; boil until reduced to 8 cups, about 10 minutes. Stir in the curry base and lime zest.

In a small bowl mix together the cornstarch and water until smooth; add to the soup and bring to a boil, stirring. Reduce the heat and simmer for 5 minutes, stirring occasionally. Add the shrimp, red snapper, basil, sugar, and lemon juice; simmer until the shrimp and fish are opaque throughout, about 2 minutes. Season with salt and pepper. Serve immediately.

CEVICHE OF OPAKAPAKA
ADAPTED FROM A RECIPE BY ROGER DIKON, MAUI PRINCE HOTEL, MAKENA, MAUI

Serves 8

Fresh fish is the mainstay of the new and the old Hawaii cuisine. One of the best ways to appreciate fresh fish is to "cook" it in an acid marinade, which retains the texture and flavor of the fish and cuts its natural oiliness. This excellent recipe calls for Opakapaka (pink or crimson snapper), but it is equally good with red snapper.

For the marinade:
- 9 tablespoons fresh lime juice
- 2 tablespoons fresh orange juice
- 1 tablespoon olive oil
- 2 cloves garlic, minced
- 1 jalapeño pepper, finely chopped
- 1 teaspoon finely chopped fresh cilantro
- ¼ teaspoon salt
- ⅛ teaspoon freshly ground black pepper

For the ceviche:
- 1 pound fresh opakapaka, cut into ¼-inch dice
- 1 avocado, cut into ¼-inch dice
- 2 medium tomatoes, peeled, seeded, and cut into ¼-inch dice
- 2 hearts of palm, sliced into ¼-inch rounds
- 2 tablespoons chopped fresh cilantro
- Salt and freshly ground black pepper
- Lime slices

Thoroughly mix all the marinade ingredients in a medium bowl. Fold in the fish, making sure all pieces are coated with marinade. Cover with plastic wrap and marinate in the refrigerator for at least 2 hours.

Just before serving, fold in the avocado, tomatoes, hearts of palm, and cilantro. Adjust the seasoning, if necessary. Serve, garnished with lime slices.

POHOLE FERN SALAD WITH WAIMEA TOMATOES, MAUI ONIONS, AND SESAME DRESSING

ADAPTED FROM A RECIPE BY AMY FERGUSON-OTA,
THE RITZ-CARLTON MAUNA LANI, BIG ISLAND

Serves 4

There's nothing as refreshing as crisp greens with a tangy, spicy dressing. In Hawaii some of the ingredients in this combination (particularly the pohole fern) may be a bit arcane, but this salad will work almost as well with watercress, arugula, and/or spinach. The real key is the dressing, which makes any salad brilliant.

Dressing:
- ¼ cup rice wine vinegar
- 2 tablespoons chopped Japanese pickled ginger
- 1 clove garlic, minced
- ¼ cup sesame oil
- 1–2 tablespoons soy sauce

Salad:
- 1 pound pohole (hō ʻi ʻo) fern shoots, cleaned
- 2 Waimea tomatoes, seeded and julienned
- 1 Maui onion, peeled and julienned
- 1 teaspoon toasted sesame seeds for garnish

In a small bowl, mix together the vinegar, pickled ginger, and garlic. Slowly whisk in the sesame oil. Season with soy sauce. Toss with the salad ingredients, sprinkle with sesame seeds, and serve.

Optional: Mix in cooked bay shrimp, sliced cuttlefish, and/or cubed ahi tuna.

ISLAND FISH CAKES WITH WASABI BUERRE BLANC

ADAPTED FROM A RECIPE BY BEVERLY GANNON, HALIIMAILE
GENERAL STORE, MAUI

Makes 6 fish cakes

This classic Hawaii Regional Cuisine recipe is one of the General Store's most popular dishes. It uses panko flakes, packaged Japanese bread crumbs available in most Asian stores. (Plain white breadcrumbs are an adequate substitute.)

- 1 pound fresh fish, such as opakapaka, tuna, mahimahi, swordfish, or yellowtail snapper, finely chopped
- 1½ cups panko flakes
- ½ cup mayonnaise
- ¼ cup finely chopped red bell pepper
- 2 green onions (scallions), finely chopped
- 2 eggs, lightly beaten
- 1 clove garlic, minced
- ½ teaspoon salt
- ¼ teaspoon freshly ground black pepper
- Peanut oil, for frying
- 1 cup dry white wine
- ½ cup (1 stick) chilled, unsalted butter, cut into small pieces
- 2 tablespoons wasabi paste
- 2 teaspoons soy sauce
- Additional finely chopped green onions (scallions), for garnish

In a medium bowl, combine the fish, ½ cup of the panko flakes, the mayonnaise, bell pepper, green onions, eggs, garlic, salt, and pepper. Blend well with a fork. Cover and refrigerate for at least ½ hour.

Form the mixture into 6 fish cakes, about 4 inches in diameter. Place the remaining panko flakes on a dinner plate and coat both sides of the cakes with them. Heat ½ inch depth of peanut oil in a large skillet over medium-high heat. Fry the fish cakes about 6 minutes or until golden brown, turning once. Drain on a paper towel–lined baking sheet. Set aside and keep warm.

In a small saucepan over high heat, reduce the wine to 2 tablespoons. Quickly whisk in the butter, piece by piece, until melted and emulsified. Remove from the heat and whisk in the wasabi paste and soy sauce. Serve immediately, spooned over the fish cakes. Sprinkle with the additional green onions.

SASHIMI AND MIXED GREENS WITH GINGER-CITRUS VINAIGRETTE
AND WASABI-CITRUS AIOLI
ADAPTED FROM A RECIPE BY AMY FERGUSON-OTA, THE RITZ-CARLTON MAUNA LANI, BIG ISLAND

Serves 4

The profound Japanese influence on Hawaii, which began in the nineteenth century, is evident in this delightful dish.

- 2 cloves garlic
- 1 egg yolk, at room temperature
- 1 teaspoon Dijon-style mustard
- ⅓ cup olive oil
- 3 tablespoons minced pickled ginger
- 1½ tablespoons lime juice
- 1½ teaspoons wasabi paste
- 1 teaspoon soy sauce
- ¼ cup macadamia nut *or* peanut oil
- ¼ cup lemon juice
- 1 teaspoon grated fresh ginger
- Salt and freshly ground pepper
- 6 cups spring salad mix (mesclun)
- 1 pound #1 grade-A ahi tuna, thinly sliced
- Fresh chives and additional pickled ginger, for garnish

To make the aioli: Finely chop 1 of the garlic cloves in a food processor fitted with a metal blade. Add the yolk and mustard. With the motor running, slowly pour the olive oil through the feed tube until the mixture is emulsified. Scrape into a bowl; stir in 2 tablespoons of the pickled ginger, the lime juice, wasabi paste, and soy sauce. Cover and refrigerate until ready to use.

To make the vinaigrette: In a bowl whisk together the macadamia nut oil, the lemon juice, the fresh ginger, the remaining 1 tablespoon of pickled ginger, and the remaining garlic clove, minced. Season with salt and pepper. Set aside.

Place the greens in a large bowl; toss with the vinaigrette.

Divide the greens among 4 chilled plates. Layer the tuna on top of the greens. Drizzle the aioli around the tuna. Garnish with chives and additional pickled ginger, if desired.

DUCK SPRING ROLLS
ADAPTED FROM A RECIPE BY BEVERLY GANNON, HALIIMAILE GENERAL STORE, MAUI

Makes 24 spring rolls

Bev Gannon's up-country restaurant presents a delicious combination of Asian, Hawaiian, and American influences. These spring rolls are bursting with flavor and easy to make.

- 2 roasted ducks, cooled, meat removed and shredded
- 2 cups finely shredded green cabbage
- 4 green onions (scallions), finely chopped
- 1 medium carrot, finely shredded
- ¼ cup finely chopped fresh cilantro
- 1 tablespoon grated ginger
- 3 cloves garlic, minced
- 2 tablespoons toasted sesame seeds
- 1 tablespoon oyster sauce
- 1 tablespoon sesame oil
- 2 teaspoons Chinese chili sauce

- 24 (8-inch square) spring roll wrappers (available in Asian markets)
- ¼ cup water mixed with 2 tablespoons cornstarch
- ½ cup chicken stock
- ¼ cup dry white wine
- 4 shallots, finely chopped
- ½ cup Dijon-style mustard
- ½ cup grainy Pommery-style mustard
- ½ cup mango or apricot jam
- ½ cup heavy cream
- Peanut oil, for frying

Combine the duck, cabbage, green onions, carrot, cilantro, ginger, garlic, sesame seeds, oyster sauce, sesame oil, and chili sauce in a large bowl. Mix well.

To assemble each spring roll: Place ¼ cup of the filling diagonally across the center of 1 wrapper. Lift the lower triangle of the wrapper over the filling and tuck the point under the filling, leaving the upper point of the wrapper flat. Bring the two end flaps up and over the enclosed filling. Press the flaps down firmly. Lightly brush the upper exposed triangle of the wrapper with the cornstarch mixture, then roll the filled portion over it until you have a neat package. Repeat with the remaining wrappers and filling. Cover the filled spring rolls with a clean dry towel until ready to fry.

To make the sauce: Combine the stock, wine, and shallots in a medium saucepan over high heat. Reduce to ½ cup of liquid. Reduce the heat to medium and whisk in the mustards, jam, and cream. Whisk until smooth. Set aside and keep warm.

Fill a wok or other deep pot with peanut oil to a 3-inch depth. Heat the oil to 375°F. Using tongs, lower 4 or 5 spring rolls into the hot oil. Fry for 3 or 4 minutes or until golden brown and crisp. Drain on a paper towel–lined baking sheet. Keep warm while frying the remaining spring rolls. Serve with the warm sauce for dipping.

Luau

The luau is the Hawaiian version of the New England clambake (see page 24). It is a communal feast, a celebration, a cookout, a party. The luau is a secular version of the ceremonial religious feasts held by the ancient Hawaiians. Literally, "luau" is the leaf of the taro plant. The word has been broadened to signify a meal where the leaf has been used in preparation.

The center of the luau is the imu, a freshly dug pit, which is partially filled with medium and large stones. A fire is built and after the fire burns down, the hot stones are used to bake the foods for the luau. Most prominent among the ingredients of this feast is the kalua pig. Hot stones are placed in the pig and then it is carefully wrapped in ti leaves and laid in amongst the hot stones. Other foods—meats, fish, and vegetables—are wrapped in leaves and added to the imu.

STIR-FRIED BEEF ON MIXED GREENS
WITH LIME-CHILE VINAIGRETTE
ADAPTED FROM A RECIPE BY ROY YAMAGUCHI, ROY'S, HONOLULU AND MAUI

Serves 6

Then the oven is covered with earth and left to cook for several hours.

When the imu is opened, the feast begins. The pig is unwrapped. It is moist, tender, and falling off the bone. It is accompanied by poi, the purplish gray paste made from taro, which is eaten with the fingers.

Other traditional luau dishes include: laulau—pork or chicken with taro leaves wrapped in ti leaves; lomi-lomi salmon—salted mashed salmon mixed with onions, tomatoes, and rice; poke—raw aku tuna dressed with soy, ginger, and hot spices; pipi kaula—Hawaiian-style beef jerky; and haupia—a pudding made with coconut milk. Modern luaus add contemporary favorites such as salads, shrimp, and grilled fish.

To add to the celebration there are drinks, such as fruit punches, mai tais, or margaritas. And often there is music and hula dancing.

One of the great talents of fine Asian-influenced chefs is the ability to blend many ingredients into a dish while keeping the flavors harmonious and balanced. Roy Yamaguchi is a master of this elusive art.

- ½ cup hoisin sauce
- ¼ cup plus 1 teaspoon sugar
- 5 teaspoons minced fresh ginger
- 4 cloves garlic, minced
- 1 tablespoon soy sauce
- 1 tablespoon red wine vinegar
- 1 pound sirloin steak, cut into thin 2-x 1-inch strips
- ¼ cup water
- 2 tablespoons rice wine vinegar
- 2 tablespoons lime juice
- 1 tablespoon chili paste
- 1 tablespoon chopped fresh cilantro
- 1 shallot, minced
- 1 serrano chile, seeded and minced
- 1 (2-ounce) package bean thread noodles, soaked in cold water for 10 minutes and drained
- 1 tablespoon peanut oil
- 1 tablespoon sesame oil
- 1 head red leaf lettuce, washed, dried, and torn
- 1 head radicchio, washed, dried, and torn
- 1 red bell pepper, seeded and julienned
- 1 Maui onion, thinly sliced
- 1 Japanese cucumber, thinly sliced on the bias
- 1 cup blanched broccoli florets
- ¼ cup toasted, chopped macadamia nuts

To make the marinade: In a large, shallow dish, whisk together the hoisin sauce, 1 teaspoon of the sugar, 3 teaspoons of the ginger, 2 cloves of the garlic, the soy sauce, and the red wine vinegar. Add the beef; toss to coat. Marinate at room temperature for 1 hour.

To make the vinaigrette: In a small bowl, whisk together the water, rice wine vinegar, lime juice, chili paste, cilantro, shallot, serrano chile, and the remaining ¼ cup sugar, 2 teaspoons ginger, and 2 cloves garlic. Set aside.

Bring 1 quart of water to a boil in a large saucepan. Add the noodles; cook over medium heat until tender, about 3 minutes. Drain the noodles and then cool them under cold running water. Set aside.

Drain the beef; discard the marinade. Heat the peanut and sesame oils in a large skillet over medium-high heat until almost smoking; add the beef and cook, tossing, until it browns lightly, about 3 minutes. Set aside.

Place the noodles, lettuce, radicchio, bell pepper, onion, cucumber, and broccoli in a large bowl; toss with the vinaigrette. Divide this mixture among 6 plates. Top with the beef and sprinkle with the nuts. Serve immediately.

CHICKEN SATAYS WITH INDONESIAN PEANUT SAUCE
ADAPTED FROM A RECIPE BY MARK ELLMAN, AVALON, LAHAINA, MAUI

Serves 4

Here is an inspiration from Indonesia, where satay (or sateh) is a way of life, and peanut sauce is the dip of choice.

- 1 cup plus 3 tablespoons soy sauce
- 1 onion, minced
- 3 tablespoons lime juice
- 3 tablespoons chili paste
- 3 tablespoons minced fresh ginger
- 3 cloves garlic, minced
- 2 pounds boneless, skinless chicken thighs, cut into 1-inch cubes
- ¼ cup roasted unsalted peanuts
- 2 tablespoons macadamia nuts
- 1 tablespoon sugar
- ¾ cup unsweetened coconut milk
- ⅓ cup chunky peanut butter
- ¼ cup water

In a large, shallow dish, whisk together 1 cup of the soy sauce, the onion, 2 tablespoons each of the lime juice, chili paste, and ginger, and the garlic. Add the chicken; toss to coat. Cover, refrigerate, and marinate for 4 hours.

To make the peanut sauce: Place the peanuts, macadamia nuts, and sugar in the bowl of a food processor fitted with a metal blade; pulse on and off until finely ground. Place the nut mixture, coconut milk, peanut butter, water, and the remaining 3 tablespoons of soy sauce and 1 tablespoon each lime juice, chili paste, and ginger in a small saucepan; bring to a boil, reduce the heat to medium and cook, stirring occasionally, until the sauce thickens slightly, about 7 minutes. Cool the sauce to room temperature.

Prepare the grill. Drain the chicken and discard the marinade. Thread the chicken onto four 10-inch skewers. (If using bamboo skewers, soak them in water for 15 minutes before using.) Grill the chicken until cooked through and the juices run clear, about 8 minutes.

To serve, transfer 2 skewers to each of 4 warm dinner plates, or arrange them on a platter. Serve immediately, passing the sauce separately.

HOISIN-GLAZED PORK RIBS
ADAPTED FROM A RECIPE BY ALAN WONG, ALAN WONG'S, HONOLULU

Serves 6

This superb dish demonstrates the multiculturalism of the new Hawaii cuisine. Asian and European ingredients are woven together into a seamless whole. The result is exquisite.

- 1 cup chili sauce
- ¾ cup hoisin sauce
- ½ cup honey
- 5 tablespoons soy sauce
- 5 tablespoons dry sherry wine
- ¼ cup plus 2 teaspoons white wine vinegar
- ¼ cup sesame seeds
- 6 cloves garlic, minced
- 2 tablespoons plus 2 teaspoons curry powder
- 2 tablespoons plus 2 teaspoons sesame oil
- 2 tablespoons grated orange zest
- 2 tablespoons fermented black beans
- 1 tablespoon chili paste with garlic
- 3 pounds pork baby back ribs

In a large bowl, whisk together the chili sauce, hoisin sauce, honey, soy, sherry, vinegar, sesame seeds, garlic, curry, sesame oil, orange zest, black beans, and chili paste.

Divide the ribs between 2 large shallow dishes. Brush with half of the sauce. Cover the ribs and the remaining sauce separately and refrigerate overnight.

Preheat the oven to 375°F. Transfer the ribs to heavy, large baking sheets. Roast the ribs until tender, basting frequently with some of the remaining sauce, about 1 hour. Cut the ribs into individual ribs and transfer to a platter. Heat the remaining sauce and serve with the ribs.

ONO BAKED IN TI LEAVES

Serves 4

Ono is a sleek, fast-swimming game fish with delicate, white meat that is lean and flavorful. In Hawaiian ono means "good to eat," and it is. This fish is also known as wahoo.

- 6 tablespoons peanut oil
- 1 Maui onion, thinly sliced
- 6 cloves garlic, minced
- 1 teaspoon minced fresh ginger
- 2½ cups sliced shiitake mushrooms
- ⅓ cup chopped fresh cilantro
- 1 green onion (scallion), sliced
- 2 teaspoons chili paste
- 2 tablespoons fish sauce (nam pla)
- 2 tablespoons soy sauce
- 8 ti leaves, blanched to soften and stems removed
- 4 (6-ounce) ono fillets (red snapper is an acceptable substitute)
- 1 sheet nori (seaweed), julienned

Heat ¼ cup (4 tablespoons) of the oil in a large skillet over medium heat. Add the Maui onion. Sauté, stirring occasionally, for 8 minutes. Stir in the garlic and ginger; sauté, stirring, for 2 more minutes. Stir in the mushrooms; sauté for another 3 minutes, or just until soft. Remove from the heat. Stir in the cilantro, green onion, and chili paste. Set aside.

In a small bowl, whisk together the fish sauce, soy sauce, and the remaining 2 tablespoons oil. Set aside.

Preheat the oven to 400°F. For each ti leaf bundle, lay 2 ti leaves on your work surface in a criss-cross fashion. Place one piece of fish in the center of the criss-cross. Top with some of the mushroom mixture, drizzle with some of the fish sauce mixture, and sprinkle with some of the nori. Wrap up the ti leaves to enclose the fish and toppings. Secure tightly with kitchen twine. Repeat to form 4 bundles in total. Place the bundles on a baking sheet. Bake for 20 minutes.

To serve, place each bundle on a dinner plate. Cut and remove the twine. Unwrap the ti leaves and serve immediately.

GRILLED SWORDFISH STEAKS WITH TERIYAKI GLAZE AND PINEAPPLE SALSA

ADAPTED FROM A RECIPE BY PETER MERRIMAN, MERRIMAN'S, WAIMEA, BIG ISLAND AND HULA GRILL, MAUI

Serves 4

Here are Pacific swordfish, Japanese teriyaki, Hawaiian pineapple, and Southwest salsa combined into a typically multicultural new Hawaii dish.

- 3 small tomatoes, seeded and diced
- 3 tablespoons finely chopped Maui onion
- 1 jalapeño pepper, seeded
- 2 cloves garlic
- 1 teaspoon ground coriander
- ½ teaspoon ground cumin
- 1 cup peeled and diced fresh pineapple
- 2 tablespoons chopped fresh cilantro
- 1 tablespoon rice wine vinegar
- Salt and freshly ground black pepper
- 4 (8-ounce) swordfish steaks, trimmed of any fat, skin, and dark membrane
- ½ cup prepared teriyaki glaze
- 2 green onions (scallions), sliced

To make the salsa: Place 1 of the tomatoes, 1 tablespoon of the Maui onion, the jalapeño, garlic, coriander, and cumin in a food processor fitted with a metal blade. Process until finely chopped. Scrape this mixture into a medium bowl. Add the pineapple, cilantro, rice wine vinegar, and the 2 remaining tomatoes and 2 tablespoons Maui onion; toss gently. Season with salt and pepper. Cover and refrigerate until ready to serve.

Prepare the grill. Season the swordfish with salt and pepper. Grill the fish until medium-rare, about 5 to 6 minutes, turning once. Brush the fish on both sides with the teriyaki glaze.

Serve the swordfish topped with the salsa and sprinkled with the green onions.

273

JUMPING BARBECUED SHRIMP WITH GRILLED PINEAPPLE AND GINGER PESTO SALAD
ADAPTED FROM A RECIPE BY SAM CHOY, SAM CHOY'S, KONA, BIG ISLAND

Serves 4

Sam Choy is a Hawaii native who has been prominent in the new food movement. Here he combines two common Hawaiian ingredients, pineapple and ginger, to add flavor to the barbecued shrimp. There are also elements of Japanese and Chinese cuisine in this lovely dish.

- 1 pound jumbo shrimp, with shells
- 1 cup vegetable oil
- ½ cup soy sauce
- 6 tablespoons minced fresh ginger
- 6 tablespoons minced fresh cilantro
- 3 cloves garlic, minced
- 1 tablespoon lemon juice
- 1½ teaspoons sugar
- ¼ teaspoon red pepper flakes
- ¼ cup hoisin sauce
- 2 tablespoons chili sauce
- 2 tablespoons white wine vinegar
- ¼ cup minced shallots
- Salt and freshly ground white pepper
- ½ of 1 pineapple, peeled, cored, and cut into thin spears
- ½ pound spring salad mix (mesclun)
- 6 ounces somen noodles, cooked as package directs and drained

Rinse the shrimp and cut through the top shell, but not all the way through the shrimp. Peel the shells from the shrimp, leaving the end with the tails attached. Devein the shrimp.

In a shallow dish, combine ½ cup of the oil, 2 tablespoons of the soy sauce, 2 tablespoons of the ginger, 2 tablespoons of the cilantro, and the garlic, lemon juice, sugar, and pepper flakes. Add the shrimp and toss to coat with the marinade; let stand for 30 minutes.

To make the basting sauce for the pineapple: In a small bowl whisk together the hoisin sauce, chili sauce, vinegar, and 2 tablespoons of the soy sauce. Set aside.

To make the vinaigrette: In a small bowl whisk together the remaining ½ cup of the oil, ¼ cup of the soy sauce, ¼ cup ginger, ¼ cup cilantro, and the shallots; season with the salt and white pepper. Set aside.

Grill or broil the shrimp and pineapple, brushing the pineapple with the basting sauce, for about 5 minutes, or until the shrimp are opaque throughout and the pineapple is nicely charred.

To serve, toss the spring salad mix and noodles with the vinaigrette and divide among 4 dinner plates. Top with the shrimp and pineapple.

Hawaii by Mail

Cooking sauces
Aloha Shoyu Co., 96-1205 Wai Hona Street, Pearl City, HI 96782

Fresh herbs
Hana Herbs, P.O. Box 323, Hana, HI 96713

Organic tropical produce
Hawaiian Exotic Fruit Co., P.O. Box 1729, Pahoa, HI 96778

Syrups, jams, and jellies
Hawaiian Fruit Specialties, Ltd., P.O. Box 701, Kilauea, HI 96754

Chocolate
Hawaiian Vintage Chocolate Company, 4614 Kilauea Avenue, Suite 435, Honolulu, HI 96816

Taro products
Javellana Farm, 5473 Kawaihau Road, Kapa'a, HI 96746

Nuts and coffee
Mauna Loa Macadamia Nuts, HC01 Box 3, Hilo, HI 96720

Shrimp
Molokai Seafarms, P.O. Box 560, Kaunakakai, HI 96748

Cheese
Orchid Island Chèvre
Kuokoa Farm, P.O. Box 452, Kurtistown, HI 96760

HIBACHI-STYLE TUNA WITH MAUI ONIONS AND PONZU SAUCE
ADAPTED FROM A RECIPE BY ROY YAMAGUCHI, ROY'S, HONOLULU AND MAUI

Serves 4

Chef Roy Yamaguchi

Roy Yamaguchi's name is synonymous with Hawaii Regional Cuisine. The original Roy's Restaurant in Honolulu set the standard for inventive island "fusion" cuisine, with its contemporary blend of East, West, and Polynesian traditions.

Chef Yamaguchi grew up in Tokyo, but his passion for cooking soon led him to the Culinary Institute of America. Upon graduation he moved to Los Angeles and soon had his own restaurant, 385 North. His distinctive "Euro-Asian" food won acclaim, but it wasn't long before the young chef decided to leave the Southern California spotlight for Hawaii, his father's original home.

He opened Roy's in 1988. Since then, four more Roy's have opened around the world (including one in Tokyo). Chef Yamaguchi won the coveted James Beard Award for "Best Chef in the Pacific Northwest" in 1993. His public television series, Hawaii Cooks with Roy Yamaguchi, debuted in the fall of 1993.

The Japanese influence on the Hawaii Regional Cuisine is unmistakable. Not only are many island ingredients of Japanese origin, but techniques and styles also reflect the influence. This is a lovely, fresh-flavored dish that says a great deal about the new Hawaiian cooking.

1¾ cups soy sauce	1 small Maui onion, thinly sliced
½ cup sugar	1 Japanese or ½ of 1 English cucumber, julienned
4 green onions (scallions), minced	¼ cup sliced pickled ginger
1 tablespoon minced fresh ginger	1 tablespoon vegetable oil
3 cloves garlic, minced	2 cups bean sprouts
4 (7-ounce) ahi tuna fillets	2 tablespoons rice wine vinegar
1 cup mirin	2 teaspoons toasted white sesame seeds
¼ cup lemon juice	2 teaspoons black sesame seeds
1 teaspoon red pepper flakes	Daikon sprouts, for garnish
1 large carrot, thinly sliced	

In a large bowl, combine 1 cup of the soy sauce, the sugar, green onions, fresh ginger, and garlic; add the tuna fillets and marinate at room temperature for 1 hour, turning occasionally.

To make the Ponzu Sauce: Bring the mirin to a boil in a medium saucepan and reduce to ⅓ cup, about 5 minutes. Remove from the heat and allow to cool slightly. Stir in the remaining ¾ cup soy sauce, 2 tablespoons of the lemon juice, and the red pepper flakes. Set aside.

In a large bowl, combine the carrot, Maui onion, cucumber, and pickled ginger. Heat the oil in a large skillet over high heat; add the bean sprouts and sauté for 15 seconds. Transfer the sprouts to the bowl with the vegetables and toss. Add the remaining 2 tablespoons of lemon juice, the rice wine vinegar, and the sesame seeds to the bowl and toss again. Set aside.

Prepare the grill. Remove the tuna from the marinade, discard the marinade, and grill tuna about 6 to 8 minutes, turning once, for medium. (Don't overcook; the tuna should be slightly rare in the center.)

To serve, divide the vegetable mixture among 4 dinner plates. Top with the tuna fillets and spoon the Ponzu Sauce over the fish. Garnish with daikon sprouts.

Chocolate–Macadamia Nut Tart with Toasted Coconut Crust

Makes one 10-inch tart (12 servings)

Here is a spectacular, exquisitely delicious dessert. Though fairly labor intensive, the finished tart is a wonderful reward for your hard work.

- 1⅓ cups all-purpose flour
- ¼ cup superfine sugar
- Pinch of salt
- ½ cup plus 3 tablespoons chilled unsalted butter, cut into small pieces
- 2 egg yolks
- ¼ cup toasted, grated coconut
- ¾ cup plus ⅔ cup heavy cream
- ¾ cup plus 3 tablespoons granulated sugar
- 4 ounces semisweet chocolate, chopped
- 1¼ teaspoons coffee liqueur
- 1½ cups macadamia nuts

Preheat the oven to 400°F. To make the pastry: Place the flour, superfine sugar, and salt in a food processor fitted with a metal blade. Add ½ cup of the butter and the egg yolks. Pulse on and off until the dough almost forms a ball. Add the coconut; pulse on a off until the dough forms a ball. Press the dough into a 10-inch tart pan with a removable bottom. Freeze for 15 minutes. Bake for 15 minutes, or until golden brown. Remove to a rack to cool.

To prepare the caramel: In a small saucepan, bring ¾ cup of the cream to a simmer over low heat. Set a medium saucepan over high heat and gradually add the granulated sugar in small amounts, stirring constantly, until it melts and turns golden brown. Remove the saucepan from the heat and slowly stir in the hot cream. Stir in the remaining 3 tablespoons of butter and let cool. Set aside.

In a small bowl, combine the chocolate and coffee liqueur. In a small saucepan, bring the remaining ⅔ cup of cream to a boil and pour it over the chocolate. Stir until the chocolate is melted and completely smooth. Set aside.

Reserve 15 of the nuts for garnishing, and finely chop the rest. Pour the cooled caramel into the tart shell and spread evenly. Sprinkle the chopped nuts over the caramel. Pour the chocolate mixture on top and spread evenly. Decorate with reserved nuts. Refrigerate for 2 hours or until firm.

Passion Fruit and Mango Meringue Tart

ADAPTED FROM A RECIPE BY BEVERLY GANNON, HALIIMAILE GENERAL STORE, MAUI

Makes one 9-inch tart (8 servings)

Perhaps the two most delectable tropical fruits are passion fruit and mango. Here they are combined in a stunning dessert topped with a cloud of meringue.

- 1½ cups toasted macadamia nuts
- 1 cup plus 2 tablespoons granulated sugar
- ¼ cup all-purpose flour
- 4 egg whites, at room temperature
- 3 eggs
- 2 teaspoons grated lemon zest
- ½ cup passion fruit purée
- ½ cup mango purée
- ¼ cup heavy cream
- ¼ teaspoon cream of tartar
- ¼ teaspoon cornstarch
- ¼ cup superfine sugar
- ½ teaspoon vanilla extract

Preheat the oven to 375°F. Place the nuts and 2 tablespoons of the granulated sugar in a food processor fitted with a metal blade. Process until finely chopped. Add the flour and 1 of the egg whites. Pulse on and off until the dough forms a ball. With wet fingers, press the dough into a 9-inch tart pan with a removable bottom. Bake for 15 minutes or until golden brown. Remove to a rack to cool.

In a medium bowl, whisk together the eggs, lemon zest, and remaining 1 cup granulated sugar. Stir in the passion fruit and mango purées and the cream, stirring until well blended. Pour into the crust and bake for 25 to 30 minutes until golden brown and a cake tester or a toothpick inserted into the center comes out clean. Remove to a rack to cool completely before topping with the meringue.

Reduce the oven temperature to 350°F. To make the meringue: Beat the remaining 3 egg whites in a large bowl with an electric mixer until foamy. Add the cream of tartar and cornstarch. Beat until the whites form soft peaks. Add the superfine sugar, 1 tablespoon at a time, beating after each addition. Beat in the vanilla and continue beating until stiff, glossy peaks form. Spread the meringue over the tart, completely covering the filling. Bake until the meringue is golden brown, 10 to 15 minutes. Serve at room temperature, cut into wedges.

MACADAMIA NUT MUFFINS

ADAPTED FROM A RECIPE BY MARK HETZEL,
THE FOUR SEASONS RESORT, MAUI

Makes 12 muffins

*These amazing breakfast muffins are so good they could
even pass as dessert with a scoop of ice cream.*

- ½ cup (1 stick) unsalted butter, softened
- 1 cup golden brown sugar, packed
- 3 eggs
- ¾ teaspoon almond extract
- ½ teaspoon vanilla extract
- 1 cup plus 2 tablespoons all-purpose flour
- 1½ teaspoons baking powder
- ½ teaspoon salt
- ¼ cup heavy cream
- ¾ cup coarsely chopped macadamia nuts
- ⅓ cup whole macadamia nuts

Preheat the oven to 350°F. Line 12 (2¾-inch) muffin tin cups with paper muffin liners.

Place butter and sugar in a large bowl. Using an electric hand mixer, beat until well blended. Add the eggs and mix well. Beat in the extracts. Sift the flour, baking powder, and salt into the bowl and beat just until combined. Add the cream and beat just until smooth. Fold in the chopped nuts.

Spoon the batter into the prepared muffin cups, dividing equally. Sprinkle each muffin with the whole nuts. Bake about 20 minutes, or until a cake tester or toothpick inserted into the muffin centers comes out clean. Remove to a cooling rack. Serve warm or at room temperature. These muffins make wonderful tea cakes, especially when served with sweet butter and mango or papaya jam.

BANANA-COFFEE BRULÉE

Serves 4

Crème brulée has become the nation's most popular dessert (see page 123). Here is an interesting tropical twist on this creamy, rich confection that adds flavor without altering texture or appeal.

- 2 cups heavy cream
- 1 vanilla bean, halved lengthwise
- 8 eggs yolks, at room temperature
- ½ cup granulated sugar
- 2 large bananas, sliced
- ¼ cup coffee liqueur
- ¼ cup golden brown sugar, packed

Place the cream and the vanilla bean in a medium saucepan over medium heat. Bring to a boil. Remove from the heat and allow to cool for 15 minutes. Remove the vanilla bean from the cream and save it for another use.

Place the egg yolks and granulated sugar in a medium bowl. Whisk until smooth. Pour the cream into the yolk mixture in a steady stream, whisking constantly. Return the custard mixture to the saucepan and place it over medium-low heat. Cook until thickened, whisking constantly, about 10 minutes. DO NOT BOIL. Remove from the heat. Place the saucepan in a large bowl filled with ice and water. Continue whisking until the custard is completely cooled. Stir in the bananas and the coffee liqueur. Cover and refrigerate for 1 hour.

Preheat the broiler. Spoon the custard into four ¾-cup ramekins. Sprinkle evenly with the brown sugar. Broil until the sugar caramelizes, watching carefully so that it doesn't burn. Serve immediately, or chill completely and serve.

Chef Beverly Gannon

As chef/co-owner of the Haliimaile General Store, Texas-born Beverly Gannon creates innovative menus featuring Hawaii Regional Cuisine. Her dishes are full of tropical flavors and island-fresh ingredients. She is one of the founders of the Hawaii Regional Chefs organization.

After working in the entertainment industry, Gannon turned her attention to food, enrolling first in London's Cordon Bleu and later in classes with Marcella Hazan and Jacques Pepin. She started a catering company in Dallas, then moved with her husband, Joe, to Maui where she continued in this field.

When the old Haliimaile General Store came up for sale, she decided to move her operations to the site and open a small gourmet deli there as well. Soon consumer demand encouraged her to turn the store into a full-fledged restaurant. It has since become one of Maui's most popular dining destinations.

WARM PINEAPPLE TART WITH COCONUT SAUCE
ADAPTED FROM A RECIPE BY GEORGE MAVROTHALASSITIS,
LA MER, HALEKULANI HOTEL, HONOLULU

Serves 4

*Nothing says "Hawaii" more than pineapple (even though most
of this prickly fruit is now grown in Southeast Asia). Chef Mavrothalassitis has combined
island flavors with his classical French background to create a definitive dish.*

- 1 (17½-ounce) package frozen puff pastry dough, thawed
- 5 egg yolks
- 2 tablespoons powdered sugar
- ½ cup granulated sugar
- 1 large pineapple (preferably white, if available), peeled and cored
- ½ cup coconut milk
- 1 tablespoon light rum
- 4 mint sprigs, for garnish

Preheat the oven to 325°F. Roll each piece of the puff pastry to ⅛-inch thick. Cut out four 7-inch circles and place on 2 baking sheets. Pierce the circles with the tines of a fork. In a small bowl, whisk one of the egg yolks with the powdered sugar. Brush the mixture evenly over each of the pastry circles. Bake about 15 minutes until puffed and golden brown. Cool on racks.

Whisk the remaining 4 egg yolks with ¼ cup of the granulated sugar. Set aside. In a food processor fitted with a metal blade, purée a small amount of the pineapple to make ½ cup of purée. Whisk the purée and the coconut milk into the egg yolk mixture. Simmer over low heat, stirring constantly, until the sauce coats the back of a spoon. Stir in the rum. Set aside and keep warm.

Cut the remaining pineapple into thin wedges, about ¼ inch thick and 1½ inches wide. In a large nonstick skillet, sauté the pineapple wedges over high heat to a golden brown color on 1 side only. Arrange the pineapple, browned sides up, over the pastry circles, fanning from the rims to the centers to cover the pastry completely. Sprinkle each tart with 1 tablespoon of the remaining ¼ cup granulated sugar.

Preheat the broiler. Broil the tarts 5 inches from the heat source for about 1½ minutes, watching closely so as not to burn them, until the tarts are hot and the sugar has caramelized.

To serve, place each tart on a plate and surround it with the warm sauce. Garnish with mint sprigs.

Index

Acknowledgments

A book of this scope could not have been successful without the dedication of able and talented people who devoted may months to nurturing this project from concept to completed work. To them, here are my thanks.

My wife, Kathy Blue, and the resourceful Diana Torrey carefully developed and thoroughly tested every recipe in the book. Many dishes were tested, reworked, and tested again and again. My appreciation for their patience, synergism, and high standards.

Eric Wald's research, editorial input, wit, and good nature were an essential element of the project. Alison Buttenheim's organizational skills kept us on track. My office—Jack Weiner, Carol Seibert, and Tammy Tang—kept the chefs' recipes and the faxes flowing. Thanks to my researchers—Chris Engel, Maryalice Groves, Carolyn Miller, Josh Newman, and Sarah Schneider—who tracked down obscure history and arcane derivations.

What a pleasure it was to work with the professionals at Turner Publishing. Thanks to Michael Reagan for having the temerity and foresight to enthusiastically approve the project, and to Kevin Mulroy for seeing it through with style and grace. My appreciation to Karen Smith and Marty Moore, whose visual creativity will delight your eye on every page. Thanks also to Katherine Buttler and Lauren Emerson for keeping all the pieces together, and to Jane Lahr for her perceptive marketing ideas.

The guiding light behind this project from the beginning was Shep Gordon, whose efforts on behalf of America's chefs have brought the American culinary arts to a long overdue and much deserved level of respect and honor.

Ethan Ellenberg is more than just an agent, he is a guru, a creator, and a conceptualizer whose intelligence and perception has been at the core of this project. Thanks also to Joel Gotler for his unwavering support.

Kudos to Joyce Oudkerk Pool for her thoughtful and appetizing evocations of the food, and to Stephanie Greenleigh and Diana Torrey for bringing that vision to life.

I am grateful to the amazing insight and impeccable taste of Diane Worthington, who was always there to answer questions and offer encouragement.

Additional thanks to: Cindi Dietrich, Barbara Seldin, and Cheri Walker.

Finally, Kathy and I would like to thank our children, Caitlin, Toby, Jessica, and Amanda, and our mothers, Gertrud Blue and Carol Koshland, for their love, support, and healthy appetites.